THE DEVELOPMENT OF
MANAGEMENT
THEORY
AND
PRACTICE
IN THE UNITED STATES

EDITED BY   CLARENCE J. MANN AND KLAUS GÖTZ

A RESEARCH PROJECT SPONSORED BY

**INSTITUTE FOR GLOBAL MANAGEMENT
UNIVERSITY OF MARYLAND UNIVERSITY COLLEGE
AND DAIMLERCHRYSLER AG**

Pearson
Custom
Publishing

Printed in the United States of America

10 9 8 7 6 5 4 3 2 1

Please visit our website at www.pearsoncustom.com

ISBN 0–536–60283–2

BA 990667

PEARSON CUSTOM PUBLISHING
160 Gould Street/Needham Heights, MA 02494
A Pearson Education Company

Contents

Preface   v

Overview: Cultural Themes Shaping U.S. Management
Clarence J. Mann   1

Chapters

I.   The History of American Management Thought:
A Perspective and Analysis *Michael S. Frank*   33

II.   Leadership *James P. Gelatt*   63

III.   Work and the Workplace *Richard D. Neidig*   85

IV.   Managing Diversity *Glenda J. Barrett*   111

V.   Ethics and Social Responsibility as Management
Issues *Kathleen F. Edwards*   133

VI.   Issues and Trends in Operations Management
John O. Aje   157

VII.   Managing in the Information Age *Salvatore J. Monaco*   187

VIII.   Financial Systems *Robert P. Ouellette*   207

IX.   Strategic Decision Making *Clarence J. Mann*   231

X.   Organizational Design and Structure *James P. Gelatt*   257

Conclusions *Clarence J. Mann*   277

About the Authors   283

Index   285

Preface

This book was written as a partnership between DaimlerChrysler AG and the Institute for Global Management (IGM), a research and program division of University of Maryland University College Graduate School of Management & Technology. The choice of editors from each organization reflects this partnership. Both partners wanted to produce a concise overview of U.S. management theory and practice and trace their development over the past century and a half. As part of DaimlerChrysler's publication series on management concepts, the book is being translated for publication in German. The Graduate School will use the book in its courses.

This book is the product of collaboration among nine faculty members of the Graduate School, each writing a chapter in his or her area of concentration. Royalties are being dedicated to the student scholarship fund of the Graduate School.

Special thanks to Diane Rey, an alumna of the Graduate School, who provided most helpful guidance as copy editor in assisting the authors to arrive at a standard format; and to Maxine Clark, a staff member of the Graduate School, whose patience was tested and whose help was critical in coordinating the final assembly of the manuscript.

Overview

Cultural Themes Shaping U.S. Management

CLARENCE J. MANN

INTRODUCTION

Management as a discipline has a long and honored place in the United States. Well before the birth of Frederick Taylor's scientific management in the 1920s, American industrialists were experimenting with modern methods for managing large and far-flung enterprises. The first and second industrial revolutions, ushered in by an efficient steam engine in the 18th century followed by the internal combustion engine and electricity in the 19th century, swept over the resource-rich United States in the course of about five decades during the last half of the 19th and early part of the 20th centuries. They created in their wake a huge and rapidly expanding national market crisscrossed by railroads and telegraphy. Between 1850 and 1920, for instance, the U.S. population more than quadrupled from 23 million to 106 million, fed by the burgeoning immigrant population. Scale economies, generated by breakthrough technologies and combined with this vast market, afforded American industry enormous opportunities while repeatedly calling forth new management methods and forms (Chandler, 1990). The pace of change has only accelerated to the present day.

This book is intended to provide an overview of management theory and practice as they have developed in the United States over the last century and to explore some implications for the future. Most emphasis is placed on the last 50

1

The adjectives "U.S." and "American" are used interchangeably. The noun "Americans" refers only to U.S. citizens, not to citizens of Canada or Mexico. While Canadian scholars in particular have contributed significantly over the years to the formation of U.S. management thinking, this book does not attempt in any way to draw implications for either country or its management theory and practice.

years, however, for they tend to have had the greatest impact on current management practice and will continue to do so in the future. This overview section primarily establishes a cultural context for the book, developing four themes that permeate the American character and distinguish American management thought and practice—individualism, pragmatism, free enterprise system, and professional management. It concludes with a brief summary of chapter contents. (Chapter numerals placed in parentheses indicate chapters in this book that elaborate upon subject matter discussed in the text.)

Following a historical overview, the various chapters focus on specific fields or aspects of management. While the writing styles of the chapters differ somewhat, depending on the authors, each chapter reflects three perspectives: current management issues, the causes or origin of these issues, and some implications these issues may have for the future of management in the United States. Because of the breadth of the subject matter, the authors have not attempted to be comprehensive or even to provide systematic coverage of the topics, but simply to highlight a number of critical issues in each area, to raise questions and to provoke thought. They are concerned not with plowing new ground but with harvesting the crops of ideas and practices cultivated over the years.

The world today has become a highly diverse place for management theorists and practitioners alike compared to three decades ago. At that time, the American model that J.-J. Servan-Schreiber (1968) so alarmingly portrayed in *The American Challenge* as a threat to Europe seemed about to dominate the industrialized world. The threat then, according to Servan-Schreiber, stemmed not from the size of American firms nor from the "torrent of riches" pouring into Europe and the European Economic Community from American companies, but from "a more intelligent use of skills" (p. 29). The growing dominance of American industry, he argued, was due less to technological advance itself than to "the talent for accepting and mastering change," to "virtuosity in management," and to a dynamic higher educational system that undergirds the development of science, technology and modern methods of business management (pp. 67, 75, 78, 81). "Management is, in the end, the most creative of all the arts—for its medium is human talent itself" (p. 79). Servan-Schreiber also envied the research assistance that the federal government provides American companies (pp. 65–67).

Over the last three decades, as Servan-Schreiber anticipated, the American view of management as a discipline—both as art and science—has indeed taken the world by storm. Business schools and the need to teach management at every level of higher education are no longer seriously in question. But even as Servan-Schreiber wrote, the American industrial dominance that he feared was beginning to fade. Europe and Japan were gaining ever larger shares of world markets, and the unexpected success of Japanese firms raised questions about the American style and philosophy of management. The stark contrast between the Japanese and American approach to management raised questions about the adequacy of the American business model and its educational counterpart, the MBA. In its 1990 report, the Graduate Management Admission Council reported that sweeping trends in the business world, including "massive transformations in technology, the development of a truly global marketplace, and the increasing cultural diversity of work forces everywhere," called for "radical new approaches" in management education (Schmotter, 1993). Together with concerns raised by American business executives about business education, these charges hit hard among business school administrators and faculty alike.

As a result of this critique and the realities of the marketplace, American management thinking in the 1990s has shifted significantly from the world of the 1960s. Management is rapidly becoming much more global in its outlook, cross-functional in its practice and diverse in its perspective. Indeed, the fall of the Berlin Wall and the dissolution of the Soviet Union has made this reorientation a necessity, for the market system has become (for the most part) the worldwide norm for business. For their part, business schools in the United States have been redesigning curriculum. They have begun to shift their primary emphasis on business functions and such hard skills as accounting and finance, so as to encompass the softer skills of leadership, organizational communication, teamwork and human resource management. More recently, steps are being taken to weave international and cross-cultural perspectives into the curriculum and to begin embracing the enormous potential of information technology.

Equally important, the American business model is no longer an unchallenged standard of management practice and education. Hundreds of graduate-level business programs have sprung up around the world, especially in Europe, and with increasing numbers in Asia and Latin America. Leading business schools are forming regional accrediting associations with standards keyed to the U.S.: AACSB (American Assembly of Collegiate Schools of Business), i.e., efmd (European Foundation for Management Development), CLADEA (for South America), AIMS (for India), and AMDISA (for Southeast Asia). It is notable, however, that these associations are seeking to incorporate their own regional cultures and perspectives into these standards. Thus, efmd through its *Equis* quality label is seeking "to define the added dimension which characterizes the distinctively European approach to international management education" (efmd, 1999). For Europeans, this includes a greater emphasis on international issues and on language, culture and interpersonal relationships than is found in the average American MBA program.

With this in mind, the discussion in this overview begins with the proposition that diversity in management theory and practice from country to country and region to region reflects to a significant extent differences in national and regional cultures. The point is not new. As Geert Hofstede notes (1993, p. 82), despite some resistance in the U.S. academic community, it has been recognized in U.S. management literature for over 30 years. From a global perspective, Hofstede suggests three idiosyncrasies that distinguish U.S. management theory as well as

U.S. management practices from other countries—stress on market processes, on the individual, and on managers rather than workers. While there is something called "management" in all countries, he concludes, its meaning differs from country to country due to variations in history and culture. This should present no surprise, for management is human activity and management theory is an interdisciplinary product of the social sciences (pp. 88–89).

Building and expanding on initial insights by Hofstede, this overview considers four themes or lenses for putting into perspective the chapters of this book as they trace the development of management theory and practice in the United States. To the three themes suggested by Hofstede—individualism, the free enterprise system, and professional management—a fourth is added: pragmatism. No attempt is made to turn this analysis into an international comparative study of business cultures, nor to suggest that these themes are an exhaustive statement of values underlying American management. Indeed, any one or more of these four themes may be found, albeit with distinguishing marks of its own, in management approaches of other countries. Rather, these four themes simply provide vantage points for appreciating how American management thought and practice have evolved and for reflecting on what this may mean for the future.

DEFINING CHARACTERISTICS OF U.S. MANAGEMENT THINKING

Each of the four themes discussed in this chapter is portrayed as a cluster of characteristics rooted in American culture that has shaped U.S. management thinking and practice. Each cluster consists of a dominant theme, represented by the title of the section, and one or more sub-themes that give it a uniquely American character. Thus, both U.S. and British cultures typically are ranked high on individualism (Hofstede, 1984, p. 158), but the individualism of each plays itself out in dramatically different ways due to the different history, geography and sociology of these countries. Such differences are obviously much starker when the concept of individualism in the United States is compared to China, where the Western concept of "personality" does not even exist (p. 150). This is only to say that none of these themes provides meaningful insight until it is grasped as part of the American experience itself.

These four themes are presented in sequence, with the two primary cultural aspects placed first (individualism and pragmatism), followed by the economic system (free market system), and concluding with professional management. As will be seen, these themes build on each other to a large extent. The fourth, the need for professional management, follows logically from the previous three.

Individualism

The world in large part, including most Americans, point to individualism as a defining characteristic of the United States. It permeates every aspect of American life, including management thought and practice. Alexis de Tocqueville (1945), the renowned French commentator on the sociology of American life, was one of the first to coin this "novel expression" (as he called it) to describe the American character in his 1830s study of *Democracy in America*. Of Americans he observed—

> *Individualism is a mature and calm feeling, which disposes each member of the community to sever himself from the mass of his fellows and to draw apart with his family and his friends, so that after he has thus formed a little circle of his own, he willingly leaves society at large to itself. (vol. II, p. 98)*

Tocqueville, however, did not consider individualism to be an unqualified asset. While viewing individualism as a unique and possibly necessary aspect of American democracy, he was concerned that ultimately it could dilute the bonds of human affection so critical to civil society and deteriorate into "downright selfishness" (vol. II, p. 98). He saw individualism as having both a light and a dark side.

According to Hofstede's 1980 study, the United States ranks first among 40 nations on the dimension of individualism. By "individualism" he means "the degree to which people in a country prefer to act as individuals rather than as members of groups" (Hofstede, 1993, p. 89). Persons raised in an individualistic social environment are expected to look after themselves and tend to have loose ties with other members of society, except for the immediate family. Bonds of loyalty to the group tend to be weak, and contractual relationships take on more importance. As a result, Americans are highly mobile, both geographically and in their careers. During their lifetimes, they typically inhabit several different residences and work for several different companies and possibly for themselves—at various locations across the country. According to the U.S. Bureau of the Census, approximately 5 percent of all U.S. households make a job-related move within any given five-year period (Woodruff, 1999).

Americans take pride in their individualism. They see it as exemplifying an independence of spirit, the source of personal initiative, creativity and achievement, and a defense against despotic government. They tend to see it also as a universal truth for people everywhere, as witnessed by the American Declaration of Independence: "We take these truths to be self-evident that all men . . . are endowed by their Creator with certain inalienable Rights, among these are Life, Liberty and the pursuit of Happiness." In this belief Americans are stubbornly self-confident—even enshrining it in foreign policy initiatives—although they often fall short of it in practice. As an ideal, the belief is highly appealing to those around the world who seek greater freedom or political choice. For more traditional communitarian societies, however, the ideal signals a danger threatening to disrupt the social fabric.

In fact, the rugged individualism idealized in Hollywood films tends to be more fiction than real life. American individualism has always been tempered by a strong ethic and tradition of volunteerism and an equally strong propensity, especially at the local level, to improve society through group activities. For Tocqueville (1945), these were saving graces for the youthful American democracy. In the United States, he noted, an extensive network of civil associations at the local level works together with participation in political institutions and a sense of enlightened self-interest to counteract the potentially debilitating effects of rampant individualism (vol. II, chaps. IV-VIII). This dual heritage of individualism and participative citizenship has generated both a vigorous economic life and what Francis Fukuyama (1995) has called "a relatively high trust society" in the United States (p. 276).

Given these qualifications, three perspectives—success, freedom and justice—suggest how individualism has affected the development of American management theory and practice. The concepts themselves have been adapted from the study entitled *Habits of the Heart* (Bellah, Madsen, Sullivan, Swidler, and Tipton, 1985), a phrase taken from Tocqueville's work. To a large extent, these concepts capture what is meant by "life, liberty and the pursuit of happiness" contained in the Declaration of Independence. Each provides a unique insight into individualism as practiced in the United States as well as a frame of reference for the chapters on management development that follow.

Success

Success symbolizes the ultimate goal of the good life in the United States. It can mean many things, depending on individual aspirations. Whatever these aspirations are, success means the individual has achieved them, typically by stint of his or her own efforts. This trait has been characterized as "utilitarian individualism," an ethic with its own brand-name hero: Benjamin Franklin (Bellah et al., 1985, pp. 32–35). Self-educated and self-made as a successful printer and publisher in Philadelphia, Franklin is known for his homely aphorisms and his "little book" of twelve virtues used to monitor his moral progress. For instance: "Early to bed and early to rise, makes a man healthy, wealthy and wise," and "God helps those who help themselves."

Utilitarian individualism signifies the ability of a person to get ahead using his or her own initiative. Bellah et al. (1985) define it as "a life devoted to the calculating pursuit of one's own material interest" (p. 33). Its rationale lies in the notion that if everyone vigorously pursues his or her own interests, the common good will more or less automatically emerge. The critical point is defining one's own interests. Milton Friedman takes a narrow view of this ethic for American business, as discussed in Chapter V. He eschews the existence of corporate social responsibility beyond the duty to achieve a well-managed profitable operation. Business management, he argues, should do what it does best and leave to philanthropic and government agencies the tasks of remedying social ills. The more typical position of U.S. business leaders today, supported by 95 percent of the American public, however, holds that corporations owe a responsibility to their workers and communities alike and at times should sacrifice profits to serve this purpose. (See Chapter V.)

Utilitarian individualism also tends to see success in assertive leadership. Leaders are those who take charge, are self-starters, and provide direction to a group or organization. CEOs are expected to be turn-around artists for corporations in trouble and experience very short tenure if they don't succeed. Humana Inc.'s CEO, for instance, recently resigned "following two consecutive quarters of earnings setbacks and despite a recently announced plan to get the big managed-health care concern back on track" (Carrns, 1999, B15). According to a 1978

Benjamin Franklin (1706–1790). America's hero of utiliarian individualism. Copyright © Corbis-Bettmann.

survey using the Myers-Briggs Personal Interest Inventory, a personality assessment tool widely used in the United States, 75 percent of Americans test out as extroverted and aggressive in personal relations (Keirsey & Bates, 1984, p. 16). Search firms and hiring ads regularly specify a preference for "high energy" or highly motivated people with proven leadership qualities. As David Reisman (1967) concurs, citing Seymour Martin Lipset, in Riesman's "Forward: Ten Years Later" to *The Lonely Crowd*, "Americans have always been other-directed, this being the psychological fruit of a social structure without established hierarchy and with a strong drive toward equality and social mobility" (p. xviii).

At the same time, leaders may be seen as lone heroes, who stand out from ordinary folk, combining individual capability with an inner-directed sense of personal destiny and responsibility. This reflects America's Puritan legacy where each person enjoys a direct and unmediated covenant with and responsibility to God. It cautions as well against the seductive attraction of public opinion that saps a person's integrity (Hampden-Turner and Trompenaars, 1993, pp. 49–50, 63–64). Leaders are said to be "their own man," who know "the buck stops here" and "when the going gets tough, [they] the tough get going." Writers such as Riesman (1950) in *The Lonely Crowd*, Erich Fromm (1947) in *Man for Himself*, and Arthur Miller (1982) in his play *Death of a Salesman* point to the dangers of relying outside yourself for meaning and direction. They search for ways to develop a more autonomous type of social character.

While it is fair to say that this lone hero mythology of success continues to exert a strong attraction on the American management psyche, there is reason to believe that this is changing in many respects. For one, behavioral and other types of research, beginning with the late 1940s, have opened up a broad range of leadership models and theories. These point to the possibility and need for choice of leadership styles. (See Chapter II.) For another, gender and diversity awareness and accompanying legislation have begun to dislodge prevalent masculine patterns of assertiveness in favor of a greater willingness and need to listen to and collaborate with others in decision making. (See Chapters II and IV.) Third, the growing emphasis on group dynamics and team consciousness as the foundation of effective management is undermining the leadership myth of the lone hero. Even in the days of the Lone Ranger, the cavalry came to the rescue in tight spots. The accelerated pace of change and the complexity of globalized competition necessitate drawing on all the talents and perspectives of management teams. This does not eliminate the need for leadership—for even self-empowered teams need vision and cohesion—but it is shifting the roles, styles and tasks of leadership. (See Chapters II, III, V, and X.)

Freedom

Freedom embodies a second perspective on individualism with implications for American management. While it may be seen as having two facets, "freedom to" and "freedom from," only the former will be treated here. The latter, freedom from, is considered in the subsection that follows under the concept of justice. The emphasis of freedom to has been termed "expressive individualism," reflecting in many ways a reaction to utilitarian individualism (Bellah et al., 1985, pp.

33–34). It replaces the calculating pursuit of material interests with the cultivation of personal interests, self-fulfillment, and the pursuit of an individual's bliss. From this perspective, the individual freely decides—free from the confining authority of work, family, religion and government—what to do with his or her life, time and money.

For Americans, the integrity of the individual lies in this freedom of expression. In the 19th century, it became the clarion call of the "American renaissance" writers, such as Melville, Emerson, Thoreau, Hawthorne and Whitman (Bellah et al., 1985, pp. 33–34). They ridiculed Franklin's ethical calculus of personal constraints in favor of a life that is "rich in experience, open to all kinds of people, luxuriating in the sensual as well as the intellectual, above all, a life of strong feeling. . . ." (p. 34). For the American public at large, the ultimate expression of freedom has become choice in the broadest sense of the term (Hall and Hall, 1990, p. 147), i.e., choice with respect to marriage, lifestyle, vocation, entertainment and all the material, intellectual, religious and political aspects of life. Choice is nurtured in marketing campaigns, whether as the stereotyped "Marlboro Man" on a horse, or the rebel who will "Just do it." The underlying ethos and public policy require, however, that if possible the exercise of individual choice not be at the expense of others or society at large. In fact, it often may be, for resources are scarce, markets are imperfect, and the externalities of individual and aggregated choices can generate social problems.

This legacy of freedom—of expressive individualism—has several implications for the development of American management. First, it highlights the importance of early views by some American management theorists that effective administrative authority rests largely on informed, well-trained and motivated employees in the exercise of this freedom. A major proponent of this view, Chester Barnard, a former President of New Jersey Bell in the late 1920s, saw organizations as "cooperative systems" built on the willing collaboration of subordinates. His theory is credited with pointing the way toward the behavior revolution and highlighting issues that are still current in American management. (See Chapter I.) The point is particularly poignant as management hierarchies give way to flatter organizations. (See Chapter II.)

Second, expressive individualism serves as the wellspring of the volunteer and philanthropic spirit that pervades American society. This compassion co-exists with the more acquisitive and at times selfish forms of individualism that are evident as well. It has deep roots in America's religious and republican heritage (Bellah et al., 1985, pp. 28–31) as well as its strong tradition of enlightened self-interest (Tocqueville, 1945, vol. II, p. 122). Of the latter, says Tocqueville, Americans "almost always manage to combine their own advantage with that of their fellow citizens," which "constantly prompts them to assist one another and inclines them willingly to sacrifice a portion of time and property to the welfare of the state" (pp. 121–122). The point is not that Americans are any less selfish than others, but merely that "each American knows when to sacrifice some of his private interests to save the rest" (p. 123). Further, because these actions are taken voluntarily, they heighten the expression of a person's individuality. American robber barons of whatever age take great pride in bestowing largesse on social needs.

In fact, each year Americans contribute billions of dollars and volunteer millions of hours to civic, fraternal and community associations in promoting various social service, environmental, religious, educational, youth and cultural activities. Research by the Independent Sector (1999 web site), a non-profit association supporting philanthropy and volunteer activities throughout the United States, estimates that 93 million Americans in 1995 volunteered a total of 9.233 million work years, valued at $201.5 billion, for all types of charitable activities (research/charts 2). For 1996, it found that 63.5 percent of American households contributed an average of $1,017 to charitable purposes (research/charts 1), amounting in the aggregate to $117 billion. In the same year, private sector companies contributed $240 billion, or approximately twice the amount contributed by households (images/fig2).

Volunteer activities and charitable contributions are widely seen by Americans of every social strata as a way to give back to society and to place their personal stamp of identity on social causes. They are encouraged by the federal tax code and promoted by employers and the media. Many companies actively nurture this ethic among employees as a means of showing the concern for the enterprise's community and for society as a whole. At the same time, employers must recognize that the volunteer ethic they prize for business purposes does not stop at the factory or office door. As a quality of life issue, employees also have their volunteer agendas that extend to family and friends as well as to social causes of no particular interest to the employer. (See Chapter III.)

Third, the legacy of freedom challenges social convention. Despite repeated fears raised about social conformity in the United States, as previously noted, expressive individualism fosters a mindset of entrepreneurship that has thrived throughout American history. A recent 10-nation study of European and North American countries (Flynn, 1999) by the London School of Business and Babson College found that one in 12 Americans is trying to found a new business, while

Microsoft CEO Bill Gates contributes millions to charitable and educational organizations. Copyright © Microsoft Corporation.

the ratio is one in 30 for Italy and the United Kingdom, one in 45 for Germany, and approximately one in 50 for Denmark and France. The study concludes that major barriers among European countries are "attitudes that shun risk-taking" and "a stigma of failure" as well as "social pressure to conform" (France) and "a risk-averse culture and 'safety first' mindset" (Germany). Other studies point out the correspondence between individualism and political democracy, capitalism and competition (Hofstede, 1984, p. 169).

Finally, this legacy of freedom, combined with the drive for success, is acted out daily on plant floors and in boardrooms. A substantial part of American society seeks to find value and growth through the workplace. Indeed, unemployment can threaten individual self-esteem. This means, in effect, that for many Americans, the place of employment may become a surrogate family or community, implying expectations of skill development, career advancement, social intercourse and mutual trust. There is evidence to suggest that many Americans associate personal empowerment, involvement and recognition with job satisfaction. (See Chapter III.) Unfortunately, during the past 20 years, the effects of increasing competition, accelerating technological change and corporate reorganization and downsizing are undermining these expectations and with them employees' sense of loyalty. At the same time, for the sake of survival, organizations are flattening out and calling for greater personal initiative and creativity at every level. The expressive facet of American individualism offers industry a strong foundation for innovation, as the Internet communication revolution suggests. To take advantage of this cultural strength, however, American management must be willing to re-invent itself as well. New employee-employer paradigms are emerging, but their final shapes are still unclear. (See Chapters II and III.)

Justice

The third facet of individualism, justice, is enshrined in the Bill of Rights of the U.S. Constitution. These initial amendments to the Constitution expressly prohibit Congress from interfering with the free exercise of religion, speech, peaceful assembly, and petitioning the government for redress of grievances (First Amendment). Other amendments secure individuals against a broad range of arbitrary governmental acts, including unreasonable searches and seizures and the deprivation of life, liberty and property without due process of law. In a series of decisions following World War I, the prohibitions of the First Amendment were extended by the U.S. Supreme Court, via its interpretation of the word "liberty" in the Fourteenth Amendment, to acts of individual state governments as well (Corwin, 1953, pp. 983–985).

The notable facts about this concept of justice are its focus on procedure rather than an ideal vision or an ideology and its emphasis on limiting and regulating the reach of governmental power in favor of individual initiative. Whether stated in terms of individual rights or a nation of laws rather than of men, procedural justice is a constitutional system for protecting the individual from arbitrary or unnecessary governmental interference. As such, this view of justice might best be termed "freedom from." Given the doctrine of judicial review, affirmed early on by the Supreme Court in *Marbury vs. Madison* (1803), U.S. fed-

Civil rights leader Martin Luther King, Jr. preparing for his "I Have a Dream" speech at Lincoln Memorial, 1963. Courtesy of National Archives.

eral courts have become the ultimate interpreters and chief guardians of the individual vis-à-vis federal and state action. Especially since the end of World War II, as the judiciary was called on increasingly to exercise this role and as Congress became active in legislating against discrimination of all kinds, legal doctrines and the public mindset they produced have played a major role in shaping the American workplace and employer-employee relations. (See Chapter IV.)

This constitutional background—coupled with multi-cultural diversity—goes far to explain why litigation plays such a dominant role in American life today (Hall and Hall, 1990, p. 149), even though Americans otherwise are skeptical of governmental interference. Moreover, over the past five decades, the awareness of diversity has expanded dramatically. This nation of immigrants discovered in its midst many groups—whether defined by race, color, sex, religion, national origin, age or disability—that heretofore were unheard, unempowered and often disenfranchised in and out of the workplace. The constitutional injunction against discrimination has offered these groups a sharp sword to prod Congress and state legislatures on issues they had long ignored. Momentum is now beginning to shift, perhaps, from a primary emphasis on legal measures to a realization by employers that there are significant economic advantages to be gained by employing and marketing to a wide range of minorities. (See Chapter IV.)

Beneath this legal veneer lies an ethic of fairness, of treating people impartially and without favoritism. Because of the emphasis on procedural justice, this ethic is rooted not so much in egalitarianism as in equal opportunity. Its rationale is not so much love of neighbor as enlightened self-interest. Americans fundamentally abjure any notion of class distinction in favor of their belief that individuals should succeed on the basis of their talents and the luck of the draw, even though they will readily admit that money and connections often make a difference. They dislike people pulling rank and appearing superior, while at the same time seek ways to distinguish their lifestyles and exemplify individual personality. Americans, therefore, tend to be status conscious and are sensitive to status symbols, even as they down-play titles and encourage the use of first names (Hall and Hall, 1990, pp. 175–177).

At the same time, Americans appreciate the importance of teams and team sports. They are the proving ground of fair play. Indeed, Martin Gannon (1994) proposes American football as a metaphor for understanding the American character; it celebrates individual talent and accomplishment within a team context where collaboration is necessary to win. Nevertheless, personal performance is ultimately the key: "success (wealth, health, and happiness) is an individual's responsibility and duty" (p. 310). The same is true for failure, including misery and poverty. The fairness ethic assumes that, in the absence of discrimination and the abusive use of economic power, fair treatment provides all persons an equal opportunity to use their talents to the best of their ability. It is the means for a highly diverse people—in terms of lifestyle, beliefs and cultural backgrounds—to "live and let live" and to allow individuals to be their own person. Needless to say, this does not always occur for reasons that often lie outside the corrective sphere of government and the control of individuals. (See Chapters III, IV and V.)

These three facets of individualism—success, freedom, and justice—have been and continue to be formative forces in shaping American management thought and practice. They provide a clue to both the dynamism and the tensions found in the American workplace, for in many respects the workplace is simply a mirror image of society at large. Thus, dynamism is a function of the hard-charging ethic of success and free expression that pervades the American multi-cultural immigrant environment. The pluralistic classless structure of society both attracts and provides opportunities for all forms of individualistic expression, both constructive and asocial. It has created a thriving army of entrepreneurs and significant numbers of social dropouts. The tensions arise from the widely varying lifestyles and social philosophies that this diversity generates. Burgeoning court dockets and a not-so-small industry of mediators, arbitrators, team facilitators and diversity consultants attest to the existence of these tensions in and out of the workplace. Egalitarian technologies like the Internet are creating the opportunity for even greater diversity of expression as well as the tensions that go with it. (See Chapter IV.)

The procedural approach to justice, embodied in the U.S. constitutional system, provides only a minimal framework for integrating these forces of individualism within a stable society. For the most part it seeks to give them maximum expression so far as they do not infringe on the rights of others. But there are real limits to judicial solutions for complex social issues. Instead, the functional underpinnings of the American civil fabric remain those highlighted by Tocqueville (1945) over a century and a half ago and more recently by Fukuyama (1995). This "social capital" or "prevalence of trust," as Fukuyama calls it (see Chapter III), is built around an ethic of fair play and enlightened self-interest and an inclination to voluntarily channel individual energy into the workplace and an extensive network of civil associations serving the needs of communities and society at large. This is precisely why the issues of trust in the workplace as well as in the political arena have become so poignant today. (See Chapter III.) Americans must be concerned that the effects of global competition, the onrush of electronic technology and the judicial pursuit of rights-based individualism do not overwhelm or erode the fund of social capital that American society has generated and that has sustained it over the past three centuries.

Pragmatism

A second theme influencing management theory and practice stems from the American pragmatic view of the world. Pragmatism as such, of course, is not an American invention, for it is deeply imbedded in the very practical Anglo-Saxon problem-solving way of thinking. But it also has some unique characteristics, as the following discussion will highlight. It fits well with Yankee suspicion of abstractions and intellectualism, and a penchant for results. It also fits well with the dominance of commercial culture in the United States, and with utilitarian individualism discussed previously, for business is above all results-oriented. Moreover, a number of influential writers on management were themselves experienced senior executives of major corporations, e.g., Chester Barnard (New Jersey Bell), Frederick Taylor (Midvale Steel), Alfred Sloan (General Motors). They brought very practical insight to their writings. (See Chapter I.)

As a distinguishing mark of the American character, pragmatism is sunk deeply into the American psyche. While European counterparts can be found in English and German empiricism and French liberalism, pragmatism has been called "the one philosophic outlook that is native to the United States" (Rucker, 1969, p. v). As a school of philosophy, it emerged around the turn of the 19th century, but its lineage may be traced back as far as Benjamin Franklin (Dickstein, 1998, p. 3). It counts among its founders C. S. Pierce, William James and John Dewey—whose legacies have left their mark down to the present time on philosophy, psychology, behaviorism and American education in general. Essentially, these writers rejected all forms of a priori reasoning, historical and immutable truths, and absolute principles in favor of knowledge that is constantly evolving through human experience and insight within particular historical contexts (Prado, 1987, pp. 9–11).

> *Pragmatism, like modernism, reflects the break-up of cultural and religious authority, the turn away from any simple or stable definition of truth, the shift from totalizing systems and unified narratives to a more fragmented plurality of perspectives. (Dickstein, 1998, p. 4)*

This philosophy was and remains well-suited to a pluralistic, individualistic, optimistic, democratic society which has seen few limitations on its material development.

At its heart, pragmatism rejects intellectual systems and metaphysical truth in favor of methods of inquiry based on experience. Truth is a process that continually evolves experimentally; it is a verb rather than a noun, ultimately made true by events (Dickstein, 1998, p. 7). For American intellectuals at the turn of the century, this freed them from what they considered to be never-ending fruitless debates on unresolvable and ultimately pointless philosophical issues. Instead, they advocated testing all ideas in practice and in their historical context, including all scientific, religious, philosophic and ethical beliefs. Nothing, including truth, could be grasped in isolation from the situation.

American pragmatism as a school of thought has been severely criticized at various times as "spiritually empty," as a "philosophy of adaptation," and as "little more than a rationale for America's ruthless and amoral business civilization" (Dickstein, 1998, pp. 8–9). It also has been praised as a defense against utopian and totalitarian thinking. James compared it favorably to the Protestant Reformation for he believed it empowered the individual conscience (Dickstein, 1998, p. 3). Despite a slackening of interest in the decades following World War II, "pragmatism today is not only alive and well, it is ubiquitous. References to pragmatism occur with dizzying frequency from philosophy to social science, from the study of literature to that of ethnicity, from feminism to legal theory" (Kloppenberg, 1998, p. 83).

In the field of management, several strands of pragmatism are visible in the United States. First and foremost, pragmatism shows up as time-sensitive, goal and results-oriented decision making. Being predominantly monochronic, Americans tend to compartmentalize activities and to work sequentially on one rather than several activities at a time (Hall and Hall, 1990). When one activity is completed, they move on to another. Thus, making project lists has become a fine art, fostered through books of checklists and training exercises. Time also must be managed, for it is a scarce commodity. "Effective executives," admonishes the

Results are in the numbers. Copyright © Tony Stone Images.

business guru Peter Drucker (1967), "do not start with their tasks. They start with their time" (p. 25). So business memoranda are expected to be short and pithy, and in meetings speakers may be prompted to get to the point and not dawdle on unessential details or embellishments. Steven Covey (1989) has built a highly successful enterprise around promoting techniques of time management and other essential "habits of highly effective people."

Effective executives also are urged to focus on results, often referred to as the "bottom line." Their status is earned through achievement. And rewards are expected to be comparable. Achievement, note Hampden-Turner and Trompenaars (1993), "is close to being the cultural bedrock on which the United States is founded" (p. 88). In this sense, pragmatism follows closely on the heels of the success ethic of individualism discussed earlier. After considering time, says Drucker (1967), the next critical practice of effective executives is to "focus on outward contribution. They gear their efforts to results rather than to work. They start out with the question, 'What results are expected of me?' rather than with the work to be done, let alone with its techniques and tools" (p. 24).

Drucker (1967) illustrates this very American emphasis on results by reference to a story about President Abraham Lincoln during the American Civil War. When informed that his new commander-in-chief, General Grant, was a heavy drinker, Lincoln responds: "If I knew his brand, I'd send a barrel or so to some other generals" (p. 72). Lincoln knew of Grant's ability to win battles, and was frustrated with the timidity and incompetence of other generals. Lincoln needed results. The same holds for the history of American labor unions. They have eschewed the practice of organized labor in Europe to pursue objectives through the formation of political parties and legislated representation in plant management and on company boards. Instead, American unions have tended to favor an independent free-wheeling negotiating posture with companies—playing them off against each other when possible—and using this leverage to focus on such bread-and-butter issues as improving the wages, benefits and job security of their members.

A focus on results as a management principle shows up early on in the 20th century with the development in the United States of the multi-divisional enterprise. The decentralized structure that emerged, according to Chandler, arose from "the increasing diversity and complexity of decisions that senior management had to make" as these enterprises expanded their product markets and geographical coverage (Chandler, 1990, Introduction). "This type of reorganization fixes responsibility," stated the final report of the DuPont Executive Committee to its Board in 1921. "When a man is made responsible for results, his interest is stimulated—hard and effective work follows, which brings success. We believe that the adoption of this plan will bring tremendous improvements in the morale of the DuPont employees" (pp. 111–112). This organizational design laid the cornerstones for establishing separate profit and loss centers and ultimately strategic business units serving segmented markets. The language of the report also intimates that a focus on results would have a salutary effect on managerial psychology.

A second strand of pragmatism is reflected in the affinity of American managers for quantitative analysis. In fact, in expounding his theory of pragmatism and the need to verify ideas through experience, James reverted to commercial terms such as cash-value and cash payoff (Dickstein, 1998, p. 8). For the American manager, income and cash-flow statements, balance sheets, operating budgets, etc. are essentials. Indeed, in many cases, the so-called strategic plan of a company or business unit may be nothing more than some combination of these financial statements. In making decisions, Americans rely heavily on market surveys, cost-benefit and multivariate analyses, and net present value and discounted cash flow calculations. Using statistics and probabilities, they conduct quality control, assess commercial and economic risk, and speculate about anticipated consequences. Using numbers, they assess and average personnel performance, evaluate employee morale and turnover, benchmark one company's performance against another, and establish goals, standards and quality improvement objectives. And where business objectives are not readily quantifiable—for instance in the areas of customer satisfaction and organizational learning, as proposed by Robert Kaplan and David Norton in *The Balanced Scorecard* (1996)—there is a willingness to invent alternative means for measuring results. (See Chapters I, VI and VIII.)

A third strand of pragmatism can be found in the American legal system. In contrast to the codified systems of law found on the European continent, the American system stems from English judge-made common law. Its inductive reasoning from the facts and issues and judicial precedent, rather than deduction from general legal principles and a highly integrated framework of doctrines, reflects well American thought processes (Stewart & Bennett, 1991, pp. 28–36). In the now famous opening paragraph of his landmark treatise, *The Common Law*, first published in 1881, former Supreme Court Justice Oliver Wendell Holmes confirms this point:

> *The life of the law has not been logic: it has been experience. The felt necessities of the time, the prevalent moral and political theories, intuitions of public policy, avowed or unconscious, even the prejudices which judges share with their fellow-men, have had a good deal more to do than the syllogism in determining the rules by which men should be governed. The law embodies the story of a nation's development. . . . (p. 5)*

This particular passage, indicating Holmes' emphasis on inductive experience-based reasoning within a historical context as the primary source of legal principles, has endeared him to American pragmatists.

It is fair to say that this pragmatic approach to legal reasoning pervades the entire legal system in the United States, from the lowest to the highest court and from the law of torts to the interpretation of federal statutes and the U.S. Constitution. The legal system is rendered even more amenable to experience by reliance on the jury system in criminal cases and in many civil actions. In contrast generally to the European continent, U.S. juries have broad authority to find the facts in civil cases before them and to determine damage awards. This authority tends to keep judicial decision in touch with the mores and accepted practices of society. On occasion, juries have become a vent for public indignation by granting huge compensation awards plus punitive damages to punish particularly callous actions of companies in the design of products and treatment of employees.

Recent cases involving tobacco companies and gun firms suggests that some juries may be inclined to use tort litigation to punish entire industries (Biskupic, 1999).

Over the past four decades, especially at the federal level, the role of judge-made law has been far out-paced by legislated standards. These have become of utmost importance for management and the workplace, relating to race, gender, age and other types of discrimination, sexual harassment, environmental impact, privacy of information, conflicts of interest, and truth in advertising, labeling and lending. (See Chapters III, IV and V.) Nevertheless, the interpretation and application of these federal statutes continue to be heavily influenced by inductive common law reasoning, reliance on precedence and the broad authority of juries in determining facts.

Finally, a strand of American pragmatism can be seen running through a wide variety of research affecting the American workplace. It can be found in the fields of economics, engineering, psychology and human relations, sociology, social work, mathematics and statistics, biology, and systems analysis. Clearly, the social sciences have played a large role in American management science. Researchers are as a matter of course expected to employ the quantitative methods noted previously. Some of the early insights on management thought and practice, as previously noted, have come from the trials-and-errors of seasoned managers such as Sloan, Barnard and Taylor. The latter two sparked an interest in behavioral research, whether because of or in reaction to their efforts. The 1929 research on employee motivation at Western Electric's Hawthorne plant launched a revolution in social science that is continuing into the present. Following World War II, new ground was broken in quantitative and total quality management, systems and contingency theories and population ecology. Research raising fundamental questions about the existence of firms, initiated by Ronald Coase (1937) and continued by a host of institutional economists, has generated valuable insights about the operation of markets and the utility of market transactions compared to management hierarchies. These represent only a few areas of research affecting management that have been fostered by the influence of American pragmatism. (See Chapters I, II and III.)

As this discussion indicates, pragmatism has powerful roots in American management theory and practice. It is a logical companion to individualism, for it fits well with the American view of success, self-expression and accountability. These are seen largely as personal attributes and are assessed in terms of results. Given the great diversity within American culture, standards and metrics can serve to more objectively measure results and thus ensure fair treatment and equal opportunity in keeping with notions of justice. Admittedly, pragmatism may entail some adverse implications for the workplace, especially for those with a penchant for craftsmanship. While pragmatism spurns doctrine and tradition in favor of innovative solutions, it also may cater at times to expediency. Throughout history, Gannon (1994) notes, Americans products "have been less known for their elegance than for their utility, practicality and cheapness" (p. 313). Americans are quite capable of producing top quality products and services in every field, but they are likely to do this more from challenges of the marketplace than from a sense of craftsmanship. It is appropriate then to consider now how the marketplace affects American management thinking.

Free Enterprise System

The third theme shaping American management thought and practice is the dominance of the free enterprise system. In the United States, this system combines free market pricing and competition with a strong emphasis on property rights and the ability of individuals to accumulate and invest capital. Government regulation of markets and the price system by and large is kept to a minimum. The coordination of economic signals in a competitive economy is accomplished primarily, per Adam Smith (1776) in his *Wealth of Nations*, through the "invisible hand" of the marketplace. But the invisible hand—whose driving forces are innovation and competition—can be as much an iron fist as a velvet glove, for the signals it coordinates can crush as well as create and guide enterprises. Markets are relentless, if allowed to work their will.

The market system is given maximum free play in all aspects of life in the United States. Thus, there is pressure to monetize all values, from tangible goods and services to such intangible experiences as pain and suffering in damage awards for personal injury. This ensures that values are recognized and traded in the market. Particularly in recent years, the scope of the U.S. market system has expanded significantly through industry deregulation (e.g., transportation, telecommunications, banking, natural gas, and now electric power) and privatization of some traditional government functions (e.g., municipal services, harbors, airports, hospitals, public education, policing and prison management). The work force as well tends to be viewed as a cost that can be cut swiftly in business downturns or when businesses are reorganized and downsized. (See Chapter III.) Labor tends to oblige these shifting needs of companies, for it is highly mobile geographically and relatively amenable to new skill development. Collective bargaining and individual employment contracts are negotiated through the free play of market forces.

Further, the market system has provided a framework and playing field for all facets of American individualism. Thus, utilitarian individualists are encouraged to work hard because success will be materially rewarded. Expressive individualists can be entrepreneurial and rebels, spurning social and economic convention, because the high dispersion of economic power prevents them from being suppressed by old-line power centers. And the constitutional system—reflecting a wariness of excessive governmental authority—both limits the power of state and federal government and guarantees the protection of property rights, equal opportunity, and the free play of ideas. Here is a system in many ways designed to deliver the maximum choice of goods, services and individual expression in support of a broad diversity of lifestyles. Over the past two decades, it has displayed remarkable dynamism, nearly doubling real U.S. gross domestic product (GDP).

At the same time, the market system must be organized to be effective. And, if it is to avoid political pressure for governmental intervention in the future, it must be able to balance growth in productivity and wealth creation with notions of fairness and public policy values. (See Chapter V.) Over the past two decades, contend Daniel Yergen and Joseph Stanislaw (1998), "the United States has arrived at a new consensus" about the role of market forces in achieving public

Stock traders bustle about on the floor of the New York Stock Exchange. Copyright © Prentice-Hall, Inc.

policy objectives (p. 388). "The move to the market," they contend, "has been driven by a shift in the balance of confidence—a declining faith in the competence of government, offset by a renewed appreciation of the workings of the market" (p. 375). In the United States, the general expansion of the market mechanism—through deregulation and privatization—has just been noted. At the same time, paradoxically, "the diminution of economic regulation is offset by increased government intervention in the marketplace through social-value regulation, the explosion of claims to rights and entitlements, and the machinery of litigation" (p. 388). Thus, Americans appear to be expecting more from the competitive free market, and are willing to accept more risk than most other nations to achieve this, but also want to ensure the continuance of a minimum safety net encompassing at least social security, medical care and a range of environmental standards.

Environmental pollution provides an instructive innovative application of this new consensus. It balances government standards with market discipline to address a major social issue. Pursuant to the Clean Air Act Amendment of 1990, the government controls overall pollution levels by issuing (by grant or sale) emission permits to firms. Under a system of "tradable rights," firms may either use the permits themselves or sell all or part of their emission allotment to others and use the proceeds to reduce their emissions. As a result, note Yergin and Stanislaw (1998), "environmental quality is optimized for the entire region rather than on a company-by-company or facility-by-facility basis" (p. 362). Overall, they conclude, total emission levels are being reduced much more rapidly and regulatory costs are much lower. In addition, the lower regulatory profile has the potential of reducing adversarial conflict between environmentalists and industry. The new consensus, therefore, considers markets to be viable and effective means to achieve important public policy ends.

This new consensus creates both opportunities and challenges for American management. Enormous opportunities arise from the relative free flow of production factors and technology in the United States, the well-developed capital markets, and the ability of entrepreneurs to exploit the opportunities. As noted previously, one in 12 Americans today is trying to found a new business, either as a fresh start-up or spin-off of an existing company. Equally important, except for regulating bankruptcy, government does not normally impede the decision of firms to close down divisions quickly and reallocate resources to more promising areas. "With the onset of the third industrial revolution," argues Lester Thurow (1999), "the ability to rapidly open up the new and close down the old became the central characteristic needed for economic success. . . . That is what [the American system] does best" (p. 54). In the mid-1980s, for instance, Intel turned around from a non-competitive DRAM (dynamic random access memories) manufacturer to become the world leader in microprocessors. Factor mobility—especially of labor and capital—and the ability of firms to reallocate and rapidly change the mix of their resources, marks a major difference between the United States and other less flexible market-oriented economies. (See Chapter IX.)

The vagaries of the market also have placed a premium on the role of finance in American management thinking. Finance and financial officers are assigned prominent roles in American companies. By providing a common denominator of firm performance, financial indicators have become the early warning system for possible business problems as well as indicators of success. The incessant drumbeat of market competition and the competitive intensity of financial markets mean that monthly and quarterly financial reports are critical not only for marketing and production managers, but also for stock prices and creditors. Over the years, the scope of these financial indicators has expanded to accommodate societal concerns and the need for increased productivity, e.g., SEC and tax law requirements, activity based accounting (ABC), total cost accounting (TCA), valuation of intellectual property, globalization of accounting and financial standards, and environmental accounting. (See Chapter VIII.)

Other management areas as well have been and are being shaped by the pressures of market forces. Marketing strategy and marketing management, for instance, distinguish American management thinking almost as much as the emphasis on finance. The size and scope of the U.S. market pushed market-led production into the forefront early in American history. Mass merchants like Sears, Spiegel and Montgomery Ward revolutionized marketing, first through catalogs and later, with the growth of auto ownership, through department stores. Since then, retail marketing strategy has gone through several phases, including shopping malls, specialized catalogs and boutiques, the impact of Japanese quality standards and now e-commerce. Each phase has brought with it new levels of marketing sophistication, targeting increasingly customized market segments. In the highly competitive U.S. market today, firms are forced to take their market research and product positioning very seriously. (See Chapter IX.)

Further, the increasing complexity of the marketplace and intensity of competition, especially since the end of World War II, have forced American firms to embrace strategic planning in word, if not in deed. Successful firms now revisit long-term strategic planning on an annual or at least a biennial basis, even though their planning horizon may be 10 to 20 years. The complex, rapidly changing and globalizing environment is unforgiving for firms which neglect to exercise foresight. For this reason as well, firms have been forced over the past three decades to scan the flood of research and product development in order to identify new and converging technologies. (See Chapters VII and IX.) Companies are turning to research services to extract and process this data on an ongoing basis from university treatises, independent inventors and federal and private R&D laboratories.

Market pressures, combined with information technology and the Internet, also have begun to create a revolution in management style and thinking. Americans have long had a love affair with technology (Lears, 1981). Information technology is its latest fling. In an apparently increasing trend, American companies spent over $1 trillion on IT investment in 1998. IT is affecting business management today in at least three important ways. (See Chapter VII.). First, it is increasing productivity and growth overall through the more effective management of knowledge assets. This requires management, however, to incorporate IT as a core competence into its strategic objectives and to integrate it into its corporate culture and business processes. Moreover, IT is redefining the value chain, both in the way buyers and sellers interact and through the value added. IT improves the speed, efficiencies, accuracy and richness of transactions. Third, IT is revolutionizing the process of innovation and product development by enabling firms to integrate constantly changing customer feedback with design changes and to dovetail these in turn with more customized production. As a result of these trends, the corporate information and communication officer (CIO) is taking a place alongside other senior corporate officers in major U.S. enterprises. (See Chapter VII.)

Finally, management practice has been affected by efforts to ensure transparency in the marketplace. This has occurred largely through public policies concerned with disclosure of product information, fair treatment, equal opportunity and collusive practices. At a very basic level, the retail practice of fixed prices has been enhanced considerably by legislated labeling and packaging requirements to ensure that contents are known and products can be compared, and by unfair trade laws that establish "truth" standards in such areas as advertising and loan documents. (See Chapter V.) The sale of securities is stringently regulated at both the state and federal levels by disclosure requirements and prohibitions against fraud and misrepresentation.

At another level, transparency in the labor market is promoted through equal opportunity laws that prohibit discrimination—whether based on race or national origin, religion, gender, age or disability—and thereby encourage hiring decisions based on merit. Other laws accomplish the same purpose for the purchase and sale of real estate and for bank loans. These are buttressed in many cases by industry and company codes of conduct setting guidelines for ethical behavior. (See Chapters IV and V.) At a more general level, state and federal antitrust laws promote transparency in the market by prohibiting monopolization, collusive activities to rig or monopolize markets, and agreements between firms to fix prices, set production quotas, rig bids and other unfair practices. At all three levels, these rules of conduct and fair play not only promote transparency in the marketplace, but predictability as well, for they establish minimum uniform standards which for the most part are not subject to bureaucratic discretion and interference. (See Chapter V.)

Taken as a whole, the free enterprise system highlighted here reflects a constitutional heritage where individual rights, limited government and private property are dominant values. The system functions on a daily basis, however, only by virtue of a complex network of public and private institutions which could not be covered in this book, e.g., banking system, stock markets, trade and other business associations, federal reserve system, court system and alternative means of dispute settlement. It should be noted, furthermore, that the social values underpinning this system must be highly tolerant of disparities in the distribution of wealth. In a free market system, such disparities give rein to the underlying ethos of individualism and drive the movement of production factors and the ongoing reallocation of resources. At the same time, the long-term stability of the system depends on cultivating those civilizing "habits of the heart," reflecting a sense of fairness, tolerance, equal opportunity and enlightened self-interest, that so endeared American individualism to Tocqueville over 150 years ago.

Professional Manager

The fourth and, in a sense, culminating theme running through American management theory and practice concerns the emphasis given the professional role of the manager. Hofstede (1993) argues that in the United States, the manager has been glorified as a decision-maker and cultural hero at the expense of the workers. This he attributes to "extreme individualism" combined with "fairly strong masculinity." Because rank-and-file workers are the real decision-makers, at least on a relatively simple level, he reasons, managers instead should follow workers' leads and be involved more in maintaining networks (pp. 92–93). This assessment fits nicely with Hofstede's (1984) conclusions ranking the United States first in terms of individualism and thirteenth in terms of masculinity (i.e., "assertiveness") among the 40 countries covered in his research (p. 189). While this view highlights certain salient cultural influences on American management practice, it also tends to play to a stereotype. In reality, the role of managers in the United States is more nuanced and broadly ranging than this in both theory and practice.

Historically, managers first appeared in the United States during the 1850s and 1860s. They were salaried hierarchies of executives needed to coordinate the new railway network and telegraph system (Chandler 1990, p. 408). These hierarchies soon were adopted by other industries where the scale efficiencies of mass production in capital-intensive industries could be integrated with mass distribution (pp. 410–411, 417). By the turn of the century, management hierarchies were incorporated into mass merchandising companies spawned by this revolution in transportation and communication. Ultimately, a corporate office was needed to coordinate these hierarchies as business functions became more specialized within multi-divisional enterprises (p. 422). With these developments came the need to coordinate and recruit management teams to supervise these new production processes and extensive sales networks. Similar developments, incidentally, occurred in Germany by the early 1900s—though much later in Great Britain—for larger, more capital-intensive industries (p. 428).

To gain a fuller and more balanced view of the manager in the United States, emphasis should be placed on management as a profession and how this fits with the U.S. culture and economic system. The term "professional" is employed here to mean not only the existence of commonly definable standards of management skills and good practices, but also that managers tend to be hired and judged with reference to these standards. This view fits well with the strong rule-orientation and analytical bias lying at the root of mass production and permeating the scientific management school of Frederick Taylor (Hampden-Turner and Trompenaaars, 1993, pp. 31–45). Chandler (1990) sees a close connection between the rationalizing and systematizing that dominated American management thinking and organizational change during the first half of the 20th century and the engineering training of early American industrial pioneers, e.g., Pierre du Pont (DuPont), Alfred Sloan (General Motors), General Robert Wood (Sears), Frederick Taylor, and many others (p. 317). While the generation of executives that followed these business leaders tended to adopt a more informal, personal approach, nevertheless Chandler concludes that "the rational, analytical outlook . . . has become, in recent years, the more accepted way in American business" (p. 319). Business education in the United States, discussed at the outset of this overview chapter, has tended to support and promote a strong analytical systematic bias in management thinking. (See Chapter I.)

This emphasis on professionalism does not mean that trained managers necessarily make the best or even always good business decisions. Bounded rationality, whether due to limits on time, information, resources or personal predilections, means managers do not always optimize their actions to the last degree (Simon, 1997). Nor does it mean that professional managers necessarily are likely to be successful business leaders, for the qualities of successful leadership are often as much art, political finesse and personality as skill and good practices. (See Chapter II.) Rather, the term "professional" simply connotes that management is a discipline that can be taught and learned, that it evolves through research, and that it enjoys recognized status in the United States. In many ways over the years, this fact—as promulgated through the American business school system—has helped to enlighten and possibly tame the more strident individualistic and masculine traits identified by Hofstede.

Within this historical context, the competitive structure of the American free enterprise system, just discussed, has prompted enterprises of all sizes to adopt a professional approach to management based on merit. In the first place, the intensity of rivalry in the marketplace forces firms with relatively few exceptions to compete for top-flight human resources. Nepotism of any kind threatens the quality of management decisions and warns away the most qualified talent. At bottom, it also cuts against the grain of American individualism and particularly its ethos of equal opportunity. Second, the widespread reliance on capital markets in the United States has drawn an ever-sharper line between management and shareholders. Highly dispersed, publicly traded stock and bond holdings diffuse direct ownership control over management and broaden the latter's area of operational discretion (Berle and Means, 1932). Having little direct control, the holders and potential purchasers of these securities are concerned primarily with qualifications and results, i.e., that a firm's managers are well qualified and that they regularly anticipate and respond appropriately to changes in the marketplace. For the same reasons, shareholders tend to hold management strictly accountable both short and long term for maximization of profits and poor performance.

In a recent survey (Calori and DeWoot, 1994), European managers confirmed that professionalism is a primary characteristic of American management. By this, the authors point to the rationalistic emphasis on organizational charts and position descriptions, functional and departmental specialization, segmentation into strategic business units, and strategic planning. In addition, they highlight the individualistic accent on self-achievement and mobility, a short-term profit orientation focused on shareholders, and the highly competitive marketplace centered on customer satisfaction (p. 14). Compared to Japan on the one hand and Europe on the other, European managers tend especially to prize the entrepreneurial aspects of American management stemming in large part from this combination of traits. At the same time, they are leery of the disproportionate emphasis on profit maximization and the head-to-head stand-offs between management and labor in U.S. firms that they believe threatens social harmony (pp. 32–37).

Professionalism, it is fair to conclude, is a defining characteristic of American management. It is a critical element of the "managerial enterprise" and the U.S. system of "managerial capitalism," whose evolution Chandler (1990) so well traced. And it is the focus of American business education, which has considerable status within the American university system. A 1997 survey of 1,400 CEOs found that advanced degrees in business are preferred over advanced degrees in computer science and engineering (Hahs, 1999). These results also indicate a changing profile for the American manager, which is reflected throughout the chapters in this book—one that overlays traditional analytical, technical and quantitative competencies with strong interpersonal and communication skills, sensitivity to diverse cultures, ethical sensibilities, strategic insight and "real world" practical experience.

This changing profile in U.S. management thinking was advocated as early as 1924 by noted management author Mary Parker Follett. A leading exponent of human relations principles, who was not generally recognized at the time, Follett is heralded by Peter Drucker as "the brightest star in the management firmament" of her time and by Warren Bennis as someone who anticipated his thoughts on leadership by 40 years (Nation's Business, 1997). She is said to have "transformed the ideas of modern management into human proportion, into terms of community" (Graham, 1996, p. 283), envisioning the necessity of understanding individual and group motivation and of humanizing the workplace in order to increase productivity. The professionalism that Follett endorsed—achieving harmony through a flexible leadership style conducive to conflict resolution—is widely recognized by U.S. managers today in the ways they make business decisions. (See Chapters I and II.)

Not surprisingly, therefore, the meaning of professionalism for American management has been shifting with the changing character of society and the marketplace. While it continues to encompass the dominant American themes of individualism, pragmatism and the free enterprise system, the professional role of the manager has begun to respond to the increasing diversity of the American work force, the fast pace of technological change, the communication and information technology revolution, the growing emphasis on open systems thinking, and the globalization of the marketplace. The changing role of the manager has been clarified and helped along by a large body of research and writing over the years. These changes and the forces of change are discussed throughout the chapters in this book.

CHAPTER OVERVIEWS

The four broad cultural themes just discussed cut across the various chapters of this book. While the chapters provide an in-depth look at particular subjects or topics, the cultural matrix highlights common threads in the American character that have significantly influenced one hundred-fifty years of U.S. management theory and practice. The various chapters also provide an overview of many issues facing U.S. management today and how these have come to be issues. Coverage and treatment of these issues, however, are by no means exhaustive. Instead, the reader should view these chapters—summarized below—simply as illustrating the types of challenges American managers face and what these challenges are likely to look like in the coming decades.

In Chapter I, "The History of American Management Thought," Dr. Michael Frank explores the many schools of thought that have influenced American management thinking, arguing that their emphasis has tended to shift over time from serious academic and scholarly research to ready-made formulas that meet the appetite (if not the needs) of modern American management. Many recent management writings prescribe very specific formulas or applications for increasing productivity, efficiency and profit. He questions whether this level of scholarship is sufficient to provide companies in America's rapidly advancing post-industrial society with the guidance needed for their functioning and structure 10 years hence. The critical issue for the future of American management is whether such prescriptions produce short-term or long-term value, both or neither.

Chapter II, "Leadership," points out how definitions of leadership have changed over time. Management thought has progressed from the centuries-old notion that leaders are born, writes Dr. James Gelatt, to the recognition that leadership qualities can be acquired and are adaptable to situational changes. Individuals who perform a leadership function in one context may serve by choice (or because of the situation) as a follower in a different context. A key factor in being a leader is to understand what motivates one's followers.

Chapter III, "Work and the Workplace," presents developments in the world of work. It is intended to raise issues and provide a basis for debate, says Dr. Richard Neidig, rather than present solutions. As organizations enter the 21st century and are faced with mounting domestic and worldwide competition, he asks, is the relationship between the corporation and the worker sufficiently healthy to meet the challenges? Since the industrial revolution, friction between workers and their organizations has been constant. Yet, most individuals have a need to be productive and to find value in their labor. Over the past two decades, the emergence of Generation X and the redefinition of trust and loyalty within the workplace, together with the continuing need for people to pursue professional and personal growth, have become critical realities of today's workplace. Organizations that can not deal with a changing work environment may face serious consequences.

In Chapter IV, "Managing Diversity," Dr. Glenda Barrett traces the evolution of organizational thinking about marrying individual human rights and corporate needs in a multi-cultural environment. She identifies key legal developments over four decades, recent consumer and labor market pressures, and ongoing group dynamics that converge to shape organizational strategies and programs. The chapter also reviews the current status of minorities in the U.S. workplace and discusses implications for future managers.

Chapter V, "Ethics and Social Responsibility as Management Issues," explores ethical challenges which managers face on a daily basis. Dr. Kathleen Edwards examines them in the U.S. business context of social responsibility and analyzes some of the successful ways American managers deal with these issues. In particular, she covers seven key management issues: ethical communication with stakeholders, ethical managerial behaviors in relation to employees, negotiating ethically and the dispute resolution systems for this, ethics codes and other resources, socially responsible organizational behavior, and making a profit while being socially responsible.

In Chapter VI, "Issues and Trends in Operations Management," Dr. John Aje examines how technology and globalization have revolutionized the subject. Operations management, he says, is the design and management of production systems that create an organization's products and services. He traces the evolution of operations management as a discipline, identifying significant contributions and how they have enhanced the discipline. Particular attention is paid to the quality movement and technology convergence as they have influenced the development of operations management

Chapter VII considers "Managing in the Information Age." Dr. Salvatore Monaco examines the dramatic changes in information technology and how they are fundamentally changing every industry from health care to banking to automobile manufacturing. These changes are affecting the pace of commerce; reshaping rules of engagement; placing priority on research; development and innovation; and redefining the organization and the way it interacts with stakeholders. The chapter focuses on three areas where businesses must meet these challenges: knowledge management, the customer value chain and new product development. Consideration also is given to IT as a strategic weapon and to its impact on the roles and tasks of management.

Chapter VIII, "Financial Systems," considers the central role these systems play in U.S. management. As the common denominator for all decisions made by the enterprise, Dr. Robert Ouellette points out, these systems lie at the heart of the start-up, growth, survival and profitability of the firm. Financial systems are evolving rapidly toward liberation from historical constraints and toward greater value and utility to managers at all levels of the organization. Among the important areas of liberation is the incorporation of non-financial factors in traditional accounting, the valuation of intellectual assets, and the internationalization of standards. Information technology also plays an increasingly major role in this liberation process with electronic commerce and intelligent agents leading the way. Finally, the chapter explores some of the models and theories that are providing a more solid foundation for financial system applications in an increasingly more complex environment.

"Strategic Decision Making," the subject of Chapter IX, examines the evolution of strategy as a concept in American management thinking over the past five decades. Dr. Clarence Mann focuses attention on five contrasting dimensions of strategy that continue to shape management thinking: strategy making as an emergent verses a deliberate process, market verses resource-focused strategy, a portfolio verses a core competence focus on strategy, competitive verses cooperative strategy, and strategy as a function of industry evolution verses industry creation. These contrasting dimensions imply choice, and choice entails trade-offs. The manager as strategist must be conscious of these trade-offs and proactively shape these dimensions in order to address three environmental factors: the ongoing challenge to innovate, the rapid pace of change and the uncertainty wrought by globalization.

In Chapter X, "Organizational Design and Structure," Dr. James Gelatt considers why organizations exist, how they are structured and how they function. Further, he explores the various dimensions of organizational design, including structure, culture, environment, goals and strategies and technology. He also considers stages of growth in organizations, their life cycles as well as management theory as related to organizational design and structure. Concluding sections deal with the evolution of global organizations, the management of learning organizations and the implications of this for the future of management.

CONCLUSION

Taken together, the four themes presented in this chapter—individualism, pragmatism, free enterprise system, and professional management—have shaped U.S. management theory and practice during the past century and a half. Their influence is reflected throughout the topical chapters in this book. The complexities of an increasingly diverse work force and a technologically driven and globalizing economy are forcing American managers to reconsider conventional wisdom. While the themes themselves are not likely to change, the balance of values within and among them most certainly will. This book seeks to identify what some of those changes will be.

REFERENCES

Bellah, R.N., Madsen, R., Sullivan, W.M., Swidler, A., & Tipton, S.M. (1985). *Habits of the heart: Individualism and commitment in American life*. Los Angeles, CA: University of California Press.

Berle, A.A., & Means, G.C. (1932). *The modern corporation and private property*. New York: Macmillan.

Biskupic, J. (1999, Aug. 30). Jurors vent outrage at industry. *The Washington Post*, p. A1.

Calori, R., & DeWoot, P. (Eds.). (1994). *A European management model: Beyond diversity*. New York: Prentice Hall.

Carrns, A. (1999, Aug. 4). Humana's chief executive steps down after 2 quarters of earnings setbacks. *Wall Street Journal*, p. B15.

Chandler, Jr., A.D. (1990). *Strategy and structure: Chapters in the history of the American industrial enterprise*. Cambridge: MIT Press. (Original work published 1962)

Coase, R. (1937). The nature of the firm. *Economica*, pp. 386–405.

Corwin, E.S. (Ed.). (1953). *The Constitution of the United States: Analysis and interpretation*. Washington, D.C.: U.S. Printing Office.

Covey, S.R. (1989). *The seven habits of highly effective people*. New York: Simon & Schuster.

Dickstein, M. (1998). Introduction: Pragmatism then and now. In M. Dickstein (Ed.), *The revival of pragmatism* (pp. 1–18). Durham, NC: Duke University Press.

Drucker, P.F. (1967). *The effective executive*. New York: Harper & Row.

Efmd (1999). Green light for European quality improvement system Equis: Equis key characteristics. http://www.efmd.be/html/body_equis.html, and http://www.efmd.be/html/body_characteristics.html

Flynn, J. (1999, July 2). Gap exists between entrepreneurship in Europe, North America, study shows. *Wall Street Journal*, .

Fukuyama, F. (1995). *Trust*. New York: Free Press.

Gannon, M.J., & Associates (1994). *Understanding global cultures: Metaphorical journeys through 17 countries*. Thousand Oaks, CA: Sage Pub.

Graham, P. (Ed.) (1996). *Mary Parker Follett: Prophet of management*. Boston: Harvard Business School Press.

Hahs, D.L. (1999, March). What have MBAs done for us lately. *Journal of Education for Business, 74*(4), 197–201.

Hall, E.T., & Hall, M.R. (1990). *Understanding cultural differences*. Yarmouth, ME: Intercultural Press.

Hampden-Turner, C., & Trompenaars, A. (1993). *The seven cultures of capitalism: Value systems for creating wealth in the United States, Japan, Germany, France, Britain, Sweden, and the Netherlands*. New York: Doubleday.

Hofstede, G. (1984). *Culture's consequences: International differences in work-related values* (abridged ed.). London: Sage Pub.

Hofstede, G. (1993). Cultural constraints in management systems. *Academy of Management Executive, 7*(1), 81–94.

Holmes, O.W. (1963). *The common law* (M. DeWolfe Howe, Ed.). Cambridge: Harvard University Press. (Original work published 1881)

Independent Sector (1999). Research: The state of the independent sector. http://independent-sector.org/programs/research/

Kaplan, R.S., & Norton, D.P. (1996). *The balanced scorecard: Translating strategy into action*. Boston: Harvard Business School.

Keirsey, D., & Bates, M. (1984). *Please understand me: Character and temperament types* (4th ed.). Del Mar, CA: Prometheus Nemesis.

Kloppenberg, J.T. (1998). Pragmatism: An old name for some new ways of thinking. In M. Dickstein (Ed.), *The revival of pragmatism* (pp. 83–127). Durham, NC: Duke University Press.

Lears, J. (1981). *No place of grace: Antimodernism and the transformation of American culture 1880–1920*. New York: Pantheon.

Nation's Business (1997, May). A guru ahead of her time. Anonymous.

Prado, C.G. (1987). *The limits of pragmatism*. Atlantic Highlands, NJ: Humanities Press International.

Reisman, D. (1967). *The lonely crowd: A study of the changing American character* (13th printing). New Haven: Yale University Press.

Rucker, D. (1969). *The Chicago pragmatists*. Minneapolis: University of Minnesota Press.

Schmotter, J.W. (1993, Winter). The Graduate Management Admission Council: A brief history, 1953–1992. *Selections, 9*(2), pp. 1–12.

Servan-Schreiber, J.-J. (1968). *The American challenge*. New York: Atheneum Pub.

Simon, H.A. (1997). *Administrative behavior* (4th ed.). New York: Free Press.

Stewart, E.C., & Bennett, M.J. (1991). *American cultural patterns: A cross-cultural perspective* (rev. ed.). Yarmouth, ME: Intercultural Press.

Thurow, L. (1999). *Building wealth: The new rules for individuals, companies and nations in a knowledge-based economy.* New York: HarperCollins.

Tocqueville, A. de (1945). *Democracy in America*, 2 vols. New York: Alfred Knopf.

Woodruff, D. (1999, Aug. 5). In new Europe, mobile workers find jobs in nations offering the best opportunities. *Wall Street Journal*, p. A14.

Yergin, D., & Stanislaw, J. (1998). *Commanding heights: The battle between government and the marketplace that is remaking the modern world.* New York: Simon & Schuster.

Chapter I

The History of American Management Thought: A Perspective and Analysis

MICHAEL S. FRANK

INTRODUCTORY COMMENTS AND OVERVIEW

The importance of American management thought, as is the case with any body of knowledge, lies in the lessons that can be learned from the past and applied to the future. After an evolution of more than 250 years, American managers and scholars find themselves asking "Where have we been, and where do we go from here?"

American management thought had its origins in the academic disciplines of economics, sociology, and psychology. Later, a new discipline emerged, which focused on the study of management. Although the material covered in this chapter has a business-oriented focus, the vast majority of what is written here pertains to public entities as well.

Since the mid 1970s, the application of management principles developed by contemporary writers to solve management problems has been a dominant force in shaping current American management practice. In recent years, however, many academics and business managers have begun to question whether the current discipline of management study will add real value to American management practice or, if in the quest for a "quick fix" to complex problems, the future has been undermined.

As management thought emerged and business schools developed, many of the writers who have remained the most influential in the field of management thought were themselves experienced managers. Some of these practitioners, such as Chester Barnard and Frederick Taylor, ran large corporations, New Jersey Bell (1927) and Midvale Steel Company (1884), respectively. In more recent times, others, such as Peter Drucker, Thomas Peters, and Michael Porter, were and remain consultants to a variety of organizations.

The importance of the distinction between an academic discipline, and an applied discipline, such as the hands-on approach of practitioners, espoused by modern-day consultants, should not be lost on the reader. The principles that emerge from an academic discipline have not necessarily been "field tested." Rather, they are borne of ideas and concepts that may or may not be generally applicable to circumstances or situations within a working organization. Recent management theory, which falls in this category, strokes with a broad brush, and therein lies the problem. Many recent management writings prescribe very specific applications—ready-made formulas perhaps—for organizations to follow in pursuit of increased productivity, efficiency and profit. The critical issue for the future of American management is whether such prescriptions produce short-term value, long-term value, both, or neither.

A CLASSIFICATION OF AMERICAN MANAGEMENT THOUGHT

The following classification scheme and time line are presented to give the reader a framework for understanding the development and rooting of the dominant management influences into various time periods and schools of management thought. This approach is not without flaws, however. First, there are many excellent books on the historical influence of great writers impacting the field of American management (Matteson & Ivancevich, 1996; Boone & Bowen, 1987; McCurdy, 1973). However, the authors of these works often use slightly different titles to classify the same writers within a given school of thought. Moreover, sometimes the same theorist is classified into different schools of thought. Chester Barnard, for example, has been placed in both the Human Relations School and the Classical School by different writers on the subject. Another problem is that the influence of different schools of thought overlap, making it difficult to be precise in establishing the starting and stopping points from one school of thought to another.

Despite these limitations, it is useful to develop a framework for analyzing the ideas and influences that have led to a specific management approach, doctrine or philosophy. The time line associated with each school of thought is intended to provide a rough estimate of the period of that school's major influence on management thinking and practice. The reader should note, however, that many of the different schools of thought presented in this article continue to exert influence on current writers and management practitioners.

In developing the time line and classification scheme, the author relied on numerous works. One work in particular deserves to be noted, as the names for the various schools of thought used in this article and many of the historical descriptions associated with various schools of thought are taken from Aldag and Stearns' excellent 1987 text, *Management*. At times the author has extrapolated from the material of many of the works cited herein to provide some analysis and thought-provoking ideas. Although the author has made every attempt to interpret objectively and fairly the thinking of many gifted scholars and practitioners, the author accepts blame for any error that may result from the extrapolation required to interpret and apply another's meaning to a particular context.

Milestones in American Management Thought

This section is intended to provide the reader with a historical time frame so that ideas and events can be placed in context. The dates for each school of thought represent when the primary body of academic work was developed for that school of thought and not exact starting or ending points.

Pre-Industrial Revolution (prior to 1770)

This period is highlighted by the contributions of the Romans, the Greeks, the military, and the church. Many of the management practices developed by these entities remain with us to this day.

Industrial Revolution (post 1770)

This period is marked by the growth of capitalism and for the first time in human history, productivity increases without war. Productivity gains and the rise in the production and consumption of material goods define the framework of the economic and social structure that developed in the United States during this period. American and European academics and management practitioners observed the effects of the Industrial Revolution and chronicled their impact in what many have called the Classical School of American Management (Aldag and Stearns, 1987). This school of thought exerted its impact on American management practices from the Industrial Revolution until the 1930s. However, the organization forms and strategy of decentralized decision making continue to influence much of American management practice to this day.

Scientific Management (1900–1930)

This school of thought developed from a focus on increasing efficiency in an increasingly complex industrial society. The theme of the school was on finding an appropriate match between worker characteristics and job design so as to ensure maximum efficiency. Frederick Taylor (1911), whose work is still referenced in many industries, heavily influenced this school of thought.

Human Relations (1920–1960)

It is possible that the Human Relations School developed as a reaction to the focus on humans as interchangeable parts in various mechanical processes whose efficiency could be enhanced by finding the one best way to carry out the process. That thinking developed as an integral part of the Scientific Management School. The world of American management thought was turned topsy-turvy by the work of a group of industrial psychologists from the Harvard faculty consulting at Western Electric's Hawthorne plant in 1929. Their work, which concluded that paying attention to the worker was in and of itself a powerful motivator of superior job effort and output, launched a revolution in social science. Since that time, there has been a plethora of articles, books and experiments that have attempted to link various dimensions of human needs (e.g., satisfaction, recognition, status, achievement, and so forth) to increased productivity. The belief in this approach continues unabated, although most of the "new" theories pertaining to enhanced human performance through intrinsic rewards were developed between 1930 and 1970. However, many of these links among participation, satisfaction, and productivity increases remain unsubstantiated (Yukl, 1998, p. 125).

Quantitative & Total Quality Management (1940–Present)

World War II saw the development and implementation of widespread and sophisticated computer applications for military use. This led to increased use of computers and other quantitative tools for the purpose of enhancing human decision making. The Total Quality Management (TQM) movement, which is based on reducing the amount of variance in goods production through statistical analysis, has its origin in this school of thought. Japan adopted many of these methods, and in large measure, Japan's recognition of their power in manufacturing enterprises accounts for Japan's transformation from a war-ravaged country to a major international competitor. The United States, ironically, did not begin to focus on the benefits of this approach until the late 1960s, when its manufacturing base and automobile markets experienced noticeable decline. Today, TQM is still in vogue as a tool of American management.

Systems Theory (1940–1980)

This theory sought to explain the various relationships that exist between an organization and its environment. The linkages determine the structure and function of organizational life, according to this school. Systems Theory continues to provide a useful method to study organizational functions and interactions.

Contingency Theory (1960–1990)

Organizational forms become more complex as the demand for product differentiation heightens. In an attempt to blend a variety of theories into one discipline, topologies begin to appear that indicate, for instance, that mechanistic, rule-oriented structures are appropriate for routine tasks in a stable environment, while non-routine tasks can best be conducted in organic structures (Burns and Stalker, 1961). Many argue that success is contingent on the linkages between organizations. Still other theorists think the United States is managing its way to economic decline based on the fact that the rise of lawyers, accountants, and financial experts to positions of control has led not only to a high rate of mergers and acquisitions, but to a decline in investment in research and development for new products. This thinking is still prevalent today (Hayes and Abernathy, 1980).

Population Ecology (1970–1980)

A theory developed by noted economist Oliver Williamson, the Chance Event (1975), began to take root during this period. It indicated that managerial skills have little to do with success; rather, the environment accounts for success. In other words, being in the right place at the right time has much more to do with company growth and survival than does management skill. The outcome for an organization is a function of being in the right place at the right time rather than a result of careful planning or skilled leadership (Williamson, 1983).

Theory Z (1960–1990)

The dominant issue of this period was how the United States could emulate Japan's success. According to Theory Z, the United States needed to emulate Japan's long-term focus and develop team-oriented systems, driven by worker input and control. Lifetime employment should become an objective of American enterprise. Theory Z was called into question with the recession of the late 1980s and the realization that manufacturing, particularly in steel-related industries, was no longer going to be dominated by the United States (Johnson and Packer, 1987). Further, Japan's recent economic plight, demands for equality, and its focus on quality-of-life issues such as more leisure time have highlighted the fact that industrial success may, as an evolutionary byproduct of economic success, change a nation's social values and work ethic. While Japan is of interest from the standpoint of how it will fare in the future, its style of management is no longer seen as a panacea for American concerns about its declining manufacturing base or its being able to compete effectively in a global economy.

Cookbook Approaches to Management Practices (1980–Present)

While the trend toward "cookbook" approaches that offer recipes as prescriptions to solve the perceived ills of American management first took root in the 1950s with the writings of Peter Drucker, such approaches gained momentum in the 1980s with Peters and Waterman's *In Search of Excellence* (1982), Albrecht and Zemke's *Service America* (1985), Crosby's *Quality Is Free* (1980), and Porter's *Competitive Strategy* (1980) and *Competitive Advantage* (1985). These works and others continue to influence American management thinking and practice. These prescriptions vary in that some focus on human behavior and others focus on organizational design. The American appetite for such instant approaches seems to be insatiable; however, the verdict is still out as to whether or not such recipes will be prescriptions that produce meaningful results.

The thoughts and ideas developed in this section are elaborated in the next section.

Organizational Forms Prior to the Industrial Revolution

The history of American management thought has its origins in Egyptian, Greek, and Roman society. The Greeks made a distinction between public and private goods and rejected mysticism in favor of the formation of some form of common governance to protect the use and distribution of public and private goods. The Egyptians were known for their engineering feats. The Romans had a system of specialized labor, which produced arms for barter. The Romans also had a sophisticated system of taxation.

Prior to the Industrial Revolution, in 17th century England, several organizational forms developed that utilized managers to accomplish objectives. Of primary consideration are the church and the military. Even earlier, the primitive tribes of many areas contributed much to the basic principles of justice and jurisprudence in communal life, but it is difficult to pinpoint the exact contributions of specific tribes.

The early nation-states administered the building of roads, the distribution of food supplies, the collection of taxes, and the supervision of the military. Niccolo Machiavelli's *The Prince* (1513) sets forth in elaborate detail not only the tactics of political survival within large organizations (which was required reading for John F. Kennedy's cabinet (Rourke, 1969, p. 48) and to this day still crosses the desk of many business-oriented graduate students) but highlights as well the complexity of the role of organizational management even in 15th century Florence.

The military advanced many principles of organizational life that are still in practice today. Early concepts that have been embraced by modern organizations include the chain of command as a primary mechanism for organizational decision making within hierarchies. Unity of command was based on the thought that individuals will be able to conduct their missions with less confusion and conflict if they are responsible to one supervisor. Ironically, the principle of unity of command has been supplanted by the matrix organization, where individuals report to more than one boss. Many scholars have observed that the major flaw of today's increasingly popular matrix organization is that employees become task-conflicted as a result of reporting to multiple supervisors (Daft, 1998). Moreover, American management seems to have a penchant for command and control structures and reporting mechanisms; hence, the obsession with management by objectives and centralized hierarchical decision making. Both of these practices, which are discussed below, have come under serious attack and are seen as counterproductive in fast-changing and productive environments (Kotter, 1977, 1982; Mintzberg, 1994).

Napoleon is given much credit for the concepts of delegation of authority and completed staff work. The former concept required Napoleon's officers to follow through in their specific areas of responsibility, and the latter concept required each officer to present to Napoleon three possible solutions to each identified problem. Military principles and practices continue to have enormous impact on modern organizations (Aldag and Stearns, 1987). All branches of the United States military have enormous research facilities dedicated to the development and improvement of management practices to enhance the effectiveness and efficiency of training programs, and the impact of motivational and disciplinary actions on productivity and morale (Dunnette, 1966).

The church observed many principles established by the military to structure a hierarchical chain of command. The most interesting aspect of the church's impact on organizational theory is the realization that ideology alone is sufficient to bind individuals to an organization. The understanding that the underpinnings of organization commitment are rooted in an organization's ability to influence attitudes and values provided the framework for latter-day sociologists and psychologists to study human motivation and the relationship between self-expression and self-concept. They concluded that these relationships are inseparably linked in 20th century corporate life.

The Post-Industrial Society

It has been cogently argued by Daniel Bell (1973) in one of the most important works of the past half-century, *The Coming of the Post-Industrial Society*, that the corporation has replaced the closely knit rural communities that sociologists such as Max Weber described as gemeinschaft. In gemeinschaft communities, citizens found psychological security in strong family ties and the institutions that were the backbone of agrarian life in pre-industrial America—the church and the school. This is particularly the case in advanced industrialized countries such as Britain, France, Germany, Japan, and especially the United States.

According to Bell, the United States, has become the first post-industrial society where work in the service area of the economy, which utilizes knowledge workers and produces no tangible product (e.g., government, education, healthcare, insurance, banking, and retail), has surpassed an industrial-manufacturing base as the locus of economic power. Bell's claim is supported by the research of Johnson and Packer's *Workforce 2000* (1987). Johnson and Packer report that in 1960, six of 10 workers were in white-collar occupations (p. 129). Moreover, the United States remains the only nation where the service sector accounts for more than half the total employment and more than half of the GNP (p. 15).

The movement to urban centers that occurred in tandem with the success of a burgeoning industrialized economy led to breakdowns in family and church ties. Bell's claims are well documented by a rising divorce rate and declining membership in and affiliations with organized religion among U.S. citizens.

Individuals, all of whom have a need to feel unique in a universe of others like themselves, found a replacement for the support institutions of agrarian life—the school, the church, the family—in the modern corporation (or organization, since one in six full-time American workers works outside the private sector). The consequences of this psychological fact and sociological phenomenon cannot be treated lightly.

This shifting of one's psychic alliances away from family, church and community life to the corporation or organization explains the major thrust of American management thought for nearly 100 years. The driving force behind contemporary theory has been the desire to understand the complex nature of the relationship between the individual and the corporation and how that relationship can be enhanced to make the corporation more viable and productive while at the same time providing the individual with an economically and psychologically rewarding relationship. Clearly, the focus of American management thought since Mayo's 1929 Hawthorne plant studies has been on the complex web of social and psychological relationships that exist between the individual and the corporation. Corporations, in modern American life, symbolize far more than a means to achieving economic well-being. They provide a reason for being, and in so doing, have come to manifest the individual concerns and social controversies (e.g., affirmative action, social responsibility) that confront American life in general.

Foundations for American Management Disciplines

The reshaping of American life in general and the formation of a cogent body of knowledge to enhance productivity and efficiency in America was spearheaded by the Industrial Revolution. Prior to the Industrial Revolution, 95 percent of the population of the United States lived in rural settings. Most urban centers in the early 1700s had less than 2,500 people. By 1960, 60 percent of the population lived in urban centers of 50,000 or more (Bell, 1973, p. 171; Johnson and Packer, 1987, p. 56). During the Industrial Revolution, the migration to urban centers was rapid and extensive. The impact of this movement produced radical changes in the manner of work and human socialization.

One impetus for the development of a discipline of management study was steeped in empiricism and was an outgrowth of serious scholarly work that

German philosopher Karl Marx. Courtesy of Library of Congress.

observed the ramifications of capitalism. Karl Marx (1847) is best known for the theory that capitalism was oppressive to the masses and that the end result would be the masses rising in revolt to suppress the bourgeoisie class. In the course of making his predictions, Marx did observe correctly that as capitalism emerged, it would be fueled by investment funds distinct from those of ownership. Thus, he anticipated the rise of a centralized banking system and its role in modern commerce. However, his related prediction that the banking system would hasten the revolution of the masses was incorrect. That prediction overlooked the implications of the development of a new class of worker, the professional manager. The managerial class, as it developed, became distinct from both the bourgeoisie and the proletariat (Bell, 1973, pp. 56–57).

Clearly, it was the impact of the Industrial Revolution, running in tandem with the emergence of capitalism as a dominant and viable form of economic production, that gave rise to formalized thinking about viable and necessary management practices to keep pace with the rapid spread of industry in the United States. Two pioneers and observers of the transformation of American life were Robert Owen (1771–1858) of Scotland and Charles Babbage (1792–1871) of England. Their work provided a body of knowledge that developed into the foundations for various American management schools.

Owen, prior to his migration to the United States in 1924, promoted humanism in his Scotland mill. He increased the minimum work age to 10 and provided meal breaks after $10\frac{1}{2}$ hours of work (Aldag and Stearns, 1987, p. 34). Babbage, a mathematical genius, perhaps best known for the binomial system that underpins much modern computer technology, advocated profit sharing and bonus plans in his 1835 work, *On the Economy of Machinery and Manufacturers*.

Interestingly, the ideas of Owen and Babbage took almost 100 years to take hold in the United States. Their contributions came to light as the Industrial Revolution took root and as modern capitalism succeeded. Concerns about issues of material and human inefficiency were exacerbated as competition increased. A new focus developed on cutting costs and increasing efficiency. For the first time in the history of civilization, the standard of living rose due to the increased productivity and efficiency of corporations, outside of the ravages of war, and theories of management began to develop and form discrete bodies of knowledge.

The Classical School of American Management

The brilliant German sociologist Max Weber (1864–1925) is credited with predicting the rise and significance of a managerial class created by the Industrial Revolution. Weber (1905) is most famous for coining the term "bureaucracy" to describe the characteristics of the newly emerged capitalistic structures. He realized that these new entities were growing beyond the control that could be exerted by the owners of the capital investment. A decision-making process was required that could be placed in the hands of a capable managerial class. For Weber, the expansion of the well-educated class of professional managers hired for their skills was inevitable, and he predicted that professional managers would bring a form of organizational decision making he described as "rationalism" to modern organizations (Weber, 1905, p. 5). The need for rationalism was brought about by the complexity of modern bureaucracy and implemented through a professional class of managers to provide a basis for organizations to enhance productivity and efficiency. This rationalism as a component of the organizations Weber observed was in contrast to earlier organizational forms that developed in the first stages of capitalism that followed the Industrial Revolution. During those stages, one person, primarily the owner of the enterprise, made all the technical and business decisions (Weber, 1905).

Weber's work provided the framework for a Classical School of American management. The Classical School described organizations as a totality of structures and functions yielding a desired output. Weber characterized the components of bureaucracy as follows: hierarchical structure, division of labor, rules

German sociologist/political economist Max Weber. Courtesy of Library of Congress.

and technical competence, management separate from ownership, position accounts for power, and formalized record keeping. While Weber's list of characteristics has often been interpreted to mean that bureaucracies should include these components, he intended his list only to be descriptive rather than prescriptive (Aldag and Stearns, 1987).

As American capitalism became firmly rooted in the 1900s, the organization forms needed to house the massive production required to fuel the rising appetite for consumer goods became a focus of some of America's most influential corporate executives. Sloan of General Motors, Vail, who developed American Telephone and Telegraph, and Teagle of Standard Oil, all advocated decentralization. Sloan (1964), perhaps more than any other writer, influenced the manner in which most American organizations are conceptualized and run to the present day. He wrote (to a lesser extent as did Vail and Teagle) that decentralization, where each unit is its own profit center, is the appropriate way to structure capitalistic enterprise.

Prior to Sloan's conceptualization of the modern American corporation (exemplified by Cadillac Motor Cars and Chevrolet Motor Cars, among others), the basis for a manufacturing structure was solely to increase efficiency through standardization of unit production, a concept that was attributed to the mechanical genius of Henry Ford. In 1908, Ford produced the Model T car for mass consumption. Each vehicle took 12.5 hours to manufacture. Just 12 years later, the same car was produced in a fraction of that time (Stoner, 1995, p. 29).

Sloan realized that while standardization had its merits, always producing the cheapest and most efficient brand left consumers little choice. He felt they would pay a premium for more variety (Bell, 1973, p. 277). As Chandler observed in his 1962 classic, *Strategy and Structure*, which studied 100 of America's largest companies—"structure follows strategy"—a fact attributable to Sloan's impact.

The writings of Henri Fayol (1841–1925) and Chester Barnard (1886–1961) are also found in the Classical School. Fayol, a French mining company executive, viewed work in terms of functional divisions: task, authority, discipline, command, direction, equity, initiative, and morale (Aldag and Stearns, 1987, pp. 35–36). He made no attempt to apply his descriptions, but sought to offer categories for the classification of events within emerging organizations of the industrial world.

Chester Barnard wrote *The Functions of the Executive* in 1938. The book is credited with paving the way for the behavior revolution (McCurdy, 1973). Barnard addressed many issues in his book that are still a focus of managers today. These issues include the following: equilibrium, incentives, participation, decision systems, and the preconditions necessary for subordinates to accept authority (Barnard, 1938).

Barnard was president of New Jersey Bell during the late 1920s and 1930s. Later, he headed the Rockefeller Foundation. After the U.S. stock market crash of 1929 and for the decade during the depression that followed, the New Jersey Bell company never failed to pay a dividend, even though its workers were not given pay raises. As a result, some scholars, such as Charles Perrow (1972), feel some of Barnard's work is disingenuous. They believe that Barnard was writing his book to placate employees for the harsh actions of corporations in the late 1920s and 1930s.

Whatever the motivation for Barnard's view that the organization is a "cooperative system" where authority resides in a subordinate's ability to accept or reject orders, his impact on the field of management thought was monumental. He is often cited as the most referenced management theorist. Barnard's "acceptance theory" outlined the obligation an organization has to provide a context for subordinates to accept authority. According to Barnard, four conditions must be met for employee acceptance: 1) subordinates understand the order, (2) subordinates see the order as consistent with the purposes of the organization, (3) the order is compatible with their personal interest, and (4) subordinates are mentally and physically able to comply with the order (Barnard, 1938; Aldag and Stearns, pp. 39–40).

Herbert Simon (1957), the last writer discussed here, in conjunction with the Classical School, credits Barnard with focusing his thinking on the manner in which decisions were made within organizations that grew and prospered in the hundred years before he set forth his Nobel prize-winning theories on decision making in his volume *Administrative Behavior*. The impact of Simon's work is evidenced by the continued demand for the book, which is now in its 10th printing and celebrating its 50th anniversary.

Prior to Simon's work, decision-making theory had its roots in the discipline of economics. The central point of the economic models of decision making is the notion of "rational self-interest." Individuals are seen as capable of selecting among a variety of known alternatives and to make a selection from an array of alternatives which maximizes the gain of the decision-maker.

Simon forever changed the face of modern decision-making literature, research and practice by pointing out that so much information is available that the quest for more and more information could be never-ending. At some point, the amount of information garnered would overwhelm the capabilities of any individual or group to analyze it and make a decision that was known to maximize gain. In other words, as Simon states it, the capabilities of individuals (and groups) are bounded (pp. 88–89). Therefore, one must start with the premise that during the decision-making process, rationality is bounded.

Coupled with the notion of bounded rationality is Simon's notion of "satisficing" (pp. 119–120). That term indicates that since it is not possible to evaluate all the alternatives, the decision maker must select from among those alternatives that appear to meet the objective. Since one cannot (or perhaps better stated, would not) know the maximal objective in many decision-making circumstances, one selects an alternative that leads to a less-than-maximal result; one "satisfices."

The Scientific Management School

A major movement that paralleled the Classical School of American management was the Scientific Management School. The founder of this discipline was Frederick W. Taylor (1856–1915). Taylor was a self-taught engineer who utilized time-and-motion studies to find "the one best way" to enhance productivity. "Taylorism" has been quite controversial from its inception to the present day.

Taylor worked as a chief engineer at the three largest steel companies in the United States between 1880 and 1915. The unions were fearful that his methods would lead to layoffs, and Taylor was compelled to testify before Congress. In his testimony, Taylor clearly sided with the employee position and expressed his belief that any earnings resulting from increased efficiency and productivity should be shared with the worker.

Although Taylor has been criticized for dehumanizing work based on his focus of matching physical traits to job performance, it is clear that Taylor's interest was in reducing the fatigue that results from manual labor and repetitive tasks. In the latter instance, Taylor was an advocate of cross-training to reduce fatigue and boredom. Although Taylor has been attacked for falsifying much of his empirical data, in *The Principles of Scientific Management* (1911), there is no doubt that his methods revolutionized the United States' steel industry and that his approach to management has remained a critical component of American management's attempts to increase productivity and efficiency through time-and-motion studies (Aldag and Stearns, 1987, pp. 40–42).

One of Taylor's disciples is particularly interesting, Lillian Gilbreth. Few women, when compared to men, have been recognized as influential in the development of American management thought. One notable exception was Lillian Gilbreth. She and her husband, Frank Gilbreth, expanded Taylor's ideas about "the one best way" to complete a task to include the effects of motion and fatigue on task performance. They believed that where worker fatigue or boredom could be reduced by lessening the number of steps in a task a worker performed, or by rotating assignments for a worker performing repetitive manual work, that a worker's productivity would increase. Lillian Gilbreth, a gifted scholar, focused her academic research on training methods to reduce fatigue and boredom. In 1914, when her doctoral thesis, *The Psychology of Management*, was published the publisher required that the author be listed as "L.M. Gilbreth" to avoid the reference to her gender (p. 43). Nonetheless, Gilbreth's observations expanded Taylorism to address more systematically the human needs of workers.

The Human Relations School

The 1927 work of Elton Mayo and his associates, F.J. Roethlisberger and W.J. Dickson from the Harvard Business School at Western Electric's Hawthorne plant in Cicero, Illinois, created a revolution in the field of social science in general and management studies in particular. An indirect ramification of the scientific management approach was a negative reaction to what was perceived as the school's less-than-dignified treatment of human labor. Thus, it is not surprising that this next period in American management was dominated by a highly humanistic focus.

Mayo (1880–1949), Australian-born and educated as a psychologist, is considered the founder of the Human Relations movement. Mayo and two of his colleagues on the faculty of the Harvard Business School, Fritz Roethlisberger and William Dickson, were called in to the Hawthorne plant of Western Electric in 1927 to investigate some unusual findings (Mayo, 1945; Roethlisberger and Dickson, 1939). Vernon and Wyatt, two industrial psychologists employed by

Western Electric, were investigating the effects of noise, light, and humidity on productivity (Aldag and Stearns, 1987, pp. 45–47; Schermerhorn, 1999, pp. 20–23).

Not surprisingly, Vernon and Wyatt found that productivity increased when room lighting was improved. However, what most surprised them was that productivity also increased when the lighting was decreased below its initial point in the experiment. Further, after Mayo and his associates arrived, the research found that when employees had input in to the scheduling of their rest breaks and other similar types of activities, their productivity also increased. The authors labeled these findings an "emotional chain reaction" (Mayo, 1945) and concluded that the social interactions at work in all human relationships provide a source of satisfaction on the job, leading to productivity gains (Boone and Bowen, 1987; Matteson and Ivancevich, 1996; Aldag and Stearns, 1987).

As Aldag and Stearns (1987, p. 47) point out, the "Hawthorne effect" has been misinterpreted to mean that productivity rises whenever one pays attention to workers. Actually, the Hawthorne effect refers to the fact that productivity also increased in the control group. It is important to note that the control group was informed of its role in the study. Thus, the work of Mayo had two broad implications for social science. The first was that social science experiments needed to be better designed to prevent contamination of control group effects. The second implication was the realization that productivity can be dramatically affected by simply paying attention to the worker. Some scholars suggest that the timing of the Hawthorne study, which took place prior to and during the Great Depression, accounted for the gains in productivity, given workers' fears about losing their jobs during that tight economic period. Far more scholars however, have concluded that attention paid to the worker is more important to him or her than pay and working conditions in most instances (Herzberg, et al., 1959).

The impact of Mayo's work cannot be underestimated. It shifted the emphasis from the mode of production to the psychological needs of individual workers as the compelling force behind efficiency and productivity gains. Many scholars and practitioners took note of Mayo's work and the literature devoted to human relations proliferated.

A female writer who was particularly influential during this time frame was Mary Parker Follett. Follett was a leading exponent of human relations principles. Based on her experiences as a social worker in the 1920s, Follett believed that the productivity of the industrial organization depended upon an understanding of individual and group motivation. She focused her writings on the effects of control, participation, conciliation, leadership and conflict on individual and group behavior. In 1940, Luther Gulick, credited as the founder of the school of public administration, edited *Dynamic Administration: The Collected Works of Mary Parker Follett*. That book was a compilation of her observations about the necessity to humanize the workplace to increase productivity, and it was based on a series of her major papers. The issues Follett raised in her papers regarding the effects of control, participation, conciliation, leadership, and conflict on individual and group behavior are still relevant to current organizational research efforts (McCurdy, p. 49).

Other notable writers who pursued the human relations school's line of reasoning and whose work continues to dramatically affect the thinking of American managers include Douglas McGregor (1906–1964), *The Human Side of Enterprise* (1960), Chris Argyris (1933–), *Personality and Organization* (1957), Abraham Maslow (1908–1970), *A Theory of Motivation* (1954), and Frederick Hertzberg (1931–), *Motivation to Work* (1959).

During the Human Relations period, McGregor (1960) postulated his well-known Theory X and Theory Y, whereby he argued that workers will be more productive in conditions where management strives to demonstrate its belief that workers are inherently motivated to do a good job and that they do not need prodding to do it. McGregor's work is generally interpreted as an argument to adopt a Theory Y management style which, when contrasted to Theory X's autocratic style, yields more autonomy, trust and self-motivation for the worker. McGregor's work complements that of Chris Argyris (1957, 1960, 1962, 1964). Argyris argues that workers subjected to an autocratic organization will be unable to meet their needs and that such practices will lead to human and organizational decay.

It remained for Abraham Maslow (1954) to develop a theory on the levels of fulfillment a worker can find within an organizational structure. He developed the hierarchy of needs, which has five progressive stages: (1) physiological, (2) safety, (3) social, (4) esteem, and (5) self-actualization. One cannot move to the next stage until the need associated with the preceding stage has been met. Physiological and safety needs are fulfilled by the organization's provision of an exchange sufficient for the employee to provide for food and shelter. Social needs are met by the daily formal and informal activities an employee can engage in as an extension of organizational interactions. These interactions extend from chitchat at the coffee machine to recreational trips.

The compelling force behind the need for esteem is the basic human desire for recognition. Psychologists and sociologists have argued for decades (Freud, 1910; Adler, 1954, p. v; Bell, 1973) that the human species has a need for recognition. One's feelings of uniqueness are essential to well-being. Self-actualization, the highest-order need, is an ideal and not a real state. After the employee's needs are met at the lower levels, the organization must keep an individual sufficiently challenged in order for the individual to find fulfillment and remain highly productive. Thus, in an ideal work setting, the individual is ever presented with new and rewarding challenges and opportunities (Maslow, 1954; Aldag and Stearns, 1987; Cascio, 1998). The result is continued self-growth.

The Human Relations School has had a monumental influence on the practices of American management. The focus of the school was on the importance of the individual and the relationship between worker satisfaction and productivity. The empirical results of this relationship are uneven according to many significant reviews of scholarly research (Yukl, 1998, pp. 125–127). Serious criticism of the Human Relations School has arisen. Noted British sociologist Charles Perrow (1972) observed that many of the school's observations were given impetus by the time frames in which they occurred. Much of the work of Mayo and Barnard took place in the aftermath of the Great Depression, which may have skewed the results. Some have argued that workers in the Hawthorne plant were delighted to have employment in 1933, and thus productivity went up during Mayo's studies for fear of job loss. Some scholars (Perrow, 1972; Bell, 1973) believe the focus on human relations went only so deep. To cite one example, Barnard's company paid a dividend to stockholders through the Depression, but, when asked by the workers for a 5-cent-per-hour pay raise, Barnard said, in effect, "let them get to hell" (Perrow, 1972). Perrow (1972) and others see the work of the Human Relations School as trite and predicting only the obvious (Bell, 1973).

Whatever one's view of the Human Relations School, it is clear that the impact of the body of literature from the school has been and continues to be a dominant force in American management thought. Much academic research has tested numerous hypotheses related to whether money alone is a sufficient motivator, the relationship of supervisory practices to job success, and the effects of management practice on absenteeism, illness, and job satisfaction (Hertzberg, 1959; Casio, 1998). More often than not, these studies indicate that intangible factors (e.g., recognition) are important—or more important—than tangible factors (i.e., money, chief among them), in increasing worker productivity and satisfaction.

Quantitative & Total Quality Management

The 1940s presented a diametrically opposite approach to the humanism of the preceding three decades. Computer systems and models gave rise to the application of quantitative tools to management decisions. Perhaps the most famous implementation of quantitative applications to corporate success was the use of W. Edwards Deming's work by Japan. Unable to find a market for his ideas in the United States, Deming, an American physicist and mathematician (and the statistician on the Hawthorne studies), took his ideas on Total Quality Management to Japan. He is given much credit for rapidly turning around Japan's quality management processes in a few years (Aldag and Stearns, 1987, p. 57; Walton, 1986, p. 7).

While Deming's work has been given much lip service in the United States, there may be a profound misunderstanding regarding the application of Deming's work. At the core of Deming's method was the application of the mathematical concept of variance to the manufacturing process. Deming believed that the key to improving products was to reduce the variance, i.e., the error rate. If one can reduce variance, quality and productivity go up. Standard performance evaluations and a focus on individual workers were deplored by Deming (1986, 1989). Product failures and poor service were the results of poorly built systems, not deficiencies within employees or their managers, he believed. For example, producing television sets with an error rate of 1 percent, as opposed to an error rate of 10 percent, is the key to increased quality and productivity, according to Deming. It is exactly this process that Japan mastered (Franklin, 1983; Kepner, 1982).

In the United States, the quality movement is often reduced to greater participation efforts or to improving human interaction. Often these attempts to improve human interaction boil down to efforts to improve customer service by enhancing an employee's interpersonal skills. Critics of this type of application of

Deming's work call it an attempt to impose "smile technology"—a term used by major corporate leaders in Japan to describe American management's penchant for the quick fix or easy answer (Walton, 1986).

The work of Deming continues to influence the thinking of American managers, even though many fail to grasp the fact that it is applicable only where variance can be precisely measured and improved through statistical analysis. For such a process as TQM to be successful, traditional performance evaluation and Management-by-Objectives plans must be set aside. They focus on trite measures of employee behavior and attempt to assign individual blame. The true impetus for improvement comes from the workers. Management's role should be to allow the workers to determine what work needs to be accomplished and how best to accomplish that work (Deming, 1986, 1989). Management provides resources and does not set direction or attempt to measure what management thinks it needs to measure. Traditional American management performance evaluation plans and Management-by-Objectives plans often confuse any employee motion that management can measure with actual productivity, efficiency, or creativity. Nonetheless, such plans are endemic to American management culture and therefore explain why employee empowerment has been so slow to take root in American management practice (Mintzberg, 1994; Kotter, 1982).

Systems Theory

Systems Theory came to fruition in the 1950s. Much of Systems Theory is based on the observations of biologist Ludwig Von Bertalanfly (Aldag and Stearns, 1987, p. 52). He was interested in the relationships among various subsystems forming a complete cycle. Later, Katz and Kahn (1966) elaborated on Von Bertalanfly's theories and applied the concepts of open systems and closed systems to organizations.

The concepts of open and closed systems were useful in the social sciences for establishing classification schemes to study organizational dependencies and environmental exchanges. Open systems rely on exchanges with other systems for survival. In theory, closed systems are self-reliant, producing and consuming everything they need for survival.

Katz and Kahn (1966) made an attempt to keep management theory a serious academic discipline. Their Open Systems Theory attempts to unify the individual, the organization, and the environment. While they made a valiant attempt to establish organizational theory as an academic discipline, their work appears to have found an audience primarily among scholars as opposed to managers.

Contingency Theory

Contingency theory holds that universal principles do not apply to general solutions to individual organizational problems. Each situation has unique characteristics that require managers to diagnose a specific solution for each problem an organization confronts rather than rely on a general approach. Contingency theory merges other theories and approaches. The rise of lawyers and accountants to leadership positions in American industry in recent years gave impetus to this movement. This shift in leadership base focused attention on exploiting for profit the linkages between organizations (Hayes and Abernathy, 1980). In practice, what encumbered the attention of American management in the 1970s was merger mania. Mergers are clearly the domain of lawyers, accountants, and MBA holders from select American universities. There is, however, no evidence that merger practices will work in the long term. In fact, there is compelling evidence that lines of business outside the purview of an organization's core business often lead to management turmoil, financial loss, and a lack of necessary innovation (Hayes and Abernathy, 1980). Thus, mergers today are viewed often from a variety of perspectives, financial and cultural.

Population Ecology Perspective

The Population Ecology Perspective offers a severe critique of management as a career for which one prepares. This body of thought is evidenced in the writings of economist Oliver Williamson (1983). Williamson asserts that the odds of becoming the leader of a large corporation are determined by chance, not ability. He goes on to state that organizational form, which he labels "production function," is far more important than strategy in terms of accounting for positive organizational performance.

Geert Hofstede is quick to point out that Williamson's theories (and those of other American scholars and management practitioners) are unique to the culture in which they are found and may not be applicable to other cultures (Hofstede, 1996, p. 79). There are no such things, according to Hofstede (p. 77) as universal management theories.

Williamson's focus on structure is linked to American management's historical penchant for formalized controls. Hofstede points out that the American company of Booz, Allen and Hamilton was commissioned by the German government in 1973 to review German management practice. The study resulted in a severe critique of the German concept of management, which is less formalized than its American counterpart. To support his assertions, Hofstede points out that the German economy has continuously outperformed the U.S. economy in almost every respect since the report was issued (p. 80).

Hofstede's work raises another important issue. The word "culture" has taken on new meaning. In today's world of increased competition, culture refers to the differences among nations in norms, values, customs, and beliefs that must be understood in order to bring about effective business relationships. For Hofstede, the term is a macro concept in the sense defined above.

A distinction must be made between Hofstede's use of the term culture from the micro use of that word by Edgar Schein. And while Hofstede is reluctant to do so, this distinction may explain Hofstede's criticism (1996) of Schein, a renowned academic and founder of a discipline of management thought that examines the values, norms, customs, and beliefs of organizations to explain mistakes, promote change, and improve performance. Schein views the organization as a psychotherapist views an individual patient. In order to effect change, Schein observes (1990, pp. 109–119), one must change the values, beliefs, customs, and norms that are endemic to an organization and the units within it by replacing them with new values, beliefs, customs, and norms. Such a process is time-consuming and requires a skilled practitioner to implement.

The Focus on Japanese Management—Theory Z

From 1960 to 1990, American managers were preoccupied with Japanese management styles. So dominant was the impact of Japan's industrial success in the 1970s and 1980s that it is rumored that an American MBA student, when presented with the choice of another lecture on Japanese management practice or committing hara-kiri, chose the latter.

The preoccupation with Japan was underscored by the prescriptions presented by Ouchi in his 1981 book, *Theory 2: How American Business Can Meet the Japanese Challenge*. In that work, Ouchi notes that America focuses on short-term employment, individual decision making, and a system of formal controls. In contrast, Japan's focus is on lifetime employment, collective responsibility, and informal controls. Ouchi suggested a modified American plan, which he called Theory Z. Under a Theory Z management style, American managers should focus on long-term employment, individual responsibility, and a mixture of formal and informal controls.

As it turns out, none of the principles of Japan's management practice, such as lifetime employment, were particularly applicable to American management. In recent years, the world economy has shown that Japan's practices cannot insulate Japan from the effects of recession. Moreover, Japan is moving away from commitments to lifetime or long-term employment, something the United States was forced to abandon with rigor in the late 1980s when a recession swept the nation and resulted in numerous instances of corporate downsizing. IBM, for example, was forced to abandon its commitment to a job for life as it reduced its workforce by more than 100,000 employees (Miller, 1993, p. A6).

The movement to copy Japan's management style as a quick-fix method for America's problems highlights the penchant of many American managers to grasp for "cookbook" approaches to complex issues that are deeply embedded in all aspects of one's culture. How does one isolate the decay of America's inner-city schools and the poorer-than-average performance in math and science of American students on various international exams versus students of other large industrial countries (Lapointe, Mead, and Phillips, 1989) from the overall ability of the United States to remain competitive well into the future? The literacy rate of Japan, an extremely homogeneous society, is close to 100 percent. Its family structure remains largely intact. Moreover, there is an emphasis on educational attainment based on intense competition. These attitudes must be contrasted to those of the United States, an extremely heterogeneous country, whose literacy rate is half that of Japan, and whose divorce rate now exceeds 50 percent (Johnson and Packer, 1989). Moreover, in the United States, access to schools and indeed employment is dictated by many factors other than academic achievement (Bell, 1973).

Cookbook Approaches:
The State of Modern American Management Theory

The point of the focus on the differences between Japan and the United States is to highlight a growing problem in American management theory. That problem is the failure or inability to separate complex issues from cookbook solutions.

It is clear that the focus of American management on Japan underscored the movement of contemporary management theory from a serious academic discipline to a grasp for the quick fix—a movement away from serious and rigorous analysis toward recipes and prescriptions. This propensity to draw from recipes as prescriptions seems vested in American corporate culture. American management has often been criticized for its short-term focus (Hayes and Abernathy, 1980) and its rejection of the intuitive process within workers that leads to productive and creative outcomes (Mintzberg, 1994). Instead, American management has tended to embrace command and control devices such as Management-By-Objectives and traditional performance plans that measure over a short term those results management thinks are desirable but which serve primarily to maintain management's own power base (Deming, 1986; Kotter, 1978, 1982).

It is little wonder that the quick fix has so much appeal to an American management focused on, or perhaps obsessed with, measurable short-term results. As is pointed out below, this focus on developing plans to measure short-term results became the reason IBM missed the desktop computer revolution (Carroll, 1993).

Moreover, many management consultants have achieved celebrity status (Drucker, 1950; Peters, 1983; Covey, 1989, 1991; Senge, 1990, 1994; Porter 1980, 1983). Few among them are women, however. One exception is Rosabeth Moss Kanter, a Harvard faculty member and the first female editor of the *Harvard Business Review*. She has achieved celebrity status based on her writings that address organizational innovation (1997), international and local competition (1995), organizational change management (1990, 1984) and a variety of other topics. As is the case with her male peers, her access to the leaders of America's largest corporations has led to a plethora of prescriptions to solve the dilemma faced by American managers in an increasingly complex world. The legitimate issue is whether such prescriptions offer real answers for serious problems.

It is almost an anathema to raise the name of Peter Drucker in the celebrity as opposed to management guru context, but some writers have observed that the genre of contemporary management theory has been and continues to be greatly influenced by Drucker. Drucker, perhaps as much as any other organizational theorist of the past 50 years, embodies the issue of whether or not management theory is an academic discipline or something else. The fact that Drucker was denied a chair at Yale University (Micklethwait and Wooldridge, 1996) for not being a "proper academic" reveals the vexing question for the future of management theory: Is management theory a serious body of academic literature, or is it pop psychology based on a series of "quick-fix" prescriptions, and cookbook approaches whose recipes catch on like a fad diet and go out of style with the next trend? In their *New York Times* article, Micklethwait and Wooldridge point out that Oxford's refusal to establish a separate business school focused on management as an academic discipline was in part based on the fact that one can find on the same bookshelf in a bookstore's business reference section ". . . heavyweight texts like Michael Porter's *Competitive Advantage of Nations* . . . (next to) such poppycock as *Make It So: Leadership Lessons From Star Trek The Next Generation* (1996, p. 3). While they conclude that Oxford made a mistake, this writer has a less charitable point of view. Since Porter rose to fame in the 1980s with his works based on serious academic research, he has had few if any rivals. Unfortunately, most modern-day business texts fall in the genre of cookbooks that offer recipes as quick-fix prescriptions.

Let us analyze this issue regarding management as a discipline by briefly reviewing the contributions of Drucker a bit more fully. Born in Vienna in 1910, Peter Drucker authored his first book, *The Practice of Management* (1954). That book provided an analysis of successful company practices at Ford Motor Company, Sears-Roebuck and Company and IBM contrasted with unsuccessful practices. Drucker, the founder of Management-By-Objectives (MBO) and its leading proponent, presents advice in the book on implementing MBO, marketing strategies, organizational structure and decision-making. The book has sold over 200,000 copies since it was published and continues to sell 20,000 copies a year (Boone and Bowen, 1987, p. 186).

Drucker, more than any other management theorist, personifies the modern movement of management thought from a discipline rooted in scholarly research to a collection of practical advice provided "in a lively style" and designed to captivate a wide audience of practitioners (Boone and Bowen, 1987, p. 123). His work can be contrasted to the work of Weber (1905) and Bell (1973) whose focus was to explain the issues underlying certain tendencies in social settings, such as a corporation. Drucker's focus, on the other hand, was to provide a pragmatic approach to solving particular business problems by prescribing a recipe-like solution.

In 1960, Drucker authored *The Concept of the Corporation*. In that book, he analyzed General Motors, which he labels the most successful company in social history. More importantly, from the standpoint of impact, is the fact that he touts Management-By-Objectives as a prescription for successful management. This development presents an interesting phenomenon. As a result of his access to top officials in America's most successful companies, Drucker can prescribe remedies to business leaders. Most large companies have, as a result of Drucker's work, embraced the concept of Management By Objectives.

Management-By-Objectives has come under careful scrutiny as a result of IBM's failures in the late 1980s. MBO was seen as a central cause of that failure, as Carroll points out in his 1993 *Wall Street Journal* article, "The Failure of Central Planning at IBM." Carroll argues that IBM placed too much emphasis on planning, which created a rigid, centralized structure that rewarded planning itself as a business accomplishment at the expense of true innovation.

Henry Mintzberg, the only individual to twice win the *Harvard Business Review* award for article of the year for "The Manager's Job: Folklore and Fact" (1972); and "The Fall and Rise of Strategic Planning" (1994), has questioned the role of MBO-type thinking altogether. He argues that the American managers' penchant for analysis at the expense of synthesis may lead to a loss of competitiveness. This is exactly what happened to both General Motors and IBM in the later stages of their histories.

Management, Mintzberg argues, needs to be more intuitive and less structured. He recognizes that a command and control structure is a hallmark of the American way of doing things. Managers cannot get their arms around intuition, but they can revel in the good feelings they have when they see and touch a nicely laid-out MBO plan. It is exactly this need for something tangible that Drucker awakened in the American manager, and as a result he became an American icon of folk hero status in business circles.

Many other American writers of organizational theory have sought to emulate Drucker's success. A few examples will suffice to make the point. In 1983, Peters and Waterman, two consultants from America's most successful high-end corporate consulting firm, McKinsey and Company, wrote *In Search of Excellence,* which became an international bestseller. It was read in boardrooms throughout America and accepted as gospel. Peters obtained a syndicated column and was a featured speaker on television and at Fortune 500 companies. As it turned out, most of the companies Peters and Waterman covered in the book were in serious trouble within five years of the book's writing, especially IBM. Peters and Waterman embraced IBM's management styles and practices in the same way that Drucker embraced many of General Motors' practices some 30 years earlier.

As was the case with Drucker, it was their access to corporate executives and lively style that paved the way to the bestseller list. The reader should not make the conceptual leap that writing for popular use is not a noble end and that this author frowns on popular success in the market place. Rather, the question is to what end was the work designed—scholarship that leads to gains by business readers or popular appeal based on anecdotal evidence or personal interviews of business leaders whose views may or may not be transferable from one setting to another but whose names generate market interest in book purchases.

In Search of Excellence prescribes a series of steps for companies to follow: staying close to customers to learn their preferences; being hands-on in order to stay in touch with employee roles (i.e., "management by wandering around," p. 296); remaining with the business the company knows best (i.e., "stick to the knitting," p. 292); and fostering an inclusive climate for all employees. The book's format—easy to read with plenty of pizzazz—became the benchmark for how to relay management theory to practitioners.

The overriding problem with a prescriptive approach is that the "cure" may not be applicable to a specific type of disease. IBM, for instance, dominated by a centralized management structure, continued to stick to the mainframe market it knew best, and missed in very large part the desktop revolution. It has yet to recover from that mistake. Moreover, the U.S. recession of the late 1980s downsized exactly that class of employees whose management roles (and subsequent employee output) were to be greatly enhanced by "wandering around." Technology changed the economics of scale associated with various unnecessary levels of management; accordingly, the prescription to wander around was sacrificed in the wake of a difficult to foresee but nonetheless monumental trend toward individual technological empowerment and its associated productivity gains.

A few years after *In Search of Excellence, Service America* (1985) arrived. Authored by Karl Albrecht and Ron Zemke, *Service America* looks at the key to service among successful companies and prescribes how the individual employee can make a difference. Staff departments must see those they serve as internal customers, while every employee must recognize the "moment of truth" where the employee's interaction with a customer becomes the company to that customer, the authors assert. While the book details the massive amount of money spent by companies such as Scandinavian Air to improve service through technological means, many American companies adopted the less important but quicker to implement aspects of customer service such as customer service training programs.

In the view of the author (Frank, 1994), the focus on service in terms of customer relations training and finding the right people for the job caught on because it was an objective management could meet. As the author observed in 1994, one large financial institution implemented a customer service improvement program even though that institution was already in the top 2 percent of companies providing a similar service. The customer service training issue is raised not to debate the value of good customer service; rather, it is intended to highlight the fact that an easy-to-measure program was implemented while issues that are more serious and difficult to assess, such as a better method for that institution to ensure a sound loan portfolio, did not receive attention. The institution went bankrupt in 1993 as a result of its poor loan portfolio.

After being ignored by management in the United States, Deming's work came to their attention in the 1970s as a result of its success in helping to revitalize Japan's economy. However, American practitioners did not utilize Deming's work in the same way Japan used his methods and ideas. American managers sought to capitalize on Deming's ideas in the same way that they grasped the prescriptions of Drucker, Peters and Waterman, and Albercht and Zemke. The shortcut they sought was to implement Deming's ideas, which centered around the mathematical concept of the value of measurement of statistical variance in products and systems where such measurement is precisely known (e.g., parts manufacturing). The work of many other consultants who built on Deming's ideas in a manner that appealed to American managers by simplification of his statistical processes and avoidance of the necessity to give up such command and control devices as MBO caught on in the United States. Philip Crosby, author of *Quality Is Free* (1980), exemplifies the type of approach that has appeal to American managers. He is a management consultant who offers a step-by-step approach to solve quality problems. The approach is general in nature and appears to be applicable to a variety of corporate situations. American managers were attracted to this seeming panacea, and many failed to realize what Deming pointed out so clearly; mainly that real quality improvement is limited to those systems where variance (in the mathematical sense discussed previously) can be accurately obtained, measured, and then reduced.

In 1993, Michael Hammer and James Champy wrote *Reengineering the Corporation*. American managers embraced the book, which provided yet another cookbook approach to solving management problems in corporate America. Hammer and Champy do present some interesting and worthwhile notions, however. Foremost among them is the idea that Adam Smith's concept of division and specialization in labor as presented in his *An Inquiry into the Wealth of*

Nations (1776) is no longer applicable. Modern technology makes it possible to radically redesign today's corporations. Such redesign must be driven from the top down and therefore is in stark contrast to the decades of work invested by American managers in Total Quality Management, a bottom-to-top concept that in theory empowers the lowest-level worker. This explains why Hammer (1996) notes that 75 percent of reengineering efforts fail. Many companies, based on the prescriptions found in the literature, implement both approaches simultaneously, only to be frustrated by the ensuing failure of each.

It is vastly more important to realize that many problems are inherently complex than it is to seek ready-made solutions through the most recently popular quick fix. It seems to this writer that much of contemporary management literature has been instrumental in perpetuating the belief that following simple formulas will provide meaningful results for the long term. Ken Blanchard's *One-Minute Manager* books (1982, 1984, 1986, 1987, 1990) are a case in point. In his books, Blanchard gives advice to managers on one-minute praisings, one-minute reprimands, one-minute feedback, one-minute goal setting, and the like. No doubt the issues that underlie Blanchard's prescriptions are serious academic and practical concerns rooted in the field of psychology. These books, however, which take very little time to read, became very popular in boardrooms and with chief executive officers throughout the nation based not on the strong but unrevealed scholarship that underlies the basic principles, but based on the fact that Blanchard clearly knew his market. He knew that easy-to-adopt quick fixes would appeal to many American managers.

Steven Covey has clearly become the Ken Blanchard of the 1990s. Today, prescriptions for management are outlined in his two most widely known works, *The 7 Habits of Highly Effective People* (1989) and *Principle-Centered Leadership* (1990). Covey now presides over a vast training network of disciples, who teach his program to numerous corporations and individuals. The principles of his first book provide the 7 steps to become a highly effective manager (be proactive, keep the end point in mind, put first things first, think win-win, first understand then be understood, be synergistic, self-renew). The second book provides the ingredients for successful leadership (continually learning, service oriented, energetic, trustful, adventurous, synergistic and self-renewing). The value of works such as those written by Covey and Blanchard is ultimately, as is "beauty," in the eyes of the beholder.

Senge's *The Fifth Discipline* (1990), which espouses the need for organizations to seek a method for continuous learning, has been enhanced with a field book (1994) to help managers build a learning organization through applying systems thinking, personal mastery, mental models, shared vision and team learning throughout the organization. Using a case-based approach, Senge is convinced that his principals unlock the secret to a successful organization.

It is more difficult to classify the contribution of some contemporary management theorists. Since Drucker, no writer in the field of American management had the influence of Harvard's Michael Porter. It would be difficult to find any American management textbook written in the past 20 years that does not mention the impact and scope of Porter's theories. In *Competitive Strategy* (1980),

Porter identifies five industry forces that managers must consider in their development of market strategies. The five forces are: (1) the threat of new entrants into the market, (2) the bargaining power of customers in the industry, (3) the bargaining power of suppliers in the industry, (4) the threat of substitute products or services entering the market, and (5) the price competition or other forms of rivalry among existing firms in the industry or market.

This model has proved useful to managers in understanding the various difficulties their products and services might encounter in their life cycles. Porter also envisions the importance of his model in a global economy. He pursues his theme of global competition in his 1985 book *Competitive Advantage,* where he notes that companies must select a strategy of cost leadership, which is contingent upon large market share, or a strategy of differentiation, which pursues a small market share but has the advantage. It is difficult to determine at this point in the history of American management thought whether Porter's models have widespread appeal because they actually increase competitive advantage or because they are easy to understand and apply.

If the quick-fix approach to complex issues was not bad enough in and of itself, the movement has other insidious effects when coupled with American management's penchant to measure all aspects of individual performance. Leslie Glick (1994), in his study of mid-career business graduate students, found that such students became very upset when they where asked to solve novel problems unrelated to those found in the course text or other assigned readings. This emotional distress continued, even though the feedback a student received on such assignments did not count in the course grade (p. 356). Clearly, students only wanted to be measured in situations where they felt comfortable directly applying established formulas or for which there were clearly established standards, which is how American management trains, measures and rewards its workers. There is great cause for alarm in this finding for academics and practitioners alike. What are the implications for American management, or for that matter a competitive America, if it produces and rewards a management class that seeks pat answers to novel situations?

CONCLUSION

American management thought has evolved from its origins in serious academic and scholarly research to today's ready-made formulas that meet the appetite (if not the needs) of modern American management. Since the United States remains the world's most advanced industrial nation, it is difficult to envision how today's corporations will function and be structured 10 years hence, with or without the input of additional prescriptions, although more are certain to come.

As some writers cogently argue, an organization may pass through a life cycle that is far more contingent upon natural evolution than the effects of one particular strategy or another at any particular point in time. Simply put, organizational growth and change may be more evolutionary than revolutionary (Greiner,

1972). In that case, the future of organizations is unknowable, and any prescriptions or practices to ensure future success are, at best, educated guesswork.

Therefore, this chapter closes with the state of American management thought in a quandary. Until time reveals the winning approach, one is forced to sift among serious attempts at scholarship and management practice enhancement, à la Porter's and Hammer's contributions, along with the trite observations of many writers who offer ready-made remedies for the ailments of American management practice.

REFERENCES

Adler, M. (ed.). (1954). *The major works of Sigmund Freud*. In Great Books of the Western World. (1954, Vol.54). Chicago: Encyclopedia Britannica.

Albrecht, K., & Zemke, R. (1985). *Service America*. Homewood, IL: Dow Jones-Irwin.

Aldag, R.J., & Stearns, T.M. (1987). *Study guide management*. Cincinnati, OH: South-Western College Publishing.

Anders, G. (1993, March 25). IBM's pick is talented: Some see flaws. *The Wall Street Journal*, p. A1.

Argyris, C. (1957). *Personality and organization: the conflict between the system and the individual*. New York: Harper Brothers.

Argyris, C. (1960). *Understanding organizational behavior*. Homewood, IL: Dorsey Press.

Argyris, C. (1962). *Interpersonal competence and organizational effectiveness*. Homewood, IL: Irwin.

Babbage, C. (1963). *On the economy of machinery and manufacturers* (4th ed.). New York: Augustus M. Kelley.

Barnard, C.I. (1947). *The theory of social and economic organization*. New York: The Free Press.

Baron, J.N., & Kreps, D.M. (19XX). *Strategic human resources: Framework for general managers*. New York: John Wiley & Sons.

Bell, D. (1973). *The coming of post-industrial society: A venture in social forecasting*. New York: Basic Books.

Boone, L.E., & Bowen, D.D. (1987). *The great writings in management and organizational behavior*. New York: McGraw-Hill.

Boulding, K.E. (1956). General systems theory: the skeleton of science. *Management Science*, 197–207.

Burns, T., & Stalker, G.M. (1961). *The management of innovation*. London: Tavistock Publications.

Carroll, P. B. (1993, January 10). The failures of central planning at IBM. *The Wall Street Journal*, p. A6.

Cascio, W.F. (1998). 5th ed. *Applied psychology in human resource management*. New Jersey: Prentice Hall.

Covey, S.R. (1989). *The 7 habits of highly effective people.* New York: Fireside.

Covey, S.R. (1992). *Principle-centered leadership.* New York: Fireside.

Crosby, P.B. (1980). *Quality is free.* New York: Mentor.

Culbreth, A.H., & Carey, E, G., (1948). *Cheaper by the dozen.* New York: Thomas Y. Crowell.

Daft, R.L. (1998). *Organization theory and design* (6th ed.). Cincinnatti, OH: South-Western College Publishing.

Deming, W.E. (1986). *Out of the crisis.* Cambridge, MA: MIT, Center for Advanced Engineering Studies.

Deming, W.E. (1991). *Foundation for management of quality in the western world.* Japan: Institute of Sciences.

Drucker, P. (1954). *The practice of management.* New York: Harper & Row.

Drucker, P. (1960). *The concept of the corporation.* Boston: Beacon Press.

Dunnette, M.D. (1966). *Personnel selection and placement.* Belmont, CA: Wadsworth.

Frank, M. (1994). Teaching excellence: Form and substance in management curriculum. Nineteenth International Conference: Improving University Teaching. College Park, MD: University College.

Franklin, W. (1986). *Administrative management.* New York: Dalton Communications.

Freud, S. (1910). *The origin and development of psychoanalysis.* Translated by Harry Chase. The Great Books of the Western World. (1954, Vol.54). Chicago: Encyclopedia Britanica.

Glick, L. (1994). The case for changing the grading paradigm in graduate school. Nineteenth International Conference: Improving University Teaching. College Park, MD: University College.

Greiner, L.E. (1972, July-August). Evolution and revolution as organizations grow. *Harvard Business Review*, 37–46.

Hammer, M. & Champy, J. (1993). *Reengineering the corporation: A manifesto for business revolution.* New York: Harper Business.

Hammer, M. (1995). *The reengineering revolution: A handbook.* New York: Harper Books.

Hannan, M.T. & Freeman, J.H. (1977, March). The population ecology of organization. *American Journal of Sociology*, 929–964.

Hayes, H., & Abernathy, W.J. (July-August 1980). Managing our way to economic decline. *Harvard Business Review*, 67–77.

Herzberg, F., Mausner, B., & Snyderman, B. (1959). *The motivation to work.* New York: John Wiley & Sons.

Hofstede, G. (1996). Cultural constraints in management theories. In Paton, A., et al. (eds.), *The new management reader* (pp. 77–90). London: Open University.

Hutchins, R. M. (Ed.) (1952). *The major works of Sigmund Freud.* Chicago: Encyclopedia Britannica.

Johnson,W. & Packer, A. (1987). *Workforce 2000: Work and workers for the 21st century.* Indianapolis, IN: Hudson Institute.

Kanter, R. (1984*). The change masters: Innovation and entrepreneurship in the American corporation.* New York: Simon & Shuster.

Kanter, R. (1990). *When giants learn to dance.* New York: Touchstone Books.

Kanter, R. (1993). *Men and women of the corporation.* New York: Basic Books.

Kanter, R. (1995). *World class: Thriving locally in the global economy.* New York: Simon & Shuster.

Kanter, R. (1997). *Innovation: Breakthrough at 3M, Dupont, GE, Pfizer, and Rubbermaid.* New York: Harper Business.

Katz, D., & Kahn, R.L. (1966) *The social psychology of organizations.* New York: John Wiley & Sons.

Kepner, C. (1982). *Productivity in America: Where it went and how to get it back.* New Jersey: Kepner-Tregoe.

Kotter, J. (July-August 1977). Power, dependence, and effective management. *Harvard Business Review,* 125–136.

Kotter, J. (November-December 1982). What effective mangers really do. *Harvard Business Review,* 156–170.

Lapointe, A.E., Mead, N.A., & Phillips, G.W. (1989). *A world of differences.* New Jersey: Educational Testing Services.

Machiavelli, N. (1513). *The Prince.* Translated by Allan Gilbert for Duke University. North Carolina: Durham University Press.

Marx, K. (1967). *Capital.* Translated by Samuel Moore. The Great Books of the Western World, (1954, Vol. 51). Chicago: Encyclopedia Britannica.

Marx, K. & Engels, F. (1847). *Manifesto of the Communist party.* Translated by Samuel Moore. The Great Books of the Western World (1954, Vol. 51). Chicago: Encyclopedia Britannica.

Maslow, A.H. (1954, 1970). *Motivation and personality* (2nd ed.). New York: Harper & Row.

Matheson, M. T. & Ivancevich, J.M. (1996). *Management and organizational behavior classics* (6th ed.). Santa Monica, CA: Irwin.

Mayo, E. (1933). *Human problems of an industrial civilization.* New York: The Viking Press.

Mayo, E. (1945). *The social problems of an industrial civilization.* New York: The Viking Press.

Mayo, E. (1945). *The social problems of an industrial civilization.* Boston: Division of Research, Graduate School of Business Administration, Harvard University Press.

McCurdy, H. (1972). *Public administration: A bibliography.* Washington, DC: American University.

McGregor, D. (1960). *The human side of enterprise*. New York: McGraw-Hill.

McGregor, D. (1967). *The professional manager*. New York: McGraw-Hill.

Micklethwait, J. & Wooldridge, A. (1996). *The witch doctors: Making sense of management gurus*. New York: Time Books.

Micklethwait, J. & Wooldridge, A. (1996, November). Oxford dons vs. management gurus. *Wall Street Journal*, A18.

Miller, M. (1993, January 27). Signing off: John Akers agrees to resign at IBM. *The Wall Street Journal*, A5–A7.

Mintzberg, H. (1975, July-August) The manager's job: Folklore and fact. *Harvard Business Review*, 49–61.

Mintzberg, H. (1994, January-February). The fall and rise of strategic planning. *Harvard Business Review*, 107–114.

Nadler, D.A., Shaw R. B., Walton, A.E., et al. (1995). *Discontinuous change*. San Francisco: Jossey-Bass.

Ouchi, W.G. (1981). *Theory Z: How American business can meet the Japanese challenge*. Reading, MA: Addison-Wesley.

Ouchi, W.G. & Jaeger, A.M. (1978, April). Type Z organization: Stability in the midst of mobility. *Academy of Management Review 3*, 308.

Paton, R., Clark, G., Jones, G., Lewis, J., & Quintas, P. (1996). *The new management reader*. London: Routledge.

Perrow, C. (1972). *Complex organizations*. Glenview, IL: Scott, Foresman and Company.

Peters, T.J. & Waterman, R.H., Jr. (1982). *In search of excellence*. New York: Warner Books.

Pfeffer, J. & Salancik, G.R. (1978). *The external control of organizations: A resource dependence perspective*. New York: Harper & Row.

Porter, E.M. (1980). *Competitive strategy: Techniques for analyzing industries and competitors*. New York: Free Press.

Porter, M. (1985). *Competitive advantage: Creating and sustaining superior performance*. New York: Free Press.

Roethlisberger, F.J. & Dickson, W.J. (1939). *Management and the worker: An account of a research program conducted by the Western Electric Company, Hawthorne Works, Chicago*. MA: Harvard University Press.

Rourke, F. (1969). *Bureaucracy, politics, and public policy*. Boston: Little Brown.

Schein, E. (1983). *Organization culture and leadership*. San Francisco: Jossey Bass.

Schein, E. (1990, February). Organization culture. *American Psychologist 45* (12), 109–119.

Schermerhor, J.R., Jr. (1999). *Management* (6th ed.). New York: John Wiley & Sons.

Senge, P.M. (1990). *The fifth discipline*. New York: Currency and Doubleday.

Sinclair, U. (1906). *The jungle.* New York: Doubleday.

Simon, H.A. (1997). *Administrative behavior* (4th ed.). New York: The Free Press.

Sloan, A. (1964). *My years with GM.* New York: MacMillan.

Smith, A. (1776). *An inquiry into the nature and causes of the wealth of nations.* Chicago: Encyclopaedia Britannica.

Taylor, F.W. (1911). *Principles of scientific management.* New York: Harper & Brothers.

Teich, A.H. (1993). *Technology and the future* (6th ed.). New York: St Martin's Press.

Walton, M. (1986). *The Deming management method.* New York: Putnam Publishing Group.

Weber, M. (1963). *Max Weber.* New York: Thomas Y. Crowell.

Weber, M. (1947). *The theory of social and economic organization.* New York: The Free Press.

Williamson, O. (1964). *Organization behavior: In the economies of discretionary behavior.* New Jersey: Prentice Hall.

Williamson, O. (1975). *Markets and hierarchies: Analysis and antitrust implications.* New York: Free Press.

Yukl, G. (1998). *Leadership in Organizations* (4th ed.). New Jersey: Prentice-Hall.

Chapter II

Leadership

JAMES P. GELATT

INTRODUCTION

This chapter addresses the elusive concept of leadership. Specifically, the chapter contrasts definitions of "leader" and "manager," examines theories and types of leadership, and discusses factors that are changing the role of the leader in today's organization.

Because the terms "leader" and "leadership" mean different things to different people, it might be helpful to start with a definition. "Leadership" is a comparatively new term, having been in common usage for only about two hundred years (Stogdill, 1974). Although there are numerous definitions, what is common to many is: Leadership is the process by which one person influences others to achieve goals (Rouch and Behling, 1984; Katz and Kahn, 1978).

This definition has within it several important elements:

- *Leadership is a process.*

  As one definition describes it, leadership is "the behavior of an individual when he is directing the activities of a group toward a shared goal" (Hemphill and Coons, 1957, p. 7). For leadership to be an observed phenomenon, some action must be taking place; that action is stimulated by the person we call the "leader."

- *Leadership implies followers.*

  Leadership implies a group whose members are acting in a way that is reflective of the leader's own behavior.

- *Leadership involves influence.*

  Possible definitions for "influence" include: "persuasion," "authority," "control," "power," "motivation," "inspiration." In other words, leaders may get the followers engaged by any of a number of behaviors, some of which are more directive than others.

- *Leadership implies that the leader and the followers are working toward a goal.*

  The extent to which the goal is shared will vary by situation. In some groups, there is an enthusiastic sense of shared goals; in others, there is clearly more "ownership" of the goals on the part of the leader than his or her followers. In the former, we might describe the behavior of the leader as more "inspirational;" in the latter, more "coercive."

LEADER OR MANAGER: WHAT DO ORGANIZATIONS NEED TODAY?

Much has been written in the past two decades on the importance of leadership. Some of the writers have made a distinction between "leader" and "manager."

Warren Bennis and Burt Nanus (1985) are credited with making this distinction between managers and leaders: "Managers are people who do things right, and leaders are people who do the right thing" (p. 21). Bennis and Nanus observe that the words "to manage" mean "to bring about, to accomplish, to have charge or responsibility for, to conduct." By contrast, "leading" is "influencing, guiding in direction, course, action, opinion" (Bennis and Nanus, 1985, p. 21). The distinction is between "efficiency"—using resources competently—and "effectiveness"—using resources to achieve organizational goals. In Bennis' and Nanus' view:

> *Effective leadership can move organizations from current to future states, create visions of potential opportunities for organizations, instill within employees commitment to change . . . instill new cultures and strategies in organizations that mobilize and focus energy and resources (Bennis and Nanus, 1985, pp. 17–18).*

Harvard-based management theorist John Kotter presents a somewhat similar distinction between the two, as seen in Figure 1.

Figure 1. Comparison of Management and Leadership

Creating an agenda	Planning and Budgeting—establishing detailed steps and timetables for achieving needed results, and then allocating the resources necessary to make that happen	Establishing Direction—developing a vision of the future, often the distant future, and strategies for producing the changes needed to achieve that vision
Developing a human network for achieving	Organizing and Staffing—establishing some structure for accomplishing plan requirements, staffing that structure with individuals, delegating responsibility and authority for carrying out the plan, providing policies and procedures to help guide people, and creating methods or systems to monitor implementation	Align People—communicating the direction by words and deeds to all those whose cooperation may be needed so as to influence the creation of teams and coalitions that understand the vision and strategies, and accept their validity
Execution	Controlling and Problem Solving—monitoring results vs. plan in some detail, identifying deviations, and then planning and organizing to solve these problems	Motivating and Inspiring—energizing people to overcome major political, bureaucratic, and resource barriers to change by satisfying very basic, but often unfulfilled, human needs
Outcomes	Produces a degree of predictability and order, and has the potential of consistently producing key results expected by various stakeholders (e.g., for customers, always being on time; for stockholders, being on budget)	Produces change, often to a dramatic degree, and has the potential of producing extremely useful change (e.g., new products that customers want, new approaches to labor relations that help make a firm more competitive)

Source: J. Kotter, 1995, p. 102.

As can be seen by the chart developed by John Kotter, management is often seen as being more internally directed and aimed at getting an agreed-upon job done; whereas leadership is seen as being more about getting people committed to the job that needs to be done. Recent literature has presented management in a bad light in comparison to leadership. Management is sometimes described as being "stifling," "rigid," "controlling," and "autocratic;" whereas leadership, by favorable contrast, is presented as being "enabling," "enhancing," "flexible," and "democratic" (Bennis, 1994, p. 23).

Bennis' comparison, although perhaps overstated, does reflect how we have come to think about leadership and management. Leaders are given credit for being big thinkers, able to motivate and inspire, while managers are derided for being constrictive and unimaginative. In practice, the difference between a manager and a leader is probably a lot less distinct. Many leaders are autocratic, and many managers are enabling.

Do today's organizations need leaders, or do they need managers? The truth is that both are needed in varying degrees, depending on the situation—the culture of the organization, the goals of the organization, and its life cycle stage. Each of these three elements merits closer examination in light of the issue of manager or leader.

Organizational Culture

We have come to recognize that organizational culture and leadership are intertwined. When it comes to culture, managers play a less important role. Management theorist Edgar Schein (1992) posits that cultures actually begin with leaders as the leaders impose their own set of values and opinions on the group. If the group is successful and the leaders' values and assumptions come to be taken for granted, an organizational culture emerges. In a sense, the culture then defines how group members behave—even members who are leaders themselves.

Because leadership is so linked to culture, it is not surprising that leaders emerge at those times when the organization is in need of change. New leaders begin to assert themselves in both tangible and intangible ways, and their influence can be seen in what Schein calls "overt phenomena" (Schein, 1992, p. 8): customs, "rules of the game" (behaviors that are or are not acceptable), ways of thinking, and expressed values.

How does the leader infuse his or her own culture into that of the organization? According to Schein (1992, p.8), there are several "culture-embedding mechanisms":

- What the leader pays attention to, what gets measured, what he or she controls
- How the leader reacts to serious circumstances, including crises
- How the leader allocates resources, especially sparse resources
- What part the leader plays as a role model, teacher, coach
- What the leader rewards, and the criteria by which rewards are allotted
- The means by which the leader recruits, selects, promotes, and removes members of the organization

Leaders both affect the organizational culture and are affected by it. As culture becomes ingrained, it influences behavior of all members of the organization, be they leaders, managers, or followers.

Organizational Goals

Broadly speaking, organizational goals can be categorized as primarily focused on either *efficiency* or *effectiveness*. Effectiveness refers to the degree or extent to which an organization achieves its goals. Efficiency refers to the proficient use of resources (Etzioni, 1985). Using these definitions in conjunction with Kotter's distinction between managers and leaders (above), it can be said that managers tend to be more oriented toward "efficiency," and leaders toward "effectiveness." (As with any such distinction, one should be careful not to make the differences too extreme.)

Relatively stable organizations, organizations with a clear sense of purpose and a fairly secure market share, may want to focus on operational goals—being more efficient—in order to trim costs and thus remain competitive. In this context, managers are key. By comparison, organizations in need of renewal, that are losing market share or seem unmotivated, may need leadership that will inspire the staff of the organization to rally around the leaders' own values and goals and encourage members to extend themselves, achieving more than the staff might have thought possible. (This type of "transformational" leadership will be covered later in this chapter.)

Organizational Life Cycle

Whether the organization needs leaders or managers, and the type of leader or manager needed, will vary according to where the organization is in its own life cycle. Most organizations are created by one individual (or at most a few individuals) whose vision is the driving force. The owner or owners often possess a technical skill (as was the case with Steven Jobs and Steve Wozniak at Apple Computers); they spend long hours simply trying to get the organization up and running. The issue is not management in this entrepreneurial stage of the organization (Daft, 1998); it is survival.

If the organization survives, it may move into the second stage of its life cycle, in which growth leads to the establishment of departments, and with departments a chain of command, job descriptions, and specialization (division of labor). In this collectivity stage (sometimes, "youthful" stage), the opportunities increase for managers to run the newly created departments, plan work flow, and oversee production.

As the organization continues to mature, the managerial role continues to expand as the organization becomes more formalized. The organization has "grown large with success" (Schermerhorn, 1999, p. 227), and it needs managers to keep it moving forward efficiently. Internal rules systems are put into place. If effective, they will help the organization to grow; if not, the rules and systems may lead to a clogged bureaucracy, which is characteristic of the fourth stage (elaboration). Organizations that reach this stage now need a new infusion of leadership that will revitalize the organization by getting it to rethink what it does, why and how (Greiner, 1972).

LEADERS AND LEADERSHIP: A HISTORICAL PERSPECTIVE

Although there have been leaders ever since humans first came together in social groups, the definition of what it meant to be a leader—and the way that one became a leader—have changed over time. One way of viewing leadership—that leaders were born as leaders (the "Genetic Theory") emerged with the first leader and prevailed as the single definition of leadership until the 20th century.

Figure 2 presents the major theories of leadership that have developed since 1900. They include Trait Theories, Behavioral Theories, Contingency Theories, and Current Theories, each of which will be examined.

Figure 2. Theories of Leadership

Prior to Early 20th Century	Early 20th Century	1940–1960s	1960s–1980s	1990s and on
Genetic/Great Man	Trait Theories	Behavioral Theories	Contingency Theories	Current Theories

Source: J. Schermerhorn, 1999, p. 267.

The Genetic Theory

For much of history, leaders were seen as "prophets, priests, chiefs, and kings" (Bass, 1995, p. 5). This concept of leadership assumed that leadership was genetic—that leaders were born to be leaders. This image of leadership was the underpinning for the divine right of kings, as the genes of leadership were thought to be transmitted, typically from father to son. (The Roman word for ruler was "Caesar," which in German became "Kaiser" and in Russian, "Czar.")

The power of the genetic philosophy was that it offered a ready explanation for how leadership came about. One was a leader because he or she inherited the right characteristics from his or her parents, as leadership passed genetically from generation to generation (Montana and Charnov, 1987).

Napoleon Bonaparte. Courtesy of the Library of Congress.

The Genetic Theory, also known as the Great Man Theory, was dominant for centuries; in fact, it was only in this century that it declined. The decline was caused by three factors: democracy, research, and world change.

(1) Democracy had taken a foothold in many parts of the world, and democracy was based on an assumption that all people were created equal. One thus became a leader by dint of effort, not by birth. Persons such as Andrew Carnegie, born in humble surroundings, became vastly successful through their own efforts.

(2) Research into leadership had disproved the idea that leaders were born that way. Research studies, such as the Trait Theory described below, provided an alternative to the long-held assumption that leadership qualities were genetic and could not be acquired.

(3) The final blow to the Great Man Theory came when many of the ruling families in Europe were decimated as a result of war and revolution. Over time, the Genetic Theory of leadership failed because the world changed—especially with the rise of the Industrial Revolution, wherein a new breed of leader emerged on the basis of wealth and concomitant power (Montana and Charnov, 1987).

Trait Theory

Early in the 20th century, some scholars started asking, "Is it true that leaders posses a certain trait or set of traits that sets them apart?" The answer, after exhaustive study, was that there did seem to be a set of characteristics that distinguished leaders from others. Although someone who possessed these traits might not be a leader in every circumstance, it was likely that the person who emerged as the leader in every circumstance possessed these distinguishing traits to some extent. The research also led to another important observation: that while leaders possessed certain distinguishing traits, they were not necessarily born with those traits.

As summarized by Stogdill (1995), the leadership traits identified were in five clusters:

(1) *Capacity*   Intelligence, verbal ability, judgment, alertness

(2) *Achievement*   Knowledge, erudition, achievements in athletics

(3) *Responsibility* Initiative, dependability, self-confidence, persistence, ambition to excel

(4) *Participation*   Affability, cooperation, humor, adaptability, and

(5) *Status*   Popularity, socioeconomic status (Stogdill, 1995).

Each of the five clusters is in effect a path to becoming a leader. Some leaders emerge based on their intellect, while others become leaders because they excel in a popular sport, such as basketball. Some become leaders because of their willingness to take the first step or the fact that they appear confident, and some because they are seen as likeable team players, capable of adapting to the needs of the group and to the requirements of the situation. And still others become leaders by virtue of wealth or social class.

Behavioral Theories: The Ohio State and Michigan Studies

In the late 1940s, research was conducted that focused on assessing leadership qualities by observing how leaders behaved. These behavioral studies were concentrated in two major American universities—Ohio State and the University of Michigan.

Ohio Studies in Leadership

Using a Leader Behavior Description Questionnaire, the Ohio State studies on leadership looked primarily at two factors:

(1) *Consideration*—meaning the extent to which the leader behaved in a manner that was friendly and supportive; and

(2) *Initiating structure*—meaning the extent to which the leader structures not only his or her own role, but also the role of subordinates in the interest of attaining group goals.

The two categories were considered relatively independent of one another. It is interesting to note that the Ohio State researchers started with an assumption that the effective leader would demonstrate a high capacity in both factors, consideration and task. Their research did not bear this out. In the studies, some leaders scored high on the consideration factor, some high on the initiating; some high on both; and some low on both. Those who scored high in the consideration factor had less grievances against them and less turnover compared to those with high initiating structure. Subordinates tended to be more satisfied with those leaders who showed at least a moderate level of consideration.

The studies also found that the effects of one characteristic could not be fully understood without looking at the other. In other words, examining only the degree to which an individual was task-oriented, without also considering his or her ability to work well with others, provided an incomplete picture of that individual's leadership potential.

University of Michigan Leadership Studies

The Michigan Leadership Studies sought to identify the relations among leader behavior, group process, and group performance. As summarized by researcher Rensis Likert (1961), the studies addressed three important leader behaviors: task-oriented behavior, relationship-oriented behavior, and participative leadership.

Task-oriented leaders focused on planning, scheduling, and coordinating. They guided subordinates in setting performance goals that were ambitious but doable.

Relationship-oriented leaders were more considerate, more supportive, and more helpful; they inspired trust and confidence. Their supervisory style was more general than close.

Participative leaders acted as facilitators and guides. They allowed others to participate in decision making—given them a higher level of higher satisfaction (Yukl, 1998).

Contingency Theories

Since the 1960s, another school of leadership theory has emerged. Called a "contingency approach," it is based on an assumption that what makes for an effective leader depends not only on the leader's characteristics, but also on the situation (Chemers, 1993).

Fiedler's Contingency Model

The first extensive contingency leadership model was developed by Fred Fiedler (1967) at the University of Washington. Fiedler's theory is based on the assumption that leaders are most effective when their style is matched up with a situation in which they can best function. Fiedler developed a measurement tool called the "least preferred co-worker (LPC) scale," which asked respondents to think about someone with whom they had difficulty working. Respondents then completed the LPC scale in regards to that person. The scale evaluated the degree to which respondents favored working in a situation that was more people-oriented or more task-oriented.

What Fiedler proposed in his Contingency Model was that, having determined what type of leader the person was, the best way to assure his or her success on the job was to match the person's preference (for task or people) with a situation in which he or she would be most comfortable. For example, persons who are very task-oriented will perform more effectively as leaders if they are placed in a situation that draws on their determination to get the work done. Putting a task-oriented person in a situation that largely calls for social skills would, in Fiedler's view, be a recipe for failure.

Situational Leadership Model

In contrast with Fiedler's Contingency Model, which modifies the situation to match the leader's style, the Situational Leadership model suggests that the leader should adapt his or her style to match the situation. The concept "situational leadership" was introduced by Paul Hersey and Kenneth Blanchard (1982). It approaches the role of the leader based on the abilities and interests of the worker or follower. The root concept is "readiness": Is the follower motivated to achieve? Is he or she willing to accept responsibility to get the job done? Does he or she have the ability (training, experience, skills) necessary to accomplish the job?

The Situational Leadership model (as depicted in Figure 3) has four stages, from the most controlling on the part of the leader ("Directing" or "Telling") to the most self-controlled on the part of the follower or worker (the "Delegating" style).

Directing (or *"Telling"*) is recommended when the follower lacks essential "readiness." Here, the relationship between the leader and follower is high in terms of task, and low in terms of relationship. In essence, the leader tells the follower what to do and how to do it. This highly controlling style is suggested for new employees, or for employees who are tackling a job that they have not done before.

Figure 3: Situational Leadership

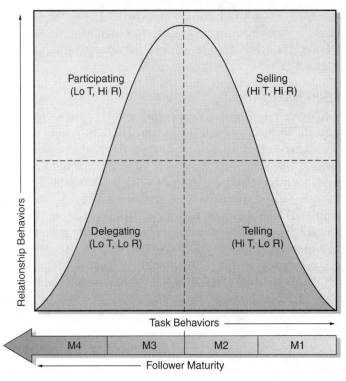

Source: Hersey and Blanchard, 1988, p. 171.

Coaching (or *"Selling"*) is the style recommended for followers who are acquiring an understanding of the job. The leader is still highly involved in terms of task, but now is also highly involved in terms of interaction. The leader is acting much like a coach on a team sport might act—giving direction and encouragement, but not being involved in actually doing the task.

Supporting (or *"Participating"*) is the third style; it is recommended when the worker demonstrates a high degree of readiness. The leader is able to reduce his or her actual direction, while retaining a high degree of interpersonal contact. In this manner, the leader can provide ongoing positive reinforcement.

Delegating is the style used when the worker clearly has the capability and the motivation to get the job done, and needs virtually no help from the leader in order to do so. As its name implies, the "delegating" style implies delegating both authority and responsibility to the employee.

Whether one favors Fiedler's approach—match the job with the characteristics of the person, or the Situational Leadership approach—adapt one's leadership style to fit the situation, one message of contingency theories is clear: No one style of leadership is right for every situation. The odds of having a harmonious and productive workplace are increased when there is a good fit between the leader's style and needs and abilities of the workers.

LEADERSHIP AND MOTIVATION

As noted earlier, leadership implies followers. Acquiring and retaining followers demands motivation. Theories on motivation can be clustered into four groups: (1) Process theories; (2) Equity theories; (3) Reinforcement theories; and (4) Content theories.

Process Theories

Process theories of motivation emphasize how and by what goals individuals are motivated. Process theories of motivation consider individual wants, the follower's preferences for certain outcomes, and the followers' belief that if he or she complies with the leader's request that it will lead to a desired outcome.

This linking between what the follower believes may be the result if he or she follows the leader is known as Expectancy Theory. Expectancy Theory says that an individual will be motivated if he or she thinks the task is worth doing; believes he or she can do the task; and feels that sufficient reward will accrue to him or her as a result of doing the task (Vroom, 1964; Porter and Lawler, 1968).

Equity Theories

Equity theories are related to Expectancy Theory in the sense that the follower looks at the possible results of his or her compliance with the leader. But equity theories have another dimension: the follower also compares the results of his or her own efforts with the results obtained by others (Adams, 1965). If the follower feels that the same level of effort is not rewarded equally, and he or she is getting fewer rewards than others, then he or she may decide not to comply, or to comply with considerably less enthusiasm.

Reinforcement Theories

Reinforcement theories deal with how consequences of previous actions influence future actions. It is no coincidence that reinforcement theories use a model similar to that of behavior reinforcement scientists such as B. F. Skinner, for Reinforcement Theory maintains that the actions of the follower are the result of learned behavior. "Behavior that results in a pleasant outcome is likely to be repeated; behavior that results in an unpleasant outcome is not likely to be repeated" (Schermerhorn, Hunt and Osborn, 1997, p. 138).

Content Theories (also "Needs Theories")

Content or Needs theories stress the importance of understanding factors within the follower that cause him or her to act in a certain way. Content theories thus center on the satisfaction of individual needs. An effective leader should understand what motivates each person and attempt to provide a setting in which personal needs and organizational needs can both be achieved. Notable among Content theories are those of Maslow, Herzberg, and McClelland.

Although the four types of motivational theory—Process theories, Equity theories, Reinforcement theories, and Content theories—look at motivation from different perspectives, they have one thing in common. Each acknowledges the importance of understanding what it is that motivates followers if one is to be an effective leader.

LEADERS, POWER AND DECISION MAKING

As noted, leadership is about influence, and influence is about power. Power is the ability of one person (call him or her Person A) to get another person (Person B) to do what Person A wants done. Leadership power can come from three sources: (1) the ability to offer or withhold rewards (salary, promotion, more interesting work); (2) the ability to punish (withholding a salary increase, demotion); and (3) formal authority (being "the boss") (Schermerhorn, Hunt, and Osborn, 1997).

One way in which leaders exercise power is in the manner in which decisions get made, and the extent to which followers get to participate in the decision making (Vroom and Yetton, 1973; Tannenbaum and Schmidt, 1958). Figure 4 displays a decision-making continuum.

On the far left in the figure is the *autocratic* decision-making style, in which the leader makes the decision without first seeking input from his or her followers. Moving toward the right on the diagram, the next approach is the *consultative* approach, in which the leader asks his or her followers for suggestions and then makes the decision after weighing follower input. Farther along the continuum is the *joint decision*. As its name implies, this approach involves both leader and followers in a mutual decision-making process. At the far right on the continuum is *delegation*, where the leader turns over the authority and responsibility for making the decision to the followers.

The extent to which the leader shares decision-making authority with his or her followers depends on several factors. One is the leader's self-confidence. If the leader feels positive about his or her ability to lead and feels respected by his or her followers, he or she may be more willing to have the followers participate in making decisions. A second factor is the nature of the decision itself. Some decisions are simple and straightforward and don't require a team to reach a decision. Other decisions are more complex, with no single right answer. When facing a more complex problem, the leader may want to involve others in order to acquire necessary information or test possible alternatives.

A third factor affecting the degree to which the leader may involve others in making the decision is when facing a sensitive issue about which people feel strongly. In this instance, the leader may opt to have the followers fully involved in making the decision so that he or she is not identified with a decision that is likely to please some and displease others.

Figure 4. Continuum of Decision Making

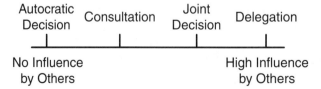

Source: Yukl, 1998, p. 124.

Sharing decision making. Copyright © Tony Stone Images.

A fourth factor is time. Some decisions must be made quickly, without the luxury of discussion. A sense of urgency may prompt the leader to make a decision autocratically simply because he or she feels it is essential that a decision be made fast.

LEADERSHIP TYPES

Leadership comes in different forms. These leadership forms have been labeled the *traditional authority,* the *legal-rational,* the *charismatic, and* the *transformational.*

In the *traditional authority* system of leadership, the role of leader was determined by heritage and custom. In some traditional authority leadership societies, the role of leader went to the oldest in the clan; in others, it went to the son of the previous leader. The divine right of kings discussed earlier is an example of the traditional authority leadership system.

The *rational-legal leadership* system (Weber, 1947) grants leader status to someone on the basis of law (for example, an elected official).

Charismatic leadership is the type that many lay persons think of when they hear the word "leader." Charismatic leaders are thought to possess qualities that set them apart from others, and it is these very qualities that give them the authority to act. Charismatic leaders often wield considerable power because of who they are, not because of their position or legal authority (Hughes, Ginnett, and Curphy, 1999). Examples would include the Ayatollah Khomeini and Mahatma Gandhi.

Charismatic leaders often emerge during times of social crisis. It is not uncommon for charismatic leaders to emerge in response to an established system of authority.

The essence of *transformational leadership* is the leader's ability to reshape institutions in order to accomplish ambitious goals. Transformational leadership often surfaces in organizations where members have wants that are not being met. Transformational leaders see themselves as change agents. They tend to be value-driven, believe in people, and are visionaries. Successful transformational leadership, as management theorist James McGregor Burns found, stimulates members to do more than they might have thought they would or could do. Members exhibit increased enthusiasm, organization loyalty, and pride. They display trust in themselves and their own goals. In this sense, they behave in a manner similar to the transformational leader (Burns, 1978).

KEY MANAGEMENT AND LEADERSHIP ISSUES TODAY

The definition of leadership and the role of the leader are undergoing dramatic changes in today's organizations. Some of the factors driving this change are: the changing the role of the leader as participant, the concept of stewardship, and the growth of empowerment.

The Changing Definition of the "Leader"

Historically, leaders have been at the center of the group and group process. The organization reflected his or her personality. Indeed, Edgar Schein (1992) has maintained that leadership and culture are two sides of the same coin. Historically, leaders have expected compliance. They have set the organization's goals and developed the plans to realize these goals. Today, society is moving away from the traditional definition of leader, as Moses represented the concept. Recent experiences with some charismatic leaders—e.g., Jim Jones, who encouraged his 900 followers to commit mass suicide in a remote area of Guyana in 1978—have led some to question this role of leader. As a result, new theories of leadership have emerged that cast the leader in a more human and less absolute context.

The role of the leader is changing in today's organization.
Copyright © Photo Researchers.

Leader as Participant

The advent of Contingency Theory (Fiedler, 1967) and Situational Leadership (Hersey and Blanchard, 1982) heralded a new approach to decision making in which the role of leader varied by circumstance. In some instances, the leader continued to be directive and controlling, but in others, his or her role shifted to a more facilitative, coaching, or supportive style.

The concept of stewardship has also recently emerged. In this approach, the leader works less to advance his or her own agenda and more to advance the agenda of the organization. Stewardship implies a sense of partnership with others in the organization (Block, 1996).

Teams in organizations have become an increasingly popular way of doing business. In some organizations, hierarchical decision making is giving way to team-based decisions, and traditionally managed teams are giving way to self-managed teams.

Empowerment

Empowerment takes delegation one additional step. Whereas delegation implies that the leader assigns tasks to his or her followers and then gives them the authority and responsibility to get the job done, empowerment shifts overall control for the job to the individual or team. In an empowered environment, the follower in a sense ceases to be a follower; he or she "owns" the job and has the power to do what is required to see that the organization's goals as related to this job are met. Unfortunately, the term "empowerment" is often misused. At its best, the term—as reflected in Figure 5—represents a complex shift in the leadership paradigm that starts with hiring the right staff, giving them the tools to make decisions, and providing a climate that fosters empowered behavior.

There are several factors that have led to a redefinition of leadership: the knowledge and information explosion, global and cultural differences, generational and psychographic differences in the work force, and the increased pace of change. Taken together, these factors are making it impractical if not impossible to lead organizations according to old-line definitions of that term.

Knowledge/Information Explosion

One consequence of the information explosion is that the term "leader" cannot readily be applied to the person who possesses all of the requisite knowledge or skills necessary to run the organization. The working world has seen an increase in knowledge-based workers, which in turn has meant less of a role for the directive form of leader/manager. As American industry moves from an industrial model of management to an information-based model, organizations will need to "rethink their traditional approaches to directing, coaching, and motivating employees" (Barner, 1996, p. 16). The role of the leader or manager may also change in this information-based model. If workers possess the requisite knowledge and skills, the manager may need to become more of a facilitator who smooths the way for the knowledge worker to get the job done.

Global and Cultural Differences

As the world becomes more interconnected, and the United States more culturally diverse, American leadership styles will need to adapt to new situations. The

Figure 5. Elements of Empowerment

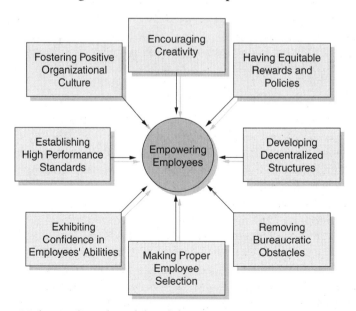

Source: Nahavandi and Malekzadek, 1999, p. 396.

leader or manager capable of functioning effectively in a culturally diverse environment will need a new set of traits. According to Schermerhorn, Hunt and Osborn (1998, p. 19), today's leaders and managers must have the ability to:

- Adapt to a variety of business environments;
- Respect differing value sets, beliefs, and practices;
- Solve problems quickly in unfamiliar surroundings;
- Communicate with persons of various cultures (including the ability to speak more than one language);
- Understand dissimilar governments and political systems; and
- Show enthusiasm and respect when interacting with others.

Generational and Psychographic Differences in the Work Force

D. Quinn Mills (1987), a professor and management theorist at Harvard University, observed some key differences between persons born before or during World War II and those born shortly thereafter (frequently referred to as Baby Boomers), many of whom grew up in the Vietnam era. Mills found that those born prior to World War II:

- Tended to follow orders;
- Gave persons respect based on their title (Lieutenant, Boss, etc.); and
- Assumed that those in authority were the leaders.

By comparison, Mills noted, those who were born after World War II and grew up in the Vietnam War era:

- Followed orders if those orders seemed to make sense;
- Gave persons respect when that respect was earned, and not on the basis of their title; and
- Assumed that leadership was a shared characteristic not unique to those in authority.

Baby Boomers in the Work Force

Baby Boomers (those born in the United States between the years 1946 and 1964) have had enormous influence on organizations. It can be assumed that some of the greatest changes in the work force culture—changes in dress code, flextime, empowerment—were driven by the Baby Boomers in the work force.

The oldest Baby Boomers turned 50 in 1996. They are no longer questioning the Establishment; they are the Establishment. One organizational challenge faced by Baby Boomers is a consequence of their sheer numbers. There are more of them than there are managerial and other higher-level positions in organizations. This means that for decades there will be a glut of people at the peak of their working capability, ready to lead organizations, but with no place to go. As a result, some Baby Boomers are looking at options—including a heightened interest in moving out, starting over in a new position in a new organization, or going it alone with one's own business.

Generation X

The term "Generation X" loosely applies to persons born between 1968 and 1986 (or thereabouts). A focus group conducted by the author with CEOs found that these CEOs expressed both fascination and frustration with their "Gen X" employees. When motivated, these employees tended to be highly productive, hard working, and goal-oriented. They were bright and computer literate. They played as hard as they worked. And they had no hesitation in moving on to another employer when the opportunity arose or they became bored.

One CEO in the focus group said that her organization had become accustomed to having to hire new employees constantly; that Gen Xers rarely stayed more than 18 months to two years. She had to recognize that if she wanted the talent they could bring, she had to make adjustments in the workplace.

What surveys and focus groups such as this reveal is that Generation Xers value achievement and wealth, while personal and physical security rank higher with "mature" adults.

The point for leaders is clear: Motivation may vary by circumstance, including generation. To be effective, today's leader needs to understand that some factors tend to motivate generations differently. The leader also needs to appreciate that generational observations should be made with caution and tempered by an understanding of individual differences.

Increased Pace of Change

One of the most talked about factors affecting management and leadership today is the speed with which change occurs. Management theorist and consultant David Nadler and his colleagues (1994) coined the term "discontinuous change" to describe the turbulent environment in which organizations find themselves today. Note the changing role for leaders in this environment of disequilibrium:

> *The companies that survive in the coming decades will be those that are able to respond quickly and effectively to changing environmental conditions. This puts a premium on certain capabilities—adaptiveness, flexibility, and responsiveness. Successful firms will learn to act at a faster rate than the competition, and their leaders will have no choice but to be effective anticipators and managers of large-scale change (Nadler, Shaw, Walton, and Assoc., 1994, p. 3).*

What is needed, according to Nadler and others, is a kind of transformational leader who can transform the organization, who is able to create new vision, gain commitment, and institutionalize change (Bass and Avolio, 1994).

IMPLICATIONS FOR THE FUTURE OF MANAGEMENT AND LEADERSHIP

This chapter concludes with a look at emerging thought on leadership in the next millennium.

Leading in a Changing Organizational Environment

Most of our understanding of what it meant to be a leader or a manager was formed during an era when change occurred not overnight, but over a generation; when people worked for the same company all of their lives; when managers were needed to pass information down the chain of command. The stable, predictable organization of the early 1900s has given way to a workplace in which it is said there only two kinds of managers—the quick and the dead.

Rosabeth Moss Kanter, former editor of *Harvard Business Review*, notes that leaders and managers need to understand that the environment in which they operate has changed in the following ways:

- The number of channels through which action can be taken and influence exercised has increased dramatically;

- Influence is shifting from the vertical to the horizontal—from chain of command to peer networks;

- The distinction between manager and managed is blurring, especially as it relates to access to the external environment, access to information, and control over work; and

- Relationships outside the organization are becoming increasingly important as sources of internal power and influence (Kanter, 1989, pp. 85–92).

The workplace that Kanter describes demands that we rethink traditional definitions of leader and manager. To be an effective leader means being able to encourage a willingness to change, and knowing how to listen and adapt to what one hears from his or her followers. And it means being able to inspire others because of one's values and commitment to a vision.

Leader as Change Agent

According to John Kotter (1997), today's leaders need to transform their organizations by establishing a sense of urgency for change; providing a vision of where the organization should be—and then empowering others to act on that vision; and moving the change process forward by creating short-term wins and leveraging improvements (Kotter, 1999).

The dilemma that presents itself to leaders who would be change agents is that, paradoxically, companies are attempting to become leaner while at the same time empowering their workers. One consequence of downsizing has been that those employees who survive the personnel cuts are less willing to take risk, fearing that they may be the next to be let go. For leaders to be successful as change agents, they will need to discover ways to involve those in subordinate roles—those who are close to the customer, those who have the essential knowledge and skills—in actively managing the organization.

In other words, the challenge facing the leader as change agent is how to lead the organization through radical change while at the same time securing essential employee initiative and commitment (Conger, Spreitzer, and Lawler, 1999).

The Leader's Ability to Listen and Adapt

Peter Senge (1997), who coined the term "the learning organization," says today's leader must be a learner, which means he or she must have a willingness "to be ignorant and incompetent. . . . In the old model, the job of the people at the top was to figure out what was going on, make all the key decisions and . . . translate top management's decisions into coordinated actions." (pp. 139–140). By comparison, what is needed on the part of today's leader, Senge maintains, is to accept that decisions should be made and implemented at the level where the action is occurring.

Leader as Embodiment of Values

Author Steven Covey (1992) argues for "principle-centered leadership," that is, leadership that is rooted in and responsive to core values. For Covey, leadership means valuing basic principles above the organization. To be successful, leaders will need both character and competence; one without the other will be insufficient.

Importance of a Shared Vision

Several authors and management theorists writing today stress that the way to get through these tempestuous times, to lead the organization toward success despite all the changes occurring around it, is through a sense of shared vision—what Joel Barker, who coined the term "paradigm shift," calls the vision community. (Barker, 1990).

Providing the vision is not enough. That vision must be shared by persons throughout the organization, and it is the role of the leader to make that happen.

REFERENCES

Adams, J. S. (1965). Inequity in social exchange. In L. Berkowitz, ed. *Advances in experimental social psychology*, vol. 2. New York: Academic Press.

Barker, J. (1990). *Discovering the future: The power of vision*. Videotape.

Barner, R. (March-April 1996). The millennium workplace: Seven changes that will challenge managers—and workers. *The Futurist*, 30:6, 14–18.

Bass, B. M. (1995). Concepts of leadership. In J. L. Pierce & J. W. Newstrom, eds. *Leaders and the leadership process: Readings, self-assessments, and applications*. Boston, MA: Irwin McGraw-Hill.

Bass, B. M. & Avolio, B. J. (1994). *Improving organizational effectiveness through transformational leadership*. Thousand Oaks, CA: Sage Publications.

Bennis, W. (1994). The material quoted is from a presentation on leadership by Dr. Bennis, Washington, DC.

Bennis, W. & Nanus, B. (1985). *Leaders: The strategies for taking charge*. New York: Harper & Row.

Block, P. (1996). *Stewardship : Choosing service over self interest*. San Francisco: Berrett-Koehler Publishers

Burns, J. M. (1978*). Leadership.* New York: Harper & Row.

Chemers, M. M. (1993). An integrative theory of leadership. In M. M. Chemers & R. Aymans, eds. *Leadership theory and research: Perspectives and directions.* New York: Academic Press.

Conger, J. A., Spreitzer, G. M., & Lawler, E. E. III. (1999*). The leader's change handbook: An essential guide to setting direction & taking action.* San Francisco: Jossey-Bass Publishers.

Covey, S. R. (1992). *Principle-centered leadership: Strategies for personal and professional effectiveness.* New York: Simon & Schuster.

Daft, R. L. (1998). *Organization theory and design.* Cincinnati, OH: South-Western College Publishing.

Etzioni, A. (1985). *Modern organizations.* Englewood Cliffs, NJ: Prentice-Hall.

Fiedler, E. E. (1967). *A theory of leadership effectiveness.* New York: McGraw Hill.

Hemphill, J. K. & Coons, eds. *Leader behavior: Its description and measurement.* Columbus, OH: Bureau of Business Research, Ohio State University.

Hersey, P. and Blanchard, K. (1988). *Management of organizational behavior.* 5th ed. Englewood Cliffs, NJ: Prentice Hall.

Hughes, R. L., Ginnett, R. C., & Curphy, G. J. (1999). *Leadership: Enhancing the lessons of experience.* Boston: Irwin McGraw-Hill.

Kanter, R. M. (November/December 1989). The new managerial work. *Harvard Business Review*, 89:6, 85–92.

Katz, D. & Kahn, R. L. (1978). *The social psychology of organizations*, 2nd ed. New York: John Wiley & Sons, Inc.

Kotter, J. P. (1995). *The new rules: Eight business breakthroughs to career success in the 21st century.* New York: Free Press.

Kotter, J. P. (1999). Leading change: The eight steps to transformation. In J. A. Conger, G. M. Spreitzer, & E. E. Lawler, III., eds. *The leader's change handbook: An essential guide to setting direction and taking action.* San Francisco: Jossey-Bass Publishers.

Likert, Rensis. (1961). *New patterns of management.* New York, McGraw-Hill Publishers.

Mills, D. Q. (1987). *Not like our parents: How the baby boomer generation is changing America.* New York: Morrow.

Montana, P. and Charnov, B. H. (1987). *Management.* New York: Barron's.

Nahavandi, A. & Malekzadeh, A. R. (1999). *Organizational behavior: The person-organization fit.* Upper Saddle River, NJ: Prentice-Hall, Inc.

Porter, L.W. & Lawler, E. E. (1968). *Managerial attitudes and performance.* Homewood, IL: Richard D. Irwin.

Rouch, C. F. & Behling, O. (1984). Functionalism: Basis for an alternative approach to the study of leadership. In J. G. Hunt, D. M. Hocking, C. A. Schriesheim, & R. Stewart, eds. *Leaders and managers: International perspectives on managerial behavior and leadership*. Elmsford, NY: Pergamon Press.

Schein, E. H. (1992). *Organizational culture and leadership*, 2nd ed. San Francisco: Jossey-Bass Publishers.

Schermerhorn, J. R., Jr. (1999). *Management*, 6th ed. New York: John Wiley & Sons, Inc.

Schermerhorn, J. R., Hunt, J. G. & Osborn, R. N. (1997). *Organizational behavior*, 6th ed. New York: John Wiley & Sons, Inc.

Schermerhorn, J. R., Hunt, J.G. & Osborn, R. N. (1998). *Basic organizational behavior*, 2nd ed. New York: John Wiley & Sons, Inc.

Senge, P. (1997). Through the eye of the needle. In R. Gibson, ed. *Rethinking the future*. London: Nicholas Brealey Publishing.

Stogdill, R. M. (1974). *Handbook of leadership: A survey of the literature*. New York: Free Press.

Stogdill, R. M. Personal factors associated with leaders: A survey of the literature. In J. L. Pierce & J. W. Newstrom, eds. *Leaders and the leadership process: Readings, self-assessments, and applications*. Boston, MA: Irwin McGraw-Hill.

Yukl, G. A. (1998). *Leadership in organizations*, (4th ed). Upper Saddle River, NJ: Prentice Hall.

Vroom, V. H. (1964). *Work and motivation*. New York: John Wiley & Sons, Inc.

Weber, M. (1947). *The theory of social and economic organizations*, trans. A. M. Henderson & H. T. Parsons. New York: Free Press.

Chapter III

Work and the Workplace

Richard D. Neidig

OVERVIEW

Introduction to the Topic

This chapter is about the meaning of work to employees today, selected trends in the workplace, and the resultant impact on managers, leaders and organizations. While the United States is the country of primary focus, the content of the chapter should prove of interest and value to readers from many parts of the world. We will briefly explore the historical perception of work, from the workers' perspective; view the current realities of work and emerging work-related issues of importance to individuals and organizations; and ask a few questions which must be answered by each of us as we enter the 21st century world of work. As author, I claim the right to provide some degree of personal opinion, which should be considered as the thoughts of an optimist sometimes prone to philosophizing and lecturing on the importance of passion in our lives. These personal thoughts are to be dealt with as the reader sees fit. Still, the vast majority of the material contained within this chapter is grounded in today's realities, having evolved from the history of work, and containing very real meaning for the leaders and managers of today, tomorrow, and the foreseeable future.

Emerging characteristics of today's worker and 21st century organizations are reshaping employer-employee relations and will determine the future of work from both individual and organizational perspectives. Frankly, some of the news from the world of work is troubling. After reviewing the literature on the concept of "trust" in modern organizations, Whitener, Brodt, Korsgaard, and Werner (1998) posited that the American worker's trust in employers has hit rock bottom. At the same time, employers may or may not have trust in their workers, in apparent contradiction to programs such as empowerment, self-managed teams and telecommuting. As technology and the information age exert their rule, many organizations and their employees are engaged in a historic struggle over employee monitoring, such as electronic surveillance, drug testing, and archiving of employee communications (Cranford, 1998; Greenlaw & Prundeanu, 1997; Hatch & Hall, 1997; Mishra & Crampton, 1998).

Many workers, faced with aging parents or the need for childcare and possessing new work-life values, are seeking employment with organizations that support the personal concerns of their work force. Yet, Mackavey (1999) believes that while more organizations appear to be trying to deal with their employees' need to find and manage an appropriate balance between work and family, closer inspection shows that "work and family are still, generally, considered two separate domains . . . if one is to give priority to either one, the organization expects you to give it to work" (p. 3).

In sum, many people view their jobs with negative attitudes. What are the potential implications of an estranged work force? Dutton (1998) noted that "in corporations, as in nations, disenchantment leads to a loss of innovators, a withholding of energy and even to sabotage or espionage" (p. 51). This does not read as a formula for competitive advantage or individual self-actualization.

The overview continues with a brief look at the importance of work to the individual. The remainder of this chapter will focus on some of the key issues and trends that characterize modern workers and their organizations. In the end, the reader may have more questions than answers, but hopefully a commitment to "make a difference" will guide the pursuit of the answers to those questions you see as important.

The Meaning and Importance of Work

A substantial case can be built for the premise that "work," or a dedication to productive labor, has always been a basic need of humankind for both survival of the species and nurturing of the human spirit. Historically, and still today in much of nature (and in many corporate boardrooms and on many shop floors), "survival of the fittest" might be restated as "survival of the industrious." This appears to be a proposition held by many of us—those who work the hardest are likely to be not only the survivors but also the leaders of a species or a corporation. While this may not be an accepted tenet for everyone, there is most likely less argument with the claim that work is a necessary part of most of our lives and we each perceive our work in somewhat different ways.

People come to their jobs with individual attitudes and intentions, toward the organization, their jobs, and their motivations. As Bellman (1996) stated in discussing the meaning of work, "we are purposeful people . . . there is intention behind our actions; there is purpose behind our performance" (p. 55). Even without an exhaustive review of the "meaning of work" literature, one can still easily build a case for the premise that people seek identity in life, and our "employment" represents important opportunities and threats to establishing a positive self-image as we shape our individual identities.

The challenge for managers and leaders in today's organizations, and for each of us as individuals with the power to find value and growth through work, is how do we align individual needs and values with those of our organizations? Do people still both value and dread their jobs in the same ways as 10 years ago, 30, 50, a century back? The final answer will not be found within this chapter. In fact, the answer is probably beyond the limits of most organizational behavior research, which focuses on group data rather than dealing with the power of individual differences.

The answers to questions about worker values and individual perceptions of work itself are probably somewhere around "it depends." It depends on many things, from who you are, where you came from, where you hope you are headed, how you find your satisfactions in life, where you need to journey to reach your life's goals, and which goals you choose to pursue.

Today's worker is in part a product of the evolution of work itself and the self-perceptions that accompanied changes in the nature of work. As technology and globalization increase the pace of change in organizations, workers and corporations will continue the process of evolution, particularly in the area of human resource management.

The Evolution of Worker Perceptions

Chapter I reviewed the history of management, with particular emphasis on the dramatic changes in the nature of work brought on by the Industrial Revolution. As business investors gave rise to mass labor and sought to maximize organizational productivity, there arose an almost immediate incentive to study the nature of work, the worker, and those who manage the work process.

Today, the corporation continues to be economically dependent on the collective productivity of its work force. To a very large extent, the individual needs and values of each worker present the greatest frustrations to many managers and the variance in the human resource that often determines organizational success or failure. Therefore, while work has typically been studied according to certain "group" characteristics, the individual differences among workers within any work group should also be viewed as critical variables in any attempt to understand the relationship between effective management practices and the concepts of worker satisfaction, motivation and productivity.

We vary even as to the labels we attach to our work, and these labels may provide insight into our, or our organization's, view of the meaning of work. People involved in work as a "livelihood" may be engaged in this activity primarily in exchange for pay. It is how we maintain our lives or lifestyles. A "job" may encompass the tasks that we contract to do. Those activities that occupy most of our waking day would constitute our "occupations." When we view work as using our knowledge, skills and abilities in some socio-economic order, labor becomes "employment." If I am working at something I feel called upon to do, it may well be my "vocation." Beyond the semantics of this exercise, it is clear that work has not one, but many meanings for most of us. It is labor, even if a labor of love, because by definition it requires the investment of energy. Work can be fulfilling and indeed a necessary contributor to mental health for most people. It can also produce ulcers, alcoholism, depression, suppression of output, sabotage and other forms of individual and collective destruction.

Harpaz (1998) cited evidence that "for most people, the meaning of work has generally been expounded by three propositions . . . of which the most prominent is economic or instrumental, the second concerns commitment to work as part of human nature and human needs, and the third is socio-psychological"(p. 143). In other words, workers need income and want to be paid fairly; they want to be part of a productive endeavor, where they feel as though their input is making a difference; and they need to be part of an organized effort at achieving a positive output. In his review of previous research on the goals of workers from various cultures, Harpaz referenced research that indicated that the two most dominant goals for workers across a number of countries are similar: they want interesting work and good pay. The convergent findings for these logical goals are reassuring from a human resources strategy standpoint. To some degree, diverse people appear to share a common value system with respect to the basic goals they hope to achieve on their jobs. Complexity, of course, is added by individual and group differences in what defines interesting work and what is perceived as "good pay."

There are key constructs that allow workers to achieve the meaning from their work that they seek and organizations to reap the maximum benefit of worker commitment. The concept of trust is one such construct.

TRUST

A recurring theme in organizational behavior literature is that trust is a key ingredient in shaping the definition of work for many of us. If you and I agree on what we want to accomplish, have the talents and resources to make it happen, and possess an understanding of why the goal has value to both us and the organization we work for, "making it happen" should be relatively easy to accomplish.

However, there are two additional dimensions that will help distinguish our joint performance, or serve as corrosive barriers to our efforts if we run low on these qualities. I am a strong believer in the importance of *trust* among people to allow for maximum synergy and the energizing power of *passion* for the goal.

Trust can be defined as the level of confidence we share in each other's ability and dependability to contribute positively to task accomplishment. Trust does not necessarily mean we like each other, let alone have a sense of affection. These may be pleasant aspects of our relationship, but they are neither necessary nor sufficient for a trusting, effective working relationship. What we achieve, when trust is present, is an understanding that we can work together effectively, accomplish things as a team that are less likely individually, understand what our roles are, and count on each other to get it done. We also believe that one will not abandon the other as the journey proceeds.

Passion is the importance of that journey and the level of commitment we have for the undertaking. Lucas (1997) asserted that a fatal illusion of some organizations is that if there is a good plan in place, the organization need not be concerned about the passion within its people. He noted that "all organizations have passion. The passion may be active or latent, positive or negative" (p. 168). Passion may well differentiate a vocation from a job.

Trust allows for maximum synergy in an organization. Copyright © Tony Stone Images.

After more than 40 years of research on trust the concept remains a critical construct to the success of current and future organizations (Lewicki, McAllister, & Bies, 1998). With the rapidity of changes in employer-employee relationships, in the nature of work, in the responsibilities for career management, in the definitions of loyalty, what is the current state of trust in and within modern organizations? Whitener et al. (1998) offered a bleak conclusion: "At the same time that trust in organizations has hit 'rock bottom,' researchers have shown that interpersonal trust has significant relationships with many organizational variables, such as the quality of communication, performance, citizenship behavior, problem solving, and cooperation" (p. 513). Other researchers echo the concern with the perception of a betrayal of trust between organizations and their work forces (Elangovan & Shapiro, 1998).

Most authors on the dimension of trust stress the complexity of the construct. However, complexity characterizes most of our relationships in life, those that can be labeled trusting and those that lack trust. In the world of work, perhaps trust can be redefined as a mutual understanding shared by companies and their employees over how things are, the basis of this reality, and the shared investments, opportunities and rewards that can characterize successful business interactions within organizations. It requires open communication, mutual respect, reliability, character and competence. These are not "warm and fuzzy" niceties; they are bedrock determinants of a healthy organizational culture.

Trust determines an organization's ability to successfully implement meaningful change. For example, "empowerment" emerged as one of the power terms of the 90s. Empowerment involves leaders and managers in helping others acquire and use the necessary power within an organization to make decisions that affect themselves and their work (Schermerhorn, Hunt, & Osborn, 1997).

Empowerment is one of the change goals and change energizers in modern organizations. However, "empowerment is only likely to enhance cooperation and, ultimately, organizational performance . . . if trust exists in the organization" (Jones & George, 1998, p. 531).

As Jones and George (1998) discussed, trust includes a certain level of emotion. That is, trust is based on both factual data (e.g., the behavior of other people) and our acceptance or rejection of these behaviors. Again, the emotional outcome need not be one of liking or disliking, but of confidence and a sense of security in a particular relationship, even if time-bound rather than life-long. Similarly, Borowski (1998) viewed the relationship between management and employees as basically a human relationship that should be governed by guidelines that would oversee any human relationship. In healthy interactions, this means respect, open communication, empowerment and trust. Organizations that are able to add a dose of passion to the mix can see the results and reap the rewards.

Is there a relationship between trust and passion in an organization's culture and the concepts of job security and loyalty? This question appears to have a much more complex answer today than twenty years, or perhaps even a decade ago.

JOB SECURITY, CAREER MANAGEMENT, AND LOYALTY

Organizational behavioral experts are increasingly studying concepts such as empowerment, employee disenchantment, downsizing, self-managed careers, contingent workers, family-friendly workplaces and trust as key variables in the mosaic of modern organizational life. Are today's employees turned-on by and loyal to their organizations, or are they disillusioned and disenchanted? Dutton (1998) believed that employee disenchantment leads to a loss of innovators within corporations, and as disenchantment deepens, employees may withhold their energies or even resort to sabotage. Dutton notes that an increasing number of companies offer "family" programs, such as childcare, eldercare and corporate gyms in recognition that an investment in retaining the "best and brightest" is a wise business decision.

At the same time, the definitions of job security and loyalty are being rewritten. O'Hara-Devereaux and Johansen (1994) concluded that lifelong employment for the majority of workers within many countries, especially the United States, is over. Job security, therefore, is less likely to be defined as an understood contract between corporation and employee based on a sense of mutual loyalty. Instead, job security becomes closely related to maintaining and enhancing employability, where individual workers assume the responsibility for their own career management.

As the United States witnesses these changes in the nature of work, the historic importance of work to the self-esteem of the American worker must not be forgotten. To be unemployed in the United States has historically meant that self-esteem is threatened and psychological and physical health are perhaps endangered (Ferraro, 1998). While people may adapt to the new realities of work, maintaining a strong employability record will continue to be important, beyond pure economic reasons, to the American's sense of worth and well-being.

O'Hara-Devereaux and Johansen (1994) pointed out that workers are spending less time with more employers. Workers in the United States are responding to organizational changes, including "downsizing" and "right-sizing" with greater self-awareness. The individual is more likely to be aware that lifetime, and perhaps even extended, employment with one organization is unlikely and that job security is more than ever entrusted to the individual worker. Milkovich and Boudreau (1997) sent a blunt message: "No one owes you a job, a career, or future security. Globalization and faster change means that you alone will be responsible for charting a successful career" (p. 362).

At the extreme, one could envision an end to the concept of the "permanent employee." Instead, the work force may be characterized by individuals who manage their own career movement and are committed to lifelong learning, career and employment flexibility, specific project completion, and professional interdependence.

An interesting dilemma surfacing for 21st century organizations is that managers want dependable, skilled workers; but employers are hesitant to make long-term economic commitments to employees who may move in the near-term to another company. As workers of the future become more mobile and demand greater employment flexibility to meet lifestyle goals, employers may need to reassess the types of career and training investments they will make to what may be short-term employees.

A recent *Newsweek* article on the "new American career" focuses on many of the forces that are shaping the changes in the definitions of job security and career management. McGinn and McCormick (1999) cite Robert Reich, former U.S. Labor secretary, as concluding "loyalty is dead," and it appears to be dead in both directions (corporation and worker). Reich notes that self-employed workers are rapidly expanding and already constitute up to twenty percent of the U.S. labor force.

Harris (1999) believes that "loyalty is being defined more in terms of working together to make something happen rather than the company taking care of the employee for life" (p. 2). As contingent workers increase in numbers and as even those employees currently working for a company define themselves as paid consultants, "self-employed" may soon characterize an even higher percentage of the work force.

McGinn and McCormick (1999) are most likely correct when they state that the shift to a more independent worker is probably born, to a large degree, of fright. Widespread prosperity within the economy has not protected companies from the global competitive pressures and the demands of investors. "Sadly, one thing hasn't changed: employees are usually the first costs that get cut" when the competition threatens a corporation's earnings estimates (McGinn & McCormick, 1999, p. 44).

Does all this mean that organization-based career management, succession planning, and long-term professional development programs are dead? The answer is definitely "no."

While the 1960s and 1970s perhaps saw the greatest proliferation of "fast track" programs for "star potential" employees, these programs still exist. Larsen and London (1998) stated that "despite the academic debate and a number of organizational and economic dynamics that would suggest their demise, high-flyer programs have shown surprising resiliency and still constitute the backbone of career management in many large organizations" (p. 64). However, Larsen and London also noted that beginning in the 1980s, as organizations began the transformation to flatten structures and experienced the economic pressures of increased competition resulting in rapid cost-cutting, not as many fast-track trainees were included in career-focused development programs.

Job security, career management and loyalty take on particular importance for an emerging generation of workers. The youth in America's work force offer wonderful opportunity and very real challenges to 21st century organizations.

JOB VALUES AND GENERATION X

The meaning of work can vary according to the generation each of us was born into. American workers represent three different generations: "traditionalists," "Baby Boomers" and "Generation Xers" (Thiedke, 1998). While these groupings represent generalized assumptions that aren't necessarily valid for each individual within a particular generation, comparison across the three sources of workers is interesting and potentially valuable as a source of guidance for organizational and management practices.

Traditionalists are those born before 1946; they frequently combine a practical outlook on life with a strong work ethic. They accept, even value, the hierarchical organization with the embedded authority of position power (Thiedke, 1998).

The Baby Boomers are generally viewed as those born between 1946 and the mid-1960s. Thiedke (1998) noted that these workers were optimistic as they began their careers and often were driven in pursuit of their careers. In contrast to the traditionalists, baby boomers have had a love-hate relationship with authority. (Interestingly, much of the position power in American organizations can be found among baby boomers, although the flattening of many organizations has put middle managers at risk, the organizational level where boomers have often settled-in.)

From the mid-1960s through the early 1980s, a new wave of American worker was born. These are the Generation Xers. According to Thiedke (1998), "they're generally skeptical of and unimpressed with authority . . . They reject boomers' workaholism and materialism and are determined to lead more balanced lives. They are willing to be led but only by those who demonstrate competency. Many Xers feel they've had to accept jobs that aren't commensurate with their education" (p. 65).

Minerd (1999) discusses a number of misconceptions about Generation X workers and provides suggestions for mangers as they attempt to maximize performance and satisfaction of this group of workers. (Unlike Thiedke, 1998, Minerd classifies Generation Xers as born between 1963 and 1977, a more limited time frame.) Minerd relies heavily on Tulgan's (1997) published work on Generation X in listing the misconceptions of disloyalty, arrogance, unwillingness to pay one's dues to the organization, and lack of ability to delay gratification as characteristic of Generation X workers.

Minerd (1999) believes there is a difference between disloyalty and wariness. Generation Xers are more wary than other generations because they have witnessed widespread downsizing of people who were loyal and hardworking employees; this has also resulted in their cautious response to organizational expectations of "paying one's dues." Minerd states that Generation Xers tend to be very self-confident, but this is not necessarily arrogance.

Generation Xers view employment security as based on their own abilities, rather than secured through company retention policies (Tulgan, 1997). Abilities, of course, are quite transferable across jobs and organizations, which reinforces a sense of independence for people who might otherwise fear organizational dependence. With respect to delay of gratification, Tulgan stated that Generation X workers demand more detailed and more consistent feedback on their performance. They like to see tangible results of their work, the sooner the better.

Recommendations for managing this generation of workers include providing independence in self-study and professional development, with concrete learning objectives; provide a work environment rich in feedback, with tangible work outcomes; and develop managers to provide mentoring support to Generation Xers (Minerd, 1999; Tulgan, 1997).

Ironically, while business and management schools include organizational behavior as part of their curriculum, there is some concern that their faculty members are also struggling with the Generation X student. Payne and Holmes (1998) examined the attitudes of undergraduate management faculty towards their Generation X students. The faculty members were 35 years or older (i.e., baby boomers or traditionalists), with terminal degrees in management or organizational behavior. The perception from a majority of respondents was that generation-based problems in faculty-student communication are real.

While faculty-student disagreements might be claimed as an eternal struggle, future research must focus on how universities and organizational training programs can provide the most effective learning environments for Generation Xers. There is evidence that these students prefer experiential activities to traditional lecture and testing (Payne & Holmes, 1998; Tulgan, 1997). Of course, adult learning theory has historically emphasized the importance of hands-on methodologies in teaching and training, so the issue here may relate more to some university faculty members or corporate trainers than to a new generation of students.

Thiedke (1998) discussed the concern many managers have with Generation X workers' seeming unwillingness to work their way up an organization's hierarchy and "distractions" caused by their concern with life outside the office. As Thiedke pointed out, Generation Xers can claim they have a strong desire to contribute to an organization, while not accepting the notion of company-based career management as a realistic expectation, based on the numbers of people they have seen downsized at the very time they entered the work force. (Martin, 1999, estimates that Generation Xers grew up in an era where up to 75 percent of American families were impacted by corporate downsizing.) Furthermore, Xers value (often demand) that an organization provides the opportunity to achieve a balanced life, where work is an important variable in that balance, but not the entire recipe.

Thiedke (1998) provided a list of the assets that Generation X workers bring to an organization. These include adaptability (Xers have grown up with change being the constant), creativity (the very rejection of parts of the status quo can lead to innovation), and comfort with technology. Thiedke avers that Generation Xers can be the people who lead organizations into the Information Age, as they visualize and develop uses for technology that baby boomers and traditionalists would never imagine.

To provide an appropriate culture for Generation X workers, Thiedke (1998) recommended:

- A casual and friendly environment where relationships are collegial, not hierarchical;
- High-quality training;
- Clear expectations about job performance;
- Ample opportunities to excel;
- Feedback that is frequent, timely, accurate and specific;
- An environment of respect in which Generation Xers' opinions are taken seriously and they're seen as valued members of the team;
- Managers whose words and actions are consistent and who see wisdom in pursuing a balanced life. (p. 66)

Since all three generations of workers populate our organizations, a significant responsibility of modern managers is to help people who embody quite different organizational values to work together productively. The increasing diversity of the work force in terms of demographics other than age greatly increases the challenge to managers, as they deal with both individual differences and group differences arising from the many facets of diversity within the human resource.

Regardless of the generation of worker, the nature of work and work organizations is about performance and output. If an organization provides a culture that leads to the "happy worker," will productivity naturally follow?

JOB PERFORMANCE, JOB SATISFACTION, AND WORKER MOTIVATION

The relationship among job satisfaction, worker motivation, and job performance has proven to be one of the most complex paradigms in social-science research. At the most basic level, this research has tried to determine whether there is a causal relationship, such as where satisfaction increases productivity. It seems like organizations have generally adopted the hypothesis that a happy worker will be a productive worker. Current concepts such as employee empowerment, the virtual organization and employee monitoring most likely have very real effects on worker satisfaction; the relationship to productivity is less clear.

Are There Causal Relationships?

Technology, globalization, work force diversity, increased competition and many other realities are shaping modern organizations in terms of job redesign, worker expectations and management practices. However, one of the constants since the Industrial Revolution and the arrival of organized efforts to deliver goods and services has been the focus on worker productivity as a key ingredient in organizational success.

The 20th century has seen major research investments in both maximizing job performance (productivity) and attending to worker needs and desires (job satisfaction). An early, and continuing, research hypothesis was "a happy worker is a productive worker," which implies a causal relationship between the two outcomes. This relationship was often viewed as satisfaction influencing productivity (although some researchers developed a model based on the hypothesis that it is productivity that determines worker satisfaction). A popular belief continues to be: the more satisfied the employee, the more productive the worker.

Yet, the relationship between worker attitudes and productivity has, for the most part, eluded precise determination. More than four decades ago, Brayfield and Crockett (1955) published a seminal review of research on employee attitudes vis-a-vis employee performance that documented no clear relationship between the two measures. While Brayfield and Crockett's research was met with disbelief and denial by more than a few business schools and management "experts," the message was clear; a happy worker may or may not be productive and there certainly was no consistent causal effect between the two phenomena.

There was and is more substantial evidence that job satisfaction may be related to certain employee withdrawal measures; e.g., absenteeism and turnover. That is, if I find my job seriously unpleasant, I will try to avoid as much of the unpleasantness as possible. Absenteeism and turnover are two ways to escape the unpleasant work situation. Even here, however, there are external factors such as the labor market, which will moderate employee response to dissatisfaction. For example, turnover is more likely if there are expanding job opportunities (Schultz & Schultz, 1998).

After countless additional studies on satisfaction and performance, McCue and Gianakis (1997) could only conclude from the literature that job satisfaction is an intensely studied variable across organizational research. They further noted that the debate on the nature of the relationship between satisfaction and productivity has continued in vigorous form since the Brayfield and Crockett (1955) review. Perhaps the safest statement on the satisfaction-performance issue is that almost any causal proposition is still contentious (McCue & Gianakis, 1997). Having said that, there is little doubt that employee productivity, job satisfaction, and worker motivation will continue to be targets of theory, research and speculation well into the next century, and probably beyond.

Are happy workers productive workers? The answer is unclear. Copyright © Tony Stone Images.

In a recent study on employee satisfaction, Johnson and McIntye (1998) surveyed over 8,100 government employees and found that the attributes of organizational culture most strongly related to employee satisfaction were empowerment, involvement and recognition. With respect to work climate, communication showed the strongest relationship to satisfaction. These findings appear to be in line with continuing trends in many organizations towards empowerment of the work force and increased attention to improving organizational communication.

The Impact of Empowerment on Satisfaction and Productivity

The logical relationships among empowerment, recognition and communication seem apparent. As Dover (1999) notes, the goal of empowerment programs is to create a shared purpose and increased collaboration among employees resulting in greater value to the customer. "With effective empowerment, employees . . .

become self-directed decision makers aligned with the shared purpose—and they receive the reinforcement and support needed to optimize the value provided to customers" (Dover, 1999, p. 51).

Lucas (1997) stated, "We as managers have to empower people by helping them to see and set high but achievable goals for themselves. Empowerment begins with establishing the expectations, not just achieving them" (p. 79). So, is the empowered worker both happy and productive? Once again, the answer is probably, "it depends." A simple, causal relationship among empowerment, satisfaction and productivity will undoubtedly be difficult to document through research across organizations, unless individual differences are factored into the research design.

While employee empowerment is endorsed by numerous theorists and consultants and most likely desired by many employees, there are related concerns. Dover (1999) points to several potential pitfalls with empowerment programs. Managers can view such programs as threats to their authority and resist or sabotage empowerment efforts. Employees, who suddenly find new opportunities for decision making, may mistake empowerment for discretionary authority, where they assume unilateral power to make decisions. Newly empowered employees may lack the skills needed to attain collaborative decision making, and management may be unwilling to fund or engage in required training. Finally, there are some workers who prefer not to assume the responsibilities of empowerment and offer resistance from the worker perspective

Lucas (1997) concluded that empowerment can be a good or bad idea. He presented three ill-bred reasons for empowerment. Empowerment becomes a panacea if it arises from the strategy of "we'll fix things by getting everyone involved" (p. 127). Empowerment is a cop-out, if "we don't know what we're doing, so let's pass the buck down to the front line" (p. 127). Finally, empowerment can be a dangerous strategy to deal with downsizing, where we "'empower' (i.e., overload) the survivors, who don't have the time, energy, or creativity to think about today (much less the future)" (p. 127).

The bottom line on empowerment is probably that of most every organizational development tool. It requires careful analysis of the need for change, development of the appropriate change procedures, training and reinforcement for employees throughout the organization, and planned monitoring and revision as needed. Can carefully designed and implemented empowerment programs raise employee satisfaction, allow for motivated employees to better accomplish the goals of the organization, and result in measurable gains in productivity? I suspect the answer is "yes." Effective goal setting alone has been shown to increase productivity. The catch obviously is in determining what is an effective empowerment program for an organization, a work unit and the individual employee—a challenge of substantial proportion.

While empowerment may provide workers with a sense of independence in decision making, the move to virtual organizations can add independence in the area of face-to-face human contact. Telework offers benefits such as flexibility and less commuter stress. Virtual corporations provide exciting, fast-paced potential for business success. However, research has yet to fully explore the impact of the virtual environment on the interpersonal aspect of work and the specific interpersonal needs of many workers.

The Impact of "Virtual" Work Relationships

High job satisfaction, control over the conditions of work, and social support are three factors that may reduce the effects of stress caused by or present on the job (Schultz & Schultz, 1998). The rapidity of change in modern organizations, including continual modifications in job design and the workplace itself, have implications for job satisfaction and a sense of control (or lack thereof) over one's working conditions. As telecommuting and e-mail replace face-to-face interactions in the "workplace," many Industrial Age ways of establishing human relationships and acquiring social support in organizations are being threatened or eliminated.

Today, more than 15 million American workers are performing their jobs at home, and this number is expected to rise dramatically in the 21st century. This change can increase worker satisfaction and help with the work-family balance; however, it can also create problems that may lower job satisfaction and challenge the development of trust within organizations.

As we move further into the Information Age with the accompanying technologies shaping the nature of work, basic human interactions are being redefined. For example, extensive research has shown the importance of non-verbal communication in determining the interpretation of words and the formation of interpersonal relationships. Tone of voice, facial expressions, gestures, posture, office decor, personal attire and scores of other non-verbal cues are all processed by humans as we attempt to understand messages and to make decisions about people. Now, we must learn new ways to test the meaning of words and to establish working relationships that cannot as readily rely on many of the traditional non-verbal aspects

Telecommuting and e-mail have replaced Industrial Age ways of establishing human relationships in organizations. Copyright © Tony Stone Images.

Home office. Today, more than 15 million American workers are performing their jobs at home. Copyright © Tony Stone Images.

of communication. The impact of these changes on worker satisfaction, including both physical and mental health, will be an area of important research.

Hallowell (1999) presents chilling commentary on the potential negative effects that can result from lack of adequate face-to-face, same space communication. As a practicing psychiatrist and a faculty member at Harvard Medical School, Hallowell has observed and studied the importance of what he calls "the human moment at work" (p. 58). He believes that people "need to experience . . . the human moment: an authentic psychological encounter that can happen only when two people share the same physical space" (p. 59), and Hallowell says these encounters must include the work part of life, not just social encounters. "The human moment has two prerequisites: people's physical presence and their emotional and intellectual attention" (p. 59).

Hallowell (1999) is concerned that human moments are disappearing in modern organizations, with troubling consequences. He notes that technology has made face-to-face interactions far less necessary and less frequent over the past decade. Hallowell believes the human moment is being replaced by worry, in part "because electronic communications remove many of the cues that typically mitigate worry. Those cues—body language, tone of voice and facial expressions" (p. 61).

Hallowell (1999) discusses senior executives whom he counsels on anxiety disorders. He states, "I can tell you without a doubt that virtually everyone I see is experiencing some deficiency of human contact . . . I am increasingly sought out because people feel lonely, isolated or confused at work" (p. 60). Hallowell does not rest his case solely on observations provided through his clinical practice. He also cites "strong evidence from the field of brain science" (p. 61), where brain chemistry has shown the debilitating effects of even partial isolation.

"Toxic worry," anxiety that has no basis in reality, is one of the most serious consequences of the disappearing human moment, according to Hallowell (1999). His advice to organizations is not to retreat from the Information Age or refute technology and all the tremendous opportunities it provides. Rather, he cautions us to carefully plan how we will preserve our human moments and to then make them happen. For example, he cites one CEO who has developed a policy where all virtual employees must come into the office at least once each month for unstructured face-to-face time.

Employee Monitoring

Another rapidly expanding practice influencing the satisfaction-performance paradigm is directly related to the increasing use of technology within organizations. Employee monitoring is on the rise. While the exact number of employees who are electronically monitored on the job varies by author, there is no doubt that elec-

Electronic surveillance on the rise at work. Copyright © John Sutton, John Sutton Architectural Photography.

tronic monitoring is already widespread and growing. For example, Greenlaw and Prundeanu (1997) cite various estimates on the use of electronic monitoring that include a figure as high as 20 percent of the work force, and that was in 1990.

Various reports indicate that U.S. organizations spend over $1 billion annually on electronic monitoring. This includes telephone call accounting; telephone service surveillance; computer monitoring; location monitoring, such as computer chips in employee badges; and video monitoring (Greenlaw & Prundeanu, 1997; Mishra & Crampton, 1998).

Of course, not all employee monitoring is electronic. Mishra and Crampton (1998) list other types of monitoring systems that are used in American workplaces. These include undercover operatives, spying (live observers), and teams of investigators posing as friends of the worker. Add drug testing, and the employee monitoring business is big business indeed.

Convincing cases have been built both in support for and opposition to widespread employee monitoring. For example, Cranford (1998) cited estimates of costs to employers resulting from drug abuse that run as high as $60 billion per year. At the same time, Mishra and Crampton (1998) stated that "while many motives [for employee monitoring] are positive and help protect employees, the activities raise questions about invasion of privacy and even health" (p. 4). DeTienne (1993) pointed to the probable financial impact on organizations if employers are found unjustifiably liable for employees' stress-related illnesses caused by various forms of monitoring. As an additional cost, some organizations have experienced extreme employee turnover in response to electronic monitoring (Mishra & Crampton, 1998).

While employee monitoring is not a new phenomenon, the rapid increase in electronic monitoring and drug testing does add a significant issue to the characteristics of today's work and workplace. The import for this chapter is the immediate and long-term impact of employee monitoring on employee satisfaction and job performance. The results are not in, but it is certain to be an area for continuing research, debate, government legislation, collective bargaining and litigation. One could hypothesize that, similar to employment testing within the United States, business necessity and validity may be prudent criteria for organizations to pursue as they attempt to support various monitoring approaches.

At the same time, individual workers and collective bargaining units may be well-served to consider both employee and employer needs as they wrestle with privacy vs. productivity debates. Ethical considerations appear to be relevant to both employers and employees. Society expects organizations to recognize the rights and responsibilities of individuals and to use their assets in a socially responsible manner (Cordeiro, 1997). Society also has the right to expect workers to focus on customer value, in terms of product and service quality, cost and safety.

Thus, the interrelationships among practices, job satisfaction, worker motivation and productivity are not easily broken-down into cause and effect relationships. Still, best practices within modern organizations must include how human resources are viewed and respected. The dignity of each individual worker supports a corporate effort at inclusion; competition for the best workers may demand special organizational attention to both external and internal environments.

EMERGING PARADIGMS

This section provides a brief look at several out-of-the mainstream movements gaining strength in modern organizations. These are certainly not the only emerging issues, nor even necessarily the most popular within the organizational behavior literature, but they are worthy of discussion. The movements discussed include spirituality and work, emotional intelligence, quality of life issues, and the response of human resource development programs.

Spirituality in the Workplace

Spirituality in the workplace is one of the newer organizational behavior paradigms. Leigh (1997) described the movement toward recognizing and nurturing human spirituality at work:

> *It's about acknowledging that people come to work with more than their bodies and minds; they bring individual talents and unique spirits. For most of the 20th century, traditionally run companies have ignored that basic fact of human nature. Now, they explore spiritual concepts such as trust, harmony, values, and honesty for their power to help achieve business goals. (p. 26)*

Leigh concluded that many companies are joining the effort to reestablish the meaning of work as a reaction to the downsizing that began in the 1980s. She also believed that the craving for meaning in the workplace is not just a baby boomer journey, but rather spans all generations. Similarly, Laabs (1995) saw a desire among people worldwide to establish congruence in their lives and find meaning in their work.

An important aspect of spirituality programs is the organization's involvement in helping employees establish appropriate work-life balance, through programs such as daycare, flexible work schedules and telecommuting. Leigh (1997) cited research that indicates a relationship between employee involvement in such programs and effective work outcomes.

McKnight (1998) wrote that most people view their work as a continuing struggle to prove their worth, while fearing loss of their jobs. He concluded that many people do not like what they spend a good part of their lives enduring— their jobs. He pointed to research that has shown Americans highly value meaning and direction in their lives. McKnight presented spirituality as a possible path for organizations and individuals to pursue in their quest to alter the negative perceptions of work.

McKnight (1998) defined spirituality as a life force that energizes people to purposes beyond the inner-self. To realize this level of what might be called self-actualization, a person needs the opportunity to establish a totally integrated life, where work is a key component. McKnight concluded that organizational leaders and managers must change their definitions of the purpose of business to allow for the positive aspects of spirituality in the workplace. He stressed the importance of recognizing that critical products of any organizations are its internal culture and its impact on society. In the 21st century, work groups may become an increasingly active force in introducing spirituality into the workplace, where values shift from fear and competition to trust and cooperation (Laabs, 1995).

Emotional Intelligence

In addition to spirituality, another emerging organizational paradigm is "emotional intelligence." Emotional intelligence has a logical relationship with spirituality. From the study of American organizations and high-performance executives, Goleman (1998) asserted strong empirical evidence for the impact of emotional intelligence in determining performance within organizations. He found that almost 90 percent of the variance between star performers and average ones in senior positions within the organizations studied was due to emotional intelligence dimensions, rather than cognitive abilities.

Goleman (1998) provided four key attributes of emotional intelligence: self-awareness, self-regulation, motivation and empathy. People with high self-awareness understand that feelings do affect them and everyone within an organization. Self-regulation allows people to experience and benefit from feelings (emotions), but not be controlled by them. Self-regulation is a key ingredient in the establishment of trust. Motivation is seen as a passion for challenge, for continual learning, for doing the job well. Empathy allows an individual to consider feelings, especially those of other workers, when making decisions. Goleman believes empathy has increased importance to modern organizations due to the increased use of teams, globalization, and the need to retain critical talent among a highly mobile work force.

Cultivating an organizational culture that develops and reinforces emotional competencies is viewed as solid business strategy by a growing number of supporters. Goleman (in Salopek, 1998) viewed these competencies as critical to the success of any organization, yet insufficient attention is being paid to the development of such qualities he noted.

Cooper (1997) concluded that research has shown how emotions drive trust, loyalty and commitment. Cooper saw leaders worldwide increasing their awareness of the importance of emotions in the workplace and the potential of feelings (passion) to determine productivity. Since satisfaction is also an attitude, or feeling, a plausible hypothesis is that emotion, or passion, can influence both productivity and gratification.

> *Research suggests that people with high levels of emotional intelligence . . . experience more career success, build stronger personal relationships, lead more effectively, and enjoy better health than those with low [emotional intelligence]. People with high emotional intelligence motivate themselves and others to greater accomplishment. (Cooper, 1997, p. 32)*

Cooper stated that emotional intelligence can be learned.

Goleman (in Salopek, 1998) agreed that people can be trained on the various aspects of emotional intelligence, although he expresses concern over the training approach used in many organizations. Goleman believes training on competencies related to emotional intelligence must be tailored to fit the needs of individuals and the organization, and a proper learning environment is necessary.

Cooper (1997) stressed the importance of trust to the development and achievement of emotional intelligence. He stated that the development of trust depends on making emotional contact with people, and without trust, innovation in organizations will not occur.

Cooper (1997) eloquently described the power and limitations of individual differences, when he noted that none of us can do everything well; yet, each of us can do some things better than many other people—a reality not recognized by many organizational practices that suppress the uniqueness of individuals. Cooper encouraged people to develop strengths, rather than trying to "fix" what are viewed as weaknesses. Goleman (in Salopek, 1998) recommends making change self-directed, where people design their own development plans.

Certainly, these thoughts on individual development, emotional intelligence and spirituality appear compatible, even reinforcing, principles. Furthermore, they appear to fit many of the needs of each of the generations of workers in American organizations, including those of Generation X. There is also a logical connection between the emotional intelligence and spirituality relationship and self-managed careers.

Evers, Rush, and Berdrow (1998) discussed the skills students need to succeed in the modern workplace. The essential skills were seen as managing self, communicating, managing people and tasks, and mobilizing innovation and change. "Being aware of oneself and surroundings, being able to lead oneself and manage one's career" (Evers et al., p. 53) rings familiar to the content of this chapter.

Quality of Life Issues

There seems to be little doubt that many workers today seek a healthy balance among the many elements of their lives—family, work, leisure and continued growth. There also appears to be little doubt that many people are finding it increasingly difficult to establish this balance. There is research evidence that a certain level of balance is important to physical and psychological well being. Pearson (1998) reported on research, which indicated that job satisfaction and leisure satisfaction were significant predictors of psychological health.

Stress for each of us is real, and it comes from many sources. The conflicts between work and family can be a significant source of life stress (Schultz & Schultz, 1998). We can't avoid life stress, but as individuals and with the assistance of progressive organizational practices, perhaps we can reduce and better manage stressors that emanate from our work.

To the extent that quality of life includes the psychological well being of workers, employers' responsibilities are being addressed by case law in the United States (Fisher, Schoenfeldt, & Shaw, 1999). American organizations have responded to quality of life issues by developing programs such as employee assistance, on-site daycare and flexible working conditions.

Nevertheless, as noted earlier, Mackavey (1999) is concerned that many organizational programs that deal with balance of life issues are more cosmetic than substantial. She believes that often these programs focus more on how employees can better organize their life activities to make them more available for work than

Many workers today seek a healthy work-life balance.
Copyright © Tony Stone Images.

on how they might realize a truly balanced existence. Whether this is a valid criticism or not, it is most likely true that Americans are still trying to define the
meaning and demands of a balanced life. Individual and organizational responses will evolve as the journey continues. The good news is there appears to be a
growing recognition of the importance of the human spirit, of emotions and feelings, and of work-life balance. Mega-dollars are being spent on employee monitoring, but there has also been an increasing investment in employee quality of
life issues. Those who log on to the World Wide Web can initiate a search for
work and life management information and watch the sources scroll across
screen. The issues are real, and the response is growing.

Human Resource Development

Many of the issues raised in this chapter relate to training and development of the work force at every organizational level, including a path of lifelong learning for each of us. As more people adopt the belief that job security is only achieved through continued learning and skill development, there may be an expanding movement to jointly determine training goals within organizations. Individual workers as well as collective bargaining forces may increase their efforts to influence the investment of training dollars. Working together, employees and organizations may be able to transform the perception of training from a cost to an investment.

Leading-edge organizations, as defined in the 1999 *American Society for Training and Development* annual "state of the industry" report, ranked high on all of the following factors:

- percent of employees trained
- training expenditures per employee
- use of innovative training practices
- use of high performance work practices
- use of innovative compensation practices
   (Bassi & VanBuren, 1999, p. 3)

The direct investment in training is not the only indicator of organizational commitment to change and growth. Rouiller and Goldstein (1993) report that a positive organizational transfer climate is also an important condition to allow for learned behaviors to be transferred to the job. A positive transfer climate requires management practices that facilitate rather than inhibit the application of new knowledge and behaviors. Tolerance for risk and the time required by employees to develop new learning curves with respect to job performance are key attributes of a positive transfer climate.

Rothwell (1995) discussed "human performance technology (HPT)" as a focus on integrating all we know about improving human performance in organizations. "HPT recognizes that human performance is influenced by many factors working separately and collectively. Performance is not solely the result of individual efforts" (p. 4). As we move into the next century, the nature of work and the workplace will likely continue its rapid rate of change. How we develop the human resource to effectively mange these changes will be a key to organizational success.

SUMMARY: A PERSONAL PERSPECTIVE

This chapter represents an olio of current and emerging issues that relate to the world of work, primarily from the workers' perspective but also from the viewpoint of the organization. No claim is made that the issues raised are exhaustive—quite the opposite is the assertion. For example, we did not touch upon critical organizational factors in America such as the learning organization, workplace violence, the state of equal employment opportunity, harassment, or trends in collective bargaining. These factors continue to impact organizations and the people who work within American companies. The issues presented within this chapter were chosen because they deal with the worker at the individual level, their impact is often misunderstood, and they are factors that show probable interaction effects.

Preparing this chapter reinforced a rather simplistic observation about the complexities of life. Each of us must strive to recognize and manage the many variables that impact us and others, in our lives and in our work, and strive individually and collectively to achieve what is the right and necessary balance across these variables. Will we succeed in the effort? It most likely depends on our definition of success. We are not powerless. We can develop personal leadership and have a positive influence on our work climates and perhaps help determine organizational culture. Often individual effort will make a difference; at times we will need to develop sufficient trust to work together on shaping our organizations and determining the gestalt of our lives.

Clasping yet another draft of this chapter, I was lowering my creaking body into the chair from which I do much of my reflective reading when I noticed a newspaper article that was on the abutting end table. "Why Are We Human" read the grabber. In *The Washington Post* article, Potts (1999), of the Smithsonian Institution, describes a variability hypothesis connecting different evolutionary steps with the adaptability of the human brain. Near the end of the article, Potts writes, "In light of the variability hypothesis, the human brain is adapted to a world prone to changing conditions, novel problems and multiple options. This view seems to explain nicely why the greatest brain enlargement coincided with the period of most habitat instability" (p. H5).

Potts' (1999) comments were with respect to the past several million years, rather than the present world of organizations. Nevertheless, "changing conditions, novel problems and multiple options . . . habitat instability" read awfully close to the issues we are dealing with today.

While the human brain may keep on "growing" as the species continues writing its history, I am convinced that we need not wait on future physical evolution to sculpt the kind of "world of work" we want to inhabit. Frankly, our brains can handle this challenge right now. Most people within our organizations know what needs to be done to help align work with overall life challenges and how to combine work and the responsible life into a meaningful and individually unique existence. In sum, it is less a question of the brain than of the heart.

REFERENCES

Bassi, L.J., & VanBuren, M.E. (1999). The 1999 ASTD state of the industry report. *A Supplement to Training & Development Magazine*, 1–27.

Bellman, G. (1996). Working on purpose. *Training & Development, 50* (6), 55.

Borowski, P.J. (1998). Manager-employee relationships: Guided by Kant's categorical imperative or by Dilbert's business principle? *Journal of Business Ethics, 17* (15), 1623–1632.

Brayfield, A.H., & Crockett, W.H. (1955). Employee attitudes and employee performance. *Psychological Bulletin, 52,* 396–424.

Cooper, R.K. (1997). Applying emotional intelligence in the workplace. *Training & Development, 51*, (12), 31–38.

Cordeiro, W.P. (1997). Suggested management responses to ethical issues raised by technological change. *Journal of Business Ethics, 16* (12/13), 1393–1400.

Cranford, M. (1998). Drug testing and the right to privacy: Arguing the ethics of workplace drug testing. *Journal of Business Ethics, 17* (16), 1805–1815.

DeTienne, K.B. (1993). Big brother or friendly coach? *The Futurist, 27* (5), 33–37.

Dover, K. (1999). Avoiding empowerment traps. *Management Review, 88* (1), 51–55.

Dutton, G. (1998). The re-enchantment of work. *Management Review, 87* (2), 51–54.

Elangovan, A.R., & Shapiro, D.L. (1998). Betrayal of trust in organizations. *The Academy of Management Review, 23* (3), 547–566.

Evers, F.T., Rush, J.C., & Berdrow, I. (1998). *The bases of competence*. San Francisco: Jossey-Bass Publishers.

Ferraro, G.P. (1998). *The cultural dimension of international business* (3rd ed.). Upper Saddle River, NJ: Prentice Hall.

Fisher, C.D., Schoenfeldt, L.F., & Shaw, J.B. (1999). *Human resource management* (4th ed.). Boston: Houghton Mifflin.

Goleman, D. (1998). What makes a leader? *Harvard Business Review, 76*, (6), 93–102.

Greenlaw, P.S., & Prundeanu, C. (1997). The impact of federal legislation to limit electronic monitoring. *Public Personnel Management, 26* (2), 227–244.

Hallowell, E.M. (1999). The human moment at work. *Harvard Business Review, 77*, (1), 58–66.

Harpaz, I. (1998). Cross-national comparison of religious conviction and the meaning of work. *Cross-Cultural Research, 32* (2), 143–170.

Harris, J. (1999, January). Does love still make the business world go round? *American Management Association International, 2*.

Hatch, D.D., & Hall, J.E. (1997, August). Video surveillance presents HR challenges. *Work force, 76* (8), 67.

Johnson, J.J., & McIntyre, C.L. (1998). Organizational culture and climate correlates of job satisfaction. *Psychological Reports, 82* (3, Pt. 1), 843–850.

Jones, G.R., & George, J.M. (1998). The experience and evolution of trust: Implications for cooperation and teamwork. *The Academy of Management Review, 23* (3), 531–546.

Laabs, J.J. (1995). Balancing spirituality and work. *Personnel Journal, 75* (9), 60–68.

Lawson, H.H., & London, M. (1998). High-flyer management-development programs. *International Studies of Management & Organization, 28* (1), 64–90.

Leigh, P. (1997). The new spirit at work. *Training & Development, 51* (3), 26–33.

Lewicki, R.J., McAllister, D.J., & Bies, R.J. (1998). Trust and distrust: New relationships and realities. *The Academy of Management Review, 23* (3), 438–458.

Lucas, J.R. (1997). *Fatal illusions.* New York: AMACON.

Mackavey, M.G. (1999, January). Shared purpose: Linking family and company values. *American Management Association International*, 3–4.

Martin, C.A. (1999, March). In "Change management: AMA's training conference report. *American Management Association*, 2–4.

McCue, C.P., & Gianakis, G.A. (1997). The relationship between job satisfaction and performance. *Public Productivity & Management Review, 21* (2), 170–191.

McGinn, D., & McCormick, J. (1999. February 1). Your next job. *Newsweek,* 43–44, 45.

McKnight, R. (1998). Spirituality in the workplace. In J.D. Adams (Ed.), *Transforming work* (pp. 160–178). Alexandria, VA: Miles River Press.

Milkovich, G.T., & Boudreau, J.W. (1997). *Human resource management* (8th ed.). Chicago: Irwin.

Minerd, J. (1999). Bringing out the best in Generation X. *Futurist, 33* (1), 6–7.

Mishra, J.M., & Crampton, S.M. (1998). Employee monitoring: Privacy in the workplace? *S.A.M. Advanced Management Journal, 63* (3), 4–14.

O'Hara-Devereauz, M., & Johansen, R. (1994). *Global work.* San Francisco: Jossey-Bass Publishers.

Payne, S.L., & Holmes, B. (1998). Communication challenges for management faculty involving younger 'Generation X' students. *Journal of Management Education, 22* (3), 344–367.

Pearson, Q.M. (1998). Job satisfaction, leisure satisfaction, and psychological health. *Career Development Quarterly, 46* (4), 416–426.

Potts, R. (1999, April 14). Maybe evolution favored an all-terrain animal. *The Washington Post,* H1, H4-H5.

Rothwell, W.J. (1995). Beyond training and development. *Management Review, 84* (9), 4.

Rouiller, J.Z., & Goldstein, I.L. (1993). The relationship between organizational transfer climate and positive transfer of training. In Russ-Eft, D., Preskill, H., & Sleezer, C. (Eds.), (1997). *Human resource development review* (330–344). Thousands Oaks, CA: Sage Publications.

Salopek, J.J. (1998). Train your brain. *Training & Development, 52* (10), 26–33.

Schermerhorn, J.R., Hunt, J.G., & Osborn, R.N. (1997). *Organizational behavior* (6th ed.). New York: John Wiley & Sons.

Schultz, D.P., & Schultz, S.E. (1998). *Psychology and work today* (7th ed.). Upper Saddle River, NJ: Prentice Hall.

Thiedke, C.C. (1998). How you can keep your Generation Xers on staff. *Family Practice Magazine, 5* (10), 65–66.

Tulgan, B. (1997). *The manager's pocket guide to Generation X*. Minneapolis, MN: Lakewood Publications.

Whitener, E.M., Brodt, S.E., Korsgaard, M.A., & Werner, J.M. (1998). Managers as initiators of trust: An exchange relationship framework for understanding managerial trustworthy behavior. *The Academy of Management Review, 23* (3), 513–530

Chapter IV

Managing Diversity

Glenda J. Barrett

We hold these truths to be self-evident, that all men are created equal, that they are endowed by their Creator with certain unalienable Rights, that among these are Life, Liberty, and the pursuit of Happiness. (Declaration of Independence, July 4, 1776)

INTRODUCTION

The United States has always been a multi-cultural nation, so diversity is not a new issue. Applying the principle of equality in the workplace crowded with diverse individuals, however, is a recent development. In the last 35 years, changes in legal frameworks, consumer markets, labor supply, and other economic pressures have emphasized the need to cultivate human resources and employ them wisely.

This chapter outlines major events in diversity management for the last four decades and traces the evolution of thought from protecting individual rights to creating a diverse portfolio of talent that gives the corporation a competitive edge.

The key questions it addresses are: What is diversity management? Why is it relevant to American companies? How have organizations responded? What is the current status? What are the implications for managers?

DEFINITIONS

The American Heritage Dictionary (1996) defines "diversity" as simply "difference." *Managing diversity* in American organizations, however, is a complex proposition. In fact, there is a diversity of opinion on exactly what the concept means.

At one end of the spectrum, many think "managing" primarily means complying with the law. In this context, managing diversity is a renaming or repackaging of the programs used to satisfy federal or state equal employment opportunity (EEO) and/or affirmative action (AA) requirements. The key questions are: Do the specified groups have equal access to the opportunities and resources of the organization? Are they being treated in an equal, non-discriminatory manner?

Others argue that while access issues are still relevant, "managing" should be focused on how the diverse human resources are actually used. Roosevelt Thomas (1990), who coined the phrase, described it as a way "to get from a diverse work force the same productivity we once got from a homogeneous work force, and to do it without artificial programs, standards—or barriers" (paragraph 14). Managing diversity is, he explained, "a comprehensive managerial philosophy designed to enable managers to tap the potential of all employees, regardless of how diverse they might be" (Thomas, 1990b, paragraph 10). He even speculated that tapping such potential could provide competitive advantages in productivity. Thus, using the broader view, managing diversity becomes not just adherence to legal frameworks, but a mindset, an organizational culture.

How an organization defines "managing"—whether it assumes the legal or the developmental approach—shapes the scope, goals, functions, and evaluation methods it employs. For instance, if the narrower, legal definition is used, managing diversity would be required only where U.S. law prevails. Under this definition, an American company that hires a diverse work force from within the U.S. would certainly need to manage diversity. So, too, would a large domestic company that imports labor into the U.S. or a company that sends an American expatriate to a host country, such as Japan.

Questions arise, however, about various other international work arrangements. For instance, if the U.S. had a joint venture in another country, such as Korea, should the employees hired locally also be considered in the scope? Or, should a third-country-national employee, such as a Dutch citizen, working for an American firm in a foreign host country, such as France, be included in the definition? Conversely, would a German corporation that transferred its own staff as expatriates to work in the U.S. need to "manage diversity"? As the labor pool globalizes, these questions become more important. Legislation has begun to consider non-traditional staffing configurations, and international case law is beginning to develop precedence. Nevertheless, the legal jurisdictions and margins are currently confusing and fluid (Carnell, Davidoff, & Eidenberg, 1998). Of course, theoretically, all of these international configurations could be included in "managing" diversity if the broader, developmental definition is employed.

The operational definition of "diversity" is also debatable. U.S. law provides some guidance by identifying the protected categories, such as race, color, sex, religion, national origin, age, and disabilities (Milkovich & Boudreau, 1997). Nevertheless, the specific dimensions of these characteristics are often questioned. For instance, the Americans with Disabilities Act (ADA) defines "disability" as a "physical or mental impairment that substantially limits one or more of the major life activities; a record of such an impairment; or being regarded as having such an impairment" (U.S. EEOC-ADA, 1997, paragraph 1). However, "there is no definitive list of impairments that are considered to be disabilities. Courts are directed to reach determinations based on a case-by-case analysis. This determination is not made on the basis of the name or diagnosis of the employee's impairment but, instead, on the basis of the effect of the impairment on her or his life" (Bennett-Alexander & Pincus, 1998, p. 362).

Recently, three cases, involving nearsightedness (*Sutton v. United Air Lines*, 1999), blindness in one eye (*Albertson's, Inc. v. Kirkingburg*, 1999), and hypertension (*Murphy v. United Parcel Service*, 1999), raised a central issue: If a condition can be corrected, such as by wearing glasses or taking medicine, should it be considered a disability? (Lash, 1999) When the U.S. Supreme Court ruled that it should not, advocates of a broader interpretation of the law said they would ask Congress to revise the statute (Biskupic, 1999). Thus, although the U.S. law provides an outline of the protected groups, detailed clarification is an ongoing process. Therefore, an organization that considers "diversity" to be limited to legal protections still has considerable risk to "manage."

An organization that looks at diversity in a developmental framework encounters even more complexity. In addition to deciphering and satisfying the legal requirements, it must also ask whether those characteristics (race, color, sex, religion, national origin, age, and disabilities) are, in fact, the crucial ones. Are they the relevant traits in terms of work group interaction? Or, should other dimensions, such as socioeconomic status or personality preferences, be included? For example, when a conflict arises between two "diverse" members of a staff, is it due to one of the protected differences, such as race or age, or is it a clash of introverted vs. extroverted personality styles? The laws were written to ensure constitutional human rights and to address social-political concerns, not to foster organizational productivity. Consequently, the characteristics the law protects may not be the salient ones in terms of working together.

The ambiguous definitions of "managing" and "diversity" raise several important issues. For instance, who decides what is a "legitimate difference" between people, something that needs to be "managed"? (Dale, 1998) In the United States, for example, race is considered to be a key trait; but in many European Union countries, it is not (Milkovich & Boudreau, 1997). How do the traits interact? Is there a priority structure? For instance, is gender more important than age, religion, or work ethic? Loden & Rosener (1991) list six primary dimensions of diversity (age, ethnicity, gender, physical abilities/qualities, race, and sexual/affectional orientation) and eight secondary dimensions of diversity (educational background, geographic location, income, marital status, military experience, parental status, religious beliefs, and work experience). What else might be included? There is no universally accepted listing of human differences.

If it isn't clear what "diversity" is, is it clear what it is not? What are the similarities among humans? What shared traits might serve as a foundation for productive interaction? When conflicts arise, finding common ground can be an effective strategy. In "managing diversity," there are still many questions that beg intelligent, operational answers.

RELEVANCE—THREE PARADIGMS

For organizations, these dancing definitions create the proverbial Pandora's Box. Nevertheless, most corporations forge ahead, trying in some fashion to manage diversity. Why? The rationale has changed over the last 35 years, but it has consistently been fueled by some type of business necessity.

Thomas and Ely (1996) describe three paradigms to explain what are essentially economic forces that underlie the evolution of diversity management in the United States. The first paradigm is a response to legal developments, the second one is driven by external market conditions, and the last one addresses internal operations. Reviewing each paradigm in more detail reveals the trends and factors contributing to its development.

Discrimination and Fairness

The first paradigm, Discrimination and Fairness, is described as:

> *Prejudice has kept members of certain demographic groups out of organizations such as ours. As a matter of fairness and to comply with federal mandates, we need to work toward restructuring the makeup of our organization to let it more closely reflect that of society. We need managerial processes that ensure that all our employees are treated equally and with respect and that some are not given unfair advantage over others. (Thomas and Ely, 1996, paragraph 15)*

While social justice may play a role in an organization's stance on diversity, in this paradigm, a powerful business motive is cost avoidance. Companies want to minimize the direct and indirect expenses associated with the legal environment. Avoiding legal costs was a predominant justification for managing diversity during the 1960s and 1970s, and it remains an ongoing concern today.

Navigating the legal risk is not easy, however. There are many federal and state laws that govern a variety of discrimination issues. The major federal provisions are shown in Table 1. Each state can also create its own set of supplemental protections. For instance, while federal law does not directly protect affiliation orientation under Title VII of the Civil Rights Act, several states and many cities do include some level of protection for gays and lesbians (Bennett-Alexander & Pincus, 1998).

Coordination between the levels of government protection as well as among the federal laws themselves can be problematic. Adding to the complexity is the fact that laws are not fixed; they are dynamic. Each provision changes through legislative revision, judicial review, and/or executive action. A closer look at the historical developments of two key federal provisions, the Civil Rights Act and affirmative action, illustrates how the requirements can fluctuate and, thereby, make it difficult for organizations to contain legal costs.

Table 1. Major Federal Employment Discrimination Provisions

Year	Title	Purpose
1963	Equal Pay Act of 1963 (EPA)	Outlaws gender discrimination in compensation for substantially similar work under similar conditions
1964	Title VII of the Civil Rights Act of 1964, as amended; includes the Pregnancy Discrimination Act of 1978	Prohibits employment discrimination based on race, color, religion, sex, or national origin
1965	Executive Order 11246, with the 1967 amendment that added sex to the list of protected categories (E.O. 11375).	Prohibits employment discrimination for federal contractors that do at least $10,000 worth of business with the government
1967	Age Discrimination in Employment Act, as amended (ADEA); includes the Older Workers Benefit Protection Act of 1990 (OWBPA)	Outlaws age-based employment discrimination against individuals who are at least 40 years old
1973	Section 501 of the Rehabilitation Act of 1973, as amended	Outlaws employment discrimination against federal employees with disabilities
1974	Vietnam-era Veterans Readjustment Act	Outlaws discrimination against Vietnam-era and disabled veterans
1990	Title I of the Americans with Disabilities Act (ADA)	Outlaws disability-based employment discrimination in both the public and private sector, excluding the federal government
1991	Civil Rights Act of 1991	This major amendment to the Civil Rights Act of 1964 clarifies previously contested provisions regarding disparate impact, provides options for jury trials and monetary damages, and extends coverage to international assignments.

Sources: U.S. Equal Employment Opportunity Commission, Statutory Authority (1998b);
U.S. Department of Labor, EEO E.O. 11246, as Amended (1965);
U.S. Department of Labor, Small Business Handbook (1997);
Kelly & Dobbins, 1998.

The Civil Rights Act of 1964-Title VII (as amended) is the landmark federal legislation that prohibits discrimination in employment decisions based on race, color, sex (gender), religion, or national origin unless the characteristic is a bona fide occupational qualification (BFOQ). Under this law, someone who feels he/she was denied opportunities that are available to others, that he/she was treated differently, and that the different treatment was due to one of the protected characteristics (i.e., race or gender) could sue the employer for unlawful discrimination. For instance, if an employer states that a master's degree is required for a job then interviews four male applicants who have the degree but does not interview the one female applicant who also has the degree, it is possible that illegal discrimination based on gender has occurred. It appears that she has been treated differently because she is a woman. This type of complaint is known as "disparate treatment." For several years, this was the only form of complaint.

In 1971, the U.S. Supreme Court expanded the Title VII scope by introducing disparate impact theory. Under this argument, the effect a policy has on a protected group is considered. In the ground-breaking case *Griggs v. Duke Power Co.* (1971), the Court ruled that the educational level and tests the company used to screen applicants for a position were not related to job performance and that the higher-than-necessary requirements prevented blacks from being considered. In other words, the screening criteria were racially-biased. Chief Justice Burger wrote:

> The (Civil Rights) Act proscribes not only overt discrimination but also practices that are fair in form, but discriminatory in operation. The touchstone is business necessity. . . . Good intent or absence of discriminatory intent does not redeem employment procedures or testing mechanisms that operate as "built-in-headwinds" for minority groups and are unrelated to measuring job capability. (Bennett-Alexander & Pincus, 1998, p. 73)

Avoiding legal costs was a predominant justification for managing diversity in the 1960s and 1970s. Copyright © Joe Sohm, Uniphoto Picture Agency.

Expanding the unit of measure from an aggrieved individual to adverse impact on a protected group was a significant development in discrimination law. It occurred just before Congress extended Title VII protection in 1972 to government employees and empowered the Equal Employment Opportunity Commission (EEOC) to sue employers (EEOC, Strategic Plan, 1997). The combined government actions sent a loud wake-up call for organizations to check their personnel policies and procedures more closely and monitor them in more sophisticated ways. Organizations frequently responded in the 1970s by creating Equal Employment Opportunity specialists on their staff to manage the developments (Dobbin, Sutton, Meyer, & Scott, 1993). Many also established internal grievance systems, even in non-union environments, in order to avoid costly and embarrassing lawsuits by handling problems in-house.

The government expanded the scope of specific protected characteristics, too. For instance, in 1976, the U.S. Supreme Court ruled that discrimination based on pregnancy was not covered by the gender provisions of Title VII (*General Electric Co. v. Gilbert*, 1976). Congress contradicted this judicial opinion by passing a new amendment, the 1978 Pregnancy Discrimination Act, to include this protection.

Similarly, before the mid-1970s, courts were reluctant to consider sexual harassment under the sex provisions of Title VII. When they finally did in 1976 (*Williams v. Saxbe*), the acceptable argument was "quid pro quo." This means that, in order for sexual harassment to occur, "the employee is required to engage in sexual activity in exchange for workplace entitlements or benefits such as promotions, raises, or continued employment" (Bennett-Alexander & Pincus, 1998, p. 204). A decade later, the U.S. Supreme Court broadened the criteria for sexual harassment by acknowledging that it could occur in a "hostile working environment" even when no quid pro quo was evident (*Meritor Savings Bank, FSB v. Vinson*, 1986). The new criteria worried organizations because the conditions for a "hostile" work environment were vague. In the early 1990s, the courts decided that a "reasonable person standard" would be used to assess the conditions (*Ellison v. Brady*, 1991; *Harris v. Forklift Systems, Inc.*, 1993). The clarity of that refinement also made organizations nervous. A wave of sexual harassment training for supervisors and employees flooded corporate America.

Organizations actually did appreciate several U.S. Supreme Court rulings in 1988–89 since the rulings made it more difficult for employees to win their cases. For instance, in *Wards Cove Packing Co. v. Antonio* (1989), the Court shifted the burden of proof. Employees now had to prove that a discriminatory policy was not job-related rather than have employers prove that it was (Bennett-Alexander & Pincus, 1998). Furthermore, in *Price Waterhouse v. Hopkins* (1989), the U.S. Supreme Court decided that an employee would not win the case if the employer could show that the same employment decision would have been made based on nondiscriminatory reasons.

In response to these rulings, among others, however, Congress passed the Civil Rights Act of 1991. It returned the burden of proof to the employer, negated the "mixed motives" factor, and instituted several other provisions that increased the cost risk for organizations. For instance, the 1991 amendment added optional jury trials, which tend to be more unpredictable. It also increased possible sanctions by allowing compensatory and/or punitive damages. Furthermore, it extended coverage of the law to U.S. citizens who are employed in American organizations outside the United States as well as to foreign employees who are working in the U.S. (Bennett-Alexander & Pincus, 1998).

The changes in the scope, definitions, and enforcement provisions of Title VII were not unique. Affirmative action (AA) mandates have been even more controversial and have ridden stormy waves of legislative, judicial, and executive maneuvers.

Affirmative action is related to equal employment opportunity (EEO); but, theoretically, it is different. Whereas EEO strives to reduce barriers for everyone, AA prescribes proactive initiatives, such as preferential treatment, for protected groups in remedial situations. In other words, AA requires positive steps to promote adequate representation of diverse groups where it hasn't existed before (Milkovich & Boudreau, 1997; Bennett-Alexander & Pincus, 1998).

History shows that the practical boundary between EEO and AA is often unclear. While limited affirmative action mandates were issued as early as 1941 when President Franklin D. Roosevelt signed Executive Order 8802 to curtail discrimination in defense contracts, the primary foundation for affirmative action today is Executive Order 11246, as amended, which was signed by President Lyndon Johnson in 1965. It prohibits discrimination in employment for federal contractors that provide at least $10,000 of goods and services to the government. Employers who contract at least $50,000 of business must also create an affirmative action plan, and larger employers must conduct a work force analysis that shows the distribution of protected groups by job category and identifies areas of underutilization (Bennett-Alexander & Pincus, 1998; U.S. DOL-Small Business Handbook, 1997). The Office of Federal Contract Compliance Programs, which is part of the U. S. Department of Labor, administers this executive order and defines underutilization or underrepresentation as "having fewer minorities or women in a particular job group than would reasonably be expected by their availability" (Bennett-Alexander & Pincus, 1998, p. 121).

In 1978, a landmark case, *Regents of the University of California v. Bakke*, challenged the practice of affirmative action and asserted that it was, in effect, reverse discrimination. In it, Mr. Bakke, a white male, applied for admission to the medical school at the University of California at Davis. After he was rejected, he learned that less qualified non-white applicants were accepted under a special admission program that reserved a number of seats for minority applicants in order to increase diversity at the campus. He claimed that his rights under Title VII of the 1964 Civil Rights Act and the Equal Protection Clause of the Fourteenth Amendment to the U. S. Constitution had been violated since the special admission program discriminated based on race or ethnic status. The U.S. Supreme Court ruled in favor of Mr. Bakke, stating that the design of the admission program did violate the Fourteenth Amendment; but the Court did not prohibit considering race or ethnic background in general.

The following year, an employment-related affirmative action plan was contested because minority workers were admitted to a training program before white craftsmen with more seniority. In *United Steelworkers of America, AFL-CIO v. Weber* (1979), the Supreme Court ruled that a policy that reserved 50 percent of the openings for an in-house training program for blacks was permissible because Title VII of the 1964 Civil Rights Act "did not prohibit voluntary race-conscious affirmative action plans undertaken to eliminate a manifest racial imbalance, the measure is only temporary, and it did not unnecessarily trample the rights of white employees" (Bennett-Alexander & Pincus, 1998, p. 126). Thus, the demographic conditions as well as the program design are important considerations in determining whether affirmative action plans are legal.

While the courts sorted through the legal intricacies, national debate about affirmative action found a voice in the presidential campaign of 1980. Republican candidate Ronald Reagan argued against it. When he was elected, he reduced executive branch staff and funding to support it. He appointed staff members and "federal judges who were opposed to regulation in general and to affirmative action in particular. . . . Clarence Thomas, as chair of the EEOC, told the general counsel of his agency not to approve conciliation agreements that included employment goals and timetables" (Kelly & Dobbin, 1998, paragraph 19). In 1991, President Bush appointed Clarence Thomas to the U.S. Supreme Court with Congressional confirmation after highly publicized Senate hearings about his questionable interaction (alleged sexual harassment) with EEOC staff assistant Anita Hill.

In 1995, *Adarand Constructors, Inc. v. Pena* tested a federal affirmative action policy in the courts. Most federal agency contracts contain subcontract compensation clauses that provide financial incentives for the prime contractor to hire certified small businesses controlled by "disadvantaged" individuals. These clauses require the prime contractor to presume that "disadvantaged" individuals include minorities. In this case, the prime contractor of a federal highway construction project chose an Hispanic firm that was certified as a small disadvantaged business. Adarand Constructors, Inc., who lost the subcontract although it was the lowest bidder, filed suit, claiming the assumption that Hispanics are disadvantaged was faulty. The U.S. Supreme Court ruled that a "strict scrutiny" standard should apply and ruled in favor of the plaintiff.

After this ruling, President Clinton "advised federal department heads to review their race-conscious policies and suggest revisions to uphold the Adarand standard. He concluded that affirmative action had not outlived its usefulness, but he ordered agencies to eliminate or reform any practice that created quotas, led to the placement of unqualified individuals, discriminated against majority group members, or continued after its goals had been met" (Kelly & Dobbin, 1998, paragraph 37).

In 1996, the people of California passed Proposition 209, the California Civil Rights Initiative, to ban preferential treatment in public hiring, contracting, and education. The anti-affirmative action referendum won 54 percent of the votes (Rowan, 1996). After it passed, Congressional Republicans were expected to seek a similar national law (Seib, 1996) while the Democratic Clinton administration announced it would take the matter to court to have the initiative declared unconstitutional (Yeager, 1996).

Thus, over the years, companies have received mixed messages about if or how affirmative action should be enacted. Today, while they may be contractually obligated to practice it, the judicial and political support needed to enforce it seems questionable.

Affirmative action is a dilemma for other countries as well. For instance, European practices typically ban the use of preference programs. In a 1995 *New York Times* article on job discrimination in Europe, Richard Stevenson wrote:

> The European Court of Justice, which applies the legal directives adopted by the European Union to cases in the member nations, struck down a program in the German city of Bremen that required municipal agencies to give preference to women over men in job categories where women were underrepresented, assuming the women had at least equal qualifications. The court held that the program violated a 1976 European Union directive that requires equal treatment for men and women in employment, even though the directive provided for exceptions in cases where a measure was intended to remove existing inequalities. (paragraph 13)

Thus, no one seems certain about how to reduce underrepresentation in the workplace. Finding models that provide immediate solutions is unlikely.

Title VII of the Civil Rights Act and affirmative action are only two of the discrimination provisions in the United States. All of the major laws have complexities. Overall, in the last 40 years, the cumulative effect of several significant pendulum swings has been to broaden the scope of employee protection, to be more inclusive, rather than less. In fact, the only two groups that have consistently been excluded from employment opportunities have been children and illegal immigrants.

For organizations that want to be ethically fair and legally correct, the inclusive trend presents a managerial challenge and increases the financial risk. Companies cannot afford to ignore the issue, however, since neglect can be costly. Several recent cases can attest to that. The EEOC (1998) reports that Lockheed Martin agreed to pay $13 million in back pay in an age bias settlement, Mitsubishi Motor Manufacturing of America agreed to pay $34 million to settle a sexual harassment case, and Wal-Mart was charged by a jury with a $3.5 million verdict under the ADA. Of course, not to be forgotten is the largest settlement for race discrimination: In 1995, Texaco agreed to pay $176.1 million—after considerable front-page news coverage (Bennett-Alexander & Pincus, 1998).

Cost, however, is not the only consideration. In the 1980s, organizations began to eye the impact diversity might have on revenue. Generating revenue was a primary motive in the highly competitive economic climate. Economic recessions and globalization pressured organizations to find new sources of income. How could diversity management relate to that corporate goal?

Access and Legitimacy

Thomas and Ely (1996) address this question in their second paradigm, Access and Legitimacy. They explain that diversity can be used to penetrate new markets. The rationale is:

> We are living in an increasingly multicultural country, and new ethnic groups are quickly gaining consumer power. Our company needs a demographically more diverse work force to help us gain access to these differentiated segments. We need employees with multilingual

skills in order to understand and serve our customers better and to gain legitimacy with them. Diversity isn't just fair; it makes business sense. (paragraph 30)

Whereas organizations had previously tried to continue the melting pot illusion by assimilating minority groups into the existing corporate culture, in the 1980s they saw the benefit of highlighting their differences. Thus, people were hired to bridge the gap between the organization and a diverse external consumer market. They were expected to help the organization understand the new customer groups and to flash them a brightly lit welcome sign.

While critics have argued that this bottom-line approach still does little to reduce the tokenism and stereotypical thinking that foster resentment and erode self-confidence, others have adopted it as one means to negotiate. The National Association for the Advancement of Colored People (NAACP) recently used this rationale when it announced a 1998 boycott of Best Western International, Adam's Mark Hotels & Resorts, and Omni Hotels for failing on the Economic Reciprocity Initiative Hotel Industry Report Card. According to the NAACP, the three hotel chains scored poorly on "key diversity issues such as employment, vendor development/procurement opportunities, equity and ownership, advertising and marketing, and philanthropy" (Whitford & Higley, 1998, paragraph 7). Kweisi Mfume, the NAACP President and CEO, said the association and 72 co-sponsoring organizations "intend to keep consumers informed so that they can decide where, and where not, to spend their dollars" (Whitford & Higley, 1998, paragraph 4).

Over the years, human resource managers viewed the move from tolerating to valuing diversity as a step in the right direction. They fostered the perception as part of a wider effort to increase the appreciation of people's roles in organizational performance and to elevate the human resource management (HRM) profession within the corporate structure.

While promoting diversity to address consumer demands, HRM professionals also urged organizations to diversify their personnel due to the shifting labor pool. This supply-side, competitive-edge argument intensified in 1987 when the Hudson Institute released its study, *Work force 2000*. In this highly publicized report, commissioned by the U. S. Department of Labor, Johnston and Packer (1987) projected:

The work force will grow slowly, becoming older, more female, and more disadvantaged. Only 15 percent of the new entrants to the labor force over the next 13 years will be native white males, compared to 47 percent in that category today. (p. xiii)

The report also cautioned policymakers to "maintain the dynamism of an aging work force . . . reconcile the conflicting needs of women, work, and families, and . . . integrate black and Hispanic workers fully into the economy" as part of its list of recommendations (Johnston & Packer, 1987, p. xiv).

The Hudson Institute later claimed that "some ambiguous wording in *Work force 2000* led to misinterpretation of the data" and that the interpreted rate of diversifying was exaggerated (Judy & D'Amico, 1997). However, in its sequel report, *Work force 2020*, it still implies that gender, ethnic, and age diversity will

Two businessmen examine paperwork during a business meeting. The U.S. labor force is slowly becoming more ethnicly diverse. Copyright © Prentice-Hall, Inc.

continue as significant issues. For instance, the report notes that "women now account for about 46 percent of the work force, up from only 29 percent in 1950; in the years immediately ahead, they will approach parity with men" (Judy & D'Amico, 1997, p. 53). The institute also reports:

> . . . the U.S. labor force continues its ethnic diversification, though at a fairly slow pace. Most white non-Hispanics entering America's early twenty-first century work force simply will replace existing white workers; minorities will constitute slightly more than half of net new entrants to the U.S. work force. Minorities will account for only about a third of total new entrants over the next decade. Whites constitute 76 percent of the total labor force today and will account for 68 percent in 2020. The share of African-Americans in the labor force probably will remain constant, at 11 percent, over the next twenty years. The Asian and Hispanic shares will grow to 6 and 14 percent, respectively. Most of this change will be due to the growth of Asian and Hispanic work force representation in the South and West. The changes will not be dramatic on a national scale. The aging of the U.S. work force will be far more dramatic than its ethnic shifts. (Judy & D'Amico, 1997, p. 6)

Thus, it appears that multi-faceted diversity is here to stay, especially in the virtual environment where people from the Northeast may easily work with demographically different staff members or consumers in the Southwest regions of the country or even with people in other nations.

In response to consumer market demands and labor supply projections, many organizations have created human resource policies to attract and retain non-traditional employees. For instance, alternate work arrangements, such as job sharing, temporary or part-time employment, a compressed workweek, flextime, and telecommuting have grown, in part, to accommodate the needs of a diverse labor pool. Similarly, creative recruitment strategies have been designed to tap non-traditional groups, such as retirement communities and organizations that support disabled populations. Companies have also established mentoring programs for new staff members to avoid high turnover costs and to help women and ethnic groups succeed. Accordingly, some organizations have also made their compensation programs more flexible. For instance, they have developed core cafeteria benefit plans. These provide employees with a standard minimum level of benefit, such as basic health insurance, but allow the individual staff members to select other types of benefits, such as child or elder care, to meet their individual needs.

In short, many organizations have seen that in a globalized economy diversity management means more than legal compliance. They have seen value in having a diverse staff to attract new consumers and to provide superior customer service. They have also seen that the many-faced labor supply may give them no choice. So, the question becomes: How can organizations tap the best talents of all their employees and create synergy among them?

Connecting Diversity to Work Perspectives

This question is at the heart of Thomas and Ely's (1996) third framework. Calling it an "emerging paradigm," they label it "Connecting Diversity to Work Perspectives" (paragraph 40) and describe it as one that "organizes itself around the overarching theme of integration" (paragraph 45). They explain:

> *Assimilation goes too far in pursuing sameness. Differentiation . . . overshoots in the other direction. The new model for managing diversity transcends both. Like the fairness paradigm, it promotes equal opportunity for all individuals. And like the access paradigm, it acknowledges cultural differences among people and recognizes the value in those differences. Yet this new model for managing diversity lets the organization internalize differences among employees so that it learns and grows because of them. Indeed, with the model fully in place, members of the organization can say, we are all on the same team, with our differences—not despite them. (paragraph 45)*

This third paradigm shifts the focus of diversity management from legal concerns and market conditions to group dynamics and organizational development. It looks at how organizations can use diverse perspectives to generate more creativity and flexibility without producing debilitating "diversity tension," such as conflict and miscommunication (Roosevelt, 1990, paragraph 18). Thus, it examines team-building methods, such as building trust, and "learning organization" (Senge, 1990) issues, such as experimenting with new approaches and transferring knowledge quickly and efficiently throughout the organization (Garvin, 1993)—but in a multi-cultural context.

Previously, if corporations included cross-cultural issues in human resource development, it was primarily for international staff. For example, American expatriates might learn that Germans value technical expertise in a leader whereas, in the U.S., the leader may be chosen because he/she has effective interpersonal skills, not technical knowledge. Or, they might learn that German meetings tend to be more structured and decision-oriented than American sessions (Schneider & Barsoux, 1997).

Today, similar analysis of cultural values among the ethnic, gender, and age groups inside the U.S. needs exploration. For example, perceptions of time and the importance of punctuality can vary across groups. The gender composition of a work group can affect the way people communicate with one another. Or, expected leadership roles and styles can differ by group (Ferraro, 1998). Not surprisingly, companies turn to training to facilitate the interaction among people with diverse backgrounds.

An industry of diversity consultants and associations has arisen to promote and support diversity initiatives through training, organizational development and change management (Lynch, 1997). For example, in 1993, the Society for Human Resource Management, a prominent professional association, introduced its Mosiac program to emphasize diversity issues and techniques. The services include publications, training, and conferences as well as a "diversity toolkit" (SHRM, 1999). The Conference Board, another well-known business organization, launched its programs in diversity management in 1994. It provides conferences to discuss diversity issues, and it has established a Council on Work force Diversity to facilitate the exchange of "best practices" information (Conference Board, 1999).

In summary, history shows that managing diversity has not been easy. Defining the task and determining why it is important are still debatable issues. The three paradigms—Discrimination and Fairness, Access and Legitimacy, and Connecting Diversity to Work Perspectives—demonstrate how perspectives have evolved over 35 years and represent strategies that are still used today. Over that time, all of the major human resource management functions, from employee relations, job analysis and design, recruitment and selection, performance management, and compensation to organizational development and training have struggled with this issue. It takes a coordinated effort to capitalize on diversity. Given the efforts expended, how well are organizations doing?

CURRENT STATUS AND IMPLICATIONS

Knowing the current status of diversity management in organizations is difficult. Measurement is a substantial problem; various validity issues arise. For instance, construct validity depends on which paradigm is used. In other words, managing diversity must be defined before it can be measured.

In the first paradigm, discrimination and fairness indicators might include the number of employee grievances or lawsuits and the dollars associated with those, underutilization rates, and the number or value of any federal contracts lost due to non-compliance with affirmative action requirements. In the second paradigm, access and legitimacy indicators might include correlations between staffing changes and changes in the client base, account revenue, or customer feedback. It might also include the number of vacant positions or correlations between the number of minorities or women hired and the recruitment methods used. In the third paradigm, diversity patterns in performance measures, such as turn-around time, reject rates, absenteeism, turnover, employee satisfaction, or workplace violence might be used to indicate whether diversity is enhancing or detracting from organizational processes.

Obviously, multiple measures are needed, even within one paradigm. Diversity industry consultants often recommend a cultural audit to capture multiple perspectives. There isn't a standard format for a cultural audit. The design is based on a specific corporation's situation and should involve sophisticated research principles and methods. Often these include quantitative and qualitative approaches, such as analysis of personnel records, employee surveys, or focus groups.

At the national level, the current evaluation of diversity management is based on the first paradigm, Discrimination and Fairness. The primary measuring methodology is quantitative, such as using EEOC case records or Census data; but the recent Federal Glass Ceiling Commission used qualitative measures, such as public hearings and focus groups, as well.

The Civil Rights Act of 1991 authorized a bipartisan commission to "identify the glass ceiling barriers that have blocked the advancement of minorities and women as well as the successful practices and policies that have led to the advancement of minority men and all women into decision-making positions in the private sector" (Glass Ceiling Commission, 1995, p. 3).

This 21-member Commission, appointed by President Bush and Congressional leaders, and chaired by the Secretary of Labor, found:

> *Despite the growing awareness among corporate leadership of the bottom-line value and economic imperative of including minorities and women in senior corporate management, progress has been disappointingly slow, and barriers persist which stop able people from achieving their full employment potential. (Glass Ceiling Commission, 1995, p. 7)*

Specifically, the Commission notes that a "a survey of senior-level male managers in Fortune 1000 industrial and Fortune 500 service industries shows that almost 97 percent are white, 0.6 percent are African American, 0.3 percent are Asian, and 0.4 percent are Hispanic" (Glass Ceiling Commission, 1995, p. 9).

The statistics on the status of women in high-level jobs are equally dismal:

> *The data show that minorities and white women are increasingly earning the credentials that business needs. However, data also show that women hold only 3 to 5 percent of the senior-level jobs in major corporations. Moreover, only 5 percent of the women who hold those senior-level jobs are minority women. (Glass Ceiling Commission, 1995, p. 10)*

The Commission also found substantial differences in salaries between the groups. The report notes:

> *In 1992, U.S. Census data reported the ratio of female to male earnings in management jobs ranged from a low of 50 percent in the banking industry to a high of 85 percent for managers in human services. An analysis of 1990 U.S. Census data shows that black men*

who hold professional degrees and top management positions earned 79 percent of what white men earn. Black women, also with professional degrees and in top management positions, earn 60 percent of what white men in comparable positions earn. (Glass Ceiling Commission, 1995, p. 13)

In a separate study, the Catalyst organization, whose mission is to facilitate the success of women in the workplace, found that in 1997, women held "10.6 percent of total board seats on Fortune 500 companies (643 of 6,081 board seats), up from 10.2 percent in 1996, and 8.3 percent in . . . 1993" (Catalyst, 1997, paragraph 1).

Thus, while the government and other organizations do recognize companies using "best practices" by giving public awards, such as the Frances Perkins–Elizabeth Hanford Dole National Award for Diversity and Excellence in American Executive Management or the Catalyst Award, and while they do acknowledge that some progress has been made, overall, advocates of diversity initiatives must be disappointed, if not depressed. Equal employment opportunity is still an American dream, not corporate reality.

What are the barriers to full use of human resources? Are the problems in the organizational systems and/or in human psychology? The Glass Ceiling Commission listed characteristics of successful initiatives. (See Table 2.)

Others echo similar suggestions, but there is no consensus about what is needed next. A popular cry is for accountability. The Conference Board recently released a study that indicated improvement in this area. Yet a recent Society for Human Resource Management survey found that more than half of the Fortune 500 companies polled said they did not tie compensation and performance to diversity goals, while 79 percent of randomly selected smaller companies said they did not (Digh, 1998).

Table 2. Characteristics of Successful Initiatives

They have CEO support.
They are part of the strategic business plan.
They are specific to the organization.
They are inclusive—they do not exclude white non-Hispanic men.
They address preconceptions and stereotypes.
They emphasize and require accountability up and down the line.
They track progress.
They are comprehensive.

Source: Glass Ceiling Commission Report, Executive Summary, 1995, p. 9.

While many feel that refinement of the current structure is required, such as increased leadership commitment or improved accountability, others (Dale, 1998; Cross, 1996; Ferris, 1994) assert that true equality is unlikely, if not impossible, without significant reform of organizational culture and the distribution of power in American companies. Gormley (1996), Director of Corporate Social Responsibility at Sisters of St. Francis, questions whether it is even feasible to "manage" diversity, saying "the very act of managing defeats the goal of integration—that is the incorporation of equals" (paragraph 6). She elaborates:

> *A we-they, manager-managed dichotomy seems incompatible with integration and emphasizes some of the fundamental obstacles to it. These obstacles include but are not limited to traditional assumptions about hierarchical structure, sources of power, need for control, and definitions of success. We are not recommending anarchy but rather wishing to focus leaders' efforts on themselves, the organizational culture, and the environment rather than on the workers and the work. (Gormley, 1996, paragraph 6)*

In short, the national data indicate only a trickle of improvement over the years. The glass ceilings and the flagrant, costly violations found in world-famous corporations reveal a significant gap between theory and practice. The uncertainty about what to do next stems from the disagreement in the definition of diversity management and the corresponding lack of strong measurement data, especially in the second and third paradigms, about what works successfully.

Thus, managers of the new millenium are faced with more questions than answers about how to handle diversity. Undoubtedly, some will be tempted to ignore the complex issues. Since human resources are becoming more diversified in the U.S. and global connections are increasingly common, however, a laissez-faire approach does not seem prudent. Diversity initiatives should be actively incorporated into each of the human resource management functions; they should support the overall HRM strategies for the organization.

CONCLUSION

Managing human resources wisely is a fundamental business necessity. Even corporations whose competitive health hinges on creative financial portfolios or technical advancement, in fact, really depend on the people who make and implement those strategic decisions. Thus, the value of the human element should not be underestimated.

Diversity complicates the challenge to employ people well, but it also offers opportunities to find more effective ways to work. In the 35 years since the signing of the Civil Rights Act of 1964, a combination of economic considerations have stretched the concept of managing diversity from a limited EEO/AA function to a broader human resource management strategy. Some would even argue that it represents an attempt at social reform. Nevertheless, changing the system appears to be a slow process. Examples of poor diversity management are easy to find, and relatively little progress is evident in the national statistics.

The pressures that have shaped diversity management during the last 35 years—expanding legal requirements, multi-cultural consumer markets, demographic shifts in the labor supply, and concerns for competitive internal operations—will continue into the 21st century. While corporations can still elect to pursue diversity management only in terms of legal requirements, as was commonly done in the 1960s and 1970s, such a strategy seems short-sighted and anemic for the global environment of the new millennium. Instead, organizations need to focus on productivity and capitalize on their investment. They need to remove artificial barriers and use their human resources to their full potential. Why shouldn't organizations build inclusive, flexible systems that can elicit—not oppress—the optimal performance of each employee?

The task is not easy, and the way is not paved. Currently, conceptual and operational definitions are problematic. Tools and practices are rudimentary at best, as are the evaluation criteria and methods to test them. Moreover, commitment and motivation are questionable. Indeed, the new millennium managers will have much to do to convert diversity into a diamond, to continue the American dream.

Copyright © Grant Heilman Photography, Inc.

REFERENCES

Adarand Constructors, Inc. v. Pena, 515 U.S. 200 (1995). [Online]. Available: Academic Universe, Lexis-Nexis, as of 5/14/99.

Albertson, Inc. v. Kirkingburg, No. 98–591 (1999 U.S. Lexis 4369). [Online]. Available: Academic Universe, Lexis-Nexis, as of 6/24/99.

The American heritage dictionary of the English language (3rd ed.). (1996). New York: Houghton Mifflin Co.

Bennett-Alexander, D., & Pincus, L. (1998). *Employment law for business* (2nd ed.). Boston: Irwin McGraw-Hill.

Biskupic, J. (1999, June 23). Supreme court limits meaning of disability. *The Washington Post*, pp. A1, A10.

Carmell, W. A., Davidoff, P. K., & Eidenberg, J. N. (1998, October). *Application of U. S. antidiscrimination laws to multinational employers.* New York: Law firm of Winston & Strawn. Material presented at the International HRM Certificate Program, Society for Human Resource Management in Chicago.

Catalyst. (1997). *Census of women board directors of the Fortune 500.* New York: Author. [Online]. Available: www.ilr.cornell.edu/lib/earchive/GlassCeiling/facts/facts.html as of 5/3/99.

Conference Board. (1999). *The Conference Board's programs for human resources & organizational effectiveness.* [Online]. Available: www.conference-board.org/expertise/orgs.cfm as of 5/14/99.

Cross, E. (1996, November/December). Managing diversity. *Harvard Business Review*, p. 178ff. [Online]. Available: Academic Universe, Lexis-Nexis, 1206 words, as of 4/6/99.

Dale, K. (1998). Successful diversity management initiatives: a blueprint for planning and implementation. *Industrial Relations Journal, 29* (1), p. 92ff. [Online]. Available: Academic Universe, Lexis-Nexis, 1537 words, as of 3/18/99.

Digh, P. (1998, October). The next challenge: holding people accountable; organizational commitment towards diversity. *HRMagazine, 11*(43), p. 63ff. [Online]. Available: Academic Universe, Lexis-Nexis, 2374 words, as of 5/3/99.

Dobbin, F., & Sutton, J. R. (1993, September). Equal opportunity law and the construction of internal labor markets. *American Journal of Sociology, 99* (2), pp. 396–428.

Ellison v. Brady, 924 F. 2d 872 (9th Cir. 1991). [Online]. Available: Academic Universe, Lexis-Nexis, as of 5/14/99.

Ferraro, G. (1998). *The cultural dimension of international business* (3rd ed.). Upper Saddle River, NJ: Prentice Hall.

Ferris, F. (1994). Why is it so hard to value diversity? Ask the white male. *The Public Manager: The New Bureaucrat, 23*(4), p. 27ff. [Online]. Available: Academic Universe, Lexis-Nexis, 1961 words, as of 3/18/99.

Garvin, D. (1993, July/August). Building a learning organization. *Harvard Business Review 71*(4), 78–91.

General Electric Co. v. Gilbert, 429 U.S. 125 (1976). [Online]. Available: Academic Universe, Lexis-Nexis, as of 5/14/99.

Glass Ceiling Commission. (1995). *Executive summary: the glass ceiling fact-finding report. Good for business: making full use of the nation's human cap-*

ital. [Online]. Available: www.ilr.cornell.edu/lib/e archive/GlassCeiling/ as of 5/3/99.

Gormley, D. (1996, November/December). Managing diversity. *Harvard Business Review*, p. 177ff. [Online]. Available: Academic Universe, Lexis-Nexis, 1054 words, as of 4/6/99.

Griggs v. Duke Power Co., 401 U.S. 424 (1971). [Online]. Available: Academic Universe, Lexis-Nexis, as of 5/14/99.

Harris v. Forklift Systems, Inc., 510 U.S. 17 (1993). [Online]. Available: Academic Universe, Lexis-Nexis, as of 5/14/99.

Johnston, W., & Packer, A. (1987). *Work force 2000*. Indianapolis, IN: Hudson Institute.

Judy, R., & D'Amico, C. (1997). *Work force 2020*. Indianapolis, IN: Hudson Institute.

Kelly, E., & Dobbin, F. (1998, April). How affirmative action became diversity management. *American Behavioral Scientist, 41*(7), p. 960ff. [Online]. Available: Academic Search FullTEXT Elite, 25 pages, as of 3/18/99.

Lash, S. (1999, May 2). Even justices unsure about disability law; three cases question the intentions of statute. *The Houston Chronicle*, pp. A1. [Online]. Available: Academic Universe Lexis-Nexis, 1566 words, as of 5/3/99.

Loden, M., & Rosener, J. (1991). *Work force America—managing employee diversity as a vital resource*. New York: McGraw-Hill.

Lynch, F. (1997, July/August). The diversity machine. *Society, 34* (5), p. 32ff. [Online]. Available: Academic Search FullTEXT Elite, 13 pages, as of 3/18/99.

Meritor Savings Bank, FSB v. Vinson, 477 U.S. 57 (1986). [Online]. Available: Academic Universe, Lexis-Nexis, as of 5/14/99.

Milkovich, G., & Boudreau, J. (1997). *Human resource management* (8th ed.). Chicago: Irwin.

Murphy v. United Parcel Service, Inc., No. 97–1992 (1999 U.S. Lexis 4370). [Online]. Available: Academic Universe, Lexis-Nexis, as of 6/24/99.

Price Waterhouse v. Hopkins, 490 U.S. 22 (1989). [Online]. Available: Academic Universe, Lexis-Nexis, as of 5/14/99.

Regents of the University of California v. Bakke, 438 U.S. 265 (1978). [Online]. Available: Academic Universe, Lexis-Nexis, as of 5/14/99.

Rowan, C. (1996, December 29). Judge forces new look at affirmative action ban. *The Houston Chronicle*, p. Outlook3. [Online]. Available: Academic Universe, Lexis-Nexis, 649 words, as of 5/14/99.

Schneider, S., & Barsoux, J. (1997). *Managing across cultures*. London: Prentice Hall.

Seib, G. (1996, December 10). GOP Congress debates an attack on affirmative action. *Wall Street Journal*, p. A24.

Senge, P. M. (1990). *The fifth discipline*. New York: Doubleday.

Society for Human Resource Management (SHRM). (1999). *Diversity initiative.* [Online]. Available: www.shrm.org, as of 5/14/99.

Stevenson, R. (1995, November 26). Job discrimination in Europe: affirmative laissez faire. *The New York Times*, Section 1, page 10. [Online]. Available: Academic Universe, Lexis-Nexis, 1401 words, as of 5/14/99.

Sutton v. United Air Lines, No. 97–1943 (1999 U.S. Lexis 4371). [Online]. Available: Academic Universe, Lexis-Nexis, as of 6/24/99.

Thomas, D., & Ely, R. (1996, September/October). Making differences matter: a new paradigm for managing diversity. *Harvard Business Review*, 74(5), p. 79ff. [Online]. Available: Academic Universe, Lexis-Nexis, 9314 words, as of 2/2/99.

Thomas, R. (1990, March/April). From affirmative action to affirming diversity. *Harvard Business Review*, p. 107ff. [Online]. Available: Academic Universe, Lexis-Nexis, 6107 words, as of 4/6/99.

Thomas, R. (1990b, September/October). Questions and answers about managing diversity. *Black Collegian 21*(1), p. 120ff. [Online]. Available: Academic Search FullTEXT Elite, as of 3/18/99.

United Steelworkers of America, AFL-CIO v. Weber, 443 U.S. 193 (1979). [Online]. Available: Academic Universe, Lexis-Nexis, as of 5/14/99.

U.S. Department of Labor (DOL). (1997, November). Employment of Vietnam era veterans and special disabled veterans. *Small business handbook—workplace standards for federally assisted or funded contracts.* [Online]. Available: www.dol.gov/dol/asp/public/programs/handbook/vietvets.htm as of 5/14/99.

U.S. Department of Labor (DOL). (1965). *Equal employment opportunity Executive Order 11246 As Amended.* [Online]. Available: www.dol.gov/dol/esa/public/regs/statutes/ofccp/eo11246.htm, as of 5/4/99.

U.S. Equal Employment Opportunity Commission (EEOC). (1998, December 10). *EEOC enforcement activities.* [Online]. Available: www.eeoc.gov/enforce.html, as of 5/4/99.

U.S. Equal Employment Opportunity Commission (EEOC). (1997, January 15). *Facts about the Americans with Disabilities Act.* [Online]. Available: www.eeoc.gov/facts/fs-ada.html, as of 5/4/99.

U.S. Equal Employment Opportunity Commission (EEOC). (1998b, December 10). *Statutory authority.* [Online]. Available: www.eeoc.gov/statauth.html, as of 5/4/99.

U.S. Equal Employment Opportunity Commission (EEOC). (1997, November 3). *Strategic plan: Introduction.* [Online]. Available: www.eeoc.gov/plan/intro.html, as of 5/4/99.

Wards Cove Packing Co. v. Antonio, 490 U.S. 642 (1989). [Online]. Available: Academic Universe, Lexis-Nexis, as of 5/14/99.

Whitford, M., & Higley, J. (1998, July 20). NAACP's latest card targets three chains. *Hotel and Motel Management, 213* (13), pp. 1, 25. [Online]. Available: ABI/Inform, as of 3/18/99.

Yeager, H. (1996, December 21). President to take on Prop. 209; Calif. law ended affirmative action. *The Houston Chronicle*, p. A13. [Online]. Available: Academic Universe, Lexis-Nexis, 509 words, as of 5/14/99.

Chapter V

Ethics and Social Responsibility as Management Issues

KATHLEEN F. EDWARDS

INTRODUCTION

Since the dawn of recorded time, human beings have faced ethical issues. Sometimes referred to as conscience, sometimes discussed as morality—ethical issues have always presented challenges. The ways in which early writers discussed ethical behavior continue to serve as a foundation for present day management behaviors. Aristotle, Plato, and Diogenes each offered guidance on moral behavior. Shakespeare, in *Richard III* (c. 1590–94/1983) identified ethical stances. And, Bolt, in *A Man for All Seasons* (1962), described the agony of Sir (Saint) Thomas More who wanted to be loyal to his king but who needed first to be honest with himself and his God.

In the world of business, managers probably face ethical challenges on a daily basis. Managers and organizations also come in frequent contact with situations that require socially responsible actions. The purpose of this chapter is to identify selected key management issues related to ethics and social responsibility. It will also provide the reader with some of the ways successful managers in the United States attempt to deal with ethical dilemmas and how some U.S. managers handle corporate social responsibility. Another purpose is to discuss reasons for the selected ethical and social responsibility opportunities in business in the United States. A final purpose of this chapter is to present views on the managerial implications of identified ethical challenges, along with some of their potential solutions.

It is hoped that this discussion will support the already well-developed ethical and social responsibility base brought to it by its readers. The chapter may also offer an opportunity for readers to further reflect and explore their ethical and socially responsible actions, in pursuit of the "defining moment" (Badaracco, 1998). A defining moment lets each manager know how far he or she has come in becoming a truly ethical person.

This chapter begins with a brief discussion of terms, concepts and issues that are relevant to ethics and social responsibility. Then, separated into various headings, are presented seven key management issues. Two of these management issues (Ethical Communication with Stakeholders and Ethical Managerial Behaviors in Relation to Employees) are further subdivided into specific areas for discussion.

SOME BASIC ETHICS TERMS, CONCEPTS AND ISSUES

Before entering a discussion of current U.S. management issues related to ethics and social responsibility, a brief review of relevant terms, concepts and issues is presented in this section. Ethics is defined and normative and descriptive ethics are differentiated. Selected ethical principles are presented. Some ethical issues with which managers deal are emphasized and values are brought into the discussion. The section concludes with brief remarks on social responsibility.

Ethics is considered a study of standards of conduct or moral judgment. Ethics describes the gray area in which most of us generally function: somewhere between totally free will at one end of the spectrum and codified law at the other end.

Ethics is described as a gray area because it is neither black nor white, and the answers are never clear (Rakich, Longest, & Darr, 1992). Ethical challenges are called "dilemmas" because there are usually two opposing possibilities, sometimes both equally desirable and sometimes both equally undesirable.

There are two parts of moral philosophy with which managers deal: descriptive and normative ethics. Descriptive ethics is ". . . concerned with describing or characterizing the morality or behavior of people or organizations. . ." Descriptive ethics presents what ". . . managers, organizations, or individuals are doing." Normative ethics is ". . . concerned with supplying and justifying a coherent moral system" (Carroll, 1998). Normative ethics helps the manager answer the question of what should be done to deal with ethical dilemmas.

The general ethical principles upon which reasonable people base their ethical decisions come from ethics theories and principles and the application of them. Some of the more frequently relied on ethical bases include: doing something because it represents a societal good (beneficence); doing no harm (non-malfeasance); doing something because it will benefit the many and not just the vocal few (utilitarianism); doing something because it is the right thing to do in a certain situation (respect for person, shown by truth telling; respecting a person's autonomy; keeping confidential what should be, and keeping one's promises, known as fidelity); and doing something because it is fair (justice or equity) (Rakich, Longest, & Darr, 1992).

A few other terms related to the study of ethics may prove helpful to an exploration of ethics. An ethical concern is an active state of uneasiness, uncertainty, or conflict about how to determine a response to a situation that may have moral implications. An ethical issue is a situation that requires a judgment that considers questions and the controversial implications about which moral standards or norms of conduct apply (Maryland Nurses Association, March, 1999).

Ethical issues that generally affect management and governance include: fiduciary duty (the relationship has certain obligations and duties); conflict of interest (when a person has multiple obligations that demand loyalty and the decisions are in conflict); the handling of confidential information (especially if the information could be used to benefit the manager or others or if the information is used to harass or injure others); and, ethics and marketing (various ethical issues arise around the marketing issues of service, consideration, access and product promotion). Depending on the industry, there will also arise special areas of ethical challenge: e.g., the issue of biomedical research in the health services industry.

An underlying premise of most discussions of ethics is that a person or an organization has "values." A value is a principle, standard, or quality regarded as worthwhile or desirable (*Webster's II New Riverside University Dictionary*, 1984, p. 1275). Drucker (1999) writes that we manage ourselves in business by knowing our strengths, knowing how we perform and understanding our values. Becoming an ethical manager requires not just the acquisition of information about the ethical bases for actions but also the willingness and ability to apply it to personal values and work behaviors. As individuals refine and enhance their values and ethical action bases, they contribute to the organization's ethical status.

Along with ethical decision making on the one-to-one or one-to-group level, ethics is represented in the business world under the rubric of social responsibility or corporate social responsibility (CSR). Social responsibility implies that an organization is aware of its impacts on its physical, social, cultural and legal constituencies. In recent years, U.S. organizations have come much more to understand the importance of their potential positive and negative effects on multiple stakeholders, including the broader community. No organization functions alone, nor does it function merely within the borders of its own homeland. The global marketplace and access to global information make known to all what a company is about.

CURRENT KEY MANAGEMENT ISSUES

With an understanding of some key ethics terms, concepts and issues, the reader is invited to consider a number of current key management issues in the United States from the standpoint of their ethical and social responsibility connections. By referring to the "definitions" of the terms, concepts and issues explored in the previous section, the reader should be able to more clearly understand how applying them can help solve the ethical challenges discussed in the following sections. This section is separated into six key management issues, with two of those issues being further subdivided to focus on especially timely topics.

There are numerous management issues in the United States that relate to ethics and social responsibility and this chapter will focus on the following key management topics, within the framework of ethics and social responsibility:

- Ethical Communication with Stakeholders
  - Ethics in Marketing
  - Risk Communication
  - Internal Communication
- Ethical Managerial Behaviors in Relation to Employees
  - Provision for Whistle-Blowing
  - Conflicts of Interest
  - Confidentiality of Information
  - Sexual Harassment
- Negotiating Ethically and Establishing Appropriate Dispute Resolution Systems
- Ethics Codes and Other Ethics Resources
- Socially Responsible Organizational Behavior
- Making a Profit while Being Socially Responsible

In discussing each of these key management issues, the causes of the issues and the implications of the issues for the future of management will be explored. Some of the implications of these issues will be presented as suggestions for management success in the areas of ethics and social responsibility.

ETHICAL COMMUNICATION WITH STAKEHOLDERS

Any business, no matter what its product or service, has multiple stakeholders. Sometimes called "constituencies," these individuals and groups are the organization's customers, clients, suppliers, employees, investors, financiers, regulators, surrounding communities, media representatives and interested others all over the world. Communicating with individuals and groups with connections to an organization can provide several ethical challenges.

How much information to share, in what manner (or medium), and at what time are three crucial aspects of corporate communication. Argenti (1996) suggests that corporate communication is actually a discipline unto itself. He includes within corporate communication the following functions: image and identity of a corporation; corporate advertising; media relations; financial communications; employee relations; community relations and corporate philanthropy; government relations; and crisis communications.

In this section, three areas of stakeholder communication will be discussed: ethics in marketing, risk communication and internal communication. These three areas were chosen for emphasis because of the author's interest in them and because of the potential they have for causing managerial angst.

Ethics in Marketing

In each of the corporate functions identified by Argenti, there is the potential for ethical action as well as threats to ethical performance. The first area of emphasis in this section is ethics in marketing. According to Smith & Quelch (1993), it is not surprising that the unethical practices in business marketing often show up in the press. The marketing aspect of business is closest to the consumer, very visible and, as a result, unethical business practices "more frequently involve marketing activities" (p. 4). Smith & Quelch advise that some marketing people may behave more unethically than other business people because ". . . the pressures and opportunities to which marketing management is exposed are such that marketing may remain the source of most misconduct in business" (p. 4).

In the United States in recent years, there have been numerous examples of marketing practices where ethics seem to have been overlooked. One case surrounded a baby food manufacturer that sold a baby juice product labeled as apple juice that actually contained no apple juice at all. A second example of ethics in marketing in the U.S. concerned a major automobile repair organization that encouraged its service supervisors to "find" needed repairs on automobiles brought in for maintenance, whether the vehicle needed the repair or not. A third example, however, surrounded a manufacturer of pharmaceuticals that immediately withdrew from store shelves across the country all bottles of an over-the-counter pain reliever because a few bottles had met with tampering.

Techniques that are sometimes used to explain unethical marketing include: denial of responsibility, denial of injury, denial of the victim, condemning the condemners, and appealing to higher loyalties (p. 7). These techniques are linked with the stance that marketing is value neutral. This position is rejected by Smith and Quelch, who posit that if marketers ignore ethics, customers will go elsewhere. They may also seek legal remedies, and such a stance is likely to encourage a "dog-eat-dog" mentality in an organization's culture, its motivation of employees, and the type of employees it attracts and retains (p. 8). Good ethics, therefore, is good business but having high ethics and high profits may not always be possible.

Incorporating ethical considerations within marketing decision making is certainly challenging. The basic reason why marketing ethics should be advocated is the ethical precept of respect and concern for ". . . those affected by their [marketing managers'] decisions" (Smith & Quelch, 1993, p. 9). The decisions made in marketing are founded in ones values and how one chooses to live her life (p. 10).

The marketing challenges generally discussed in business ethics books surround product safety, price-fixing, bribery, deception and the adverse social influences of advertising. Even though the issues may change, the ethical principles do not. For example, privacy problems today resulting from database marketing, brought on by technological advances, still relate to a need for the ethical handling of confidential information (Smith & Quelch, 1993, p. 10).

The five major ethical issues identified as most difficult by members of the American Marketing Association were: bribery ("money under the table"); fairness (inducing customers to use services not needed); honesty (lying to customers to obtain orders); price (differential pricing); and product (exaggerated performance claims) (Smith & Quelch, 1993, p. 12).

How then does an ethical marketing manager act? Smith & Quelch (1993) proffer several suggestions. In the area of personal selling and sales force management, codes of conduct are encouraged but laws and regulations are still very much needed. Areas where improvement is needed include preserving the anonymity of marketing research subjects; not exposing marketing subjects to stress; not involving marketing participants without their knowledge; not using deception or coercion nor causing embarrassment to subjects; accrediting the marketing researchers themselves; and creating appropriate rules for inclusion and exclusion of marketing subjects (pp. 162–170 and 186–195).

In the area of product design and positioning, one area for consideration includes refraining from using advertising aimed at product differentiation that may harm those who see it and attempt to replicate product use under those sometimes-harmful conditions. An example would be the portrayal of a sport vehicle attempting to scale a vertical cliff. Suggestions for improving marketing's ethical stance in the area of product packaging and labeling include: greater use of warning labels on products; expansion of informational labels (e.g., nutritional content, packaging recyclability); and using the least expensive packaging. The consumer is benefited by purchasing products whose packaging adds less cost to the total product and whose recylability adds the least to waste.

Ideas for product recalls include the establishment of appropriate product recalls for product failures and dealing with aging machines and equipment. Finally, in the area of the product and the environment, Smith and Quelch (1993) suggest even greater attention to packaging and other pollution-control methods (pp. 287–294).

In the area of pricing, standards are evolving. Historically, antitrust legislation and enforcement were used to deal with pricing concerns. Today, U.S. consumer groups are even more concerned with pricing; therefore, the interpretability of price information will continue to be a topic for exploration and resolution (p. 402).

Advertising and sales promotions are being dealt with under two different frameworks: moral and legal. The moral way calls for nondeceptive advertising; the legal way suggests following the American Association of Advertising Agencies' Creative Code. According to Smith and Quelch (1993), it seems that ethics to advertising professionals equals simply using the legal way. The Code referred to contains statements that are seen as narrowly legal, not focusing at all on the moral issue which suggests that persuasion is created to induce purchase rather than to simply provide information on which an informed consumer can make a decision. Legal, yet possibly amoral, persuasion includes those selling strategies aimed at persons not mature enough to distinguish product claims (toys and candy for children) as well as those marketing techniques geared to certain purchasing groups (expensive athletic shoes to disadvantaged youth) when those youths' values and self-esteem may be victims of such sales.

This focus by marketers on the legal and not the moral aspects of advertising and sales is seen as insufficient by Smith & Quelch who suggest that theories need to be tested empirically by persons knowledgeable of moral as well as of legal issues, via studies that focus on the potential harm to consumers of a lifetime's bombardment by marketing messages (advertising) (pp. 619–625).

Risk Communication

In addition to ethics in marketing, a second area of importance for ethical communication with stakeholders is "risk communication." Risk communication refers to those processes of communication where a complex situation has potentially negative consequences for communities and interested others. The risk may be financial, legal, societal, environmental, etc. One example is the need to communicate with homeowners the potential risk from leaking underground petroleum storage tanks such as those found on many farms in rural America. Organizations today are under siege from a variety of constituents: regulators want their rules met; employees and employee representatives (e.g., unions, advocacy groups, families) want employees protected from undue harm; and shareholders want profit. Any of these situations can produce risk for the organization. When a crisis does arise, the risk communication with each constituency takes on a very serious tone.

Corporations in the U.S. can face ethical challenges in the area of risk communication when dealing with events where, for example, the corporation's products, processes and services may damage the environment. The lead agency for environmental protection in the United States is the Environmental Protection Agency (EPA). The EPA has over 20 years of experience in communicating with citizens about environmental risk situations, and it offers Seven Cardinal Rules of Risk Communication (Covello & Allen, 1988). They are:

1. Accept and involve the public as a legitimate partner.
2. Plan carefully and evaluate your efforts.
3. Listen to the public's specific concerns.
4. Be honest, frank, and open.
5. Coordinate and collaborate with other credible sources.
6. Meet the needs of the media. (Note: This is complex and takes much skill and rapport.)
7. Speak clearly and with compassion.

These "rules" were not explicitly created for ethics discussions; rather they were created to assist federal, state and local public health and environmental protection officials in dealing appropriately with citizens in crisis situations. An ethical base, however, seems clearly discernible in the EPA's rules: respect for person, as evidenced by truth-telling, listening, and sharing all available information.

Internal Communication

In addition to ethics in marketing and risk communication, a third area of importance in ethical communication with stakeholders is internal organizational communication. Respectful, honest and open communication with stakeholders stems from an ethical base. Communicating clearly and openly with employees is equally important as with any other company constituency. Many employees complain that they never know what is happening in their organizations. They express their frustration by relying more and more on informal communication systems, such as the grapevine, electronic messages, and cartoons and jokes placed at key locations in the work environment. What is needed in most organizations is a demonstration of respect for workers. What types of action this respect will take may vary, depending on the leadership, mission and goals of the organization.

Some successful tools in use in the United States to deal with employees' feelings of disenfranchisement include town meetings, where all employees come together on a regular basis in an unstructured setting to discuss relevant organizational topics. Also used are informal "hallway" conversations with managers and peers to encourage open dialogue. Cross-unit or ad hoc team projects can also increase interorganizational communication. What is key in each of these methods is the ethical principle that underpins them. If the communication methods chosen are not based on honesty, respect for individuals and sharing the same information with all workers, then attempts at enhancing communication and trust may have an opposite effect. The stronger the ethical base that supports the organization's communication methods, the better the chances that employees will demonstrate their positive feelings for being well-treated by wanting to stay longer with the company and wanting to buy in to the organization's mission and goals.

In addition to ethical communication with employees, there are several other areas of ethical importance to employees. One of the most crucial is that of managerial behaviors in relation to employees.

ETHICAL MANAGERIAL BEHAVIORS IN RELATION TO EMPLOYEES

How is it known whether behavior in organizations is generally ethical? In the U.S., managers rely on what they read and what they hear. Managers consult the literature to learn what the latest research has shown. They scan newspapers and rely on selected news services and industry summary reports to determine what is "hot" in their work settings. They pay attention to who is suing whom and winning in the court system and what damages juries and judges are awarding in work-related suits and allegations.

Over the last 20 years, the United States has seen an increase in the number and types of legal cases brought that have affirmed the rights of workers over unilateral control by management. Less tolerance is exhibited in the United States now for discrimination in the areas of equal employment opportunities, including persons who are differently abled, physically and mentally; sexual harassment; unfair or unsubstantiated advertising claims; price gouging; insider financial trading; and unsafe consumer product sales.

Awareness by U.S. citizens, the judicial system, the media, and workers and business managers has led to sanctions for inappropriate workplace behaviors, especially in the areas of interpersonal contact (e.g., sexual harassment) and worker safety (e.g., safety code violations).

One of the first ethical responsibilities that an organization has in relation to its employees is that of simply being an ethical organization. In the past, organizations were expected to comply with existing laws and to generally avoid doing harm to workers. Today, however, a higher standard of ethical organizational performance is expected. The shift is from a compliance mode to an "integrity-based" mode (Paine, 1994). This means several things: it means that the ethical strategies developed are deeper and more demanding and that there is no one right integrity strategy. The integrity-based strategy consists of guiding values and commitments that make sense and are clearly communicated. The organization's leaders are personally committed, credible and willing to take action on the values they espouse. The espoused values are integrated into company decision making and the company's systems and structures support and reinforce those values.

A final point made by Paine (1994) is that managers in integrity-based organizations are expected to have the decision-making skills, knowledge and competencies needed to make ethically sound decisions on a day-to-day basis.

The requirements, then, for being a manager in an ethical organization are high. Managers demonstrate their competence to make ethical decisions by appropriately dealing with employees in several ways. Some of these ways are: strongly supporting employees' rights to whistle-blow, dealing proactively with potential conflicts of interest, and showing no tolerance for sexual harassment.

Provision for Whistle-Blowing

Whistle-blowing is ". . . an expression used to describe an employee disclosing illegal, immoral, or illegitimate practices by the employer" (Daft, 1994, p. 92). In the area of whistle-blowing, managers have a key role to play.

For years, the model employee was probably the one who kept his mouth shut when wrongdoing was observed, for fear of reprisal by management or peers. Over time, U.S. society has demanded that workers be given protection from peers, management, and the organization itself if they come forth in good faith to announce wrongdoing they believe has occurred.

Possibly stemming from abusive situations in many industries, organizations in the United States have created written policies to encourage the whistle-blower to communicate what is believed to have occurred. Companies have established hot lines where employees can call anonymously to report unsafe working conditions as well as fraudulent, wasteful, illegal or abusive practices.

In its earlier days, whistle-blowing was not rewarded; now it is encouraged. The United States federal government includes in its agencies' codes of ethics such affirmative statements as: "Employees shall disclose waste, fraud, abuse and corruption to appropriate authorities" (National Institutes of Health (NIH) Ethics Program, 1989).

Whistle-blowers are protected from retribution and given freedom to offer their observations. This can sometimes be uncomfortable for management, depending on the issue. Awareness of the need for whistle-blowing and an appreciation of its uses in any company with which one does business in the U.S. could be wise practices.

Conflicts of Interest

Nowhere does ethical behavior hit home more often than in the area of conflicts of interest (COI). When one works in the business community, friendships and networking are common. Oftentimes, the persons involved in relationships that have personal and business dimensions may have access to information, and even decision making which could advantage or harm another person or organization. Knowing when to recuse oneself from being privy to information, sharing information, voting or otherwise making decisions on potentially ethically challenging situations can be key to success. Recusal will be discussed in this section.

Tools in place in the United States to assist in preventing conflict of interest situations generally take the form of conflict of interest statements, guidelines and agreements. The National Institutes of Health, the largest health related research organization in the United States, follows the United States federal government's guidance on conflict of interest. On the NIH Web site, COI is discussed. A COI ". . . arises when an employee is involved in a particular matter as part of his/her official duties with an outside organization with which he/she also has a financial interest, or one which is imputed to him/her, i.e., the employee's 1) spouse, 2) minor children, 3) an organization in which the employee serves as officer, director, trustee, partner, or employee, or 4) a person or organization with which the employee is negotiating for prospective or has an arrangement for prospective employment. Conflicts can be real or apparent" (NIH Ethics Program, 1989).

Due to the high degree of potential for COI in the workplace, organizations such as the NIH have a very comprehensive set of requirements to assist employees in dealing ethically with a potential conflict of interest. One set of tools consists of written documents called waivers or authorizations. Waivers are used to resolve actual conflicts of interest and they are generally based in law. Authorizations allow certain actions, even though these actions continue to appear to represent conflicts of interest. In essence, these tools "waive" or "authorize" certain actions, which are considered acceptable under certain sets of circumstances, set forth clearly in writing.

Another tool to assist in dealing with COI is the "recusal" or self-disqualification from the conflict of interest. In recusal, a written statement is signed by the employee which spells out ". . . the scope of the disqualification and the precise nature of the conflicting interest or activity. The disqualification should also identify the individual who will deal with the matters from which the employee is disqualified" (NIH Ethics Program, 1989).

Financial disclosure statements, either public or confidential, may be required of employees to protect against conflict of interest. "Cooling off" periods may be imposed. Such a requirement provides that a set amount of time must elapse before certain persons and organizations may appropriately do business with each other again.

Finally, organizations may require that upon termination of employment, a certain period of time must elapse before the employee may assume employment with certain other businesses and organizations.

Through all of these mechanisms, employees are helped to avoid actual and apparent conflicts of interest.

Confidentiality of Information

The ethical principle of respect for persons is often demonstrated by the manner in which organizations keep confidential certain information. Privacy of a person's employment history, health condition(s), financial situation and personal matters is absolutely protected by federal law in the United States. Other areas of ethical concern in relation to confidentiality include the electronic storage and sharing of information, trade secrets and intellectual property, and other business transactions. The fact that there are breaches of information in the workplace suggests that more than federal-level statutes are needed to deal with this ethically charged area.

The area of confidentiality of information is one in which the manager can lead by example. The ethical manager will not engage in gossip, nor tease or ridicule, even by innuendo or facial expression. Sarcastic comments, humor at the expense of another, or of another's ideas, and intolerance of the differences of others as demonstrated by leaking information, are unethical and disrespectful.

The United States has seen in recent years a strong current of intolerance for behavior in social and business settings that is perceived to be demeaning of a person's age, gender, color, race, sexual preference, religious views, and physical or mental abilities. If the reader is wondering how in the world can a manager prevent her or himself from disrespecting someone in one of these categories, one suggestion is to disrespect no one. Keeping confidential most of what is known is probably another good practice.

Sexual Harassment

Continuing with the discussion of ethical managerial behaviors in relation to employees, attention now turns from whistle-blowing, conflict of interest, and confidentiality of information to sexual harassment. In the United States, the issue of sexual harassment has risen to prominence in the past 15 years. The United States Supreme Court, the highest court in the land, has sent a clear message to companies: ". . . Put your [sexual harassment] policy in writing, communicate it to every employee, and follow up on complaints." (Barrier, 1998). The message is clear and it is getting out.

In its 1998 rulings, the Supreme Court handed down two sexual harassment decisions that affect workers and managers in the U.S. The two rulings in combination state "If a supervisor takes a 'tangible employment action' against a sexually harassed employee. . . . the employer is always liable for damages. It doesn't matter if the owners or top managers of the company had no knowledge of the supervisor's actions. Neither does it matter if they tried to prevent such harassment" (Barrier, p. 15).

The high court's rulings also conclude: "If a supervisor's harassment of an employee is 'severe or pervasive' to the point that it creates a 'hostile work environment', the company can be liable for damages even when the supervisor didn't take any 'tangible employment action' (Barrier, p. 15).

The Supreme Court did offer guidance to companies on protecting themselves from liability. The Court recommends that companies have in place an effective sexual harassment policy and be able to prove that the person alleging harassment failed to take advantage of it. This means that companies must have sexual harassment policies, must put them in writing, must make sure that everyone in the company has read them and then it must truly enforce them.

The last procedure (enforcement) implies that managers know how to deal with sexual harassment allegations and to follow up. This generally requires training. Many companies in the United States now have in place a mandatory sexual harassment training program for all employees, with special attention for managers.

Unfortunately, no matter how well trained are managers, and no matter how communicative are employees and managers, there will always be disputes in organizations, because the key component in business is people. However, managers have a role to play in determining how often, or if at all, sexual harassment will occur in their organizations. Badaracco (1997) observed ". . . managers are the ethics teachers of their organizations" (p. 65). He feels that whether they intend to teach or not, they do, and that this function is an integral part of their managerial roles.

NEGOTIATING ETHICALLY AND ESTABLISHING APPROPRIATE DISPUTE RESOLUTION SYSTEMS

Even with Badaracco's prophetic statement about managers as ethics teachers, readers may still wonder a bit why negotiating and handling disputes are discussed in a chapter on ethics and social responsibility. In addition to the omnipresence of organizational conflicts, there are other reasons. In everyday life, as well as in business, people negotiate. Most do so with the goal of achieving a desired end, but sometimes they go about it in ways that are often counterproductive. They may eventually get part of what they want, but they may leave in their wake a trail of resentment, anger and barriers to future cooperation.

Most people in business, including many managers, have not had formal preparation in negotiating. They negotiate the way they have seen others negotiate, or they have created their own style over time as they have gained experience in settling disputes. These tried-and-true methods may not have taught them much about being successful at negotiating, about not doing damage to relationships or preserving self-respect and comfort among the parties.

People generally negotiate in one of two ways, either as the "hard" bargainer or the "soft" bargainer. Neither style works very well, so Fisher and Ury

(1991) have created what they term "principled negotiation." This style of negotiation contains four key points which are: separate the people from the problem, focus on interests, not positions, invent options for mutual gain, and insist on using objective criteria.

The part of Fisher and Ury's book that is most relevant to this chapter concerns the acceptance of the other person's (or organization's) needs and wishes when negotiating. Acceptance of the importance and validity of the other party's interests is demonstrated by respecting the differing interests of the other party (or parties) and the value of the party's positions. The negotiator is functioning from an ethical base in trying to achieve not just what s/he sets out to accomplish but will also aid the other party in achieving that person's goals. How can this be?

The truth of it is that respect for the other, the true desire to really learn what the other person needs, wants and is willing to change in order to successfully conclude the negotiation, creates an open attitude. This mind-set brings about a sense of openness, trust and honesty that encourages ethical and principled behavior, enabling both parties to work toward meeting both parties' goals.

Consider that when one negotiator, or bargainer, focuses solely on what she or he wants from the "deal," the possibilities for considering other ways to have only her or his needs met will diminish considerably. By listening to the other party, allowing another way to handle the situation to enter consciousness, and exploring each and every possible way to settle the negotiation, the negotiator may actually end up with all that she wanted, and more. By blocking the opportunity for other options, the negotiator limits her ability to win what she wants most. The process, itself, may also open doors for new negotiation on other areas of interest.

Just as individuals can identify their usual conflict and dispute issues and can use principled negotiation as a base for formulating dispute settlement techniques that are ethically based, so too, can organizations. Ury, Brett and Goldberg (1988) have described ethical dispute resolution systems applicable to organizations.

The dispute resolver begins with the least expensive, simplest and closest-to-the action format to resolve disputes. It is based on the real "interests" of each party, what the parties really want as opposed to what they *say* they want. The goal is to reconcile the interests of the parties in the dispute. If the dispute is not solved at this first level, the organization may move to a dispute settlement mode that is based on the relative "rights" of each party. Again, this is based on the ethical principles of fairness, honesty and doing the right thing. However, as Ury et al. (1988) point out (p. 7), rights are rarely clear, and there can be numerous rights which enter into a dispute settlement: law, custom, precedent, standards. If the dispute is not settled via an interests or rights-based method, the entity with the greatest amount of perceived "power" in the conflict may "win." Some aver that using this third level of dispute resolution means that disputes are not actually resolved at all.

In summary, ethical performance in settling disputes is based on fairness, equity, justice, honesty, truth-telling, respect for the other party, keeping confidential certain information and doing the right thing. In order to solve ethical dilemmas and situational disputes, employees and managers need to have help in performing ethically in today's world. This means that all workers may benefit from training in principled negotiation, and that organizations would do well to establish an ethical dispute resolution system.

ETHICS CODES AND OTHER ETHICS RESOURCES

Knowing and understanding the bases for ethical decisions and how to negotiate ethically does not protect one from being ethically challenged. In addition to knowing about principles, one needs practice in applying them. One begins by analyzing the ethical situation at hand: What are its causes? Who is involved? Why? What led to the predicament? What has already been tried? Who will be affected by the decision, in either direction? Can the decision be postponed while additional information is gathered?

Once data are gathered, a plan for ethical action is created. Time, however, is not always on the manager's side; quick decisions are often the norm. One dubiously positive thing about the frequency of ethical challenges for managers is that managers get a lot of practice with them.

A tool that can help managers when faced with ethical challenges is an ethics plan. The ethics plan describes the organization, its potential for ethical challenges, its most commonly experienced ethical dilemmas and its plan for dealing with them. Ethics plans are becoming more and more important to organizations as they attempt to become more ethical and more socially responsible; consequently many organizations have such a document. Others are preparing them.

Codes of ethics are generally written documents that support the concept of dignity as the central factor that drives human interaction in the workplace (Karp and Abramms, 1992). They set boundaries for what constitutes ethical behavior, and they are visible, reflecting the organization's values. They have a behavioral focus and are responsive to day-to-day conditions. Karp and Abramms (1992) suggest that four phases are helpful in developing a code of ethics: clarifying values; establishing the individual ethics for the organization; training employees in the why, how and what of the ethics code; and providing follow-up training.

For some employees, for example, attorneys, physicians and others, there will be codes of ethics to which they should adhere in carrying out their individual professional duties. However, these codes are valuable in all business settings. Adherence to professional codes of ethics should benefit the overall ethical climate of an organization. Mary Parker Follett, the noted management theorist who discussed in the 1920s and 1930s many of the key management concepts relied upon today, encouraged business professionals to develop their own professional standards. She wrote that business people also were capable of high levels of professionalism in their careers. She believed that how a manager conducted himself contributed to the profession of business:

> *The way in which you give every order, the way in which you make every decision, the way in which you meet every commitment, in almost every act you perform during the day, you may be contributing to the science of management. (in Graham, 1996, p. 274)*

One example of a U.S. firm that demonstrates professionalism by its positive expectations for management behavior is the General Motors Corporation. It has created *Guidelines for Employee Conduct* (1997). The guidelines offer assistance to employees in the areas of compliance with the law, equal employment opportunity, conflict of interest, gifts and gratuities, interests in other businesses, outside employment, public service and conflict of interest, the Foreign Corrupt Practices Act, political activity and government relations.

Other organizations use various techniques to help managers appropriately deal with ethical conflicts. In the area of conflict of interest, companies may circulate policy statements to which managers can refer when the manager is unsure if a true conflict of interest exists. Managers can also consult with their supervisors or with their peers to help determine if a COI exists. If a conflict of interest does exist, procedures are described that will help the employee remove her or himself from any decision making on that issue.

In addition to ethics plans, ethics guidelines and codes of ethics, some companies use the services of ethicists. Whether hired as employees or employed on retainer, ethicists are educated professionals whose sole purpose is to advise clients on the ethical nature of issues. It is not unusual for health care organizations, especially those that deal with beginning-of-life and end-of-life decisions, to use the services of professional ethicists. Some organizations, instead, will use an "ombudsperson" who is an official of the organization and who acts as the "corporate conscience" (Daft, 1994, p. 92).

In addition to an ethicist or ombudsperson, organizations may invite representatives of various fields to assist in creating an ethics committee where decision makers can discuss and examine all facets of a thorny ethical issue. Panelists who sit on these ethics committees may represent the organization's industry (e.g., marketing, sales, or health care), the community, the religious/spiritual community, and the ethics community. The ethics committee may also be empowered to monitor company ethics overall.

There are numerous books, journals and adult education courses on ethics. It is hard to pick up a business journal without finding an article on an ethical challenge. The bibliography at the end of this chapter is just a small sample of relevant ethics and social responsibility literature. In addition to books, reports and journal articles, there are electronic resources available to assist managers with ethical concerns. There are general business Web sites (e.g., www.bbb.org for the United States Better Business Bureau or www.depaul.edu/ethics for the DePaul University Institute of Business and Professional Ethics) as well as ethics sites by special interest area (e.g., www.prsa.org/profstand.html for the Public Relations Society of America Code of Professional Standards).

Even if a company is committed to ethical behavior, uses an ethicist or ombudsperson, has an ethics plan, uses an ethics committee, and refers to relevant ethics resources, it will not meet its goal of being an ethical organization unless employees are regularly trained in ethics matters. As most managers know, creating ethics policies, reviewing relevant reference documents and consulting with subject matter experts is not enough. Employees must *know* that ethics is an important company value and have this view instilled in their minds and hearts in order for it to be reflected in their actions.

This means that if the leaders of the organization do not "walk the talk" of ethics, all of the organization's ethical strategies may be for naught. Gellerman (1989) writes that the ethical example set by senior managers is "vitally important" (p. 73). He also states that "Management is responsible for creating and sustaining conditions in which people are likely to behave themselves, and for minimizing conditions in which they may be tempted to misbehave" (p. 74). This is no small matter to consider. An organization's employees can be tempted to act unethically in a number of ways. The inducement may be very appealing, and if people are placed in situations where an ethical choice is just too difficult to manage, the organization really is not able to attribute the employee's ethical lapse just to weakness. The organization may also be at fault.

Gellerman suggests that in addition to having codes of ethics and having senior management embody ethical actions in their behavior, further steps are needed to ensure that employees are working in an atmosphere that can produce the most ethical behavior possible. He proposes that organizations draw a clean line between behavior that is acceptable and behavior that is not; emphasize the ethical code in place, not just treat it as "window dressing;" communicate sound advice about interpreting the organization's code of ethics; and establish disclosure mechanisms. Whistle-blowing, discussed in this section, is an example of such a mechanism.

As organizations identify ethical behavior for individual employees and for the company overall, the next level of ethical behavior with which managers need to be concerned is that of socially responsible organizational behavior.

SOCIALLY RESPONSIBLE ORGANIZATIONAL BEHAVIOR

Socially responsible organizational behavior is a challenge for most organizations. Based on the premise that most managers want to be ethical people and that most organizations want to do the "right thing," U.S. managers have slowly come to accept that corporate social responsibility (CSR) is part of their individual managerial responsibility.

According to Daft (1994), social responsibility is ". . . management's obligation to make choices and take actions that will contribute to the welfare and interests of society as well as to the welfare and interests of the organization" (p. 89). Social responsibility means distinguishing right from wrong, and it covers a wide range of issues.

Daft (1994) states that in evaluating corporate social performance, one can look at several levels of social responsibility that a company may demonstrate. The first level posits that economic responsibility is the only social responsibility. Canada, the United States and Western Europe do not consider this an adequate criterion of performance. The second level of social responsibility reflects legal responsibilities, wherein businesses are ". . . expected to fulfill their economic goals within the law" (p. 90). The third level represents ethical responsibilities, and the fourth level indicates discretionary responsibilities which are "purely voluntary" and reflect the organization's ". . . desire to make social contributions not mandated by economics, law or ethics" (p. 91). A company can position itself anywhere on the continuum from having a desire only to make a profit to making a profit and also being committed to helping achieve certain social standards.

Carroll (1998) indicates that corporate social responsibility today is sometimes referred to as "corporate ethics" and sometimes as "corporate citizenship." He describes four "faces" of corporate citizenship. "Good corporate citizens are expected to: be profitable (carry their own weight or fulfill their economic responsibilities); obey the law (fulfill their legal responsibilities); engage in ethical behavior (be responsive to their ethical responsibilities); and, give back through philanthropy (engage in corporate contributions)" (paragraph v).

One can compare Carroll's concept of a good corporate citizen with Paine's concept (1994) of an integrity-based organization. Just as integrity-based firms go beyond mere compliance with the law, good corporate citizens are in compliance with the law and are also ". . . imbued with a quest to display ethical leadership in the communities in which they reside" (Carroll, 1998, paragraph xxvii). Carroll describes the exemplary corporate citizen as an organization that strives to maximize profit while simultaneously ". . . fulfilling its citizenship obligations to others" (paragraph xxxviii).

The types of activities in which companies participate to demonstrate their social responsibility include making philanthropic contributions that are voluntary and for which no benefit to the company is expected, as well as carrying out activities that the community does not necessarily expect the organization to perform.

In 1997, the United States federal government presented the first Ron Brown Award for good corporate citizenship. Named after a United States commerce secretary who died on a United States trade mission in 1996, the Brown award honors organizations that meet five criteria for corporate citizenship. These criteria are: the corporations have "family-friendly" policies, good health and pension benefits, a safe workplace, training and advancement opportunities, and policies that avoided layoffs. Winners of this award for 1997 were the IBM Corporation for its diversity programs and Levi Strauss & Co. for its antiracism program (Carroll, 1998).

The Council on Economic Priorities in Washington, D.C. presented in 1997 Corporate Conscience awards to the Kellogg Company, for technical assistance and direct services to African-American men and boys in their communities, and to Toys R Us for addressing child labor and fair labor practices around the world (Carroll, 1998).

Not all agree that corporate social responsibility is a useful idea, however. Freeman and Liedtka (1991) propose seven reasons to abandon the concept of corporate social responsibility. Their reasons are: the concept of CSR derives from economics, without including themes from history, religion and culture; the CSR models extant all accept Milton Friedman's argument as a basis (that the only responsibility of business is to increase profits); CSR accepts the business language of fully accepting capitalism or of totally abandoning it; CSR is "inherently conservative" and it encourages managers to delve into areas in which they have no expertise: i.e., fixing social ills; CSR divides business and society; and social responsibility uses the language of rights and responsibilities, which is limiting and irrelevant to managers.

This author disagrees with Freeman and Liedtka. The bulk of extant literature, as well as common sense and logic, all point to social responsibility as rising above each of the components of Freeman and Liedtka's argument.

For instance, Pava (1996) suggests that the Talmudic concept of "beyond the letter of the law" can serve as a basis for supporting social responsibility. Pava discusses the classical view of business, espoused by Friedman, which suggests that social responsibility is a "subversive" doctrine. Pava also refers to Rodewald (1987), who states that the only deviation from profit should be that which is authorized by law or government regulation.

Pava and other social responsibility advocates suggest that law is primarily a reactive institution, not in touch with local ethics. Just as most politics is local, most ethical dilemmas are found in a contextual realm, not easily or neatly solved by relying on law or viewing the bottom line of a financial spreadsheet.

The proponents of the classical view of CSR and the pro-social advocates can each accept some of the wisdom of the other. Friedman accepts the need for some corporate obligations "beyond mere legal requirements" (Pava, 1998). The pro-social groups recognize some truth and advantages in the classical view. Pava concludes, therefore, that the Talmudic concept of beyond the letter of the law may serve as a jumping off point for further discussions between the two sets of thinkers because this concept aims at integrating law and ethics. Just as the Catholic tradition suggests that capitalism can be affirmed when it integrates both law and ethics (Novak, 1993), the Talmudic concept of *lifnim mishurat hadin* also attempts this integration.

MAKING A PROFIT WHILE BEING SOCIALLY RESPONSIBLE

Mary Parker Follett noted in 1925, "We all want profit and as much as we can get. And this is as it should be when other things are not sacrificed to it" (in Graham, 1996, p. 280). Follett notes that managers are motivated by a number of goals, for example, by the love of work and satisfaction for a job well done, by a desire for personal development, by wanting to perform a service and by wanting to make a profit. She suggests that rather than giving up any of these goals, managers should strive toward achieving as many of them as possible.

A 1996 *Business Week*/Harris Poll stated that "95 percent of Americans surveyed thought U.S. corporations owe something to their workers and communities and that they should sometimes sacrifice profit 'for the sake of making things better for their workers and communities'" (Carroll, 1998).

Demonstrating social responsibility includes analyzing the organization's impact on its environments, gathering supporting or refuting data, and preparing plans to deal with possible negative effects of its organizational actions. Whether the outcome of such an analysis includes increasing one's level of volunteerism in the community or improving one's methods for handling garbage, an organization can always find ways to improve its level of social responsibility.

Angelidis and Ibrahim (1993) write that corporate executives know the law and understand criminal and civil sanctions. They know these vary by locality but executives are sometimes perplexed when they discover that a business practice is tolerated in a certain community but not in another. These authors see the scope of a business organization as being "determined both by the organization itself and by society's expectations" (paragraph xii). No longer is it sufficient for the board of directors, the CEO and the mangers to conjure mission, goals and objectives in a vacuum. Community awareness, consumer input and customer satisfaction are assuming even greater importance in an organization's ability to be successful.

Angeledis and Ibrahim (1993) go so far as to posit that, "Failure on the part of an organization to understand and satisfy the various demands of the social segments within which it operates will lead to its rejection by society and its eventual demise" (paragraph xii).

Consider, however, Milton Friedman's *New York Times Magazine* article (1970) "The Social Responsibility of Business is to Increase Its Profits." In that article, Friedman quotes from his earlier book ". . . there is one and only one social responsibility of business—to use its resources and engage in activities designed to increase its profits so long as it stays within the rules of the game, which is to say, engages in open and free competition without deception or fraud" (p. 91). Few would argue with the view that if a company were not at least marginally financially profitable, it would have difficulty remaining viable. However, in the time since Friedman's book and article were published, the world and many facets of society have changed. The seemingly narrow and insular view expressed by Friedman has been refined by expectations for business that are broader, deeper and more inclusive of other than simply monetary return on investment as a guarantor of organizational success.

It is not enough for a company to have a balanced "bottom line." There are expectations that companies will "give back" to the community and even to the people, as represented by government, in the course of conducting their business. Beyond giving back to various stakeholders, companies are also expected to be socially responsible. There is a general sense, for example, that companies should be conducting audits before implementing actions which may harm the environment. Knowing the potential effects of a product or service on the physical, mental and emotional health of people and other aspects of the environment has become key to being considered a good partner, a good business and a socially responsible "corporate citizen."

Even Milton Friedman specifies "moral rules" that corporations should follow: e.g., compete openly, do not deceive, and do not engage in fraudulent activities (Smith & Quelch, 1993, p. 2). Smith and Quelch (1993) quote Donaldson who writes, "If corporations neglect moral issues, society will look outside the corporation for remedies" (p. 6). And Levitt, also quoted by Smith and Quelch, states that profit is insufficient as a purpose of business, "If no greater purpose can be discerned or justified, business cannot morally justify its existence." (p. 7)

Daniel Bell (1973) developed a view related to social responsibility not too long after Friedman's often-quoted statement. Bell posits that the corporation is "made up of people" (p. 287) and one cannot treat people as things. Over time, corporations have come to replace the formerly communitarian institutions of family, church and town. The occupational group, Bell states, has become the reference group for many people, with its values and expressions reflecting the human response to otherwise unmet social needs.

When a business assumes this level of importance from a sociological standpoint, it has obligations to its members (today called stakeholders). Bell suggested that satisfaction on the job, minority employment, relative pay, responsibility to a community, responsibility for the environment and confrontation with moral issues were emerging topics that the corporation in a social world was required to address.

Beyond having the "direct responsibility" to make as much money as possible for its stakeholders, Bell stated that corporate executives needed to be concerned with ". . . conforming to the basic rules of the society, both those embodied in law and those embodied in ethical custom." (p. 292) He also quoted Clausen who argued that ". . . nobody can expect to make profits . . . if the whole fabric of society is being ripped to shreds" (p. 292).

The corporation was viewed by these authors as an autonomous enterprise which should become ". . . an instrument for service to society in a system of pluralist powers" (Bell, 1993, p. 293). In responding to various of Friedman's points about double-taxation, Bell concluded that U.S. society had "rested on the premises of individualism and market rationality," but that it had moved to "a communal ethic, without that community being, as yet, wholly defined" (p. 298).

Though the communal ethic may still not yet be wholly defined for the United States, there is some anecdotal evidence that making a profit and being socially responsible will be more important to future managers in the U.S. At over 30 U.S. college campuses nationwide, as of May, 1999, graduates are taking a "pledge" that asks the graduate to "explore and take into account the social and environmental consequences of any job I consider or any organization for which I work." The hoped-for outcome of the nonbinding pledge is encouraging college graduates to find socially responsible jobs and to stick to their convictions. The program reports U.S. college graduates as saying that ethics is now near the top of their list for lifetime goals (College grads, 1999).

SUMMARY

Business people in the United States today reflect a variety of management theories and leadership styles. The impact of one's generation on one's way of approaching work, working with colleagues and seeking satisfactions seems clear. Something that is also observable in U.S. managerial circles today seems to be a desire to be more open than in the past, more inclusive of differences and more desirous of personal growth and satisfaction. Numerous managers from all industries speak of wanting more "fun" as they journey through their careers, of desiring more productive experiences with a variety of people and situations, and of trying to be open to things they have not necessarily planned.

This may signal a change to an era when managers in forming ethical positions attempt to balance their personal and professional needs and goals with the needs of their stakeholders. This new era may develop into one in which a manager feels that meeting her or his own goals is of equal importance as meeting those of other organizational stakeholders. Such a reciprocal view may add complexity to evaluating the advantages and disadvantages of a manager's ethical decisions.

As a manager wrestles with those ethical choices, and as the number and types of choice increase, the manager's ethical challenges will continue to increase. Further exploration of this concept is needed.

In closing this chapter, it seems appropriate to return to its opening. Any interested businessperson may well want to consider the writings from early history and the humanities in her or his pursuit of a personal guiding ethical framework. Boardman (1998) recalls a story that Cicero penned in 44 B.C. about a merchant and one of his business challenges. In the unfolding of the tale of the famine in Rhodes, Greece, Cicero presents a story of insider information and the opportunities and challenges it posed for a merchant. Should he tell the citizens that another ship laden with grain would soon be in port, thus lowering his immediate potential for higher profit on his ship's load of grain? Should he keep his counsel, given that he is not able to judge if the second ship will actually arrive? If he does share the information about the second ship, however, is it possible that he might gain future business from those who now trust him because of his openness? Viewing Cicero's tale through the prisms of game theory, agency theory and corporate responsibility/government regulation, Boardman offers insights about how an honorable person makes ethical choices.

What it boils down to, as Cicero advises his son, is that the honest person has many choices. What is decided may have long-term ramifications for business prospects as well as for how well one sleeps at night. Having a firm ethical base should make it easier for a manger to become the truly ethical person that Badarraco (1998) describes. Such a person examines with each ethical challenge the feelings and intuitions that are coming into conflict. The manager explores the values that are in conflict and determines what combination of ". . . expediency and shrewdness, coupled with imagination and boldness, will help . . . implement . . . what is right" (Badaracco, 1998, p. 119).

The "defining moment" comes to each person at a different time and place. Defining moments ask the manager to choose between two or more ideals they believe in. In so doing, these moments "form, reveal and test" (Badaracco, 1998, p. 116). The skills used to resolve these situations aren't found in job descriptions, and they help craft personal identities. Being open to recognizing ethical issues and seeking help in dealing with them will benefit the manager enormously toward becoming a truly ethical person.

REFERENCES

Angelidis, J., & Ibrahim, N. (Summer/Fall, 1993). Social demand and corporate supply: A corporate social responsibility model. *Review of Business, 15,* 7–11.

Argenti, P. (August, 1996). Corporate communication as a discipline: Toward a definition. *Management Communication Quarterly,* 73–98.

Badaracco, J. (1997). *Defining moments: When managers must choose between right and wrong.* Boston, MA: Harvard Business School Press.

Badaracco, J. (1998, March/April). The discipline of building character. *Harvard Business Review,* 115–124.

Barrier, M. (December, 1998). Sexual harassment. *Nation's Business.*

Bell, D. (1973). *The coming of the post-industrial society: A venture in social forecasting.* New York, NY: Basic Books.

Boardman, C. (Fall/Winter, 1998). Cicero's Merchant. *Financial practice and education, 93–101.*

Bolt, R. (1962). *A man for all seasons.* NY, New York: Random House, Incorporated.

Brown, M. (1999). *The ethical process: An approach to controversial* issues (2nd ed.). Upper Saddle River, NJ: Prentice Hall.

Brown, M. (1998). *Case studies in business, society, and ethics* (4th ed.). Upper Saddle River, NJ: Prentice Hall.

Bucholz, R., & Rosenthal, S. (1998). *Business ethics: The pragmatic path beyond principles to process.* Upper Saddle River, NJ: Prentice Hall.

Buller, P., Kohls, J., & Anderson, K. (1997, June). A model for addressing cross-cultural ethical conflicts. *Business and Society, 36, 2, 169–193.*

Carroll, A. (1998, Jan. 1). The four faces of corporate citizenship. *Business and Society Review.*

Cassell, C., Johnson, P., & Smith, K. (1997, July). Opening the black box: Corporate codes of ethics in their organizational context. *Journal of Business Ethics, 16, 10, 1077–1093.*

Cavanaugh, G. (1998). *American Business Values With International Perspectives* (4th ed.). Upper Saddle River, NJ: Prentice Hall.

Clark, M., & Leonard, S. (1998, April). Can corporate codes of ethics influence behavior? *Journal of Business Ethics, 17, 6, 619–630.*

College grads take pledge to be socially responsible. (1999, May 9). *The Baltimore Sun.*

Covello, V., & Allen, F. (1988). *Seven cardinal rules for risk communication.* Washington, D.C.: U.S. Environmental Protection Agency.

Daft, R. (1994). *Management* (3rd ed.). Fort Worth, TX: The Dryden Press.

DeGeorge, R. (1999). *Business ethics* (5th ed.). Upper Saddle River, NJ: Prentice Hall.

Desai, A., & Rittenburg, T. (1997, June). Global ethics: An integrative framework for MNEs. *Journal of Business Ethics, 16, 8, 791–800.*

Donaldson, T. (1999). *Ethical issues in business: A philosophical approach* (6th ed.) Upper Saddle River, NJ: Prentice Hall.

Drucker, P. (March-April,1999). Managing oneself. *Harvard Business Review,* 66–74.

Ferrell, O., & Fraedrich, J. (1997). *Business ethics: Ethical decision making and cases* (3rd ed). Boston, MA: Houghton Mifflin Company.

Fisher, R., & Ury, W. (1991). *Getting to yes.* New York, NY: Penguin Books.

Freeman, R., & Liedtka, J. (1991, July/August). Corporate social responsibility: A critical approach. *Business Horizons, 34, 92–99.*

Friedman, M. (1970, September 13). The social responsibility of business is to increase its profits. *The New York Times Magazine,* 87–91.

Gellerman, S. (1989, Winter). Managing ethics from the top down. *Sloan Management Review,* 73–79.

General Motors. (1998). *Guidelines for employee conduct.* Author.

Graham, P. (Ed.). (1996). *Mary Parker Follett: Prophet of management.* Boston, MA: Harvard Business School Press.

Hallowell, E. (1999, Jan.-Feb.). The human moment at work. *Harvard Business Review,* 58–66.

Hemphill, T. (1997, March-April). Legislating corporate social responsibility. *Business Horizons, 40,* 53–59.

Jackson, K. (1997, Sept.). Globalizing corporate ethics programs. *Journal of Business Ethics, 16,* 12/13, 1227–1235.

Karp, H., & Abramms, B. (1992, Aug.). Doing the right thing. *Training and Development,* 37–41.

Kourzes, J., & Posner, B. (1992, May). Ethical leaders: An essay about being in love. *Journal of Business Ethics, 11,* 5/6, 479ff.

Lewicki, R., Saunders, D., & Minton, J. (1997). Ethics in Negotiation. In *Essentials of Negotiation* (Chap. 11). Chicago, IL: Irwin.

Manzoni, J., & Barsoux, J. (1998, March-April). The set-up-to-fail syndrome. *Harvard Business Review,* 101–113.

Maryland Nurses Association. (1999, March). Ethical assessment framework. *The Maryland Nurse.* Author.

Mellema, G. (1994, Feb.). Business ethics and doing what one ought to do. *Journal of Business Ethics, 13,* 2, 149ff.

Moore, J. (1995). Historicity in Shakespeare's *Richard III.* In *Richard III Society American Branch: Primary Texts and Secondary Sources On-line.* [On line]. Available: http://www.webcom.com/r3/bookcase/moore1.html

National Institutes of Health. (1989). Conflicts of interest. *NIH Ethics Program Overview.* Available: http://ethics.od.nih.gov/topics/coi.htm

Nill, A., & Shultz, C. (1997, Fall). Marketing ethics across cultures: Decision-making guidelines and the emergence of dialogic idealism. *Journal of Macromarketing, 17,* 2, 4–19.

Novak, M. (1993). The creative person. *Journal of Business Ethics, 12,* 975–979.

Owen, C., & Scherer, R. (1993). Social responsibility and market share. *Review of Business, 15,* 11–17.

Paine, L. (1994, March-April). Managing for organizational integrity. *Harvard Business Review,* 106–117.

Pava, M. (1996, Sept.). The Talmudic concept of "Beyond the letter of the law": Relevance to business social responsibilities. *Journal of Business Ethics, 9.*

Rakich, J., Longest, B., & Darr, K. (1992). *Managing health services organizations* (3rd ed.). Baltimore, MD: Health Professions Press.

Rodewald, R. (1987). The corporate social responsibility debate: Unanswered questions about the consequences of moral reform. *American Business Law Journal, 25,* 443–466.

Shakespeare, W. (1983). *Richard III.* New York, NY: Pocket Books.

Shrivastava, P. (1995, Spring). Industrial/environmental crises and corporate social responsibility. *Journal of Socio-Economics, 24,* 211–228.

Smith, N., & Quelch, J. (1993). *Ethics in marketing.* Homewood, IL: Irwin.

Teal, T. (1996, Nov.-Dec.). The human side of management. *Harvard Business Review,* 35–44.

Thompson, L. (1998). Social justice, fairness, and social utility: All's fair. In *The Mind and Heart of the Negotiator.* (Chap. 11). Upper Saddle River, NJ: Prentice Hall.

Ury, W., Brett, J., & Goldberg, S. (1988). *Getting disputes resolved: Designing systems to cut the costs of conflict.* San Francisco, CA: Jossey-Bass Publishers.

Velasquez, M. (1998). *Business ethics: Concepts and cases* (4th ed.). Upper Saddle River, NJ: Prentice Hall.

WEBSTER'S New University Dictionary. (1984). Boston, MA: Houghton Mifflin Company.

Zaleznik, A. (1997, Nov.-Dec.). Real work. *Harvard Business Review,* 53–62.

Chapter VI

Issues and Trends in Operations Management

JOHN O. AJE

INTRODUCTION

An organization is essentially made up of production systems. Production is the conversion or transformation of resources available to an organization into goods and services. Operations management is the management of production systems.

A production system consists of four principal components: inputs; a conversion, a creation or transformation process; outputs and feedback. This is illustrated in Figure 1.

The mission of operations management is the effective and efficient management of the transformation process. This process involves the ability to understand, explain, predict and change the four principal components of production, viz, inputs, transformation, outputs, and feedback, strategically and tactically. Examples of activities in operations management are product design, procurement, locating facilities, management of inventory, human resources management, work scheduling and quality management.

Several functional areas interact with and impact on the production system of an organization. Typical ones are finance, marketing, purchasing, engineering, accounting, information systems, research and development and personnel

Figure 1. A Model of Production System

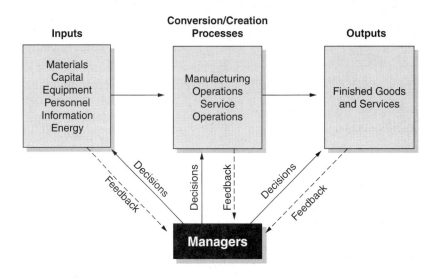

Source: Evans, et al., 1990, p.11

(Evans et al. p. 15). Figure 2 illustrates these relationships and this is followed by a brief discussion of the role of each functional area.

The decisions that are made by the finance department affect the choice of manufacturing equipment, the trade off between production resources, cost-control strategies and price-volume decisions.

The coordination between marketing and operations management is critical for the success of any organization. Operations management depend on marketing for the defining of customer needs, generating and maintaining of demand for the firm's products, ensuring customer satisfaction and developing new markets and products. It is important that the operations management group work closely with the marketing group to predict demand, project workloads and ensure sufficient capacity to handle the demand and deliver finished goods on time.

Ideas for potential products usually come from the research and development group and these are translated into product specifications and production methods by the engineering group. The purchasing department is responsible for making sure that the materials and supplies that are necessary for the production and the distribution of the finished goods are available in a timely and efficient manner. The human resources or personnel department recruit and train employees, ensure that they are equitably compensated and that all employment rules and regulations are followed. As shown in Figure 2, all these functional areas are linked together with the production system.

A production system is an open system. It is impacted by external factors such as economic conditions, government regulations, competitors, technology and customer demands. This is illustrated in Figure 2.

Figure 2. The Production System and Its Environment

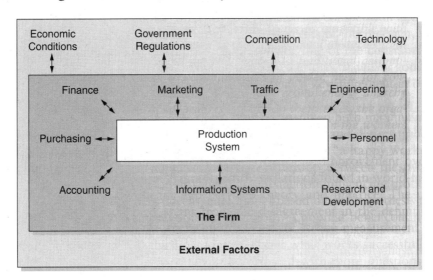

Source: Evans, et al., 1990, p.15

Perhaps the most critical and unpredictable of all the external factors is customer demand. Customer demand is based on customer expectations, which tend to change with changes in education, product knowledge, income levels, competitors' actions, advertising and government regulations and actions. In the automobile industry, the demand for quality is an example of this. In the early 1980s, quality was an important issue in the automobile industry. At that time there was a big difference between the quality levels of Japanese, European and American cars. The Japanese cars, in particular, were considered superior to American ones. Quality ratings were published by popular automobile magazines or consumer reports, and these were used by consumers as guides in their purchases. The 1990s have produced a convergence in quality levels; customers now expect quality in every automobile and the manufacturers now have to look for alternative tactics or features for distinguishing themselves and attracting customers. This is the challenge of operations management.

THE EVOLUTION OF OPERATIONS MANAGEMENT

Operations management has its roots in the Industrial Revolution of the 1770s, but most of the important developments are fairly recent. Figure 3 illustrates the significant events in operations management.

Before the Industrial Revolution, production centered around crafts and craftsmen. Skilled craftsmen and their apprentices produced goods for individual customers from studios in their homes. Every item they produced was unique, handcrafted and made entirely by one person. Craft guilds were formed to protect and foster the interests of craftsmen (also known as artisans) and to study

Figure 3. Significant Events in Operations Management

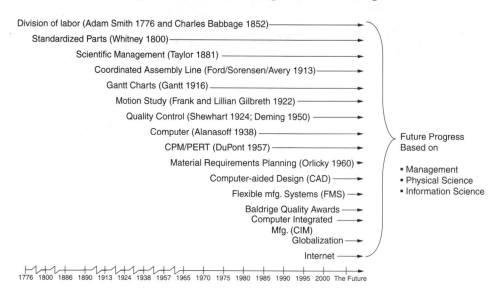

Source: Heizer and Render, 1999, p. 5

and codify the best practices. The master craftsmen or artisans transferred their knowledge and skills to apprentices and trainees with much time and attention. (Starr, p. 18)

The Industrial Revolution produced many inventions which allowed goods to be manufactured in larger quantities with greater ease and speed. Some examples of these are Hagreaves' spinning jenny (1770) and Cartwright's power loom (1785) which revolutionized the production of textiles; James Watt's steam engine (1785), which provided power for mechanization; and Maudslay's screw cutting lathe (1797), which helped to establish the metal-fabrication and machine-tool industries. These inventions made possible the modern factories and reduced the need for individual craftsmen. In textile mills, grain mills and metal metalworking and machine-making facilities, these machines replaced laborers as the primary factor in production.

Around the same time that these machines were being introduced into production processes, new methods of planning and organizing work were being developed. Adam Smith, in 1776, proposed the division of labor in his book, *The Wealth of Nations* (1776). He contended that productivity can be improved through a division of labor in which the production process is broken down into different functions, each of which is performed by a different worker. Smith reasoned that by making a worker specialize in a limited, repetitive task, he would become more proficient in his task and industry could then develop specialized tools and machines for performing the jobs more efficiently. He also stated that this would eliminate the time lost from changing jobs. The concept of division of labor, even though it has been modified over the past 100 years, continues to influence how we get jobs done (Russell & Taylor, p. 5).

Eli Whitney, in 1798, introduced the concept of interchangeable parts and paved the way for modern manufacturing. The Henry Ford assembly line in the early 1910s benefited greatly from this idea. Interchangeability means that the parts or components of one production item can be used for another. For example, for automobiles, headlights, fenders, tires and windshield wiper blades do not have to be produced separately for each one. This idea spread quickly throughout other American industries and was a major impetus for standardization and quality control. In order to achieve interchangeability among several producers in an industry, standards must be set and there must be quality control in manufacturing. The standards, which generally include the specification of tolerance limits, are set by industry, professional bodies or government agencies.

In 1832, Charles Babbage, a British mathematician, refined and extended Adam Smith's work by developing the use of the scientific method for solving some factory problems. He was the first mathematician to bring a scientific mind and method to bear on production. In his book, *On the Economy of Machinery and Manufacturers*, (1832), he agreed with most of the principles of Adam Smith but noted that the great economist overlooked an important point. That point is that with the division of labor, payment need be made only for the right amount of skill needed in a task not for craftsman-level of skills for operations. He contended that by hiring workers with different skills and paying them according to the level of skills required, the total cost of a product could be reduced. He also did some study on organizational structures, human relations, economic location analysis, research and development and price-volume-profit relationships. Babbage's other significant contribution was the invention of what was at that time called the "analytical engine," the forerunner of today's computer (Starr, pp. 790–794).

For about 50 years after the work of Babbage, the factory system continued to develop, producing products at lower cost and higher volume than was possible with the handicraft system and developing larger markets. During this period, there was no major development in management theory and practice.

In early 1900s, Frederick Taylor, an enterprising laborer at Midvale Steel Company who later became an engineer, began a management movement that would later earn him the title of father of scientific management. Taylor and his associates, Henry Gantt and Frank and Lillian Gilbreth developed principles and practices that ultimately revolutionized the field of production and operations management

The essence of Taylor's scientific management philosophy was that how much a worker can produce per day is governed by scientific laws; that managers should discover and use these laws in the operation of productive systems, and that workers should carry out managers' wishes without question. (Taylor, 1911).

Taylor believed that a business could operate more efficiently by:

1. Using managers as work planners by gathering traditional knowledge about the work and reducing it to standardized procedures for the workers.

2. Methodically selecting, training and developing each worker on an individual basis.

3. Striving for cooperation between management and the worker to simultaneously obtain both maximum production and high worker's wages.

4. Dividing the work between management and the workers so each is working on what they are most proficient in doing

Taylor, through observation, measurement and analysis identified the best method for performing each job. Once this was done, the methods were standardized for all workers, and economic incentives were established to encourage workers to follow the standards. His ideas were embraced and extended by his associates, Henry Gantt and Frank Gilbreth. Gilbreth stressed applications of the principles of motion study to the most minute details of tasks in an attempt to identify the "one best way" (most economical) of performing a given task. Gantt developed the famous Gantt chart for scheduling and monitoring work.

Taylor's approach met with resistance from some of his contemporaries and workers' unions. There were several instances of abuse of power by managers who embraced Taylor's philosophy but did not do their part to organize and standardize the work. This led to some cases of overwork and reduction of per piece payment by managers if the production rate was considered too high. The unions demonstrated this abuse by claiming that one of Taylor's subjects in several of his time-study experiments, a steelworker called Schmidt, died from overwork as a result of following Taylor's methods. They distributed a picture of what was supposed to be his grave, but in reality Schmidt, whose real name was Henry Nole, was alive and well and working as a teamster. Nevertheless, they achieved their objective because a bill, prohibiting the use of time study and incentive plans in federal government operations, was introduced in Congress in 1913 even though it was defeated (Chase and Aquilane, p. 13).

In 1913, Ford Motor Company's moving assembly line for the production of Model T cars and the ensuing spread of rapid production methods kicked the industrialization of American into overdrive and completely changed the way people work and live worldwide. Before the assembly line was introduced, each automobile chasis was assembled by one worker and it usually took about 278 hours to assemble a car. William C. Klann, a foreman in Ford's engine-assembly shop, and some of his colleagues had visited some slaughterhouses and were impressed by how conveyors carried hogs and cattle through a disassembly process. This gave them the idea of using a conveyor to speed up the assembly of one component of the Model T engine.

They first tried this with the magneto coil, part of the Model T's then revolutionary ignition system. They assembled it on a conveyor that was over 200 feet long. That was the very first belt conveyor for assembly, according to Klann. The factory bosses then started to introduce a moving line into every department. The time required to assemble a car was drastically reduced from a high of 728 hours to $1\frac{1}{2}$ hours. This made the production of Model T cars in high volume or "en masse" possible. Thus "mass production" was born.

For the next 50 years, American manufacturers perfected these methods and dominated the production market worldwide.

Ford's use of the assembly line launched the process of mass production, kicking the industrialization of America into overdrive. Copyright © Corbis-Bettmann.

Conveyer belt at meat slaughterhouse. Copyright © Corbis-Bettmann.

Model T Ford assembly line. Courtesy of Library of Congress.

Mathematical and statistical development was an important aspect of the mass production movement. Models of operations management, such as the Economic Order Quantity (EOQ) inventory model, were formulated by F.W. Harris in 1914. In 1931, H.F. Dodge, H.C. Romig and W. Shewhart, co-workers at Bell Telephone laboratories, developed the procedure of "sampling inspection" for quality control. They published statistical sampling tables, based on inference and probability theory, which are still used extensively. Their work not only paved the way for the field of quality control, but led to the acceptance of probability and statistical concepts in forecasting, inventory control and other production activities.

A new viewpoint on operations management began to emerge in the 1930s as a result of studies conducted at Western Electric's Hawthorne plant in Illinois. These studies which were conducted by Elton Mayo, created a greater awareness of the human and social factors in work. They emphasized that workers are not just production factors, as in Taylor's perspective, and that worker motivation is critical to productivity.

These experiments, which were actually motivated by Taylor's work, were designed to study the effects of certain environmental changes on the productivity of assembly line workers. The researchers were intrigued by the fact that changing the level of illumination in the work area, whether decreasing or increasing it, did not produce the kind of impact they had expected. The productivity of workers increased whether desirable or undesirable changes were made in the lighting of their work environment. The researchers hypothesized that because of the special attention paid to the group, a special relationship had developed between the members. The morale of workers increased and this led to higher productivity. Each member of the group felt an obligation to the group to keep the output high irrespective of the changes in the conditions of the work environment.

This discovery led to a growing interest in the psychological and physiological aspects of operations management. Organizations began to recognize that to increase productivity, both the technical methods, as advocated by Taylor, and behavioral approaches for improving employee motivation are important. This led many organizations to ultimately institute personnel management or human relations departments. Researchers such as Abraham Maslow (hierarchy of needs—1940s), Frederick Herzberg (hygiene factors—1950s) and McGregor (Theory X and Theory Y—1960s), made major contributions to the knowledge base of this field.

Around the same period, between 1947 and the 1960s, a new interdisciplinary body of knowledge spurred by the complex demands of logistics control and weapons systems of World War II began to develop (Chase & Aquilano, 1990). Operations Research (OR) is a multifaceted discipline that brings together diverse fields such as mathematics, psychology and economics. The quantitative tools such as linear programming, waiting line theory, PERT/CPM and simulation models that were developed as a part of this academic discipline are now used extensively in operations management.

One of the most significant developments in operations management was the broad use of computers in operations problems beginning in the 1970s. This enabled the development of a materials requirement planning (MRP) systems.

Chase & Aquilano (1990) state ". . . for manufacturers, the big breakthrough was the application of materials requirement planning (MRP) to production control. This approach ties together in a computer program all the parts that go into complicated products. This program then enables production planners to quickly adjust production schedules and inventory purchases to meet changing demands for final products. Clearly the massive data manipulation required for changing schedules on products with thousands of parts would be impossible without such programs and the computer capacity to run them. The promotion of this approach (pioneered by Joseph Orlicky of IBM and consultant Oliver Wright) by the American Production and Inventory Control Society (APICS) has been termed the MRP Crusade." (p. 22)

The developments in technologies, human relations skills, and management philosophies and techniques that have been discussed enabled the United States to achieve a leadership position in the production of goods and services, as well as the supply of managerial and technical expertise from the Industrial Revolution through the 1960s. Figure 4 shows a steady growth of productivity, output per worker-hour, in the manufacturing industry from 1870 to 1980.

Around 1970, increases in productivity in the U.S. manufacturing industry compared with the rest of the world started to take a downward turn. In the 1970s, U.S. productivity rose an average of 1.3 percent per year, and in the

Figure 4. One Hundred Years of Productivity Growth. Output per Worker-Hour in United States Manufacturing, 1870–1980.

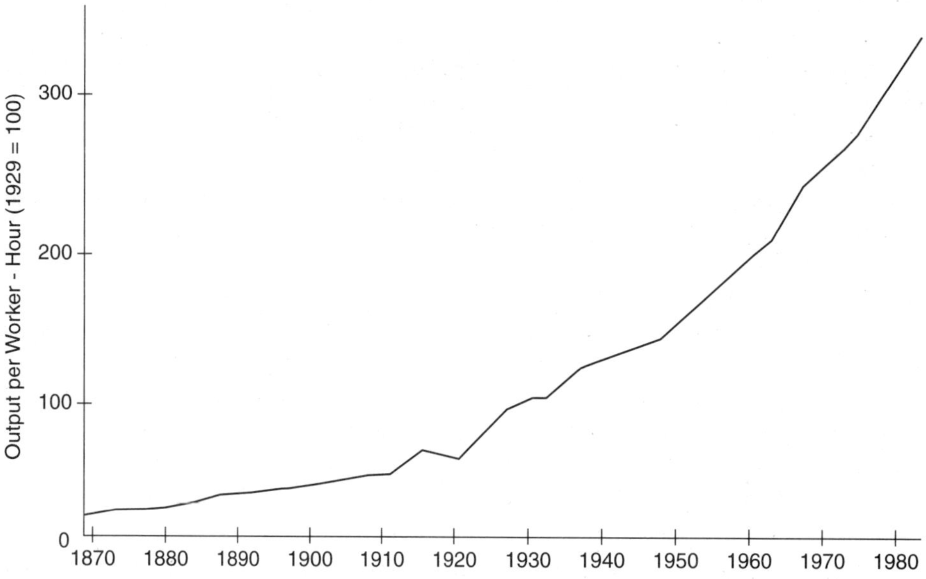

Source: Starr, 1994, p. 792

1980s productivity averaged only 0.2 percent per year. The productivity changes for some years during this period were actually negative. For example it was 2.4 percent in 1974 and 0.3 percent in 1980. While this was happening, many foreign competitors were enjoying productivity growths of 4 percent and higher (Table 1).

Table 1. Change in Manufacturing Productivity for Six Countries, 1973–1980

United States	Canada	Japan	France	West Germany	United Kingdom
1.7	2.2	6.8	4.9	4.8	1.9

Source: Starr, 1994, p. 796

By 1980, U.S. industries started to lose their share of the market in important areas such as electronics and automobiles. Japanese products in particular dominated the U.S. market. U.S. companies that were unable to compete started to close down or downsize. Many people lost their jobs. Initially, there was an attempt to rationalize what was happening by blaming it on unfair competition by Japanese companies, U.S. government regulations that did not favor domestic companies, cultural differences between U.S. and Japanese workers and so on. Most of these were dispelled when the U.S. companies came to the realization that they were in the middle of a new revolution, the "Quality/Technology Revolution."

First of all, new product-process technologies such as numerical controls, robotics, computer-aided designs/computer-aided manufacturing (CAD/CAM) and flexible manufacturing systems (FMS) became available in the late 1970s and 1980s. U.S. companies, compared with Japanese companies, were slow in adopting these advanced technologies. As one General Electric business executive explained it, "they thought mass production had solved the 'problem' of production, so they delegated the function of manufacturing to technical specialists (usually engineers) who ignored changes in the consumer environment and the strategic impact of operations."

Mass production can produce large volumes of goods quickly, but it cannot adapt very well to changes in demand. Today's consumer market is characterized by product proliferation, shortened product lifecycles, shortened product development times, changes in technology, more customized products, and segmented markets. Mass production does not fit that type of environment. Japanese manufacturers changed the rules of production with an adoption of mass production known as lean production. Lean production prizes flexibility (rather than efficiency) and quality (rather than quantity). (Quoted from Render & Heizer, 1999, p. 58.)

Process technology on an assembley line—robotic arms spraying car bodies. Copyright © Tony Stone Images.

OPERATIONS MANAGEMENT AND THE QUALITY REVOLUTION

Apart from a revolution in technologies, the 1980s also marked the beginning of a revolution in the management philosophies behind operations management. For example, just-in-time (JIT) production was pioneered by the Japanese. This management philosophy ensured minimal inventories of parts and high-volume production as it integrated several production activities.

Perhaps the most important management philosophy in the 1980s, one that became more pervasive in the 1990s, was Total Quality Management (TQM). W. Edwards Deming, Philip B. Crosby and Joseph M. Juran were the pioneers in the development of this management philosophy and its global adoption.

Deming is credited with the major turnaround in Japanese industry after World War II. Deming with his academic background in physics, mathematics and statistics, worked for the Bureau of War Department in 1939. During World War II, Deming developed a technique for quality control which guaranteed high quality and on-time delivery. After the war he tried to convince the U.S. industries to adopt this management approach but was shunned. There was no incentive for them to listen. The demand for U.S. products was high at that time and nobody was complaining about quality. There was little or no competition in both the domestic and foreign markets for U.S. products. U.S. companies failed to realize that the lack of competition was not because U.S. products were superior but was the result of a world devastated by war. U.S. products were sometimes the only ones available to consumers.

Table 2 shows that in the 1970s and 1980s, American products such as automobiles, semiconductors, air conditioners and color televisions were considered inferior by consumers.

**Table 2. A Comparison of American and Japanese
Products in the 1970s and 1980s.**

Quality of Automobiles	TGWs (things gone wrong) in	
Chrysler	285	
GM	256	
Ford	214	
Japanese (avg.)	132	
Toyota	55	
Quality of Semiconductors	**U.S. Companies**	**Japanese Companies**
Defective on delivery	16%	0%
Failure after 1000 hours	14%	1%
Quality of Room Air Conditioners	**U.S. Companies**	**Japanese Companies**
Fabrication defects	4.4%	<0.1%
Assembly line defects	63.5%	0.9%
Service calls	10.5%	0.6%
Warranty cost (as % of sales)	2.2%	0.6%
Quality of Color TVs	**U.S. Companies**	**Japanese Companies**
Assembly line defects per set	1.4	0.01
Service calls per set	1.0	0.09

Source: Russell and Taylor, 1998, p. 10

In 1950, the Japanese Union of Scientists and Engineers invited Deming to address industrial leaders. The domestic economy of Japan was shattered by the war, and Japanese products had a reputation for poor quality. Though skeptical at first, Japanese companies committed themselves to Deming's methods, and there was an impressive turnaround. Very soon industries all over the world adopted the Total Quality Management philosophy.

The U.S. government showed its support for Total Quality Management through several actions and initiatives such as the Malcom Baldrige National Quality Award, which was started in 1986 under the direction of the American Institute of Quality Control and the National Institute of Standards and Technology. Every Baldrige Award recognizes companies that have demonstrated quality management systems.

In the early 1990s, some executives started to question the appropriateness or adequacy of Total Quality Management for their organizations. There were several stories of organizations that were dissatisfied with the results of their TQM initiatives and some that went bankrupt actually blamed it on TQM. A survey of American managers showed that up to two-thirds of them thought that TQM had failed in their companies. The number of companies applying for the prestigious Malcom Baldrige Award peaked around 1991 and fell sharply in the 1990s (Nolan, 1993).

The dissatisfaction with TQM produced two notable results. The first was the rise of a new "cottage industry" of consultants who can best be referred to as "TQM pathologists." They specialized in diagnosing the reasons for the failure of TQM and in turning around failed programs. Many managers of American companies that initiated failed TQM programs still believe in its basic management concepts and are baffled that an approach that seemed to work so well for Japanese companies failed so miserably in their organizations. Hundreds of articles and books have been written to explain the reasons for the perceived failure. Some of the common reasons that have been identified are a non-supportive organizational culture or leadership, a tendency to regard it as a panacea and a quick-fix, focusing too much on the bottom-line instead of on customers' needs, a poor planning and implementation process, not empowering employees and not recognizing or rewarding them on quality criteria.

The second probable consequence of dissatisfaction with TQM was the embracement of a new management philosophy, "Business Process Re-engineering." According to the two major advocates of this philosophy, Michael Hammer and James Champy (1993), "Re-engineering isn't another idea imported from Japan. It isn't another quick fix that American managers can apply to their organizations. It isn't a new trick that promises to boost the quality of a company's product or service or shave a percentage off costs. Business re-engineering isn't a program to hike worker's morale or to motivate the sales force. It won't push an old computer system to work faster. Business re-engineering isn't about fixing anything. Business re-engineering means starting all over, starting from scratch" (p. 1).

Several business leaders, probably feeling that re-engineering offered them an opportunity to regain some credibility, believed they lost through failed TQM efforts quickly jumped on the bandwagon. As Payl O'Neill, the chairman of ALCOA explained, it, "I believe we have made a major mistake in our advocacy of the idea of continuous improvement." Here is why TQM failed according to O'Neill:

> *Continuous improvement is exactly the right idea if you are the world leader in everything you do. It is a terrible idea if you are lagging in the world leadership benchmark. It is probably a disastrous idea if you are far behind the world standard . . . we need rapid, quantum-leap improvement. We cannot be satisfied to lay out a plan that will move us toward the existing world standard over some protracted period of time . . . say 1995 or the year 2000 . . . because if we accept such a plan, we will never be a world leader. (Quoted in Nolan, Richard et al., 1995.)*

The 1990s has clearly been the decade of re-engineering. The term means different things to different people in the business world, even though it appeared that a consensus began to develop towards the end of the decade. The academic or "classical" view describes it as a "radical redesign of broad cross-functional business processes with the objective of order-of-magnitude performance gains, often with the aid of information technology" (Davenport, Harvard Business School notes, 1995, p. 2).

There are two extreme views of re-engineering both in practice and in the literature. At one end of the spectrum are people like Richard Nolan and David Croson (1995) who view re-engineering as a long-term transformation involving "creative destruction" of the dominant functional hierarchy of the Industrial Economy to the "IT-enabled network" of the Information Economy. It involves a major and simultaneous organizational transformation in culture, strategy, processes, structure and information systems. At the other end is a less radical approach which views re-engineering as any attempt to change how work is done, even if it involves only incremental changes of small, sub-functional processes.

Most of the early proponents of re-engineering had their roots in the field of information technology (IT). It is generally believed that the impetus for many re-engineering efforts was how to make better use of IT in businesses, especially in the service sector, which spent billions of dollars in the 1980s on hardware and software with no perceived increase in productivity. In reality, the problem was not that there was no increase in productivity, but that the traditional way of measuring productivity did not capture some of the benefits of information technology.

A few companies reported having a degree of success with re-engineering. Some of them are shown in Table 3. On the other hand, several studies have shown that about 50 to 70 percent of re-engineering efforts have failed. Some of these failures caused permanent morale damage in their organizations because of accompanying downsizing. This left the management with a human relations nightmare.

Table 3. Reported Reengineering Successes

Company	Process	Reported Benefit
Siemens Rolm	Order fulfillment	• Order to installation completion time improved by 60% • Field inventory cut by 69%
CIGNA Reinsurance	Many	• Operating costs reduced by 40% • Application systems reduced 17 to 5
CIGNA	Many	• Savings of more than $100 million
British Nuclear Fuels	Fuel Processing	• Doubled fuel processing rate

(continues)

Table 3. Reported Reengineering Successes (continued)

Company	Process	Reported Benefit
Eastman Chemical	Maintenance	• 80% reduction in order cycle time • Savings of $1 million/year
American Express	Many	• Cost reduction > $1.2 billion
Amoco	Capital allocation	• 33% staffing reductions
Xerox	Supply chain	• 30% inventory reduction
Rank Xerox	Billing	• Cycle time reduction of 112 days to 3 • Annual cash flow increase of $5M
Aetna	Many	• Annual savings of $300–$350M
Federal Mogul	New product development	• Cycle time reductions from 20 weeks to 20 days
AT&T Business	Many	• Product quality improved tenfold • 75% reduction in key cycle

Source: Nolan, 1995, p. 32

The reasons for the failures of re-engineering efforts are varied, but there are some common observations. In many organizations, the re-engineering effort was driven by tactical necessities such as cost reduction or downsizing which were usually a reaction to a loss of competitiveness. Many of these companies did not clearly define what they were trying to accomplish or how to accomplish it. They were anxious to see results and probably did not stay the course long enough for this to happen.

Another reason that some re-engineering efforts failed is that some companies used a bulldozer approach to re-engineering. These companies took too literally the advice of some of the proponents of re-engineering that you have to start "with a clean slate." They attempted to re-engineer all their processes, and this became too expensive and disruptive. A successful re-engineering effort should focus mainly on strategic and value-added processes; it does not necessarily have to be exhaustive. It should be done from the point of view of the customers and must produce unique capability and variety in the company's products.

OPERATIONS MANAGEMENT AND THE TECHNOLOGY REVOLUTION

The competitive thrust in the 1960s was cost, in the 1970s it was market, in the 1980s it was quality and in the 1990s it is time and globalization.

The key to successful operations management in the 1990s and the future is the recognition that the world is a global marketplace that demands on-time delivery of products. Technology plays a paramount role in achieving the on-time objective. There are two general categories of technologies, manufacturing or

Modern automobile assembly line. Copyright © Corbis-Bettmann.

process technology, which apply to the production process, and information technology, which applies to managing information (Noori, 1990). Manufacturing technologies are those that are used directly by the firm in the production of a product or in the provision of a service. Information technologies generate and transmit information essential to support the production of goods and provision of services. Table 4 shows some examples of manufacturing technologies and Table 5 some examples of information technologies.

Table 4. A Short Description of Some of the Advanced Manufacturing Technologies

Technology	Description
Numerical Control (NC) Machines	A tape-driver machine tool.
Computer Numerical Control (CNC)	A single machine tool controlled be a dedicated computer.
Direct Numerical Control (DNC)	A number of machine tools controlled by a central computer.
Industrial Robots	A general purpose, multifunctional, controllable machine.
Computer Processing Monitoring (CPM)	The use of a computer to gather information about the manufacturing process.
Computer-Aided Manufacturing (CAM)	The computer range of computer applications in direct manufacturing activities.

(continues)

**Table 4. A Short Description of Some of the
Advanced Manufacturing Technologies (continued)**

Technology	Description
Computer-Aided Design (CAD)	The use of a computer to create or modify engineering designs.
Computer-Aided Engineering (CAE)	Computerized testing of designs.
Computer-Aided Process Planning (CAPP)	Computer-generated process plans.
Machine Vision	Computerized vision systems used in manufacturing to inspect, recognize, gauge, guide, and control parts.
Automated Materials Handling	The use of computers to direct the movement of inventories.
Manufacturing Resource Planning (MRP II)	A computerized system used to plan the resources of a manufacturing company.
CAD/CAM	The integration of computer-aided design and computer-aided manufacturing.
Flexible Manufacturing Systems (FMS)	A group of machines joined by an automated materials handling system and controlled by a computer.
Computer-Integrated Manufacturing (CIM)	The computerized integration and control of all of the functions of the manufacturing system.
Just-In-Time (JIT)	A philosophy which advocates the elimination of excess (waste) in all areas of the operation that does not add value to the final product.
Group Technology (GT)	The organization of machines into cells, with each cell being used to produce a different family of parts.

Source: Noori, 1990, p. 47

**Table 5. A Short Description of Some of the
Advanced Information Technologies**

Technology	Description
Computerized Database System	A collection of data stored on a computer.
Common Database System	A centralized database containing all the data used by an organization.
Relational Database	A common database that is easy to understand and flexible to use.
Distributed Database	The distribution of common data among many computers.
Manufacturing Automation Protocol (MAP)	A communications standard which enables component technologies to be interconnected.

**Table 5. A Short Description of Some of the
Advanced Information Technologies, Continued**

Technology	Description
Artificial Intelligence (AI)	The ability to apply reasoning to solve a problem.
Machine Intelligence	Computer programs that use "if-then" logic to respond to various environmental stimuli.
Expert Systems (ES)	Computer programs that apply heuristic reasoning to solve problems that do not have a discernible optimal answer.

Source: Noori, 1990, p. 54

Space does not permit a full discussion of each of these technologies. The point to keep in mind is that the effective utilization of one category of technology depends on the other. For example, an effective computer-aided manufacturing system (CAM) is one which effectively integrates advanced manufacturing technologies with advanced information technologies (Noori, 1990, p. 48). This issue of technology integration is considered critical for the factory of the future. Many organizations operate as islands of information and production technologies. This is because many assumptions that underlie the concept of technology integration and CAM systems are at odds with actual practice. The assumptions include the following: (Duimering, 1993)

- *Computer systems can handle most manufacturing information.* This is not quite so. Most information that can be numerically coded can be handled by computers. Unfortunately, many important pieces of information that are critical to effective operations management are derived from soft data. In addition, even if the data can be coded into forms computers can handle, not all units may find it appropriate for their use.

- *A reduction in information transmission time will reduce throughput times.* This is a conceptual error. The throughput time between two processes, A and B consists of three components: The processing time, at A, the transmission time between A and B and the processing time at B. Of these three, the processing time at A and B, not the transmission time, is where most of the bottlenecks occur. Examples of this can be seen in design engineering, marketing and accounting activities. If an organization wants to reduce the throughput times, managers should focus on deducing the processing times through a better coordination of the various functions.

- *Organizations are not integrated because they lack appropriate information transmission technology.* This "if you build it, they will come" philosophy is not true. The lack of integration in many organizations is not due to a lack of information transmission technology but rather a lack of motivation on the part of individuals to use the resources available or to share them with members of other units. Weick (1969) states that most large organizations behave as loosely compiled systems in which functional units often have little desire to integrate their activities with one another.

Duimering (1993) identifies four reasons for differing functional goals that work against integration. They are:

1. *Different Functional Perspectives*: Each functional unit may have a unique perspective on its contribution to the organizations' outputs.

2. *Survival Techniques:* Functional units naturally tend to be more interested in the well-being and survival of their own units and will not hesitate to draw resources away from other units with even more pressing needs.

3. *Performance Measurement Systems:* Units focus more on performance measurements that are more important to their units. A purchasing unit, for example, which is measured on how inexpensively it can purchase materials or how low it can keep its raw material inventory levels, will try to achieve this even if it jeopardizes the activities of the production unit.

4. *Means and Ends Inversion:* Cyert (1968) describes this as a situation in which the means of achieving an organizational goal can sometimes take on the characteristics of a goal and become detrimental to the overall aim of the organization. Duimering et al. (1993) give the example of one organization in which "design engineers were provided with computer-aided design (CAD) systems to improve design effectiveness. The designers used the systems to incorporate complex design features that had been impossible to draw before. These features added elegance to the design but also added significant costs to the manufacturing process. The designers had replaced the goal of creating effective designs with the new goal of using the CAD systems to their limit." (p. 51)

Figure 5 is a model that was developed by Ebner and Vollman (1988) for technology integration in operations management.

The most important point that needs to be emphasized in this section is that technology can enhance operations, but it cannot compensate for inherent organizational flaws. As Duimering (1993) put it: ". . . true organizational integration amounts to correcting the problems that have created poorly integrated, loosely coupled organizational systems in the first place. If these problems—which are essentially organizational rather than technological—are ignored, CIM implementers run the risk of institutionalizing ineffective organizational procedures and communicational linkages by automating them rather than correcting them" (p. 52).

THE FUTURE OF OPERATIONS MANAGEMENT

The competitive environment of today and of the future is global, intense and dynamic. The operations manager is confronted with an ever-changing world. He

Figure 5. Integration of Islands of Information

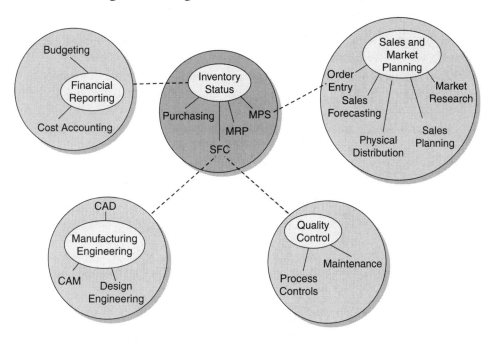

Source: Ebner and Vollman, 1988, p. 324.

is expected to produce more, better and cheaper products faster and at any time. The future of operations management will be characterized by a number of challenges that are taking shape today and can be foreseen and some that cannot yet be predicted. Five of these challenges are particularly critical for U.S. firms that have historically viewed themselves as operating in a large, mature and primarily domestic market.

Globalization and Intense International Competition.

The trend is toward "global market," "global products," "global factory," and "global village" (Heizer & Render, 1999). The ability to integrate operations from different countries and view the world as a single marketplace is critical to the success of most organizations. Abernathy (1981) uses the U.S. automobile industry to illustrate the impact of the global marketplace:

> Up until recently developments in the U.S. auto industry were determined mostly by government policies and economic forces particular to North America. The sheer extent of the U.S. market and its productive base had long guaranteed the industry a largely self-contained posture. Over the past 15 years, however, the competitive boundaries have expanded drastically until now they are virtually worldwide in scope. (p. 71)

Some of the reasons for the acceleration of international competition in recent years are: (Heizer & Render, 1999, pp. 54–67)

1. Improved communication and transportation networks that have blurred the boundaries between states, countries and continents.

2. A reduction of trade barriers. Agreements between countries (such as NAFTA) have made it easier for countries to be trade partners.

3. Increased technology transfer (both basic and advanced industrial know-how) between countries. The knowledge and technology required to compete is now easily available through all kinds of means to many nations. These means include joint ventures, co-production, education and training, licensing and technological consortiums.

4. Several countries have developed large manufacturing capabilities and need to market their products outside their borders.

5. Small firms, especially in technology intensive businesses, are able to compete by focusing on niche markets.

Heizer and Render (1999, p. 56) give the following examples of how some companies have responded to global operations:

- Boeing is flourishing because both its sales and production are worldwide.
- Italy's Benetton moves inventory to stores around the world faster than its competition by building flexibility into design, production and distribution.
- Sony purchases components from suppliers in Thailand, Malaysia and around the world for assembly in its electronic products.
- Coleco, the U.S. toy company, meets surges in demand for Cabbage Patch dolls by contracting with firms in China and Hong Kong—and then whisking the dolls to the U.S. Christmas market in jumbo jets supplied by global carriers such as Singapore and Korean Airlines.

These companies have figured out how to compete successfully in the global marketplace. International operations management hinges on three complex and important issues according to Griffin & Pustay (1996, pp. 584–586):

1. How the products should be designed and where the plants and offices should be built.

2. Where and how the resources needed for producing the goods and services should be obtained.

3. What means of transportation/communication and inventory management should be employed.

According to Schniederjams (1998), Ferdows (1997), and Heizer & Render (1999), the major reasons why a domestic company will decide to internationalize some aspects of its operations are to:

1. *Reduce costs.* This could be in the form of lower taxes and tariffs, lower labor rates, and less stringent government regulations on operations practices such as environmental control.

2. *Improve the supply chain.* The supply chain can be improved by locating facilities close to where critical resources such as expertise, labor or raw material are available.

3. *Provide quick and adequate goods and services.* Many of the customers of U.S. companies are in overseas countries. By moving some production facilities to these countries, the companies are better able to respond in a timely fashion to the changing product and service needs of these customers. Another advantage of maintaining a local presence is that the company is better able to customize its products and services to satisfy the unique cultural needs of different foreign markets.

4. *Develop new markets.* Companies are always looking for an opportunity to expand their markets or develop new ones. International operations involve interactions with local customers, suppliers, businesses, etc. that can provide unique opportunities for new markets, products and services. Sometimes a product has reached the maturity phase of its life cycle and may be moving toward the decline phase. One way to extend the life of the product is to introduce it into a foreign country where it may represent the state-of-the-art. An example of this is the market for personal computers in the late 1990s. It has reached the maturity phase in this period in the U.S., but it is in the introductory phase in some developing countries such as China and some eastern European countries.

5. *Exchange knowledge and skills.* The free flow of ideas which comes from interactions and collaborations with other companies is beneficial not just to the companies but to the industry as a whole. General Motors was able to improve its operations by collaborating with the Japanese in the building and running of an auto assembly plant in San Jose, California. GM contributed its capital and knowledge of U.S. labor and environmental laws while the Japanese contributed production and inventory management ideas. The U.S. Saturn plant and operations are based on Japanese production concepts.

6. *Recruit and retain superior employees.* Global companies offer greater opportunity for advancement and usually better security against economic downturn. Generally there are more opportunities to relocate personnel from one site to another in companies that are global in scope.

Table 6 shows that most of the well-known and successful corporations have a high percentage of their sales, assets and work force outside their home countries. This trend will continue in the future. Alvin Toffler, quoted in "Recipe for

Table 6. Some Multinational Corporations (MNCs)

Company	Home Country	% Sales Outside Home Country	% Assets Outside Home Country	% Foreign Work Force
Citicorp	United States	66	51	NA
Colgate-Palmolive	United States	65	47	NA
Daimler-Benz	Germany	61	NA	25
Dow Chemical	United States	54	45	NA
Gillette	United States	68	55	NA
Honda	Japan	63	36	NA
IBM	United States	59	55	51
ICI	Britain	78	59	NA
Nestle	Switzerland	98	95	97
Philips Electronics	Netherlands	94	85	82
Siemens	Germany	51	NA	38
Unilever	Britain/Netherlands	95	70	64

NA = Not Available

Sources: *The Wall Street Journal*, September 26, 1996, p. R6; *Forbes*, July 18, 1994; and *Fortune*, July 25, 1994, p. 143.

Intelligence," *Information Today*, March 1994, pp. 61–63, states that international firms will become stateless as decisions are increasingly made on economic, not national merits.

Time to Market

Time to market has become and will continue to be the most critical factor for success in all markets. The rapid changes in technology are causing rapid accelerations in product life cycles. New products and services depend on technology either in the manufacturing process or as a part of the product itself. As new technologies become available, they are introduced to new products which are usually cheaper, bigger, faster or "better" in some other performance criteria. These new products replace old ones that incorporated or were manufactured with old technology. The combination of continuous technological change and the pressure to minimize time to market puts new challenges on operations managers. Time to market creates opportunities for bigger market share, market leadership and increased profits. A study by McKinsey and Company showed that a product six months late to market misses out on one-third of the potential profit over the lifetime of the product. This opportunity cost is shown in Table 7.

Table 7. Speed-to-Market (in terms of probability)

If your company is late to market by:

6 Mo.	5 Mo.	4 Mo.	3 Mo.	2 Mo.	1 Mo.

Your gross profit potential is reduced by:

–33%	–25%	–18%	–12%	–7%	–3%

Improve time-to-market by only 1 mo., profits improve:

+11.0%	+9.3%	+7.3%	+5.7%	+4.3%	+3.1%

For revenues of $25 Million, annual gross profit increases:

+$400K	+350K	+300K	+250K	200K	+150K

For revenues of $100 Million, annual gross profit increases:

$1600K	$1400K	$1200K	$1000K	$800K	$600L

Source: McKinsey and Company.

The strategic advantages of competing on time to market were made obvious by the Japanese and some small North American companies in the early 1980s. These companies compressed the time required to develop, manufacture and distribute their new products. These "time-based competitors" have been able to offer a broad array of products, cover more market segments and increase the technological sophistication of their products rapidly. Table 8 shows the basic response times for the fundamental value delivery systems of the major competitors in the automobile industry in Japan and the Western countries during the 1980s.

Table 8. The New Pace of Competition: World-Class Automobile Companies

Value Provided	Representative Cycle Times	
	Western	Japanese
Sales, order and distribution	16–26 days	6–8 days
Vehicle manufacturing	14–30 days	2–4 days
New vehicle design and introduction	4–6 years	$2\frac{1}{2}$–3 years
Median age of product offering	5 years	3 years

Source: Stalk and Hout, 1990.

Some of the advantages of decreasing time to market are: (Stalk & Hout, 1990, p. 31)

- *Productivity is increased.* Studies have shown that with every halving of cycle time and doubling of work-in-process turn, productivity is increased by 20 to 70 percent.

- *Companies can charge more for products.* The first to market advantage makes it possible for the company to charge more. Customers of time-based competitors are generally willing to pay more for products and services for both economic and subjective reasons.
- *Reduction of risks.* An advantage of the compression of time is the reduction of risk. Over or under-forecasting of sales has a financial impact on businesses. The further into the future the forecast, the higher the probability that the forecast will be wrong.
- *Market Share Advantage.* The company that gets its product to the market ahead of others has the advantage of capturing a larger share of the market and maintaining it due to brand loyalty.

There are, of course, some downsides to time competitiveness. Christopher VonBraun discusses this in detail (VonBraun 1990, 1991, 1993). One of his main points from his research is that everything else being equal, an average shortening of life cycles (usually a consequence of time-based competitiveness): ". . . would initially lead to a surge in overall company sales, but later, as life cycles settled down to a shorter period, overall sales would decline more rapidly. That is, over a product's life, a shorter product life cycle would result in a smaller sales volume." (VonBraun, 1998, p. 13)

As shown in Table 8, Japanese companies were on the average two to three times faster than the best Western companies in performing the necessary operations functions. This usually translates into better product offerings and higher market share.

The biggest challenge for time to market is the coordination of the different units that are involved in the production process. Several strategies, such as concurrent engineering and integrated product development teams have been developed to enable the process. Irrespective of what strategy is used, four tasks must be accomplished by the management of a company in order to become a time-based competitor:

1. Formulate a clear target and a concentrated action plan.
2. Provide the right tools.
3. Establish policies and procedures that unify various development functions.
4. Make the value-delivery systems of the company more flexible, responsive and faster than those of the competitors.

Accelerating Pace & Increasing Importance of Information Technology

In an earlier section on operations management and the technology revolution, there was a discussion of the impact of information technology. With increased demand for quick-response operations, a wide variety of customized products and short product life-cycles, information technology will continue to be a major competitive weapon. New information technology tools such as powerful desktop personal computers, client-server architectures, and open standards for information sharing have enabled operations managers to have greater control over their information systems. A study of a sample of manufacturing companies by the National Research Council showed that computer integrated operations reduced overall lead time by about 30 to 60 percent, increased operations productivity by about 40 to 70 percent and the quality of products by a factor of two or three.

The general prediction is that the factory of the future will require no direct labor. This will be enabled by the integration of product-process technology and the decision making and control managerial technology. Figure 6 illustrates how

Figure 6. Computer Integrated Factory of the Future

Computer	CAD/CAM
	Product Design and Analysis for Quality Assurance. Specifications to CAM to Plan for Manufacturing Plans and Feedback for CAD/CAM Interface

Physical Flow ⟶
Information Flow --►

Computer	Marketing
	Orders Fed in by Telecommunication Information on What to Make Including Special Designs Fed to CAD

Computer	Factory Management
	Planning, Scheduling, Materials Management, Costs, Quality Assurance, Shipping, and Distribution

Central Computers

Computer	Computer Aided Fabrication
	Parts Fabrication on NC and FMS Systems, Involving control and materials Movement

Computer	Automated Warehouse
	Robotic Movement of Materials for Storage and Order Picking. Automated Order Preparation and Delivery.

Computer	Automated Assembly
	Robotic Movement of Materials and Assembly. Automated Quality control and Production test.

Source: Starr, 1994, p. 799.

such a system would work. It has six major components, marketing, CAD/CAM, factory management, computer aided fabrication, automated assembly, and automated warehouse which are linked with one another and with a central corporate computer system.

The volume and the nature of information technology required to run operations will continue to increase at a dramatic pace. This will create new options and opportunities for meeting the needs of an increasingly diverse and demanding market. Wheelwright and Clark (1992) state:

> *Developing novel technologies and understanding existing technologies increase the variety of possible solutions available to engineers and marketers in their search for new products. Furthermore, the new solutions are not only diverse but also potentially transforming. New technologies in areas such as materials, electronics, and biology have the capacity to fundamentally change the character of a business and the nature of competition."* (p. 30)

Increasing Importance of Service Operations Management

Service operations are becoming increasingly more important because of the fact that the United States is now predominantly a service economy. The growth of services in our economy is going to continue.

Service operations differ from manufacturing in many ways. Services are intangible, generally labor intensive, consumed as they are created and usually involve subjective assessments.

A major challenge to operations management in the future will be how to improve the productivity of these services. In some cases, techniques and approaches that have been used in the manufacturing sector to handle scheduling problems, quality management, cost control and other operations problems can be adapted for the service sector. In other situations, totally new approaches must be developed.

Fragmented, Demanding Markets

It is becoming increasingly important for organizations to develop flexible production systems that enable mass customization of products and services. Changes in technology competition and consumer demands have accentuated the importance of mass customization. Pine (1993) emphasizes this through several examples such as in cars, where Buick has a suspension system that allows a driver to choose between a soft or a sport ride; in computers, where Toshiba alone produced more than 30 varieties of laptop computers between 1986 and 1990; and in diapers, where Procter and Gamble Pampers Phases line has 13 different product designs for different stages of growth in infants as they grow to toddlers. For an operations manager, this implies a vast increase in the number of styles or types produced and a sharp decline in the length of production runs.

CONCLUSION

A brief historical overview of the development of production/operations management was presented in this chapter. Starting with the Industrial Revolution, the United States became a leading producer of goods by developing mass manufacturing. In the 1980s and 1990s, however, U.S. companies have faced aggressive and efficient competitors from Japan, Taiwan, South Korea and Germany. These new competitors have succeeded not because they relied on abundant, cheap or low-cost labor and capital. Instead, they have introduced innovative procedures and approaches to the operations management problem.

As we approach the 21st century, companies are faced with new challenges in operations management. The competitive environment of rigorous international competition, fragmented market segments and niches, and diverse and rapidly accelerating technological change has created new demands on operations management. Speed, efficiency and quality are critical success factors. To succeed, companies must be able to respond effectively to constantly changing customer demands and the moves of global competitors. They must be fast, but they must also be efficient. With an increase in the number of new products and new process technologies and shrinking life cycles, firms must utilize substantially fewer resources for their operations in order to remain competitive.

Being fast and efficient is not enough. A firm must ensure that the products and processes it introduces meet a constantly changing customer demand for value, reliability, and unique or distinctive performance.

Firms that are able to accept these challenges will enjoy a significant competitive advantage and will prosper in the 21st century.

REFERENCES

Abernathy, W.J., Clark, K.B., & Kantrow, A.M. (1981, September–October). The new industrial competition. *Harvard Business Review*, 68–81.

Albrecht, K. (1992). *The only thing that matters*. New York: Harper Business.

Chase, R.B., & Aquilano, N. J. (1995). *Production and operations management, manufacturing and services*. Chicago: Richard D. Irwin.

Chase, R.B., & Garvin, D.A. (1989, July–August). The service factory. *Harvard Business Review* 67(4), 61–69.

Chase, R.B., & Prentis, E.L. (1987, October). Operations management: A field rediscovered. *Journal of Management, 13*(2), 351–366.

Cole, R.E. (1992, Winter). The quality revolution. *Production and Operations Management 1*(1).

Davenport, T., & Short, J. (1990, Summer). The new industrial engineering: Information technology and business process redesign. *Sloan Management Review*, 11–27.

Drucker, P.F. (1954). *The practice of management*. New York: Harper & Row.

Drucker, P.F. (1990, May–June). The emerging theory of manufacturing. *Harvard Business Review*, 94–102.

Duimering, P.R., Safayeni, F., & Purdy, L. (1993, Summer). Integrated manufacturing: Redesign the organization before implementing flexible technology. *Sloan Management Review*, 47–56.

Dumaine, Brian. (1989, February 13). How managers can succeed through speed. *Fortune*, 54–59.

Evans, J. R., Anderson, D.R., Sweeney, D.J., & Williams, T.A. (1990). *Applied production and operations management*. New York: West Publishing.

Giffi, C., Roth, A.V., & Sea, G.M. (1990). *Competing in world class manufacturing: America's 21st century challenge*. Homewood, IL: Business One Irwin.

Griffin, R.W., & Pustay, M.W. (1996). *International business*. Reading, MA: Addison-Wesley.

Heizer, J. & Render, B. (1999). *Principles of operations management*. New Jersey: Prentice Hall.

McClain, J. O., Thomas, J.L., & Mazzola, J.B. (1992). *Operation Management*. New Jersey: Prentice Hall.

Melynk, S., & Denzler, D. (1996). *Operations Management, A Value–Driven Approach*. Chicago: Richard Irwin.

Nolan, R.L., Stoddard, D.B., Davenport, T.H., & Jarvenpaa, S. (1995). *Reengineering the organization*. Boston: Harvard Business School Publishing.

Noori, H. (1990). *Managing the dynamics of new technology*. New Jersey: Prentice-Hall.

Pine, B.J., II. (1993). *Mass customization: The new frontier in business competition*. Cambridge, MA: Harvard Business School Press.

Plossl, G.W. (1991). *Management in the new world of manufacturing: How companies can improve operations to compete globally*. Englewood Cliffs, NJ: Prentice-Hall.

Russell, R., & Taylor III, B. (1995). *Operations management; Focusing on quality and competitiveness*. New Jersey: Prentice Hall.

Stalk, G., & Hout, T. (1990). *Competing against time*. New York: The Free Press.

Starr, M.K. (1989). *Managing production and operations*. New Jersey: Prentice-Hall.

Starr, M.K. (1975). *Management: A modern approach*. New York: Harcourt Brace Jovanovich.

Whyte, W.H., Jr. (1956). *The organization man*. New York: Simon & Schuster.

Von Braun, C.F. (1997). *The innovation war*. New Jersey: Prentice-Hall.

Chapter VII

Managing in the Information Age

Salvatore J. Monaco

OVERVIEW

The invention of the microchip by Texas Instruments in 1958 launched a technology explosion that has changed everything. Some 40 years after its birth, society still has not assimilated all the innovation that has resulted from this phenomenal invention. And in no field is this more apparent than in information technology.

The remarkable applications of this technology have fundamentally changed every industry, from health care to banking to automobile manufacturing. It has also changed the way individuals communicate, work, shop and play.

IT has changed the pace of commerce, the rules of engagement, and the very definition of organization. No other influence has had a more profound effect on business and on the way businesses interact with stakeholders. But one of the most important changes brought about by this technology, and one that is often overlooked in corporate training programs, is a change to the way organizations manage people and processes and the way they measure success.

The Need for Strategic Managers

Traditional management styles emphasize decision making, problem solving and risk avoidance. This is a result of compensation and incentives which emphasize the achievement of targeted performance goals, such as maximizing earnings or shareholder value. Faced with these reward structures, it is easy to see why senior management tends to focus on "managing by exception;" that is, an emphasis is put on eliminating or dealing with perturbations and preserving order within chaos. This style often takes a scientific approach by focusing on identifying, framing, and analyzing the most beneficial opportunities and implementing the chosen set of alternatives.

Although this has been a very successful model for the 70s, 80s, and even the first half of the 90s, corporate boards are now beginning to recognize the need for more innovative and strategic management styles. Today's managers are being asked to create new business cultures that involve crafting partnerships and building alliances that go beyond traditional business relationships. The information age has forced managers to re-think traditional paradigms and find new ways to compete, as most of the assumptions about business and organization have outlived their time.

Peter Drucker (1998) points out that today even "basic economics is turned on its head. The new basic resource, information, differs radically from all other commodities in that it does not stand under the scarcity theorem. On the contrary, it stands under an abundance theorem." And management must understand the implications of such change. Because information is not industry-specific, nor does it have a single end use, managers must constantly look outside their own industry for new customers and new technologies that will impact their business tomorrow.

IT As a Force of Change

Not only is IT redefining the economics of information, but it is also defining the new economics of corporate growth. In 1998 corporations spent over 1 trillion dollars on IT investment (Albrecht and Cortada, 1998)—and most analysts see this as an increasing trend (see Figure 1). It is obvious that firms perceive improvements in IT infrastructure as necessary for their very survival. But this worldwide growth in IT spending is about more than a pursuit of productivity by putting newer and more powerful networked work stations on employees' desks. It is about using technology to preserve and grow market share; to find new customers for existing products and services; and to identify new products and services to serve new markets. It is about maintaining and improving competitive advantage in a rapidly changing economy—one in which traditional industry norms are falling and new companies with emerging technologies are displacing corporate giants.

IT is allowing smaller and more flexible firms, often start-ups, to compete effectively with established market leaders. Companies like Federal Express, Wal-Mart and Amazon.com, have used information technology to redefine traditional standards, create competitive advantage, and become market leaders. In the case of Federal Express, innovative logistics combined with information technology allowed a small but more flexible private firm to become a world wide leader in small package delivery. This move was possible because Federal Express used information technology to exploit a market need—fast, highly reliable business-to-business delivery.

Figure 1. Growth in Corporate IT Spending

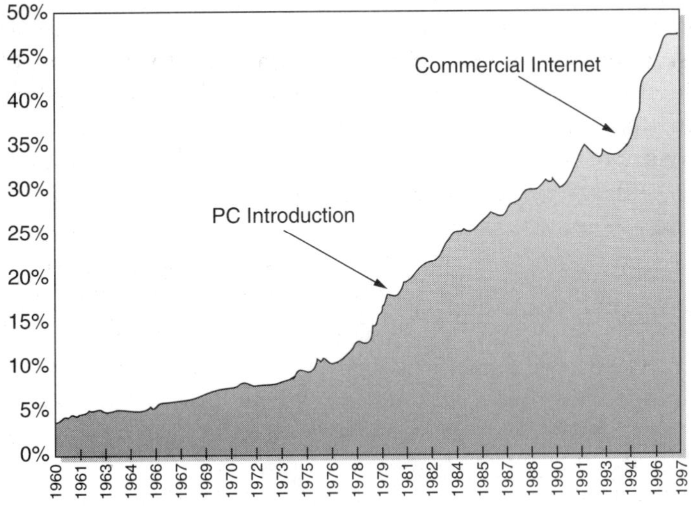

Source: U.S. Department of Commerce.

Sam Walton saw an opportunity to use state-of-the-art information technology to integrate inventory and distribution to reduce costs and manage its supply chain, overtaking K-Mart as the U.S. discount retailing giant. Jeff Bezos combined the power of the Internet with the needs of the consumer to create the almost perfect Internet business—Amazon.com. Perfect because the essence of a great bookstore is its stock of titles and the ease of finding the one title that a customer wants. With the virtual Internet store, Amazon.com's virtual stacks are essentially unlimited, allowing them to offer over 2.5 million titles, while even the largest superstores would be hard pressed to offer one tenth of that inventory.

But the success of Amazon.com was not just due to the number of titles it could carry, it was due largely to the use of a simple search engine to allow consumers to rapidly search in the convenience of their home or office for titles, authors, or subjects, combined with helpful information such as book reviews and summaries. In addition, the Amazon bookstore uses an intelligent agent to remember user preferences and alert and advise readers when new works reflecting their favorite subjects or authors are available.

None of these innovations would have been possible without advances in information technology—from automated inventory, ordering and shipping to electronic commerce over the Internet. In fact, Bezos is so aware of the importance of IT and Wal-Mart's competencies in it that he has hired many of Wal-Mart's IT employees and consultants since September 1997 to create Amazon's IT department (Leibovich, 1999). Wal-Mart, fearing its intellectual property was being pirated, filed a law suit against Amazon.com which was eventually settled out of court.

Federal Express used IT to exploit a market need—speed and reliability. In the case of Wal-Mart, IT changed the way inventory processes were managed and introduced just-in-time to retailing. And with Amazon.com, IT changed the way customers were serviced and fulfillment was managed.

As these examples illustrate, IT represents a significant opportunity for business. It also represents a significant challenge because firms that fail to effectively use IT as a strategic weapon will be quickly left behind. If knowledge, service, value and innovation are important, this challenge must be met if the successful firms of today are to endure.

IT Challenges

In this chapter we will examine how IT is challenging the skills, training and knowledge of managers by exploring three important ways IT is changing the nature of today's businesses:

- IT is increasing productivity and growth by providing the capability and tools to effectively manage knowledge assets.
- IT is redefining the traditional value chain and changes the rules of competition.
- IT is driving innovation by revolutionizing innovation and new product development.

IT AND KNOWLEDGE MANAGEMENT

Although knowledge management is the latest "management jargon," its definition is hardly an industry standard. For the purpose of this chapter, knowledge management will be defined as the effective communication of competencies, skills and collective wisdom that underlie a corporation's business success. Consulting firms have successfully implemented knowledge management in order to re-use models, processes, procedures, techniques and other "knowledge assets" that have been developed in the course of doing business. They have also used knowledge management techniques to solve clients' problems brought about by changes in the work environment caused by reengineering, downsizing and other change-producing mechanisms.

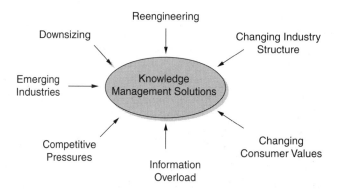

The majority of corporate executives generally agree on the benefits of managing these intellectual assets and see the need to do so. In a 1998 survey of 1,626 senior managers by the American Management Association (AMA), 53 percent said they either had or expected to have a knowledge management program in place, although they differ widely on how to do so (Wah, 1999).

Unfortunately, the literature does not provide a series of successful models to use as guides in knowledge management. Nevertheless, we can identify the processes which are necessary—the collection, cataloging, communication and distribution of intellectual assets.

IT is an enabling technology for effective knowledge management that can help implement these processes in three ways. First, it can supply the database to store explicit knowledge assets such as patents, proposals, copyrights, licenses, key contacts and relationships, and other proprietary information representing core capabilities and corporate best practices. Second, IT is the tool for the development of a cataloguing and retrieval system, i.e., a search engine, to make it easy for employees to identify and find these assets when the need arises.

Hansen, Nohria, and Tierney (1999) refer to this process as "codification." The natural outcome of this is the development of a flexible, interactive, document management system that codifies, stores, disseminates and allows "re-use" of knowledge. This typically requires a heavy investment in IT infrastructure to allow employees ready access to networked databases often enabled by a stand-alone Data Management Center.

A firm that employs the "re-use" model very well is American Management Systems. AMS has perfected the concept of "re-usable software" by developing modular software systems. This allows the company to adapt software built for one customer to other markets. AMS has not only been very successful at this, but the company considers this adaptation ability a core competence and competitive advantage (Schilleref, 1999).

A third way IT can help manage knowledge assets is by developing an interactive knowledge sharing environment—specialized networks to link employees who are then responsible for personal distribution of this knowledge. Here, tools such as video-conferencing, e-mail, intranets, and extranets are used to help build a personal networking and communication system that encourages the sharing of information.

Xerox researchers at Palo Alto Research Center (PARC) developed a system called "Eureka" which allows service representatives to easily enter their service tips in the form of "war stories"—an approach found to be very successful at facilitating the learning and transfer of this information. The system is easy to use, and Xerox management encourages its use by providing incentives to employees for helpful tips that are verified by an independent group. This employee recognition creates a self-sustaining system of contributions. Another example of interactive IT applications is at the World Bank, where experts and task leaders use the Internet to share knowledge and experience in solving economic development problems (Wah, 1999).

The critical requirement for success with this model is "encouraged sharing," and consequently, this type of process relies heavily on a supportive corporate culture. In the AMA survey, the most frequently cited obstacles among firms that had a knowledge management system were lack of employee involvement, the inability to measure results, and getting people to share their knowledge (Wah, 1999).

These knowledge management models are not mutually exclusive, and the best elements of each can and should be incorporated into a firm's knowledge management strategy. For that reason, it is helpful to view these models as IT processes that facilitate the strategic objective of creating a knowledge management system within the firm. Hansen, Nohvia and Trevney (1999) argue, however, that these models are distinctive enough that in most cases, firms rely on a single model for their strategy. The authors point out that firms tend to fall into two categories—those that focus on building an efficient system for "re-use," and those that focus on person-to-person sharing. Firms that use the re-use strategy tend to be growth driven and focus on business volume. Thus, the automated nature of this model supports rapid expansion, streamlines training, and requires a heavy investment in IT.

Firms with high profit margins, low sales volume, high interaction with customers and customized application tend to focus on developing systems that allow knowledge sharing. The overall IT investment is more moderate in this case, but the cost of personalization as enabled by one-on-one interaction may be quite high. In reality, although a firm may find one model is best for its situation, it will take elements of both models in order to have an effective knowledge management strategy. Regardless of which model is most appropriate, the methodology to develop a knowledge management process can be characterized by a set of discrete processes and enabling skills and technologies needed for successful implementation.

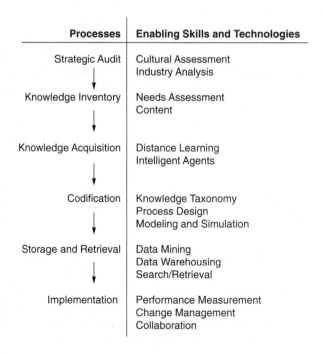

Processes	Enabling Skills and Technologies
Strategic Audit	Cultural Assessment Industry Analysis
Knowledge Inventory	Needs Assessment Content
Knowledge Acquisition	Distance Learning Intelligent Agents
Codification	Knowledge Taxonomy Process Design Modeling and Simulation
Storage and Retrieval	Data Mining Data Warehousing Search/Retrieval
Implementation	Performance Measurement Change Management Collaboration

The common result in all firms where knowledge management has been successfully implemented is higher customer and employee satisfaction, greater product and service innovation, and improved revenues and profitability. The lesson for management is that knowledge management should be viewed as a core competence and strategic objective of the firm, and IT infrastructure should be seen as a critical enabling technology. Consequently, management must provide top-down support and ensure the process employed is consistent with the culture, business model and overall strategy of the firm.

IT AND VALUE CREATION

While IT is facilitating the adoption of knowledge management in firms to create competitive advantage, managers are continuing to be challenged by the changing values of consumers. Responding to the fast pace of product innovation, consumers are continuing to demand more value from traditional products and services. Although the pursuit of best value is nothing new, the short shelf life of today's "hot products" and the abandonment of favorite brands for those offering more is a new phenomenon.

IT has enabled business to create new value relationships, i.e., to re-configure and re-invent traditional products and position these new products to capitalize on these changing values. A classic example is the demise of Encyclopedia Britannica.

Less than 10 years ago, Britannica was the dominant and high-end encyclopedia on the market. It had established a brand known for excellence and quality over decades of popular use. Yet, almost overnight, Microsoft's Encarta, a supermarket quality encyclopedia delivered on CD, overtook Britannica and World Book to become the best-selling encyclopedia ever.

What happened was a failure on the part of Britannica to recognize a basic shift in consumer values. Consumers generally purchased encyclopedias for their children's education. The increasing popularity and availability of the PC, combined with ease of use, the multimedia experience, and integrated search and copy and paste functions made Encarta the ideal tool for school-age children. Just ask an average 10, 12, or 15 year old whether he or she would rather interact with a book or a video game.

Britannica mistook the value customers formerly placed on quality and accuracy as unchangeable. But speed, flexibility, and fun won out. To compound the problem, for the same cost as a set of Britannica, consumers could purchase a PC that did much more.

Microsoft's innovation was to use IT to create a shift in values. Through the use of IT, qualities that were formally unattainable or too costly can now be achieved, creating a competitive shift in consumer buying preferences. Certainly, consumers have always preferred to listen to Mozart while researching his works, but they just did not realize it was attainable until recently.

The lesson for management is to learn how to discover and drive these potential shifts in consumer values. In Michael Porter's seminal work, *Competitive Strategy*, (1980) he points out the importance of the threat to product dominance from substitute products. Traditionally, managers have been able to monitor this threat through an awareness of trends and tracking of competitors within their industry. However, the cross functional implications of IT has challenged managers to expand their area of knowledge. Kim and Mauborgne (1999) point out that today's firms must look outside their own industry and experiences and be aware of potential substitutes (something that Britannica failed to do). Too often firms become wedded to the industry norms and fail to take advantage of new technologies, especially those developed outside the industry. Kim and Mauborgne have identified four ways that firms have created new consumer value by changing standard industry expectations: by reducing or raising certain standards, by eliminating some factors and by creating new factors (see Figure 2).

In addition to the Britannica example, consider the shift to online education. Education, particularly graduate education, has been slow to change. But some institutions, including University of Maryland University College's Graduate School, have recognized important changes in customer preferences.

UMUC's focus is adult learning, and its traditional student is in his or her mid-thirties and is working full time. The pressure of work, family, and academics is something that UMUC understands well, and it has designed its programs around high quality and high application of content to the business environment, while ensuring high convenience by offering classes in the evenings and on weekends in numerous satellite locations.

Understanding the need for convenience and flexibility led the university in the late 1980s to pioneer the "distance delivery" of graduate courses using interactive video and cable television. However, when new technologies became available, it was quick to choose Internet-based asynchronous delivery, recognizing the very high degree of flexibility this would provide.

Although the university anticipated rapid acceptance, it was unprepared for the virtual overflowing classrooms. Students rushing to online classes pushed enrollments up more than 50 percent each semester since the program's inception in 1997. And this was not just for out-of-region students. In fact, most students

Figure 2. Creating a New Value Curve

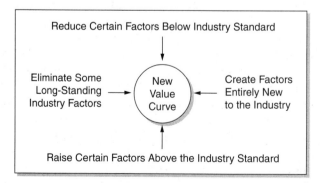

Source: Kim and Mauborgne (1999).

taking these courses were from the local area and could have chosen a tradition-al classroom course.

In short, students were willing to give up more predictable, stable and "easy-to-use" traditional face-to-face formats for courses offering a very high degree of flexibility and convenience. Busy professionals balancing job and family needs found Internet-based courses, where they did not have to set aside a fixed time period each week, and where they did not have to leave the home or office to enter the classroom, a much greater value (see Figure 3).

Figure 3. Shifting Consumer Values

Product characteristic	Britannica	Encarta
Cost	very high	very low
Quality of articles	very high	low to moderate
Accuracy of articles	very high	moderate
Ease of use	moderate	very high (search engine)
Media	text, photos	text, photos, video, audio
Editing tools	none	cut & paste into MS apps
Link to internet	none	in later versions
Updates	moderate cost new volume, not integrated	low cost, fully integrated updates

Product characteristic	Traditional classroom	On-line class
Cost	same	same
Quality	high and proven	high, but unproven
Convenience	low to moderate	very high
Flexibility	low	very high
Focus	instructor centered	student centered
Media capability	multimedia capable, but varies widely depending on instructor	limited internet-based multimedia; CD multimedia
Social interaction	moderate to high	low to moderate
Ease of use	very high	moderate to high

As more and more consumers and businesses get wired, i.e., communicate with each other electronically, the way buyers and sellers interact will continue to change the economics of competition (see figures 4, 5 and 6). Evans and Wurster (1997) identify one of the drivers in this "new economics" as a change in the fundamental business maxim of having to trade off richness for reach. The authors define "richness" as a function of:

- Bandwidth: the amount of information that can be moved from sender to receiver in a given time.

- Degree of Customization: e.g., a TV advertisement (less) vs. a one-on-one sales pitch (more).

- Interactivity: dialogue (small groups) vs. monologue (masses).

Figure 4. Worldwide Online Consumers

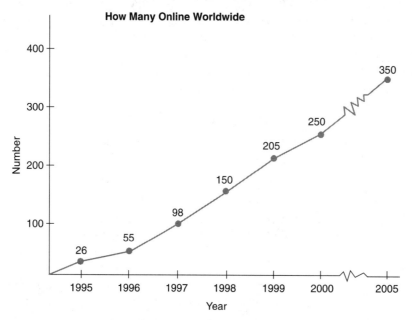

Source: NUA Internet Surveys.

Figure 5. Electronic Commerce in the U.S. (1998)

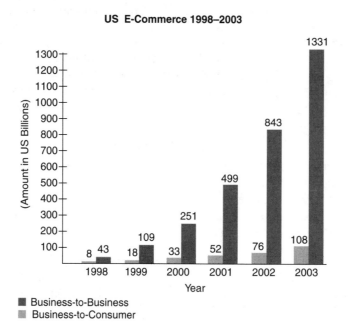

Source: NUA Internet Surveys.

Figure 6. Historical and Projected Internet Revenues

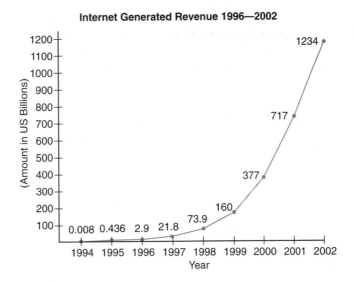

Source: NUA Internet Surveys.

Consequently, according to Evans and Wurster (1997), the greater the bandwidth, customization and interactivity, the richer the exchange.

"Reach" represents the size of the audience. In the traditional context, businesses face a very steep loss in richness as they wish to extend their reach (see Figure 7). Evans and Wurster (1997) argue that the information explosion which is connecting more people and businesses with open standards at essentially zero cost via the Internet is re-defining this relationship and flattening the curve—thus allowing both reach and richness.

Figure 7. Information Economics

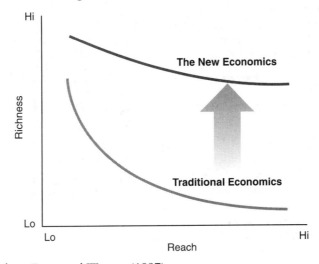

Adapted from Evans and Wurster (1997).

Firms that have successfully achieved this balance have flourished. The success of Amazon.com and other Internet stores such as Buy.com and Beyond.com and Internet portals such as Yahoo and Excite, has not been about new and innovative products or services, but about the way in which those products and services are delivered. Other examples are the changes taking place in the financial services industry. The Internet is quickly outdating the branch bank and changing the competitive landscape. Today, traditional banks are competing with online brokerages including Fidelity, Schwab, and Discover, as well as virtual banks like Security First National Bank (www.sfnb.com)—a successful bank that offers a full complement of services without bricks and mortar. It exists only on the Internet.

The implication of this new economics is important for corporate strategy as well. Effective strategic thinking is not about positioning the corporation to compete today, but in the future. Unfortunately, it is not easy to envision how traditional values and exploding information economics will continue to re-define industries, but we do know the directions they are taking and there are lessons to be learned from the remarkable changes that have already taken place. Some of these lessons are:

- Firms must recognize the value of substitution and look externally at other industries and other technologies in order to identify shifting customer values early and be ready to innovate in product, service and delivery.

- Firms must recognize that competitive advantage in certain markets can be fragile, particularly when based on established value chain relationships. Information technology can alter and change these relationships. For example, the competitive advantage of a volume discount retailer dealing in software, such as Best Buy, may be destroyed by a company like Beyond.com that has the advantage not only of selling, but in many cases, delivering software over the Internet.

- The rapid advances in information technology are creating a need for new information agents or navigators that can learn consumer preferences and help firms identify and procure the best value in products and services. Consider, for example, the impact on retail discount stores of an Internet store that can locate a brand item or service, whether it is a TV, software, flowers, or a plumber, procure it at a guaranteed low price, and schedule the delivery or service at the customer's convenience. Or consider an intelligent agent that can navigate the maze of long distance choices for consumers and identify the lowest cost service (given the day of the week, time of day and call destination), dial the required prefix and connect seamlessly. When such agents become available, a firm's strategy based on image, brand name, or discount pricing must be re-examined. For example, current research has shown that Internet shoppers show no preference for traditional retailers with an Internet presence and, in fact, prefer the new Internet start-ups (Walker, 1999).

THE ROLE OF IT IN INNOVATION AND NEW PRODUCT DEVELOPMENT

While IT can aid innovation by managing intellectual assets and by creating new value paradigms, its role is even more critical in the creation of new products and services. In the 1990s corporate managers have come to recognize an effective information system not only as essential for order fulfillment and customer service (see Figure 8), but also as an effective tool to facilitate innovation and accelerate the process of new product development.

Drucker (1985), in his seminal work on innovation, explains that innovation arises out of opportunities and can be categorized but not predicted. He cites three sources of innovation external to the firm: demographic changes, perception changes (on the part of consumers), and new knowledge (at least new to the firm or industry). Another source this author would add is industry and market creation, since technological advances have allowed visionaries and pioneers to create entirely new industries and markets, e.g., desktop publishing, digital imaging, e-commerce (see Figure 9).

Although these sources are neither exhaustive nor mutually exclusive, they serve as helpful categories for managers to better understand why ongoing innovation within a firm is largely a strategic process.

For example, those who followed changing demographics, and in particular the baby boomers, recognized that their children represented a growing teenage population with access to more technology such as cable television and videos. This led to the popularization of the music video as entertainment for this growing age group and, consequently, the creation of MTV. Similarly, the growth of the baby boomer population drove the desire for minivans and, later, sport utility vehicles.

Figure 8. The Framework for New Product Development

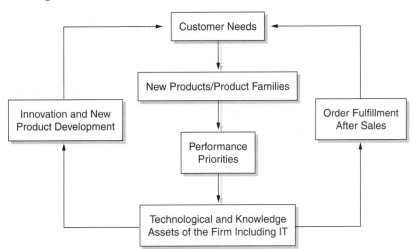

The developing trend, as the boomers now move into the 50-and-over population bracket, is a rising consumer interest in wellness centers—more user-friendly fitness centers. Rather than catering to body sculpting and intensive exercise, these centers focus on the needs of an older population that wants to stay healthy and fit.

Changes in consumer perception, another driving force behind innovation, brought about the demand for lower cost, less customized investment services for the middle class. The importance of convenience and flexibility as the traditional families were replaced by two-wage earners and single parents, together with the proliferation of home PC's, brought about the electronic revolution in online banking. As discussed earlier, educational institutions are finding this same desire for flexibility and convenience on the part of adult learners is driving new delivery models for higher education including online classes.

Besides impacting product and service delivery, breakthroughs in technology have also spawned new knowledge that has led to new products. The automobile, television, and personal computer are examples of innovation brought about by new knowledge. Although these are the type of product inventions the term innovation conveys, these pioneering efforts represent the minority of new innovation, albeit in each case they have brought substantial changes to consumers' every day lives. Finally, technology has also created entirely new industries such as digital photography, desktop publishing, and the new pervasive Internet store.

IT has served as facilitator and catalyst in most of these sources of innovation, and, in the latest advances such as the PC, distance education, and e-commerce, it has been the fundamental underlying technology. But IT helps the

Figure 9. External Sources of Innovation

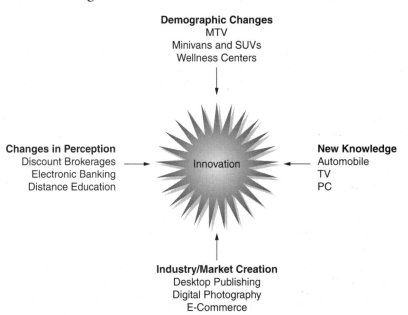

innovation process in a supporting role by helping managers gather information about what is going on not only on the outside, but inside the organization as well. Current examples of this are the new accounting tools of Activity Based Costing (ABC), Economic Value Added (EVA) and the Balanced Scorecard.

Although these accounting tools focus on the proper role of management—the creation of value rather than the avoidance of waste—they are essentially financial systems. Managers must recognize the importance of using these tools to do much more: to collect information on demographics, public perception, new technologies, and new and emerging markets that will drive future innovation in the firm.

To illustrate this point, Drucker (1998) notes that managers were surprised and unprepared for the financial collapse in Asia because of their focus on inside rather than outside information. All the data, all the symptoms and all the critical elements including country debt and balance payments were in place to predict the Asian collapse a year ahead of time. In the next 10 to 15 years, the harvesting and synthesis of this information will represent the next information frontier.

Although the intelligent community has invested heavily in this area for more than 10 years, private firms are just beginning to recognize the importance of open source information for competitive intelligence. Effective strategic planning is virtually impossible without this outside information. IT's role here is not only as a tool for data collection and management, but more importantly as a filtering agent. The real value of IT is in its ability to collect and help evaluate economic, financial, demographic and scientific information from a variety of sources. Without a filter, managers would be faced with information overload, and because of the inability to assess all the data, would hesitate to use any data at all. Intelligent agents will facilitate this filtering and evaluation process, and as this becomes more powerful and sophisticated, they will serve as one of the enabling technologies in the future of information management.

The output of the innovation process is new products and services. Information technology is allowing firms to set new competitive standards by speeding up the process of new product development. IT's inherent flexibility allows product developers to continue to define and shape products even after innovation has begun (Iasanti & MacCormack, 1997).

This is critically important in today's markets which are driven by change in both technology (new knowledge) and customer preferences during the development process. The classical product development approach has been linear and sequential. Starting with needs assessment, functional specifications detailing how the product will perform and operate are developed, a product concept is then designed, finalized, and frozen. Finally, the actual development occurs with little or no changes to the design (see Figure 10).

Most firms recognize the need for a more flexible product development process. Flexible development has been particularly critical for the emerging and rapidly changing markets of the Internet, primarily because of short product life cycles and rapidly changing preferences as new technologies emerge. It is important to be able to change the concept design late in the development process based

Figure 10. Fixed vs. Flexible Product Development

Fixed Product Development

Needs Assessment	Concept Design	Development and Launch

Flexible Product Development

Needs Assessment

Concept Design

Development and Launch

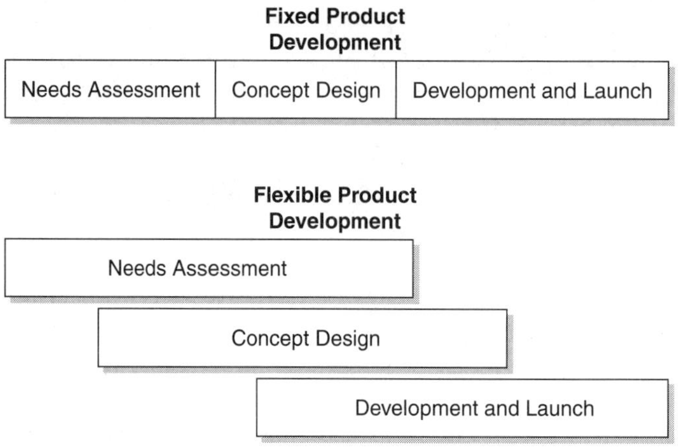

on changes in needs. Companies such as Netscape and Microsoft have made extensive use of early prototyping, testing and user feedback to fix bugs and make key design changes through releasing successively better versions of their web browsers. Whether the testing is performed on the Internet by external users, on intranets by internal staff, or by a selected set of lead users is irrelevant to the final result—flexible development leading to rapid prototyping and feedback through most of the development process.

The key to flexible development is the overlap of needs assessment, concept design, and development, facilitated by the use of information technology. IT is used to continuously assess and update customer preferences, to help designers and customers "virtualize" product performance, and to allow developers to rapidly move changes from the drawing board into production.

And software products are not the only products to benefit from this new use of technology. In fact, many traditional manufacturing firms are finding similar advantages using information technology. Iasanti and MacCormack (1997) cite an excellent example of the automaker Fiat's use of the Internet to speed the development process. At a cost of only $35,000, Fiat created a Web site to generate distance feedback on the design for the next generation Pinto, its best-selling model. Fiat's software asked customers to fill out a survey indicating their preferences for style, comfort, performance, price and safety. They were even asked to design a prototype using software that allowed them to select body style, wheel design, front and rear ends, headlamps and a variety of other features.

In three months, the company received 30,000 surveys from 31–40 year-olds with high income who were frequent auto buyers—their ideal target population. The software used not only captured the results, but tracked the sequence the respondents used to select their options. This helped designers understand the logic customers used to evaluate key design features.

Other major corporations such as GM, Boeing and Lockheed Martin use simulation and computer aided designs as well as customer feedback to test and identify the need for changes in product design. The Boeing 777, arguably the most complex commercial product ever built, was completely developed using key digital design technology.

As information technology continues to advance, managers should expect even more advances in flexible development. For years, the Japanese have been using virtual reality to enable consumers to help design home improvement projects such as new kitchens or baths. Virtual reality allows customers to experience how customized products will feel and perform for them. For example, a customer taking a virtual tour of a remodeled kitchen can see how the placement of drawers and cabinets will work, identifying storage areas that may be too high or work space that is too fragmented.

General Motors is using virtual reality software to allow customers to obtain digital tours of the next generation locomotive even as development proceeds. And the Department of Defense is considering using virtual reality to design the next generation of advanced weapons systems.

Although these products and industries differ greatly, the one thing they all have in common is the use of IT to integrate tasks, perfect and synchronize design changes, and continuously capture customer feedback. Managers should be ready for the evolution of the next generation product which may well make use of intelligent agents and the Internet to provide immediate customer feedback and self diagnostics to its designers.

LOOKING TO THE FUTURE

One of the most interesting consequences to the introduction of new information technologies to the workplace is in the way in which it has changed the traditional interaction between employees and managers. For example, new tools such as e-mail have opened new methods of communication and destroyed many traditional hierarchical barriers. Management is suddenly more accessible, and employees are not hesitating to send ideas, suggestions and comments up the chain of command.

IT is also introducing the virtual office concept, i.e., teleworking. On the surface, this seems like a win-win arrangement for managers and employees. Managers get to reduce overhead and lower costs, while employees gain increased flexibility and convenience. In theory, productivity should increase as well, as employees spend less non-productive time traveling and in meetings. However, a recent example that occurred at a large telecommunications firm illustrates what can go wrong when mangers are unprepared.

Although sales people were allowed to telework, they found they were being called together for meetings much more frequently—often two or three times per week. This was destroying the advantages of teleworking as well as the advantages for managers who wanted their salespeople out of the office visiting clients. What happened was that middle managers felt threatened by the loss of central control and oversight brought about by teleworking. To compensate, they called more meetings so they would feel more comfortable.

This example is an unfortunate reaction to the fact that IT is flattening the organizational hierarchy and allowing more flexible work environments. Managers must recognize that these changes can have negative effects on productivity and morale in the short term, but if handled properly will eventually produce the desired results. In most organizations, LANs and WANs with powerful software tools have eliminated the need for administrative layers, including, in some cases, middle management. As a result of these new productivity tools management expects employees to do more so they can recognize the cost advantages of large investments in infrastructure. Employees, on the other hand, are becoming more self sufficient, and in some cases, more isolated from their traditional support systems.

Unfortunately, this openness, while facilitating communication and the flow of ideas, can also be threatening to some managers, requiring a change in traditional communications with employees. As this trend continues, it poses a challenge for managers. They must find new ways to communicate and integrate employees into strategic activities. Here again, IT appears to offer solutions. Employees can keep in touch through e-mail and intranets with the day-to-day activities of the firm. As most managers know, interaction and communication between manager and employee is not sufficient. To be effective and productive, most knowledge workers need to interact with others so they can share ideas, tools of the trade, and best practices. The lesson for managers is that they can expect employees to be more productive and effective only if their environment, whether it is a physical or virtual office, provides the IT infrastructure to allow this type of open communication.

How fast will technology continue to change the economics of competition? Only imagination can say for sure. But consider some recent examples of how IT is changing everyday life. Cattle ranchers are managing their herds better because each steer is equipped with a microchip that continuously beams out the animal's location. The Federal Aviation Administration is experimenting with a decentralized "free flight" system allowing aircraft to choose their own flight path (Bernstein, 1998). Consumers are using "smart cards"—credit card size devices with embedded microchips and operating systems—to securely access public transportation, banking and telecommunications services (Strassel & Bank, 1998).

How will the information economy, and specifically information technology continue to shape and change the way organizations are managed? Such a forecast is not the objective of this chapter, but managers of tomorrow would do well to learn from what is working today and the factors that drive innovation and creativity (demographics, new knowledge, customer perceptions, and market creation). This chapter has discussed the obvious ones: the Internet with its open technology, scalability, efficiency and pervasive growth; also supporting technologies such as speech recognition, encryption, virtual reality and intelligent agents. The future will likely mark the use of these new and emerging technologies, and management must be able to lead in this new economy.

In this regard, management's role is difficult because it is dynamic and constantly evolving. Effective managers of tomorrow must be flexible, creative, and comfortable with uncertainty and risk. The IT revolution has insured that the era of status quo conservatism is over.

REFERENCES

Albrecht, M. & Cortada, J. (Summer,1998). Optimizing investments in information technology *National Productivity Review*, 53–60.

Bernstein, P. (1998, Nov.–Dec.). Are networks driving the new economy? *Harvard Business Review*, 159–166.

Drucker, P. (1985). *Innovation and entrepreneurship: Practice and principles.* New York: Harper & Row.

Drucker, P. (1998, Aug. 24). The next information revolution. *Forbes*, 46–58.

Drucker, P. (1998, Oct. 5). Management's new paradigms. *Forbes*, 152–177.

Evans, P. & Wurster, P. (1997, Sept.–Oct.). Strategy and the new economics of information. *Harvard Business Review*, 71–82.

Hansen, M., Nohvia, N. & Trevney, T. (1999, March–April). What's your strategy for managing knowledge. *Harvard Business Review*, 106–116.

Iasanti, M. & MacCormack, A. (1997, Sept.–Oct.). Developing products on Internet time. *Harvard Business Review*, 108–117.

Kim, C. & Mauborgne, R. (1999, Jan.–Feb.). Creating new market space. *Harvard Business Review*, 83–93.

Porter, M. (1980). *Competitive strategy.* New York: Simon and Schuster.

Schillereff, R. (1999, March 29). New at the Top. *Washington Post*, B16.

Strassel, K. & Bank, D. (1998, October 26). Microsoft to unveil smart card operating system. *The Wall Street Journal*, B6.

NUA Internet Surveys (1999, June 21). NUA Analysis Index of Graphs and Charts [Online]. Available: http://www.nua.ie/surveys/analysis/graphs_charts/index.html.

Wah, L. (1999, April). Behind the buzz. *Management Review*, 17–26.

Walker, L. (1999, April 1). Losing sleep in a mattress war. *The Washington Post*, E1, E6.

Chapter VIII

Financial Systems

ROBERT P. OUELLETTE

INTRODUCTION

Why should we care about financial systems? Because the greatest sin any enterprise can commit is to run out of money. Money and finance play a central role in the start-up, growth, maturity, decline, survival, and prosperity of any business organization. Understanding the historical roots, the development paths, the changing perspectives, and the successes and failures of financial systems in the American context can help managers, at any stage of the business cycle, to extract the lessons of history and apply them to the moment.

Besides that, financial systems is a vibrant discipline, with daily findings from research, new results from applications, and substantial changes in teaching practices. And much debate on the subject is taking place in specialized circles and in the public press. To demonstrate the value and actuality of financial systems, this review begins with a few of today's "hot" issues, such as the incorporation of non-financial factors in traditional accounting, the valuation of intellectual assets, and the emergence of international standards. This review focuses on some of the exciting changes taking place, not at the periphery, but at the heart of financial systems. Following the section on current issues, the text turns to a more traditional presentation of this burgeoning field, with an overview of financial systems; their historical roots; theories and practices; laws, regulations and standards; the impact of information technology; and finally, a look at the future of financial systems. Systems theory is used as a framework throughout this review.

CURRENT ISSUES

This section covers several current issues that shape the present and future of financial systems. These burning issues include the use of non-financial parameters in accounting (environmental protection is a case in point), the valuation of intangible assets (e.g., intellectual property), and the development of international financial standards.

Use of Non-Financial Measures in Management Accounting—The Case of Environmental Protection

In recent years, a great deal of interest has developed in incorporating in traditional accounting systems non-financial measures of performance, with the aim of better reflecting the activities of the firm. Measures such as customer satisfaction, sales volume, levels of defects and other measures have been used to better capture the full spectrum of the enterprise's operations (Hemmer, 1996).

The protection of the environment and the prevention of pollution are required under U.S. federal, state, and local laws and regulations (as described in detail below). The rising cost of environmental protection, its potentially significant impact on the income statement and balance sheet, and the financial consequences of pollution prevention programs have attracted the attention of financial managers (Bennett & James, 1997).

Effective managerial accounting of environmental issues requires the collection, analysis and reporting of two kinds of information: physical/chemical quantities, such as water and energy used and waste generated; and costs associated with use, processing and disposal. These costs might include labor, material, equipment, building, depreciation, interest, liability and permitting (White, 1993).

Total cost assessment (TCA) has become "de rigeur." TCA is a systematic process that includes four elements: cost inventory, cost allocation, time horizon, and financial indicators.

Cost inventory focuses on identifying all cost elements that belong to the analysis and includes quantification of all relevant cost and benefit elements. Cost allocation is concerned with the proper allocation of cost elements to specific processes and operations. A mass balance is usually developed for all operations and the plants to facilitate that allocation. Time horizon refers to the time element associated with an initiative. For example, profitability may be associated with pollution prevention investments. Financial indicators are the traditional indicators (net present value, internal rate of return) used to characterize return on investments.

Only such a full cost accounting can determine whether and when pollution prevention programs pay off. This full cost accounting is a natural extension of activity-based costing (Kirschner, 1994; Schaltegger & Muller, 1997). But, this is only the tip of the iceberg.

A call has been made in recent years to price all materials and products according to their societal and environmental impacts. This is a controversial, complex and conflicted program that has not been embraced by all. However, environmental accounting is slowly being implemented by American industry to incorporate non-regulatory environmental costs, to consider savings from pollution prevention, and as a method to improve decision making.

The accounting and reporting requirements for environmental liabilities and contingencies are, in principle, no different than those for other liabilities. The difficulty arises in adequately estimating actual and potential costs and meeting disclosure requirements. The accounting guidance can be found in a number of documents within the generally accepted accounting practices (GAAP) hierarchical structure (Munter & Sacasas, 1996).

The tracking of environmental components raises many issues. How much capital will be required to keep up with regulatory changes? How much of the environmental liabilities should be reported on financial statements and to regulatory bodies? Can all environment costs be embedded in the price of products and services? American industry is only starting to provide answers to these questions.

Valuation of Intangible Assets—The Case of Intellectual Property

Valuation is used in portfolio management, in acquisition analysis, and in corporate finance. Three approaches are used in valuation: the discounted cash flow valuation method, which estimates the present value of expected future cash flows on assets; the relative valuation method, which estimates value based on the pricing of comparable assets; and the contingent claim valuation method, which uses pricing models to measure the value of an asset (Damodaran, 1996). These methods have been used to value traditional assets as well as bonds, future contracts, real estate and intellectual property. In this section, the focus is on this last special case.

Intangible assets include intellectual property (such as trademarks, patents, copyrights, know-how, trade secrets, software and databases), brands, licenses, and publishing rights (Bertolotti, 1995; Elgison, 1992). Intellectual assets valuation comes into play in cases of mergers and acquisitions, fund raising and licensing agreements. There is a consensus that such "soft" assets are identifiable as separate entities and capable of being valued.

A recent review of the 500 firms in the Standard & Poor's 500 composite stock price index (which accounts for approximately 70 percent of the value of all publicly traded companies) reveals fixed assets worth $1.2 trillion in 1995. The intangible assets of the same group of companies were estimated to value $3.4 trillion (Myers, 1996). These numbers raise important issues in terms of valuation, reporting and disclosure.

Three basic methods are commonly used in intellectual property valuation. The cost method involves summing all the costs previously invested in creating the asset. Inflation rate and required rates of return, commensurate with risk, are factored into the analysis. The economic valuation method involves the quantification of the cash flows attributable to the asset and the capitalization of these cash flows. The market value method involves securing value based on prices recently obtained by other organizations in similar transactions (Bertolotti, 1995).

Development of International Financial Standards

International financial standards are coming. As in many other arenas, America may be the last country to adopt them. The International Accounting Standards Committee (IASC) is on target for standardization, and the International Organization of Securities Commission (IOSCO) has focused on a common goal to develop core accounting standards that produce reliable, high quality information (Pacter, 1998) in terms of assets, liabilities, profits and losses. The goal is to achieve global consistency in performance measurement, disclosure, and reporting.

The need for international standards is obvious. With the globalization of markets and the rise of multinational companies, investors and lenders have gone global. This globalization is favored by advances in technology and communication and national initiatives toward deregulation (Hora, Tondkar & Adhikari, 1997). Such standards would facilitate international finance activities.

The reasons that American corporations and government agencies are reluctant to favor international standards are that U.S. standards tend to be more stringent and demanding, and that the United States represents the largest economy in the world. The current position in the United States, while not uniform, is that more rigor and stringency is required. The battle lines are drawn, with the U.S. Congress, major stock exchanges, professional groups, corporations, and investors taking positions.

Adopting international standards should not be that difficult, especially when considering the willingness of foreign corporations (some 1000 of them) to comply with the generally accepted accounting practices (GAAP) of the United States in order to trade on U.S. exchanges (Byrnes, 1998). With the implementation of the North American Free Trade Agreement (NAFTA), the rise of regional alliances such as the European Union (EU), and the desire to enhance the ability of foreign corporations to access U.S. markets, the pressure will mount for the United States to adapt to the rest of the world.

OVERVIEW OF FINANCIAL SYSTEMS

The American financial system is a complex web of actors, elements, and relationships (see Figure 1). Organizational objectives, inputs, users, processes and outputs are critical components of this system. The financial systems of American firms are firmly embedded in the economic system of the country, and the country's economic system continuously interacts with other parallel and overlapping countries' economies. The environment in which the U.S. enterprise operates is peppered with legal, regulatory, standards, advisory, and participatory bodies, each with a different mission and goals (detailed below). The presence of these disparate stakeholders requires constant vigilance for changes in the disclosure and reporting of the financial health of the organization. This is the task of financial accounting. The internal environment in which the management accounting information is used is worth emphasizing. A complex web of interrelationships exists between disparate elements, with feedback loops that create a largely non-linear system that is open to the environment and sensitive to chaotic behavior (Greenberg, 1996).

Figure 1. Financial Systems Overview

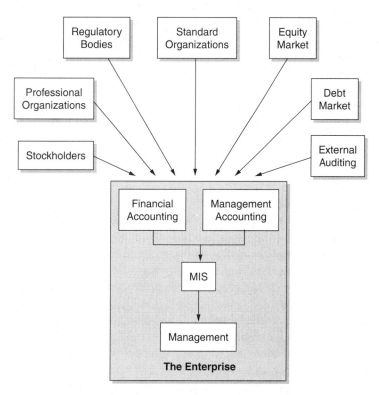

The firm or enterprise is the center of the financial system. Today, it is becoming increasingly difficult to define the boundary of the firm. Strategic alliances, virtual companies, and horizontal and vertical integration all contribute to fuzzy edges. Indeed, the modern firm can be described as a hard core of competencies, values and assets protected by a more fluid belt that serves to absorb shock and deflect attacks.

HISTORICAL ROOTS OF AMERICAN FINANCIAL SYSTEMS

In 1492, Christopher Columbus discovered America; in 1494, Luca Pacioli invented double-entry bookkeeping (Shank, 1995). Both moments have had a lasting effect on the world. Pacioli proposed an accounting system consisting of three books: a day book, a journal and a ledger, tools that are still in use today. While great strides have been made in the last 500 years, this basic three-book concept is still the core of all accounting activities. This section provides a chronological identification of defining moments and the birth of ideas, the evolution of concepts, and the modification of practices of financial systems in the United States over the last 200-plus years.

From a business point of view, the American colonies were based on mercantilism exported from Europe, with overseas trade as the main form of business transaction (Ballam, 1994). By the 1790s, this mercantilism had been replaced by Adam Smith's concepts of growth, progress, and the wealth of individuals.

Starting in the 1780s, the government promoted economic development and used its political power to mobilize U.S. resources. It encouraged transportation and shipping, reduced duties on imported goods, and subsidized domestic manufacturers (Henretta & Nobles, 1987). The period from 1780 through the 1790s saw a dramatic push in mechanized manufacturing, often portrayed as a method for young America to gain economic and political independence from previous continental ties. Before 1776, there were no banks in America, but by 1791, the Congress established the first Bank of the United States to promote monetary stability (although state-chartered banks were already in existence in several states).

Prior to the 1800s, farmers, small businessmen, merchants and artisans stood at the center of commerce. From 1800 to 1860, the population grew dramatically (from 5.3 million to 31.4 million). The non-farm labor force had grown to 47 percent and per-capita wealth was rising (Henretta & Nobles, 1987). During this period, the accumulation of foreign and domestic capital fostered a substantial increase in national prosperity that has not abated since. Already, by 1820, the United States had become a highly developed pre-industrial society with a diverse economy and a thriving export. By 1840, most corporations used charts of accounts, journals, ledgers, trial balances and periodic accounting as a guide to management. During that same period, a transition from all-purpose merchants to business specialists took place (Lookingbill, 1997). By 1850, the United States was one of the leading industrial nations. The American rail network, begun in the 1830s, helped defeat a hostile environment, linked the east and the west coasts, but more than anything else, opened access to vast resources and created a national market for goods and services.

The growth of a manufacturing economy impacted society with the rapid growth of towns and cities. Farms produced the major export material in flour, tobacco, rice, meat and cotton. The 1860 to 1920 period saw the rise of big business (Porter, 1992). The enthusiastic embracing of the market system, the growth of scientific management, and the rise in wealth spawned large-scale enterprise. By 1910, matching, accruals, depreciation, formal external reporting, and financial auditing were firmly established.

This last century, in spite of ups and downs, is a study in economic growth, diversity and prosperity, as the United States moved from a century based on steam power and engines to a century centered around electronics. The United States is now poised to enter the 21st century—the century of biology—as a leader in technology, business productivity and management acumen.

But it's not all large businesses driving the economy. In the United States, entrepreneurs have played a key role in generating technological solutions, devising marketing strategies, and improving management systems (Lookingbill, 1997). This golden age began shortly after the end of the second world war and has been fed by science and driven by technology.

By 1950, strong CEOs with financial backgrounds appeared on the scene of larger businesses, and this trend has continued to today where professional business personnel are charged with managing the firm for the owners. This period saw a focus on disclosure, financial reporting and management by exception. New, more sophisticated tools, such as break-even analysis, contribution margin analysis, and statistical estimation of cost functions were developed (Thomas, 1998).

By the 1960s, "power tools" were in use by accountants. These included five-year plans, annual profit budgets and monthly variance reports. By that time, information technology had become a close ally to accountants and finance specialists.

In the 1970s and early 1980s, developments appeared that were to lead to activity-based cost management. Today, the popular model of the firm is ecology-oriented. Concepts borrowed from biology, including competition, cooperation, evolution, co-evolution and niche, are being assiduously applied to developing, growing, and managing the firm to ensure its growth and prosperity (Moore, 1996; Carr, 1996).

EVOLUTION OF THEORIES AND PRACTICES

Financial accounting gathers information for users outside of the organization, such as shareholders, creditors, and government bodies (SEC, IRS). Managerial accounting gathers information directed at managers inside the firm, for the purposes of planning, controlling and directing operations. Both are strongly affected and motivated by theories and models of financial systems.

Models and Theories

A series of evolving models and theories provides the underpinning for the economic and financial structure erected in the United States over the last 500 years. These social, economic and political models and theories color financial systems in practice. Many stories can be told of the rise and fall of such models and theories.

Supply side economics is a philosophy aimed at stimulating economic growth and employment through improved incentives to producers and employers. The economic theory of government predicts that government officials will be swayed by their own interest, more than by the people they serve in selecting policies for implementation. Social theories recognize the centrality of social control in organizations. Contingency theory is one of many organizational theories with a decision-making perspective.

The basic tenet of these theories is that centralized organizations with tight control are applicable to organizations facing simple technology and a stable task environment, while loose control is better applied to decentralized organizations facing dynamic and complex tasks. The central idea is that organizational structures are contingent upon contextual factors where uncertainty prevails. Hopefully, both types of organizational structures can adapt to changes.

These social, political and economic theories shape the U.S. financial system. A number of models and theories have been developed over the years to provide a firmer foundation for financial decision making. Reviewed below are some of the more lasting models and theories, including the theory of the firm, the accounting model, the market efficiency hypothesis, the capital asset pricing model, the Modigliani and Miller capital structure thesis, the portfolio theory, and the theory of constraints.

Theory of the Firm

In 1932, Adolf Berle and Gardiner Means published *The Modern Corporation and Private Property*. In 1937, Ronald Coase published a classic paper titled the *Nature of the Firm*. Both publications addressed a fundamental financial question: Should ownership be divorced from control? (Bolton & Scharfstein, 1998; Holmstrom & Roberts, 1998). The situation in the intervening years has not changed, at least in the case of the larger firms. On the other hand, smaller firms tend to be employee-owned and managed. Recent studies seem to indicate that this separation between ownership and control is an inherent feature of the firm governance system and is actually a most efficient solution to decision-making problems (Bainbridge, 1995).

Accounting Model

The accounting model that emerged in the 1900s is a historical cost, transaction-based model. The current accounting model is the so-called mixed-attribute, transaction-based model that is no longer limited to historical costs but includes market values, realizable values and present values. It has been proposed that this current model should be replaced with a fair-value model, where fair market value is defined as the price obtained between a willing buyer and a willing seller (Swieringa, 1997).

Market Efficiency Hypothesis

Most financial models assume "market efficiency" and a "rational man" (used here as a generic term to refer to men, women, and computer software involved in financial transactions). We owe the hypothesis of market efficiency to the Frenchman Eugene Fama who outlined it in a paper published in 1965. The principle of market efficiency holds that competition among investors ensures that the current prices of broadly traded assets are good predictors of the future value of these securities. In other words, the full effect of information on intrinsic value is reflected in actual prices.

Many researchers and practitioners have commented that it is correct to observe that markets are frequently efficient, but it is not accurate to conclude that they are always efficient. This perspective is often lost on casual investors and professionals alike. The term "efficient market" means efficiency in terms of information. The actual definition of an informationally efficient market has four components: information has no cost and is available to all at the same time; there are no transaction costs, taxes or other barriers; price cannot be affected by a single person or organization; and all participants in trade are rational maximizers of expected utility. Obviously, these conditions are met only in utopia. In practice, there is a strong asymmetry of information, where inside managers of the firm have superior knowledge over outsiders about their own firm and its future prospects.

Economists are fond of the notion of the "rational man" and the idea that people assess the costs and benefits of their actions that have economic consequences. The notion of the rational man can be traced back to Adam Smith's *The Wealth of Nations* in 1776 and his concept of self interest and the maximization of individual profit. This rational theory of cooperation is largely untested and

Adam Smith (1723–1790). Copyright © Corbis-Bettman.

has come, lately, under attack from behavioral scientists. Their main point is that cooperation requires repeated interactions over a long period of time and requires the implementation of a complex utility function. The contribution from ecology will probably be enlarged, since evolutionary biology probably provides a better model for cooperative strategies than does economics (Dugatkin, 1999).

Capital Asset Pricing Model

The capital asset pricing model (CAPM) that postulates a relationship between risk and expected return, and that embodies the efficiency principle, was developed independently by William Sharpe, John Lintner and Jan Moissin (Ball, 1998; Litner, 1965; Moissin, 1969; Sharpe, 1964). The CAPM is the model of choice for risk, and beta (regression coefficient) is the measure of risk. The model has become the method of choice for estimating investors' expected return. The CAPM is used by institutional investors to define asset allocation and for defining the criteria for measuring performance. Industrial corporations use the same model for establishing their rate of return targets for investments.

Modigliani/Miller Capital Structure Thesis

In 1958, Franco Modigliani and Merton Miller (MM) published a theory of capital explaining how a firm should raise capital needed to acquire a variety of assets. They reached the surprising conclusion that the value of a firm depends solely on its future earning stream. The corollary is that the value of the firm is unaffected by the debt/equity mix used in financing the enterprise and that the stock price is not related to the mix of debt and equity financing. This irrelevance thesis was based on severe assumptions that were relaxed in a 1963 paper (Modigliani & Miller, 1963). The modified MM thesis is called the tax savings–financial cost trade-off theory. The conclusion is that stock price is related to debt financing, that a certain amount of debt is good, and that there is an optimal amount of debt for every firm. This review of the MM thesis provides an important lesson. Models are somewhat descriptive, but they are mostly normative; that is, they tell how investors, managers, buyers, consumers, etc. should act. When discrepancies between models' predictions and actual behaviors persist, the model requires modification.

Portfolio Theory

The modern portfolio theory is credited to Harry Markowitz (1952). The basic idea behind the theory is that investors should combine risky assets into a portfolio to minimize overall risk. The riskiness of each asset in isolation should be replaced by the contribution of each asset to the diversified portfolio.

Theory of Constraints

The idea behind the theory of constraints (TOC) is that managing product costs may lead managers to make decisions that are not in the long-term interest of the firm. TOC was developed by Eli Goldratt in the early 1980s (Goldratt, 1990). It concentrates on throughput-sales minus material costs. This measure is equated with contribution margin. Traditional accounting defines contribution margin as the difference between selling prices and all variable costs. Specifically, TOC uses measures of throughput, inventory and operating expense. A constraint is any factor that limits the ability of the firm (or a part thereof) to achieve stated goals. A wide variety of internal and external constraints are considered, including market demand, vendor quality, plant capacity, managers' skill and worker productivity (Louderback & Patterson, 1996). The central premise of the theory is that once constraints have been identified, they can be overcome, thus improving overall system performance.

TOC provides a set of well-defined measures called throughput-per-unit accounting (TA) (Ruhl, 1997a; Ruhl, 1977b). The relative merits of the theory are being recognized as more firms implement the model and obtain dramatic improvements in lead time, cycle time, product quality, and smaller inventory. (The method finds its best applicability in manufacturing and assembly line operations.) The major limitation to its broad implementation is the difficulty of reconciling its measures and results with traditional accounting.

Putting Theories to Work: Practical Applications

All of the models and theories mentioned above have had a significant impact on decision makers and, in spite of often unrealistic assumptions, they provide a useful framework for financial decision making. Unfortunately, most of these models and theories are not very good at explaining real-world behaviors, and considerable research effort is often directed to matching theories to practice. Nevertheless, most financial decisions are driven by one or more of these theories. In the sections that follow these models and theories are translated into practical applications.

Financial systems cover many aspects of the enterprise, from accounting (cost accounting, financial statements preparation, disclosure, tax), to risk management, to budgeting, to defining the capital structure, to the valuation of assets. This section reviews these current practices.

Explaining a real-world behavior. Successful investor Warren Buffett testifies in a congressional hearing. Copyright © Archive Films/Archive Photos.

Costs

Several cost concepts are important in cost accounting. Costs are clearly related to organizational, product and environmental contexts. Costs are often classified based on functions requiring an understanding of time-period costs or product-related costs. Direct costs are those that can be tied directly to material or labor used in manufacturing a product or service. All other costs are considered indirect costs. Cost drivers can be related to process units, batch, and product-sustaining or facility-sustaining activities. Collecting information about costs involves identifying activity costs and determining activity cost drivers.

The typical cost system in use today is a two-stage allocation method. It involves first determining indirect costs associated with production and support functions. The second step is identifying specific costs associated with each department. Because this simplified approach creates distortion in cost accounting, activity-based costing (ABC) has arisen. Basically, the method assigns a cost proportional to the demand for activities, material and support.

In the late 1950s and 1960s, a new concept emerged at General Electric—activity-based management (ABM). The idea behind ABM was the building of overhead cost data from information about activities. ABM can be defined by its three components: (1) an action component featuring the identification of opportunities based on on-going analysis and emphasizing performance measurement and improvement; (2) an information/cost component providing a detailed analysis of all activity costs; and (3) an evolution component that refers to constant, systematic evolution from a tedious effort to a responsive support of management decision making (Anderson, 1995).

In the 1970s and early 1980s, the idea arose in the Scovill Corporation for improving how overhead costs are constructed by tracing them back to products and other cost objects. This technique is now known as activity-based product costing (ABC) (Johnson, 1995). ABC has become popular in the United States. In 1996, approximately 49 percent of the firms were adopting ABC for strategic decision making and/or for financial reporting (Allnoch, 1997).

Activity-based costing has received considerable attention in the technical literature (Cooper, 1990; Cooper & Kaplan, 1992; Cooper, 1995; Cooper & Kaplan, 1991a, 1991b). These authors maintain that costs are driven by activities that take place at four levels: unit level, batch level, product-sustaining level and facility-sustaining level. Activities at unit-level are proportional to the volume of production. Batch-level activities are performed in proportion to the number of production batches. Product-sustaining activities are performed to support the production of a slate of products. Facility-sustaining activities are performed to maintain the production facility itself (Ittner & Larcker, 1997).

Put more simply, activity-based costing measures costs and performance of activities, assigns costs to activities, and recognizes that there is a causal relationship between cost drivers and activities (Turney, 1992).

Activity-based costing has evolved and matured and has transformed the way management looks at cost items. Because of its complexity and its demands for extensive data collection, ABC will not likely become used universally. Efforts are underway to save the basic concept while simplifying the overall effort (Brimson,

1998) and still focus on investment justification and performance measurement (Troxel & Webber, 1990).

Auditing and Control

Risk assessment, control and auditing are part of the governance function of the firm. Effective performance in this area starts with business objectives that must include profitability; the minimization of unnecessary costs; the safeguarding of assets; the avoidance of unintentional exposure; the prevention, detection, and correction of errors; the discharge of statutory and contractual responsibilities; and the production of reliable records and internal and external reports. Traditionally, these responsibilities have been placed in the hands of auditors. Auditors tend to focus on formal accounting control mechanisms and oftentimes these are not consistent with total quality management objectives. Actually, these governance responsibilities must rest with the management of the firm, and while not ignoring formal procedures, they should focus more on the control of risk, management integrity, ethics, training, management competence, morale, hiring and discharge practices, and communication.

Budgeting

Budgets are developed annually and often ignored. Budgeting is either done in a bottom-up fashion starting with profit centers, or in a top-down approach based on guidelines issued from the CEO. The bottom-up budgets rarely meet the corporate goals, and the top-down budgets are often impossible to achieve.

A decentralized approach to budgeting has recently been favored in an attempt to stimulate entrepreneurial behavior in private and public firms. When operating departments are given more discretion in planning funding and expenditures, greater effectiveness and accountability ensue (Cothran, 1993).

Two new approaches being explored are budgeting profitability and replacing budgeting with forecasting (Nolan, 1998). The first idea is to create clear links between budgets and actual measures of profitability using activity-based costing. The second idea is to use rolling forecasts to edit projections and link dynamically profit centers and operations.

Capital Structure

Many factors are involved in defining the most optimal capital structure (debt plus equity) for the firm. Leverage, liquidity, the structure of debt, and the sensitivity of liabilities to change in inflation and interest rates are all critical factors (Staking & Babbel, 1995). Corporations raise capital by selling a broad range of securities. The central idea is for the firm to sell claims to investors at a price that is larger than the cost to the firm of satisfying those claims (since financial securities are claims against the firm's assets).

Financial Reporting

Publicly traded firms are subject to exacting sets of rules on reporting and disclosure. Forms 10K and 10Q are major annual and monthly vehicles for reporting on the finance and other aspects of the firm to the Security and Exchange Commission.

Annual reports, proxy statements and annual shareholder meetings are the major methods of communication with shareholders. The rise of activism on issues such as officers' remuneration and environmental protection has forced an additional degree of formalism in these annual rituals.

The true purpose of financial analysis is the prediction of the future. The income statement, balance sheet, statement of cash flows, and ratios analysis are all part of financial analysis of the firm. Unfortunately, these analyses are often distorted by factors such as inflation, seasonal factors, and differences in accounting treatment.

Taxes

In 1773, a band of American patriots dumped chests of tea into Boston harbor in a protest of British taxation that became known as the "Boston Tea Party." Americans dislike taxation, especially without representation. Benjamin Franklin

Benjamin Franklin (1706–1790). Courtesy of Library of Congress.

summarized the view of his time: "Our new Constitution is now established, and has an appearance that promises permanency, but in this world nothing can be said to be certain except death and taxes" (Franklin, 1789). Perceptions have not changed much from his day to today.

The U.S. tax system, established by an Act of Congress on October 3, 1913, is a labyrinth of laws, rules, regulations and case law. Obviously, the Internal Revenue Service would like to collect the maximum amount of taxes, and the firm would like to pay the minimum amount of taxes. This constant tension has been a source of great creativity and frustration.

Taxation has important implications for stockholders. Returns to stockholders, in the form of dividends, are paid with after-tax dollars (or earnings), but returns to creditors are paid with before-tax income. The result of this asymmetric taxation rule is that more of a company's income is available to investors when more debt financing is used by the firm as part of its capital structure.

LAWS, REGULATIONS, AND STANDARDS

The U.S. economy and the financial systems of the firm are strongly affected by government actions. These actions are wide-ranging, but the most important are monetary policies, trade agreements, and rules and regulations related to process. Regulations represent a combination of interests: social, political and economic.

Regulations in the United States take the form of "command and control," that is, rules are enacted and violators are punished. Most controls are in the form of financial disincentives, such as fines. Regulations are here to stay. The only questions are what form they will take and what impact they will have. Clearly, regulations affect the performance of the economy and the firm, especially in global markets (Eisner, 1993).

Regulations are enacted by all branches of government following the enactment of laws by the U.S. Congress. The Congress tends to react to crisis, responds to the wishes of members' constituents, and sometimes involves itself in the development of rational plans. The United States is a very litigious society, thus the courts play a major role in interpreting legislation and regulations through opinions and rulings (Whicker, 1993).

The body of rules and regulations affecting enterprise has grown gargantuan in size, labyrinthine in scope and insidious in effect. Table 1 summarizes most of the relevant rules and regulations that impact businesses. The table is organized into four periods or regimes: (1) The market regime, which grew in response to the rise of the corporate economy and focuses on market governance; (2) The societal regime, which encompasses control and compensation for rampant capitalism and focuses on industrial stability; (3) The asocietal regime of the political economy which focuses on the prevention of hazards; and (4) The efficiency regime which focuses on supply-side economics and deregulation aimed at the elimination of policies that hinder market mechanisms (Eisner, 1993).

Table 1. Legislative and Regulatory Summary

Regulation of Markets and Unfair Business Practices

1890 Sherman Act	Prohibit agreements to restrain trade
1914 Clayton Antitrust Act	Outlaw abuses such as bribery, false statements, stifling of competition, predatory pricing
1934 The Securities Exchange Act	Create SEC
1936 The Robinson-Patman Act	Prohibits practices that lessen competition

Regulation of Management-Labor Relations

1935 Wagner Act	Rights of workers to organize and bargain collectively
1936 Walsh-Healy Act	Workers paid prevailing wage and overtime
1938 Fair Labor Standards Act	Maximum of 40 hours/week work Minimum wage
1947 The Taft-Harley Act	Protection of management and business against labor
1974 The Employment Retirement Income Security Act	Regulate and protect private pensions for workers

Regulation of the Environment and Consumer Protection

1960 The Federal Hazardous Substances Act	Preclude the introduction of any banned hazardous substance into interstate commerce
1968 The Consumer Protection Act	Truth in Lending
!969 The National Environmental Policy Act	Requires environmental impact statements
1970 The Clear Air Act	Establish emission standards
1970 The Environmental Quality Improvement Act	Mandate the protection of environmental quality
1972 The Coastal Zone Management act	Encourage states to develop programs to manage land in water use in coastal zones
1972 The Federal Environmental Pesticide Control Act	Requires registration of pesticides
1972 The Noise Control Act	Standard concerning emissions from trucks, buses, trains and other surface motor carriers
1973 The Endangered Species Act	Protect endangered and threatened species
1975 The Hazardous Material Transportation Act	Regulate the transport of hazardous material
1975 The Magnuson-Moss Warranty Federal Trade Commission Improvement Act	Rules concerning honoring manufacturer warrantees
1975 The Federal Equal Credit Opportunity Act	Prohibit discrimination among credit applicants
1976 The Federal Land Policy and Management Act	Guidelines concerning the sale of federal lands
1977 The Clean Water Act	Regulate water pollution through permits
1982 The Nuclear Waste Policy Act	Regulation for permanent repositories

Table 1. Legislative and Regulatory Summary (continued)

Supply Side Deregulation

1978 Airline Deregulation Act	Protect airlines against unreasonable competition
1980 Staggers Rail Act	Deregulate railroads
1980 Motor Carrier Act	Relax federal control over trucking

According to an analysis by the Brookings Institution (Schultze, 1999), Americans are ambivalent concerning the role of government in society in general, and in business in particular. All Americans want national security, an available retirement program, equal access to information, education, and the like, availability of health care, a clean environment, etc. Most Americans complain about the bureaucracy and inefficiency of government in dealing with the problems of a modern society. According to Schultze, society has become more complex and has forced government to intervene more frequently and more acutely in the activities and decisions of consumers and business people. This probably cannot be reversed, but the role played by government, especially the federal government, can be changed from one that forces citizens and businesses to take certain steps, to one that encourages them to achieve the same results through tax and transfer arrangements and other incentives. This would convert public goals into private interests, causing less pain.

INFORMATION TECHNOLOGY AND FINANCIAL SYSTEMS

America's financial systems have been forged in the smith shop of the economy on the anvil of the marketplace, fired by competition, fed by the oxygen of technological innovation, and hammered by laws, rules and regulations. In recent years, rapid changes in information technology have had the greatest impact on the evolution of the nation's financial systems.

Emancipation Role of Information Technology (IT)

Span of control, hierarchical reporting, linear flow of data and information are just a few of many traditional concepts being displaced by information technology. The richness of the information base, as well as the interactivity it provides between workers and management are part of a transformation process that solves traditional problems while creating new ones, such as security, sabotage, massive loss of information, and incompatibility (Moscove, Simkin & Bagranoff, 1999). The modern automated accounting information system is a delicate integration of hardware, software, data, people and procedures.

A number of American firms have sought in recent years to improve business performance through the use of more sophisticated information technology tools. Among these are knowledge-based systems (KBS), expert systems (ES) and software agents (SA).

Software agents can accomplish intelligently a number of functions traditionally assigned to humans. These activities include purchasing, negotiating price, and controlling inventory. Agents are able to perform all of these tasks because they have been imbued with autonomy, collaborative behavior, and inferential capability and given sets of objectives integrated to achieve common goals through accomplishing tasks and coordinating activities (Wang, 1999; Huhns & Singh, 1998).

Electronic Commerce: The Awakening Giant

This is the dawning of the age of electronic commerce. Business transacted over the Internet was valued at $43 million in 1998. It is projected to reach $109 million by the end of 1999 and $1.3 billion by the year 2003 (Frook & Karpinski, 1999). Originally created for consumer on-line purchases, the real niche for e-commerce is business-to-business transactions related to billing, payment, and cash management (Warner, Smith & Larson, 1999). A growing number of e-corporations, combining computers, the Web, enterprise software and extranet, are transforming the consumer marketplace, ending the tyranny of geography and creating a distributed economy (Hamel & Sampler, 1998).

Digital technology and open architecture are the primary drivers for the growth of e-commerce, creating an unprecedented "marketspace." The factors that affect the growth of e-commerce include speed, availability, reliability and security. Among these, privacy and security continue to receive the highest level of attention. Another area of concern and technology development at the forefront of e-commerce is digital signature.

Electronic commerce includes electronic funds transfer (EFT), a form of electronic cash, and computer-to-computer transactions, with suppliers and others using electronic data interchange (EDI). Billing and electronic payment, after some reticence from industrial and individual customers, are benefiting greatly from the new technology. Some 12 billion recurring bills are sent annually to consumers and businesses through the U.S. mail. Eliminating the paper, postage, and delays associated with physical handling is likely to reduce the cost per bill handling by about half (Silverman, 1998). These potential savings will force corporations to rethink and redesign their accounting systems to secure the benefits (more profit) and offer better service. But, billing is not the only choice. Businesses will be able to carry out electronically a variety of financial transactions. It is estimated that by the end of 1999, 65 percent of large American corporations will be using e-commerce routinely, enjoying savings in costs and time (Shultz, 1999).

Among the business leaders in e-commerce are financial services, the utilities, and the auto industry. Banks will find e-commerce lucrative, with an estimated 50 million households projected to be on-line by the year 2003 and 65 percent of banks offering the service (Constanzo, 1999). But, the participation rate of households will pale in comparison to commercial financial transactions. It is estimated that 40 to 50 million small and medium-size businesses and commercial customers will join the ranks of the large businesses already taking advantage of the technology. As new markets open, new entrants rapidly emerge. The breakthroughs in e-commerce are fueling competition between traditional banks and "non-banks" such as insurance companies. Nonbanks are likely to rise to become the premiere full-service financial institutions (Bloom, 1999).

The battle plans and business strategies have been developed (Mougayar, 1998) and the economics of electronic commerce appears very favorable (Choi, Stahl & Whinston, 1997).

THE FUTURE OF FINANCIAL SYSTEMS

In the 21st century, more than ever, knowledge will represent power, and intellectual capital will become the most valuable form of property. Financial managers will be knowledge integrators, providing fiduciary oversight by protecting assets and reporting extensively to regulatory bodies, integrating financial and non-financial information for planning and evaluation of performance, analyzing data and information to support decisions at all levels, and generally advising management and becoming full partners in the enterprise (Sharman, 1996).

Fundamental to this new role will be the ability to recognize the root cause of cost drivers, to account for costs through activity-based costing, outsource non-core and non-cost-effective functions, build relationships with a wide range of stakeholders including suppliers and customers, and play an external as well as a traditional internal role (Foster, 1996).

Financial systems are responding and will continue to respond to a changing economy, including the globalization and interdependence of markets, the shift to a self-service economy, the shortening of product life cycles, the primacy of the customer, and the rapid changes in technology (Boer, 1996). While the core data systems used in accounting and finance will remain the same, the need to access data and information in a timely manner, and the ability to design and produce reports on demand, will require a new flexibility and discipline (Johnson, 1995).

Cost accounting, as currently practiced, does not have much relevancy to the management decision-making process. The need for increased internal efficiencies and rapid changes in the external economic environment will call for a realignment between accounting and other functions such as engineering, marketing, and manufacturing (Rezaee & Tsuji, 1998).

SUMMARY

Financial systems are the common denominator of the enterprise and of all its activities. This chapter is addressed to managers who wish to understand the pervasive role of financial systems in the business decision-making process.

The chapter endeavors to identify major financial issues facing management today. These issues are placed in the context of the development of management theories and practices in America. Because of that context, the history, character and social circumstances of the American business shape the issues discussed. However, because of the central role of American business in the world economy, because of the globalization of markets, and because of the internationalization of standards, this review is applicable to businesses around the world.

The point of view presented in this chapter is that the practice of financial systems is evolving rapidly toward liberation from historical constraints to become a more useful tool for managers. And, that the theoretical foundation of these practices, while sometime weak, is improving as the financial edifice is being renovated and strengthened through research.

The hope of this chapter is that a systems approach will become institutionalized in the teaching, research and practice of financial systems in universities and corporations.

REFERENCES

Allnoch, A. (1997). ABC gains popularity as decision-making tool. *IIE Solutions, 29*(7), 13–15.

Anderson, T. (1995). ABC evolution. *IIE Solutions, 27*(6), 26–30.

Bainbridge, S. M. (1995). The politics of corporate governance. *Harvard Journal of Law & Public Policy, 18* (3), 671–735.

Ball, R. (1998). The theory of stock market efficiency: accomplishments and limitations, In: Stern, Joel M. & Chew, Donald H. *The revolution in corporate finance* (2–15). Malden, MA: Blackwell Business.

Ballam, D. A. (1994). The evolution of the government-business relationship in the United States: colonial times to present. *American Business Law Journal, 31*(4), 553–641.

Bennet, M. & James, P. (1997). Environment-related management accounting: Current practice and future trends. *Greener Management International, 17,* 32–52.

Berle, A. & Means, G. (1968 rev. ed.). *The modern corporation and private property*. New York: Hartcourt, Brace and World.

Bertolotti, N. (1995). Valuing intellectual property. *Managing Intellectual Property, 46,* 288–295.

Bloom, J. K. (1999). Nonbanks gave banks a run for clients' money. *American Banker, 164* (1), 17.

Boer, G. (1996). Management accounting beyond the year 2000. *Journal of Cost Management, 9*(4), 46–50.

Bolton, P. & Scharfstein, D. S. (1998). Corporate finance, the theory of the firm, and organization. *Journal of Economic Perspectives, 12*(4), 95–105.

Brimson, J. A. (1998). Feature costing: Beyond ABC. *Journal of Cost Management, 12* (1), 6–13.

Byrnes, N. (1998). Needed: Accounting the world can trust. *Business Week, 3/5/99,* 46.

Carr, C. (1996). *Choice, change and organizational change*. New York: American Management Association.

Choi, S., Stahl, D. O., & Whinston, A. B. (1997). *The economics of electronic commerce*. Indianapolis, IN: Macmillan Technical Publishing.

Coase, R. (1937). The nature of the firm. *Economica, 4,* 386–405.

Constanzo, C. (1999) 1999 Seen as e-commerce turning point for banks, *American Banker, 144*(4), 1–4.

Cooper, R. (1990). Cost classification in unit-based and activity-based manufacturing cost systems. *Journal of Cost Management, Fall,* 4–14.

Cooper, R. (1995). Activity-based costing: theory and practice. In *Handbook of cost management,* edited by B.J. Brinker, Boston: Warren, Gorham & Lamont.

Cooper, R. & Kaplan, R. S. (1991a). Profit priorities from activity-based costing. *Harvard Business Review, 69,* 130–135.

Cooper, R. & Kaplan, R. S. (1991b). *The design of cost management systems: Text, cases and readings.* Englewood Cliffs, NJ: Prentice Hall.

Cooper, R. & Kaplan, R. S. (1992). Activity-based systems: measuring the cost resource usage. *Acounting Horizons, 6,* 1–13.

Cothran, D. (1993). Entrepreneurial budgeting: an emerging reform? *Public Administration Review, 53*(5), 445–463.

Damodran, A. (1996). *Investment valuation: tools and techniques for determining the value of any asset.* New York: John Wiley & Sons, Inc.

Dugatkin, L. (1999). *Cheating monkeys and citizen bees: the nature of cooperation in animals and humans.* New York: The Free Press.

Eisner, M. A. (1993). *Regulatory politics in transition.* Baltimore: The Johns Hopkins University Press.

Elgison, M. (1992). Capitalyzing on the financial value of patents, trademarks and other intellectual property. *Corporate Cash Flow Magazine, 13*(12), 30–37.

Fama, E. F. (1965). The behavior of stock market prices. *Journal of Business, February,* 34–105.

Foster, G. (1996). Management accounting in 2000. *Journal of Cost Management, 9*(4), 36–40.

Franklin, B. (1789). Letter to Jean Batiste Leroy (dated November 13, 1789) in Bartlett, John and Kaplan, Justin (1992) *Bartlett's familiar quotation,* Boston: Little, Brown and Company.

Frook, J. E. & Karpinski, R. (1999). Electronic commerce poised for critical mass. Available January 11, 1999, http://www.internetwk.com/news0199/news011199-8.htm.

Gardiner, S. (1994). The evolution of the theory of constraints. *Industrial Management, 36*(3), 13–21.

Goldratt, E. M. (1990). *Theory of constraints.* New York: North River Press.

Greenberg, P. S. (1996). Using a systems perspective in cost/management accounting to teach learning and thinking skills. *Issues in Accounting Education, 11*(2), 297–314.

Hamel, G. & Sampler, J. (1998). The e-corporation. *Fortune, 138*(11), 80–87.

Hemmer, T. (1996). On the design and choice of 'modern' management accounting measures. *Journal of Management Accounting Research, 8,* 87–117.

Henretta, J. A. & Nobles, G. H. (1987). *Evolution and revolution: American society, 1600–1820.* Lexington, MA: DC Heath and Company.

Holmstrom, B. & Roberts, J. (1998). The boundaries of the firm revisited. *Journal of Economic Perspectives, 12*(4), 73–95.

Hora, J. A., Tondkar, R. H., & Adhikari, A. (1997). International Accounting Standards in Capital Markets. *Journal of International Accounting Auditing & Taxation, 6*(2), 171–181.

Huhns, M. N. & Singh, M. P. (1998). *Readings in agents.* San Francisco: Morgan Kauffman Publishers, Inc.

Ittner, C. D. & Larcker, D. F. (1997). The activity-based cost hierarchy, production policies and firm profitability. *Journal of Management Accounting Research, 9,* 143–163.

Johnson, H. T. (1995). Management accounting in the 21st century. *Journal of Cost Management, 9*(3), 15–20.

Kirschner, E. (1994). Full-cost accounting for the environment. *Chemical Week, 154*(9), 25–27.

Lintner, J. (1965). Security, prices and maximal gains from diversification. *Journal of Finance, Dec,* 587–616.

Lookingbill, B. (1997). Making business history: an annotated bibliography. *American Studies International, 35*(3), 4–22.

Louderback, J. G. & Patterson, J. W. (1996). Theory of constraints versus traditional management accounting. *Accounting Education, 1*(2), 189–197.

Markowitz, H. (1952). Portfolio selection. *Journal of Finance,* 77–91

Modigliani, F. & Miller, M. H. (1958). The cost of capital, corporation finance and the theory of investment. *American Economic Review, June,* 261–297.

Modigliani, F. & Miller, M. H. (1963). Taxes and the cost of capital: a correction. *American Economic Review, June,* 433–443.

Moissin, J. (1969). Security prices, risk and investment criteria in competitive markets. *American Economic Review, Dec,* 749–756.

Moore, J. E. (1996). *The death of competition.* New York: HarperBusiness.

Moscove, S. A., Simkin, M. GT., & Bagranoff, N. A. (1999). *Core concepts of accounting information systems.* 6th edition, New York: John Wiley & Sons.

Mougayar, W. (1998). *Opening digital market.* New York: McGraw-Hill.

Munter, P. & Sacasas, R. (1996). Accounting and disclosure of environmental contingencies. *CPA Journal, 66*(1), 36–41.

Myers, R. (1996). Getting a grip on intangibles. *CFO, The Magazine for Senior Financial Executives, 12*(9), 49–55.

Nolan, G. J. (1998). The end of traditional budgeting. *Bank Accounting & Finance, 11*(4), 29–35.

Pacter, P. (1998). International accounting standards: The world's standards by 2002. *CPA Journal, 68*(7), 14–20.

Polanyi, K. (1944). *The great transformation: the political and economic origins of our time.* Boston: Beacon Press.

Porter, G. (1992). (2nd edition) *The rise of big business: 1860–1920.* Arlington Heights, IL: Harlan Davidson, Inc.

Rezaee, Z. & Tsuji, A. (1998). Studies in accounting history: tradition and innovation for the twenty-first century. *Atlantic Economic Journal, 26*(2), 214–232.

Ruhl, J. M. (1997a). Managing constraints. *The CPA Journal, 67*(1), 60–65.

Ruhl, J. M. (1997b). The theory of constraints within a cost management framework. *Journal of Cost Management, 11*(6), 16–25.

Schaltegger, S. & Muller, K. (1997). Calculating the true profitability of pollution prevention. *Greener Management International, 17,* 53–69.

Schultze, C. L. (1977). *The public use of private interest.*Washington: The Brookings Institution.

Shank, J. K. (1995). Theme issue on management accounting: Wither and whence? *Journal of Cost Management, 9*(3), 3–6.

Sharman, P. (1996). Putting it all together: Management accounting in the year 2000. *Journal of Cost Management, 10*(2):3–5.

Sharpe, W. F. (1964). Capital asset prices: a theory of market equilibrium under conditions of risk. *Journal of Finance, Sept.,* 425–442.

Shultz, M. (1999). Leveraging e-commerce in purchasing transactions. *Electronic News, 45*(2251), 52–53.

Smith, A. [1776] (1996). *The Wealth of Nations.* Cannan ed. Chicago: University of Chicago Press.

Silverman, F. E. (1998). E-billing is the next step for on-line commerce. *American Banker, 163*(240), 12–16.

Staking, K. B. & Babbel, D. F. (1995). The relation between capital structure, interest rate sensitivity, and market value in the property-liability insurance industry. *Journal of Risk & Insurance, 62*(4), 690–719.

Swieringa, R. J. (1997). Challenges to the current accounting model. *CPA Journal, 67*(1), 26–32.

Thomas, J. (1998). The future—it is us. *Journal of Accountancy, 6*(23), 26–35.

Troxel, R. B. & Weber Jr., M. G. (1990). *Journal of Cost Management, 4*(1), 14–23.

Turney, P. B. B. (1992). What an activity-based cost model looks like, *Journal of Cost Management, 5*(4), 54–61.

Wallman, S. (1996). The future of accounting and financial reporting part II: the colorized approach. *Accounting Horizons, 10*(2), 138–153.

Wang, S. (1999). Analyzing agents for electronic commerce. *Information Systems Management, 16*(1), 40–48.

Warner, P. D., Smith, L. M., & Larson, L. (1999). Payment processing in electronic commerce. *CPA Journal 69*(1), 66–67.

Whicker, M. L. (1993). *Controversial issues in economic regulatory policy.* Newbury Park: SAGE Publications.

White, A. L. (1993). Accounting for pollution prevention. *EPA Journal, 19*(3), 23–26.

Chapter IX

Strategic Decision Making

Clarence J. Mann

INTRODUCTION

Strategy has deep roots in history. Beginning at least with ancient China and later Athens, it has been closely associated with military engagement and generalship and, during the last three centuries, with trade and nation-building. Today, for instance, there are strategies for economic and social development, job creation, industrial policy, trade, and export promotion. As a business notion, strategy was certainly practiced during the 19th and early 20th centuries by the moguls that built the industrial foundations of America. These business leaders knew very well that growth and success depended on their choice of long-term actions in the marketplace as well as on the way they designed and managed their businesses.

One of these early American strategists, Gustavus Swift, combined the advent of the railroads with the new technology of refrigeration to satisfy the growing demand for fresh meat in eastern cities shortly after the American Civil War. During the same period of the 19th century, Cyrus McCormick fashioned a network of franchised dealerships, supported by a distribution and sales organization, to market his reaper to farmers across America. Around the turn of the century, Julius Rosenwald developed a retail catalog strategy for Sears, Roebuck, combined with unheard of "Free Trial Offers" and "Money Back Guarantees," to become the mass merchant for middle America. And in contrast to Ford's path-breaking Model T strategy of an affordable car for all, Alfred Sloan introduced the renowned segmentation strategy of a "car for every purse" together with a multi-divisional organization to implement it. In an effort to exploit a potentially vast and growing national market, each of these entrepreneurs very consciously developed and pursued highly sophisticated strategies.

Despite these obvious successes, time has shown how fleeting success can be in the fast-changing U.S. market economy. A recent study found that only a little more than half (56 percent) of the 100 largest U.S. industrial firms in 1980 were ranked there in 1992 and that only 18 percent of them had managed to improve their ranking during that interval. Thus, 82 percent either declined in relative performance or disappeared from the list altogether during the 12-year period (Luthans, Hodgetts & Lee, 1994). Maintaining a competitive advantage, once achieved, clearly cannot be taken for granted. Strategy must be seen as a living and evolving instrument of business survival.

This chapter will examine the evolution of strategy in American management theory and practice and the key dimensions of strategy as they have emerged over time. It will identify a number of issues that have shaped this evolution, suggest how strategy contributes to business success, and indicate what role strategy is likely to play in the future for American business development.

STRATEGY—AN EVOLVING CONCEPT

Only during the past four decades has strategy become a working analytical concept for American business management. It has evolved over the past four decades in the United States in tandem with the growing popularity of American business school education. In his seminal work, *Strategy and Structure*, Alfred Chandler (1962) offers one of the earliest definitions of strategy, as "the determination of the basic long-term goals and objectives of an enterprise, and the adoption of courses of action and the allocation of resources necessary for carrying out these goals" (p. 13). Chandler's stress on long-term goals and objectives as guides for corporate action, coupled with an appropriate allocation of resources, has remained a distinctive aspect of strategy. It fits particularly well with Chandler's research, emphasizing major enterprises with long histories. It remains to be seen whether this approach works equally well for smaller entrepreneurial firms.

During the 1960s and 1970s, the strategy concept was refined further by Kenneth Andrews and his colleagues, building on four previous decades of business policy courses at the Harvard Business School. They saw it as providing focus for the whole business in lieu of simply emphasizing individual functions. Strategy was considered to be a response to the question: "What's our business?" It enables a company to focus its resources and thereby to "convert distinctive competence into competitive advantage" (Andrews, 1980, p. 15). Andrews put it this way in his second edition:

> The essence of . . . strategy . . . is pattern. The interdependence of purposes, policies, and organized action is crucial. . . . It is the unity, coherence, and internal consistency of a company's strategic decisions that position the company in its environment and give the firm its identity, its power to mobilize, its strengths, and its likelihood of success in the marketplace. (Andrews, 1980, p. 15)

While this view enables the firm to see itself as greater than the sum of its parts and adds another dimension to strategy, it was primarily conceptual without any real analytical legs.

An analytical foundation was soon added with the SWOT model—the systematic assessment of a firm's internal *strengths* and *weaknesses* in juxtaposition to its external *opportunities* and *threats*. The model is intended to assist a firm in developing the *best fit* between itself and the environment. Presumably, the best strategy(ies) would expand and leverage strengths to take advantage of opportunities while overcoming or minimizing weaknesses and threats. SWOT provides a useful set of categories for qualifying data but little insight into bridging the creative gap between a list of issues and creating or synthesizing strategies. It also provides no guidance for determining the best fit.

In his 1980 book, Michael Porter fielded a new strategy model. It was based on the structure-conduct-performance paradigm of industrial-organization economics and the insights emerging from over a half century of experience with U.S. antitrust regulation. Porter introduced a more rigorous methodology and shifted the focus of strategic analysis largely from the firm to the competitive structure of industry. His model views strategy largely as a function of industry structure and market segmentation: "The goal of competitive strategy for a business unit in an industry is to find a *position* in the industry where the company *can best defend itself* against these competitive forces *or can influence* them in its favor" (Porter, 1980, p. 4; italics added). Choices of industry and of the strategic group within the industry are the crucial decisions in positioning a firm for success. Porter's emphasis on competitive positioning, discussed in more detail below, introduced into strategic analysis a new level of analytical rigor. It also has afforded a clear target for its critics.

As if on cue, the corporate raiding and leveraged buyouts of the 1980s shifted the interest of corporate America from diversification to *value-based* strategies. The inefficiencies of many conglomerates built during the previous two decades had become evident, e.g., Mobil's acquisition of Montgomery Ward and Coca Cola's purchase of Columbia Pictures. Stock market valuations became critical, as CEOs sought to ward off hostile takeovers. Porter's second volume (1986) accommodated this shift by introducing "value chain" analysis, enabling the various activities of a firm to be disaggregated and assessed in terms of the value each adds to operations as a whole. Moreover, two of Porter's archetypal strategies—portfolio management and restructuring (Porter, 1987)—found broad and highly visible application. Either way, firms found they needed to sort out profitable from losing business units and to justify or remake their multi-business corporations.

Value-based strategies refocused strategic management toward internal analysis. Their objective is to maximize shareholder value. To do this, each business unit is assigned a market value; this in turn is compared to the price/earnings ratio of the industry, particularly of the major competitors in that industry. Other financial criteria are used as well, e.g., free cash flows discounted at the business-specific weighted average cost of capital. These are incorporated into a variety of value-based planning approaches. The movement involved the reorganization of entire corporations, such as Walt Disney, Marriott and PepsiCo (MacTaggart,

Kontes & Mankins, 1994), as well as attempts to integrate such financial criteria into management compensation and incentives.

This effort to improve productivity was also driven by a concern for the advancing pace of international competition and continuing long lead times in product development. Obvious successes of Japanese products, especially in the automotive and consumer electronics industries, highlighted the concern for what became known as "lean manufacturing"(Womack, Jones & Ross, 1990). It culminated in the impassioned pleas of such re-engineering proponents as Michael Hammer. He exhorted top management: "Don't Automate, Obliterate," referring to the unimaginative application of new technology in unsuccessful attempts to mechanize old ways of doing business. It is time, argued Hammer, "to stop paving the cow paths. . . . We should 're-engineer' our businesses: use the power of modern information technology to radically redesign our business processes in order to achieve dramatic improvements in their performance" (Hammer, 1990, p. 104).

Such re-engineering calls for discontinuous thinking, i.e., "recognizing and breaking away from the outdated rules and fundamental assumptions that underlie operations" (Hammer, 1990, p. 107). It entails such changes as: integrating activities across organizational functions, organizing around outcomes (not tasks), making decisions at points where work is performed instead of leaving procurement and quality control to others, and coordinating parallel activities on an ongoing basis as in product development. While these points are well taken, their focus primarily on operational efficiencies is a far cry from the notion of strategy introduced by Porter in his emphasis on competitive positioning (Porter, 1996).

Perhaps predictably, even as value-based strategies were being adopted across corporate America, the realization was setting in that something more would be needed to cope with rapidly changing technologies, ever-shorter product cycles, and the challenge of global competition. Indeed, this realization in large part motivated Hammer in calling for re-engineering. Driven by similar concerns, Gary Hamel and C.K. Prahalad (1994) also challenge management orthodoxy; however, they emphasize building foresight, vision, core competencies, learning and innovation into the organization. They attack excessive concern for restructuring assets and headcount. Instead, what is needed for long-term business survival is to grow the numerator of the ROI formula, i.e., new products, markets and ultimately net income. Strategy, they maintain, "is both a process of understanding and shaping competitive 'forces' and a process of open-ended discovery and purposeful incrementalism"(p. xiii). Re-engineering as well as restructuring are not without value, but they do not generate the future of the company.

These views, beginning with Hamel and Prahalad's path-breaking article on core competencies (1990), helped crystallize the emerging resource-based view (RBV) of strategy. Reflecting the earlier work of Andrews and Christensen, core competencies are based on a holistic appreciation of the corporation and the skills and technologies that can be aggregated and leveraged from across its various business units. Foresight and vision are needed to identify and dominate emerging opportunities, to stake out new competitive space, and to provide direction and motivation for developing and deploying core competencies (p. 22).

Because competition for the future consists of company vs. company rather than product vs. product, "creating the future often requires that a company build new core competencies . . . that typically transcend a single business" (p. 33). Thus, RBV represents a major departure from industry and market-driven approaches. The future is not so much about market positioning as it is about factor-driven resource development.

As this evolutionary dialogue suggests, the domain of strategy for American companies is tied to the issue of value creation—both for shareholders and other stakeholders as well as for customers, now and in the future. These two perspectives on value are inseparable; yet, there is as yet no integrating theory that enjoys general acceptance. Further, the notion of value creation itself raises two strategic questions: how should the firm define value in operational terms and, within this context, how should the firm generate value? The first question implies a business objective, the second a process for achieving it. Both pose very practical questions and must be judged by the test of feasibility. These questions are examined in more depth in the following section through the juxtaposition of several strategic dimensions.

DIMENSIONS OF STRATEGY

Strategy as a management discipline is not one thing. Nor is there one way to go about formulating strategy. Rather, as the previous discussion suggests, strategy is multi-dimensional. These various dimensions often pull in divergent, if not opposite, directions. The reason for this lies in the nature of strategy as a practical science, i.e., addressing complex real-world issues for which there is no one right answer. Not only are these issues subject to different definitions, interpretations and responses, they also are inextricably woven together. Thus, financial or marketing issues cannot be addressed strategically without taking into consideration all other aspects of the firm, e.g., technology, human relations, supplier relationship issues, etc. In short, strategy deals with what have come to be called "wicked problems" (Rittel, 1972, chap. 1).

Equally important, strategy deals with creating the future of an enterprise. This may call for the introduction of new products, automating production or business processes, investing in new plant facilities, retraining the work force, changing corporate culture, etc. In an "open system" environment, the firm's future is continually shaping and being shaped by the wider industry in largely unforeseeable ways. Thus, the future itself is a shifting and moving target.

The concept of strategy, therefore, reflects real-world complexity as well as the uncertain and interactive nature of the firm's environment. This is highlighted by the following five contrasting dimensions of strategy that have emerged in management theory and practice over the past 30 years, i.e., emergent vs. deliberate process, market vs. resource-based positioning, business portfolio vs. core competencies, competition vs. cooperation, and industry evolution vs. industry creation. These dimensions frame the variety of perspectives on strategy found in American management theory and practice. Please note that in the course of this discussion, it is necessary at times to distinguish among levels of strategy—i.e., corporate, business unit, and business function—which are so critical for larger multi-divisional firms.

Emergent vs. Deliberate Process

How are a firm's strategies formulated? Accepting Andrew's proposition, as noted above, that the "essence of . . . strategy . . . is *pattern*," i.e., "the interdependence of purposes, policies, and organized action," how does this pattern originate? Is it born full-blown from the head of Zeus so-to-speak, whether from a CEO's inspiration or a purposeful planning process, or does it gradually emerge over many months and years as the result of numerous discrete and unrelated decisions and actions taken at various levels of an enterprise? Or, in fact, as indicated by Henry Mintzberg's depiction in Figure 1, is strategy formulated through a combination of these two very different processes, sometimes one and sometimes the other? And, are there times when one approach is to be preferred over the others? Management theorists are divided on this.

During the 1960s and early 70s, the heyday of strategic planning in the United States, it was generally accepted that strategies were best generated through rational, deliberate planning efforts. Anything less would be mere guesswork and success would be pure chance (Andrews, 1980, chap. 2). A worthwhile planning effort would involve: 1) a thorough analysis of the present and future situation of the enterprise, including its industry and competitors, supported by a collection

Figure 1. Forms of Strategy

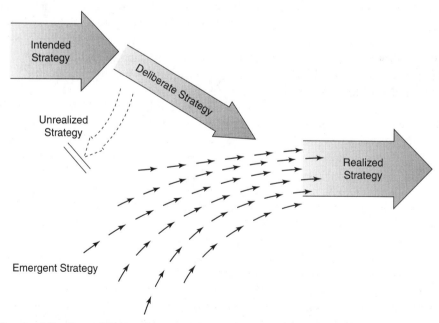

Source: Mintzberg, 1994, p. 24

of all relevant data; 2) a systematic SWOT assessment of the firm's external environment (opportunities and threats) and internal condition (strengths and weaknesses); 3) identification of a range of strategies that leverage the SOs and offset the WTs; and 4) selection of the most promising strategies from among these alternatives, based on such criteria as their consistency in reaching objectives, their likelihood in generating a competitive advantage, their feasibility, and their potential returns and risks.

A deliberate approach to formulating strategy encourages long-term purposeful thinking and provides a clear rationale for the allocation of assets. However, its value is necessarily encumbered by our limited foresight on the course of future events and our ambiguous insight into appropriate courses of action. This is inherent in the "wicked" or complex environment in which business operates, e.g., shifting consumer preferences, technology trends, regulatory initiatives, etc. Moreover, hard data often is not available, even though it typically is the preferred basis for executive decisions. Undue emphasis on measurable results and quantitative factors, which so often accompanies the planning mentality, tends to ignore or underestimate the impact of social issues and trends. It also tends to overlook the power-behavioral factors within firms—typical of turf battles and the not-invented-here (NIH) syndrome—that often determine strategic decisions and are often crucial to strategic success.

There are real limits, therefore, to rationality and the quantification of data as well as on the time and resources available for strategic planning. One response is to abandon the ideal of reaching an optimal decision from among all possible alternatives in favor of identifying a satisfactory choice from among a much more limited array of options. This entails a series of judgment calls. The *satisficing* manager selects strategies that meet or exceed a minimally acceptable set of criteria rather than delaying decision making until all possible alternatives have been identified and evaluated (Simon, 1997, pp.118–120). As this implies, the role of intuition in the process of strategy development must expand to fill the gaps created by these limits on reason and data. It is highly desirable, of course, that this intuition be as educated as possible.

Another response, termed *incrementalism*, views strategy as emerging opportunistically and gradually over time in response to various types of strategic issues. These issues could emerge in the course of a corporate reorganization, major marketing initiative or strategic alliances. Based on a review of strategic change processes in 10 major companies, James Quinn (1978) found: "Often external or internal events, over which management had essentially no control, would precipitate urgent, piecemeal, interim decisions which inexorably shaped the company's future strategic posture" (p. 9). This is only to say that top management typically prefers to deal incrementally with issues as they arise. Further, it tends to move tentatively into unknown territory, keeping options open to test assumptions, and needs time to shape and gain the support of organizational and power relationships. From this perspective, the overarching strategies of a company are to a large extent the *result* of a long line of critical decisions taken in response to urgent matters arising in various parts and at various levels of the organization.

Incrementalism correctly stresses the cognitive limits in formal planning on deciphering the future. Indeed, for companies caught in the midst of rapidly changing technology and telescoping product cycles, the future may be this very week. Incrementalism also correctly points out the process constraints involved in organizational change. Nevertheless, as Quinn points out, all companies in his sample have formal planning procedures. These procedures provide a discipline for looking ahead, however imperfectly, for improving communication about goals, issues and resource allocation, and for generating the strategic perspectives needed to focus and evaluate short-term action plans.

It appears, therefore, that these two perspectives on strategy—emergent and deliberate—must be blended. Incrementalism provides the company with a process of inductive, bottom-up reasoning tested against practical experience, while formalized planning provides a framework for reflecting on future directions. To be guided exclusively by the former exposes the organization to drift and anarchy; to be dominated by the latter runs the danger of turning strategy into controlled programming and of robbing the strategy process of creative experience. In this latter sense, warns Mintzberg (1994), strategic planning is not strategic thinking.

Market vs. Resource-Based Positioning

A second set of dimensions raises perhaps the classic dichotomy for strategists. Should strategy be formulated from the "outside-in" (market-based strategy) or from the "inside-out" (resource-based strategy)? Strategy making is foremost a management task, and it is necessarily firm-specific. But what is the primary source and type of criteria for guiding strategy formulation? Should an internal or external perspective dominate?

More conventional approaches tend to begin outside-in, i.e., by trying to determine how best to position a product or service in the market. Or, they may begin with a business or business concept and ask how best to position it among various industries or industry segments. For this purpose, Porter (1980) poses two questions: first, how attractive is an industry for long-term profitability—and under what circumstances? And second, how can a firm achieve above-average profits in an industry? The first determines which industry to enter, i.e., is the industry intensely price-competitive, highly concentrated, fragmented, growing, mature, etc.? The second indicates—by grouping firms with similar strategies (strategic group mapping)—which segment of that industry would be most favorable, and the barriers that protect each segment from head-to-head competition with firms in other groups.

Firm strategy, therefore, is viewed primarily through the prism of an industry and the five forces Porter (1980) claims shape its competitive structure (see Figure 2). These are: rivalry among competitors, threats of entry from outsiders and from substitute products and services, and the bargaining power of suppliers as well as of buyers. These forces in turn are influenced by governmental action and regulation, trends in technology, shifts in consumer values, and other variables

Figure 2. Five Forces Industry Analysis

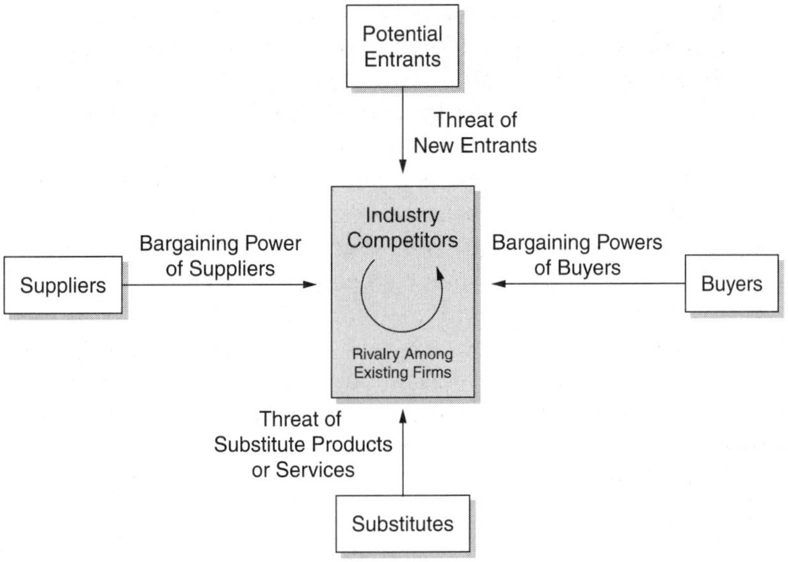

Source: Porter, 1980, p. 4

external to the industry. (Other writers have argued that government, technology and exit barriers should be treated as additional forces.) Porter's concept suggests not only that industries are dynamic and changing, but also that a firm's potential profitability depends largely on an industry's competitive structure.

Within this analytical framework, the function of strategy is to defend the firm against any of the five forces which threaten to undermine its competitive advantage and profitability as well as to take the steps needed to shape the environment in its favor. The objective of either an offensive or defensive strategy is to generate a superior return for the firm. While such strategies are numerous, Porter breaks them into three internally consistent generic types: overall cost leadership, differentiation of product or service, and focus (targeting a market segment based on cost or differentiation). The ultimate intent of these strategies is to position the firm in ways that will buffer it from the competitive forces that otherwise will undercut its profitability and survival. At one point, Porter suggests that these generic strategies "can be used singly or in combination," while at another point he argues that they are potentially inconsistent with each other. As a result, a firm's failure to develop its strategy in at least one of the three directions almost always dooms the firm to failure (by being "stuck in the middle") (Porter, 1980, pp. 34, 41–42).

In the 15-year PIMS study—*Profit Impact of Market Strategy*—of 450 companies, including 3,000 business units, Robert Buzzell and Bradley Gale (1987) give credence to the outside-in perspective. They expressly link market share to profitability. While cautioning that market share does not cause profitability, they conclude:

Large market share is both a reward for providing better value to the customer and a means of realizing lower costs. Under most circumstances, enterprises that have achieved a large share of the markets they serve are considerably more profitable than their smaller-share rivals. (1987, p. 70)

Further, this correlation does *not* appear to vary considerably from one industry or market situation to another. While the study underscores an external, industry focus to strategy, the authors challenge Porter's view that low cost leadership and differentiation strategies are necessarily incompatible. Indeed, they argue, "in the majority of cases, superior quality, large share, *and* low costs relative to competition go together" (p. 86).

On the whole, the difficulty with market and industry-led perspectives lies in the unruly and fast-changing nature of the environment itself. Just as a low cost leadership position or market niche is attained, a new technology, application or competitor bursts on the scene and industry structure changes. Nowhere has this been more evident than in the ongoing convergence of the electronic, computer and telecommunications industries over the past two decades. Moreover, the globalization of competition and markets, the information revolution and the triumph of (relatively) free market systems for the major economies are accompanied by major shifts in consumer tastes and demand around the world. Competition has become a "'war of movement,' in which success depends on anticipation of market trends and quick response to changing customer needs" (Stalk, Evans & Shulman, 1992, p. 62). How can a firm formulate strategy in such a free-wheeling and at times discontinuous environment?

Reasons like these have pressed firms to look internally for a more enduring logic to strategic analysis. This has resulted in the growing emphasize on "capabilities-based" or "resource-based" strategy (RBS). This inside-out approach differs sharply from the value-based strategies of the 1980s, discussed previously, which were dominated by financial criteria and massive corporate restructuring. Instead, RBS ties the firm intimately to customer needs and to the ongoing development of business processes to serve those needs. The virtues of the firms practicing this approach are: speedy response to customers and markets, consistency in product quality, acuity in sensing changes in customer needs, agility in adapting to different business environments, and the ability to innovate and create new sources of value. The firm must image itself "as a giant feedback loop that begins with identifying the needs of the customer and ends with satisfying them" (Stalk et al., 1992, p. 62). And the firm must be prepared to reinvent itself as the feedback indicates.

This capabilities-based approach changes competition from a chess game fought out as a "war of position" to an interactive video game played as a "war of movement." It shifts the focus of strategy from the structure of a company's products and markets to the dynamics of its behavior. Contrary to Porter's market positioning model, RBS looks for competitive advantage in terms of the distinctive resources and capabilities nurtured by industry competitors. By adopting this formula, even resource-scarce Japanese firms like Honda and Canon could successfully challenge American giants like General Motors and Xerox. And, by astutely mobilizing information technology to create logistical advantages, upstart Wal-Mart has been able to provide customers with the benefits of choice, availability and value that soon out-distanced long-established mass merchants like Sears.

In a rejoinder to this capabilities-based approach, Porter does not dispute the necessity of superior performance nor that the firm must distinguish itself from its competitors. Rather, he maintains that these alone are not enough. Operational techniques, such as total quality management, benchmarking, time-based competition, outsourcing, partnering, re-engineering, etc., according to Porter (1996), are too easily imitated, leading firms down the road of "mutually destructive competition" where improved performance fails to translate into sustainable profitability. However necessary, operational effectiveness is not viable strategy—indeed, it is not strategy at all. The only escape from this cul-de-sac is "strategic positioning," i.e. "performing different activities from rivals or performing similar activities in different ways" (p. 64). Strategic positioning, incidentally, may entail capital investment, different personnel and management approaches.

It appears that both sides of this dimension are critical to a viable concept of strategy and competitive advantage. Whether their convergence is imaged as a "giant feedback loop" involving the market, or as the necessity to support a market position with superior performance, or as some other combination, remains to be seen. In any case, both approaches seem to accept the premise that the strength each posits as primary (whether market position or firm capabilities) must distinguish the firm from its rivals in some sustainable way. The real bone of contention is what makes an advantage "sustainable."

Portfolio vs. Core Competence

The third set of dimensions is a natural companion to the second. It focuses largely on corporate-level strategy in a multi-business company, being framed by the contrast between the "portfolio" approach of focusing exclusively on individual business units and the "core competence" perspective of creating synergy across

Figure 3. Growth/Share Matrix

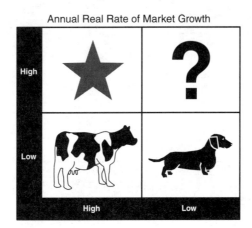

Source: Boston Consulting Group, 1970

the units. The one concentrates effort on specific markets, yielding a range of business units highly responsive and dedicated to their customers, while the other seeks to tap the strengths of all units and to build core competencies across the organization. Neither can be ignored if a firm is to remain both profitable and competitive over the long term. Both are especially critical in assessing the ultimate value of mergers and acquisitions.

The most enduring legacy of portfolio planning is Boston Consulting Group's growth/share matrix, shown in Figure 3. Its cow, dog, question mark and star metaphors are intended to provide corporate-level management of diversified businesses with a methodology to evaluate the business unit mix (Hedley, 1977).

The first step is to divide a company into its business segments and determine for each unit the overall growth rate of its market; this axis indicates the cash requirements for staying abreast of market growth. The other axis tracks the relative market share of each unit, reflecting the unit's competitive strength and likelihood of generating cash. (Note how the PIMS study by Buzzell and Gale, discussed previously, reinforces this point.) Mapping the various units of a company among the four quadrants of this matrix provides a working picture of the

Figure 4. Growth/Share Matrix for General Foods Corporation, 1980–1982

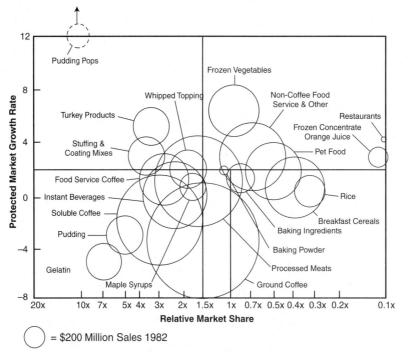

Source: Bogue and Buffa, 1986, p. 15

origin and flow of financial resources in the corporation. (See the matrix of General Foods Corporation in Figure 4.)

The second step is to assess the strategic value of the business units and to allocate resources accordingly. "Star" units, found in the high growth, high share (upper left) quadrant, require large amounts of cash to maintain their position. At the same time, they should generate large cash flows and be viewed as future "cash cows." "Dogs," by contrast, are trapped with a low share of a low-growth market. They have little potential for reaching a viable cost position and a sustainable positive cash flow. If retained, they may become a "cash trap." "Cows" are found in slow-growth, mature markets, but enjoy low costs with an entrenched superior market position. Their large cash flow surpluses are critical in funding company overhead, strengthening debt capacity and financing expansion and new initiatives, especially for the "question marks" and possibly the stars.

Question marks in many respects represent the future of the company. They are found in high or potentially high-growth markets, but their market share is presently low or possibly uncertain. They may be in an emerging industry where the product is evolving and demand has not yet fully crystallized. This was the position, for instance, of IBM (and even more so of Apple) with the advent of the PC. The cash requirements of such business units are great, while their future performance is unclear. Should the company invest or divest? A few units should become stars; the others should be liquidated. Deciding which is which is pure business judgment.

The BCG portfolio approach offers three-fold guidance for multi-business companies. First, it provides a framework for evaluating growth and market potential across a range of business units. Second, it establishes a rationale for allocating resources among diverse units, recognizing that businesses vary widely in terms of their likely future performance, their stage of development, and the nature of their contribution to the company overall. Finally, it suggests a formula for balancing the portfolio among the quadrants to ensure both internal cash flow and growth for the company.

For purposes of corporate strategy, however, the BCG matrix has been employed quite narrowly, largely for capital budgeting and to justify shifts in the portfolio through acquisitions and divestitures. Further, by viewing the company as an assortment of individual businesses, it tends to turn strategic management into investment banking. In an efficient capital market, this role and the choices it implies normally are better left to investors themselves. Most critically from a strategic perspective, the portfolio approach neglects the synergism among business units across the matrix. Such synergism provides the platform for product development and the company's overall future competitive advantage.

Precisely to combat the tyranny of portfolio management, C.K. Prahalad and Gary Hamel (1990) turned the portfolio notion on its head. Companies must see themselves, they claim, as portfolios of "competencies" rather than of businesses. This necessitates that corporate management look beneath the various end products of its business units, identify the underlying skills and streams of technology that produce them, and weave the latter together into bundles of "core competencies" that undergird a firm's competitive advantages. Any one company is likely to have only a few core competencies, but these can be harmonized, managed and leveraged in a way that contributes significantly to perceived buyer value. At the same time, they should provide a platform for developing generations of new products and entering new markets and be difficult for competitors to imitate (pp. 91–92).

During the 1980s and into the 90s, for instance, Hewlett-Packard rethought its strategic identity. It identified and then blended the unique competencies—computing, communications and measurement—underlying its three major and mostly autonomous divisions. It asked itself: "What new opportunities lie at the juncture of these three capabilities?" One of these, remote medical diagnostics, combined HP's medical instruments expertise with its computer skills, enabling patients at home to be monitored by physicians miles away. From such combinations come 'core products' and platforms for spinning off a variety of end products. A similar story can be told for 3M's core competencies in adhesives, substrates and advanced materials, whose cross-breeding has given rise to thousands of new products (Hamel, 1994).

Needless to say, the management tasks and skills implicit in developing and cross-breeding core competencies are much more complex and costly than those required for managing a portfolio of businesses. Corporate-level management must not only provide the processes and resources for integrating various aspects of research, development and engineering across product divisions, it must at the same time ensure that the cross-breeding does not disrupt the critical, ongoing product focus of the various front-line business units. It must guide, coordinate and monitor several levels of effort across the company, i.e., building and nurturing core competencies, developing core products, managing business units, and marketing end products. And it must practice the fine art of continuously improving business processes at all these levels. This is a long-term effort requiring clarity of vision, sharply focused strategies, a clearly defined action, and lots of patience. As a result, 'core competence' strategy calls for a management style at once more demanding and sophisticated than is the case for portfolio strategy.

Competition vs. Cooperation

Discussion to this point has focused largely on strategic dimensions internal to the firm and the firm's primary concern for its product markets. To ensure a sustainable competitive advantage, however, firms must also be concerned with the broader marketplace, including relationships with competitors and other industry players and the future of the industry. Consideration will now be given to dimensions of strategy involving competitors and, in the next subsection, to the evolution or re-creation of the industry itself.

The model of day-to-day or imperfect competition envisions a market where buyers and sellers deal in a relatively homogeneous product or service. Competition is not perfect, because some of the buyers and sellers are large enough to affect the market price or the product may be differentiated. In such markets, competition occurs among discrete businesses, operating in a hostile environment formed by producer rivalry, the bargaining power of suppliers and buyers, and threats from potential market entrants and substitute products. So far as possible, firms seek to buffer themselves against pressures for lower prices, higher costs and, ultimately, lower rates of return. Porter's five forces industry model (1980), discussed previously, details the source and nature of these pressures and how they shape the competitive structure of the industry. Strategies, in Porter's view, should be designed to deal with this environment, i.e., to ward off threats to the firm and to strengthen its market leverage. Strategic attention is paid to competitor intelligence, market signals and distinguishing between threatening and nonthreatening competitor moves.

Firms with this world view operate from a strategic posture favoring individualized competition among firms. They tend to view cooperation and collaboration with suspicion, either as crutches for the weak or, from the perspective of American antitrust law, attempts to gain monopoly power. In Porter's view, collaboration is a two-edged sword. On the one hand, it can achieve selective benefits, e.g., generate economies of scale, lower R&D costs, spread risk and provide access to markets. At the same time, it always involves significant costs as well as risks. These include management efforts at coordination, compromising with partner objectives, splitting profits and creating a potential competitor. Indeed, even when alliances are successful, Porter argues they "tend to ensure mediocrity, not create world leadership, . . . [for] they deter the firm's own efforts at upgrading" (1990, p. 613). Even where collaboration is justified, e.g., to undertake costly R&D or to penetrate a new market, the relationship will always be subordinated to the self-interests of the parties. As a result, Porter concludes (p. 613), alliances "are rarely a solution" and often merely a transitional arrangement.

Those opposed to this atomized view of competition emphasize organizational relationships over rivalry among independent firms. While accepting the existence of competition among firms in an industry, inter-firm relationships focus on the strategic importance of building cooperative networks among the various players in the industry. Thus, instead of playing off suppliers against each other to gain short-term cost advantages, firms should build long-term working partnerships that strive for improved business performance and buyer value. These may take the form of exclusive-dealing, licensing and cross-licensing arrangements as well as minority investments, joint ventures or other types of alliances. Similar cooperative relationships can be developed downstream as well with distribution channels and customers.

These two opposing views of strategy raise the issue of internalization versus externalization all along the value chain. At what point(s) in its operations should a firm build technological and organizational strengths internally, seek scale economies or expand the scope of its products or markets purely through capital investment? And at what point(s) should it instead outsource these activities or functions to capture new technologies and operational efficiencies? Each alternative entails trade-offs, for the management costs and competitive risks associated with collaboration may gain precious time and experience otherwise lost in "going it alone." The choice for any activity depends heavily on how a firm defines its core competencies and on its strategy for developing, leveraging and protecting them. Porter's cautionary remarks about alliances should certainly be taken to heart. Companies need to protect and nurture those competencies critical to their present and future competitive advantages. Yet, given the immense fixed costs involved in staying abreast of just technological change in almost any industry today—not to mention product development and global marketing campaigns—going it alone in every respect is becoming less and less feasible (Ohmae, 1989).

The NUMMI venture in Fremont, California, provides a classic example of two world-class auto companies who saw the need to collaborate around a defined set of objectives. New United Motor Manufacturing, Inc., is a 50–50 joint venture between General Motors and Toyota. Certainly, when it was founded in the early 1980s, this alliance was of critical competitive importance to each of the partners. In different ways, it promised to lower the operating risks for each. For GM, it presented an opportunity to learn the secrets of "lean manufacturing" for high quality, fuel-efficient compact cars. It gave the equally conservative Toyota the means to circumvent the "volunteer" export quotas restricting access of Japanese companies to the U.S. market as well as insight into American labor-management, supplier and marketing practices. It also provided Toyota with the public relations benefit of manufacturing in the United States (Yoshino & Rangan, 1995). Although head-to-head competitors, the learning objectives of each partner were completely different. At the time, however, neither of these two giants felt adequate to the task of pursuing its objectives independently.

Who won and who lost in the NUMMI alliance is still being debated. The answer depends largely on the criteria used. From a purely product perspective, the cars produced by the venture have been of high quality and well-received in the U.S. market, although the Toyota brand and reputation for service has given its models a significant price edge, even in the second-hand market (Economist, 1996). The real question is: what did the partners learn from the alliance, and how did each employ this learning throughout its operating network to improve its competitive advantage over the long term? Toyota confirmed that its management system and techniques would work for the U.S. labor force, with the result that lean manufacturing is now the standard in the auto industry. GM, on the other hand, has been a laggard among U.S. auto companies in replicating the famed Toyota production system. Presumably, GM has discovered that the Toyota approach has as much to do with social systems and people management as it does with technical skills (Doz & Hamel, 1998, p. 179). The irony for GM (as well as other American car makers) is that while the NUMMI alliance was focusing on production cost and quality, the sources of competitive advantage were shifting to design, marketing and supply-chain management.

The apparent dichotomy and choice between competition and cooperation, therefore, appears to arise largely out of the economic self-interest of firms operating within the discipline of market competition. To survive, firms must carefully identify the core competencies that provide their competitive advantage and then, because resources are ever scarce, seek to leverage them through a network of organizational relationships. Such networks can turn potential competitors into complementary partners, generate reliable, dedicated suppliers and provide the learning needed to build and strengthen core competencies. To this extent, collaboration is simply competition through other means (Doz & Hamel, 1998, p. 26). Because ultimately the name of the game is competition, however, management must carefully discern which business processes and functions to internalize and protect and which to share with or outsource to the network. These decisions necessarily are strategic in nature. Insofar, competitive and collaborative strategies may be pursued selectively and in tandem. The task of the strategist is to ensure that this mix of strategies serves the overriding objectives of the firm.

Industry Evolution vs. Industry Creation

This final set of dimensions contrasts perspectives on how firm strategy relates to the industry. Should strategy simply ride the waves of industry forces as they evolve over time, or should it pro-actively seek to influence those forces and even create or re-create the industry? While these issues share some aspects of the outside-in vs. inside-out dichotomy discussed earlier, the emphasis here concerns the ability of a firm to shape industry structure. Firms have a choice in which course to take, but it is not without costs and risks.

The more conventional view, based on Porter's early work (1980), holds that "the key *structural* features of industries . . . determine the strength of the competitive forces and hence industry profitability" (p. 4). Because these five forces (described previously) vary collectively from industry to industry, "not all industries have the same [profit] potential." Moreover, these forces are likely to change over time, due for instance to alterations in buyer preferences and sophistication; diffusion in proprietary knowledge; shifts in government policy; innovation in technology, products, marketing and business processes, etc. As these forces change, the competitive structure of the industry evolves. Because industries are complex, interrelated systems, however, they do not change piecemeal; rather, "change in one element of an industry's structure tends to trigger changes in other areas." Being able to understand and even predict these changes is important for formulating competitive strategy (Porter, 1980, chap. 8).

From this perspective, the survival and growth of firms depends largely on their ability to adapt to the particular "rules of the game" that exist and as they evolve for every industry. While firms may influence industry forces in their favor over time, their strategies are framed primarily *within* the rules or underlying economics of the industry as they exist. The strategist's role is to devise the best "fit" for the firm with its external environment. At any given time, firms appear to be much like industry observers, discerning how best to manipulate their assets among the various industry forces to provide the most favorable competitive position.

The strategist's role changes dramatically for those who argue, by contrast, that firms create industries. This means the firm has broad discretion to write or re-write the "rules of the game." As Charles Baden-Fuller and John Stopford (1994) so resolutely put it, it is the firm that matters, not the industry:

> [T]here is no economic law which says that some industries have to be less profitable than others. . . . Our first and central theme is that industry is not to blame for any shortcomings in the performance of a business. . . . The statistical evidence clearly shows that the firm is critical and the industry hardly matters at all. . . . Put simply, the correct choice of strategy appears to be at least five times more important than the correct choice of industry. (pp. 25–28)

Thus, through its point and click browser, Netscape transformed the Internet from a tool for techies to a user-friendly information system accessible to everyone. Although challenged early on by Microsoft, Netscape quickly became the industry standard by shifting to free versions of its browser and generating cash flow from advertisers. Fifteen years earlier, the "mini-mill" transformed the American steel industry from a declining to a healthy and reasonably prosperous status. It incorporated technology rejected by the major integrated steel makers, enabling it to automate, dramatically lower labor costs, feed on scrap (rather than raw steel), pinpoint products and locate near its markets.

Hamel and Prahalad (1994) put an added edge on this thinking by casting strategy as a race to the future. In this race, they caution, "there are drivers, passengers and road kill. . . ." (p. 28). The race calls first of all for industry foresight, i.e., the ability of business leaders to out-think and out-imagine the competition in influencing the directions for the industry. To do this, firms must build the best possible set of assumptions about the future, identify the types of customer benefits to provide in the next five, 10 or 15 years, build the new competencies and business processes needed for this, and reconfigure the customer interface to ensure delivery of this value. For these authors, the issue in anticipating the future is not so much that it is unknowable, for indeed it is in many respects, but that it is different. "The clues, weak signals, and trend lines that suggest how the future might be different are there for everyone to observe. There are little data critical to the development of industry foresight that are possessed by only one company" (p. 81). The challenge is to escape the present orthodoxies of the firm and industry and to focus on underlying "functionalities" (benefits and value) for meeting needs that customers have not yet recognized.

In his best seller, *The Death of Competition* (1996), James Moore poses perhaps the ultimate case for industry creation. Despite the book's title, Moore does not mean that competition is vanishing. Indeed, if anything, competition is intensifying, but in ways radically different from conventional thinking. Firms typically look for competition within their industry and in the form of individual or, possibly, groups of competitors. They need to see that their competition is, in fact, emerging new industries which are turning existing products into commodities or are making these products and their processes obsolete. The challenge, then, is to grasp competition as encompassing not simply a group of firms or even an industry, but entire business ecosystems giving birth to new industry forces.

For Moore, "business ecosystems" are "growth-oriented synergistic economic communities . . . of customers, suppliers, lead producers, and other stakeholders interacting with one another to produce goods and services" (1998, p. 169). They are similar to "force fields"—though Moore prefers comparisons to biology rather than physics—that at once underlie and are larger than any one industry. (See Figure 5, depicting core businesses in an industry interwoven with a supporting group of extended enterprises.) These in turn are sustained through complementing systems of stakeholders, regulatory organizations and competitors sharing similar business attributes, processes and organizational arrangements.

Moore's paradigm of market creation is about top management in firms "envisioning and helping to shape networks of contributions and processes" in order to "realize a workable economic future" (1996, pp. 5–6). Such visioning

Figure 5. Business Ecosystems

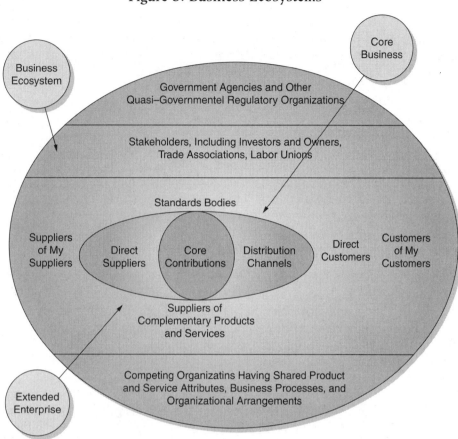

Source: Moore, 1996, p. 27

literally spawns new industries through new value paradigms, built around complex business relationships and networks of alliances. It depicts the role of the entrepreneur in Joseph Schumpeter's notion of capitalism as an ongoing "process of creative destruction" (1950).

Being a market creator, Moore believes, has been the genius of Microsoft. Microsoft anchors an ecosystem centered on microprocessing that encompasses at least four major industries: personal computers, consumer electronics, information and communication. No matter that its technology was not the most sophisticated. By grouping its core applications (e.g., Office) and leveraging them through linkages, e.g., to the Internet (Internet Explorer), Microsoft created an industry standard and an "opportunity environment" for thousands of associated suppliers, including major companies such as Hewlett-Packard and Intel. In doing so, it generated intensive cooperation and mutual adaptation among critical players in an emerging industry. Moore dubs this process of industry creation "co-evolution."

Of all the pairs of dimensions just examined, the contrast between industry evolution and industry creation presents management with the greatest challenge. If Hamel, Prahalad, Moore, et al. and their executive counterparts have it right—and there is strong evidence that in large part they do—management thinking is being wrenched out of a firm- and industry-specific chessboard mindset. Managers are forced to think expansively, relationally and proactively about firm strategy. "It involves shaping the future," warns Moore, "rather than simply defending the enterprises of the past" (1998, p. 169). This does not gainsay the need to fully understand and shape existing industry forces and trends a la Porter, but it does make clear that the strategic work of top management lies fundamentally in value and process innovation and industry creation. Unfortunately, as Moore points out, few managers have been schooled, either formally or on-the-job, in the art of envisioning new industries and in co-opting other players through collaborative relationships to make these realities.

IMPLICATIONS FOR THE FUTURE

The five dimensions or pairs of perspectives, just examined, reflect the broad frame of reference that exists among U.S. business strategists. They also reflect how diverse these perspectives can be among American firms. While any one or combination of these dimensions may be valid, depending on the context and circumstances in which it is employed, the choice implies trade-offs. The following discussion explores these choices and trade-offs in terms of two questions posed earlier in this chapter, i.e., how does strategy contribute to business success? And, what is the role (tasks) of strategy or strategy making in the future of American business development? In order to address these questions fully, it is necessary to understand the environmental factors shaping the business context for the future.

Environmental Factors

Three major interrelated factors are reshaping the environment for strategy making: the convergence of a broad range of technologies, the communication/information revolution, and the globalization of market forces. These also are primary forces shaping post-industrial society. While these factors have been chosen for their impact on American business, they are equally critical to all firms seeking to compete in a globalized economy.

The first, the convergence of a broad range of technologies, differentiates the post-industrial revolution and knowledge-based economy from its two predecessors. The first industrial revolution was triggered primarily by the invention of an efficient steam engine in the 18th century, and the second by electrification in the late 19th century. Post-industrial society, on the other hand, is being powered by at least six different, rapidly advancing, converging fields of science and technology: microelectronics, biotechnology, robotics, computers, telecommunications and man-made materials. As these basic technologies converge, new applications create the opportunity for an endless stream of new and often unforeseen products from health care to defense. The speed of this convergence is also blurring traditional lines separating industries, making it increasingly difficult for firms to gain foresight on future markets and to cost out the risk associated with the investment.

The breadth, depth and speed of this technological convergence is driven and supported by institutionalized linkages between science and technology—through industry, government and university collaboration. Over the past five decades these linkages have taken on a life of their own. As Lester Thurow (1999) puts it: "In the twentieth century, economic leadership would become a matter of systematic investment in R&D to deliberately invent new technologies" (p. 18). The deliberate, systematic character of this investment is a combination of private firms seeking to maintain their competitive edge and the demands of national policy emphasizing everything from medical research to "star wars." In the United States, 65 percent of this investment is made by industry, while 35 percent comes from the federal government and 5 percent from non-profit organizations (pp. 107, 115). Indeed, progress in scientific research and the number of Nobel laureates awarded a country, especially in the physical sciences, are worn as national badges of achievement. The four largest investors in science and technology—France, Germany, Japan and the United States—each dedicate 2.3 to 2.8 percent annually of their respective GNPs to research and development (p. 107).

The second factor of more recent origin is a product of the first and particularly of technology convergence. The communication/information revolution not only is transforming whole industries, it requires management to rethink the very nature of business. The explosion in information technology since the mid-50s has witnessed over a billion-fold improvement in processing and storage capacity—a rate that is expected to continue well into the first part of the next century. Computer-aided design and manufacturing (CAD/CAM) are reinventing the factory, while the Internet has transformed value-chain management and e-commerce is reinventing the retail industry as a whole. IT strategy has become a field of its own and is critical to success in globalizing firms. The result is the rapid pace of change and innovation in almost every part of the value chain, culminating in planned product obsolescence to pave the way for new technology applications.

The third factor, the globalization of market forces, only increases the management complexity wrought by the other two factors. These forces have been spawned by the ever-expanding liberalization of trade, investment and finance since the end of World War II, innovations in transportation (such as containerization and supertankers), and enormous improvements in telecommunications and air travel. With the collapse of Soviet communism, market forces are at work—more or less—throughout the world. They are creating a more transparent yet competitive marketplace, filled with opportunities. Globalization, however, has brought with it a large degree of unpredictability and even volatility, especially for societies without the institutional foundations, regulatory framework and value system necessary for a functioning market economy. Management as well must cope with the uncertainty and complexity of this new competitive environment.

Role of Strategy-Making

In light of this changing environment, what is the role of strategy making for the firm? Over the past 30 years, the concept of strategy has evolved from a relatively simple notion of defining the firm's business to a multifaceted concept of value creation. Or, to put it another way, it has shifted away from a hierarchically oriented strategy-structure-systems triad, where according to GE's Jack Welch "an organization has its face to the CEO and its ass toward the customer" (Ghoshal, 1995, p. 87), to a *value triad* encompassing buyers, shareholders and stakeholders alike. This is leading toward a more horizontally managed, rapid response organization where cross-cutting systems and processes shape the enterprise.

Buyer value, the focal point of this new triad, is sheer enterprise invention. In the fast-paced information/communication age, moreover, buyer value is a constantly moving target. On the one hand, value is what the customer currently perceives and wants; on the other, value is pure potential or 'white space', i.e., product opportunities addressing needs that present customers and future buyers may barely recognize. Sony's walkman, Canon's small copier, the PC and the cell phone evidence such turn of events. Only after initially rough products were introduced and critical attributes improved did the markets become fully apparent. A central strategic challenge for the firm, therefore, is to invent and continually to reinvent buyer value.

Buyer value, however, is only one leg of the value triad. Buyer value must be "appropriable" by the firm, i.e., must translate into profits for shareholders. Through his five forces analysis, Porter amply demonstrates how the structure of the industry may drain away potential profits through intense price competition and through the bargaining power of buyers and suppliers, in effect appropriating them from the firm's shareholders. IBM lost its technological lead in PCs and the resulting profits, for instance, by adopting an open standard and thereby giving a wide range of clone manufacturers cost-free entry into the market. For this reason, the firm must not only be well positioned in the market and operate efficiently, it also must nurture core competencies that distinguish it from its competitors and sustain its competitive advantage. Further, a firm's employees and its stakeholders up and down the value chain must clearly benefit long term, for their allegiance is critical to ensuring an ever-improving line of quality products and services. This necessitates a deliberate and well-managed alliance strategy that dovetails with the firm's core competencies and strategic architecture over the foreseeable future.

The central strategic challenge for the strategist, therefore, is to translate the firm's value triad into what Peter Drucker (1995) calls a "theory of the business." How well this is done and faithfully executed largely explains the successes as well as the failures of firms, for it creates a clarity of purpose that can address the management complexity wrought by the rapidly changing and globalizing environment. This theory has three aspects. First, it establishes assumptions about the environment, such as those just discussed—about society and its structure, the market, the customer, and technology. These assumptions establish what the enterprise will be paid for. Second, the theory rests on assumptions about the specific mission of the organization, or what the enterprise considers to be meaningful results. Specifically, should each enterprise image itself as impacting or shaping the market, an industry or economy? During the period before and following World War II, says Drucker, Sears Roebuck saw itself as "the informed buyer for the American family" and AT&T as "ensuring that every U.S. family and business have access to a telephone" (p. 29). Third, the theory includes assumptions about core competencies, or about the ways the enterprise must excel in order to succeed and achieve a competitive advantage. Resting on these three operating assumptions, the theory is tantamount to a business hypothesis which must be tested and revised every three or four years to remain vibrant. Obviously, many firms fail to seriously question and revise their theory until their survival is at stake. Often, this is too late, as has happened to such name brand companies as Singer and Westinghouse.

The "theory of the business" incorporates a number of the dimensions discussed in this chapter. Without denigrating the role of "emergentness" in strategy making, such a theory clearly calls for firms periodically to deliberately assess and, as needed, to revise their environmental assessment, mission and core competencies. There is no substitute for this sometimes painful process. At the same time, it argues in favor of firms seeing themselves more as portfolios of competencies than business units. This makes their potential and possibly their need for reinvention more transparent. Finally, by articulating the assumptions underlying their theories, firms are forced to see themselves as creative and proactive members of their larger environments or ecosystems. Insofar, any firm-specific atomistic view of competition must give way to one in which firms through their relationships are as much shapers and creators of industries as managers of assets and market segments. This calls on firms at times to be collaborators as well as head-to-head competitors, and sometimes at the same time with the same firm.

Given the three environmental factors largely dominating business today, most firms ultimately must take a capabilities or resource-based approach to strategy. This does not mean that they can ignore market positioning for their products and services, but only that they must not lock themselves into a one-dimensional or static view of the market. Indeed, strategy must be multi-dimensional in at least two respects. First, strategy must focus simultaneously on the corporate, business unit (or country) and functional levels, for these ultimately are the three sources of a firm's strengths (Bartlett & Ghoshal, 1998, chap. 11): its global integrative perspective, its market/buyer perspective, and its skill base. Particularly in the international arena, where complexity abounds, firms must build-in a depth of competencies at all levels which enables them to adapt their product mix and to move agilely as new technologies and technological applications emerge and as market preferences shift or new market niches become apparent.

Second, strategy must focus simultaneously on the configuration and coordination of a firm's operations (Porter, 1986; Bartlett & Ghoshal, 1998, chap. 8). The geographical location or placement of a firm's assets—as well as of its partners and markets—is particularly critical for firms with global operations. Optimum locations will vary depending on the type of business function, e.g., finance or marketing, and on constraints or opportunities in the external environment.

Thus, marketing may need to be highly dispersed among countries in order to ensure responsiveness to customers and to perform after sales service, while the finance function may need to be centralized to ensure coordination and to take maximum advantage of currency and tax issues. Manufacturing and research and development functions may vary as well by location, depending on factor costs, the strength of intellectual property rights and import restrictions. At the same time, any dispersion of a firm's operations requires appropriate means to ensure management coordination. Advances in communication and information technology are all but eliminating time delays in communications, but by no means overcoming the gaps in corporate and national culture that plague effective decision making and action. Thus, all along the value chain firms are presented with choices of how to configure and coordinate their operations. Consciously working with these choices provides the strategist with much needed flexibility.

CONCLUSION

The role of strategy, therefore, is to enable firms to envision their proactive role in mobilizing their resources and in focusing their energies on the ongoing tasks of value creation. It is also the means for firms to shape their external environment and their relationship with it. The three environmental factors—the ongoing challenge to innovate, the rapid pace of change, and the uncertainty of globalization—leave little room for error. Strategy provides the clarity for dealing with the complexity of this environment, while senior management provides the commitment and resources for its faithful execution.

Put this way, it would seem that in today's environment most firms may well favor the deliberate, resource- and competence-based, collaborative, and creative dimensions of strategy making. Still, this may not always be advisable, for the environment of firms and of each of their business units is not everywhere the same. And even though the dominant environment of a firm may favor these dimensions, their opposite dimensions can be very important for overall enterprise success. Thus, gleaning "emergent" insight from a firm's experience is always a smart way to begin a deliberate process of strategy making. The dimensions of portfolio planning and market positioning can provide useful starting points in evaluating a firm's current situation. They most likely will not, however, give firms the insight and foresight necessary to compete for the future. As a result, the contrasting and multi-dimensions of strategy as well as the theory of the business discussed here should be seen as a rich array of management tools to be used selectively as the context and circumstances indicate.

REFERENCES

Andrews, K.R. (1980). *The concept of corporate strategy.* Homewood, IL: Irwin. This is essentially as stated by Andrews in his 1971 edition. See also the writings of Christensen, C.R., Andrews, K., & Bower, J. (1965). *Business policy: Text and cases.* Burr Ridge, IL: Irwin. For a more formal planning system, see Lorange, P. (1980). *Corporate planning: An executive viewpoint.* Englewood Cliffs: Prentice-Hall; and Lorange, P., & Vancil, R.F. (1977). *Strategic planning systems.* Englewood Cliffs: Prentice-Hall.

Baden-Fuller, D., & Stopford, J.M. (1994). *Rejuvenating the mature business: The competitive challenge.* New York: Harvard Business School.

Bartlett, C.A., & Ghoshal, S. (1998). *Managing across borders.* Boston: Harvard Business School.

Bogue, M.C., & Buffa, E.S. (1986). *Corporate strategy analysis.* New York: Free Press.

Boston Consulting Group, Inc. (1970). "The product portfolio," perspectives. Boston: Boston Consulting Group.

Buzzell, R.D., & Gale, B.T. (1987). *The PIMS principle: Linking strategy to performance.* New York: Free Press. PIMS stands for "Profit Impact of Market Strategy."

Chandler, A.D. (1962). *Strategy and structure.* Cambridge: MIT Press.

Doz, Y.L., & Hamel, G. (1998). *Alliance advantage: The art of creating value through partnering.* Boston: Harvard Business School.

Drucker, P.F. (1995). *Managing in a time of great change.* New York: Truman Talley Books/Dutton.

The Economist (1996, Jan. 6). What's in a name?

Hamel, G., & Prahalad, C.K. (1994). *Competing for the future: Breakthrough strategies for seizing control of your industry and creating the markets of tomorrow.* Boston: Harvard Business School.

Hamel, G., & Prahalad, C.K. (1990, May–June). The core competence of the corporation. *Harvard Business Review,* 79–91.

Hammer, M. (1990, July–Aug.). Reengineering work: Don't automate, obliterate. *Harvard Business Review,* 104–112.

Hedley, B. (1977, Feb.). Strategy and the "business portfolio." *Long Range Planning, 10*(1), 9–15.

Luthans, F., Hodgetts, R., & Lee, S. (1994, Winter). New paradigm organizations: From total quality to learning to world-class. *Organizational Dynamics,* 5–19.

MacTaggart, J.M., Kontes, P.W., & Mankins, M.C. (1994). *The value imperative: Managing for superior shareholder returns.* New York: Free Press.

Mintzberg, H. (1994). *The rise and fall of strategic planning: Reconceiving roles for planning, plans, and planners.* New York: Free Press.

Mintzberg, H. (1994, Jan.–Feb.). The fall and rise of strategic planning. *Harvard Business Review,* 107–114.

Moore, C.F. (1996). *The death of competition: Leadership & strategy in the age of business ecosystems.* New York: HarperCollins.

Moore, J.F. (1998, Winter). The rise of a new corporate form. *Washington Quarterly, 21*(1), 167–181.

Ohmae, K. (1989, March–April). The global logic of strategic alliances. *Harvard Business Review,* 143–154.

Porter, M.E. (1996, Nov.-Dec.). What is strategy? *Harvard Business Review,* 61.

Porter, M.E. (1990). *The competitive advantage of nations*. New York: Free Press.

Porter, M.E. (1987, May–June). From competitive advantage to corporate strategy. *Harvard Business Review*, 43–99.

Porter, M.E. (1980). *Competitive strategy: Techniques for analyzing industries and competitors*. New York: Free Press.

Porter, M.E. (1986). Competition in global industries: A conceptual framework. In M.E. Porter (Ed.), *Competition in global industries* (18–60). Boston: Harvard Business School.

Quinn, J.B. (1978, Fall). Strategic change: "Logical incrementalism." *Sloan Management Review*, 20(1), 7–21. Quinn's use of the term 'logic' is not 'formal logic,' but "reasonable and well-considered" decisions to situations confronting management.

Rittel, H. (1972). On the planning crisis: Systems analysis of the 'first and second generations.' *Bedriftsokonomen*, (8), 390–396. See also: R.O. Mason & I.I. Mitroff (1981). *Challenging strategic planning assumptions*. New York: Wiley.

Schumpeter, J.A. (1950). *Capitalism, socialism and democracy* (3rd ed.). New York: Harper & Brothers.

Simon, H.A. (1997). *Administrative behavior* (4th ed.). New York: Free Press.

Stalk, G. Evans, P., & Shulman, L. (1992, March–April). Competing on capabilities. *Harvard Business Review*, 57–69.

Thurow, L. (1999). *Building wealth: The new rules for individuals, companies and nations in a knowledge-based economy*. New York: HarperCollins.

Womack, J.P., Jones, D.T., & Ross, D. (1990). *The machine that changed the world*. New York: Rawson Associates.

Yoshino, M.Y., & Rangan, U.S. (1995). *Strategic alliances: An entrepreneurial approach to globalization*. Boston: Harvard Business School.

Chapter X

Organizational Design and Structure

James P. Gelatt

INTRODUCTION

This chapter focuses on organizations—why they exist, how they are structured, and how they function.

Organizations exist for a basic reason: to get things done. "We have organizations to do things that individuals cannot do by themselves" (Hall, 1999, p. 3). Organizations are groups of people with a common purpose (Daft, 1998). Whether we are talking about formal or informal, highly or loosely structured forms, organizations are comprised of two or more people who choose to come together to pursue a common interest. We rely on organizations for basic needs—food, shelter, security; for health care; for education of ourselves and our offspring; for employment; and for amusement.

Broadly speaking, organizations can be classified as either informal or formal. *Informal organizations* are those that materialize without conscious effort—a group of people waiting for a bus, for example.

Formal organizations are those that are deliberately formed, whose activities are directed toward an agreed upon objective or set of objectives. Formal organizations may be established for profit-making purposes, as a nonprofit organization (such as The Red Cross), or as a public sector organization (e.g., a government agency). It is the formal organization that is given attention in this chapter.

The study of how organizations function is sometimes referred to as organizational theory or organizational Design. By contrast, some theorists look more at individuals within the organization and how they function; this is known as organizational behavior. Organizational theory takes a sociological perspective, while organizational behavior focuses on the psychological. To be successful as a manager, we need an understanding of both. One contributes to and complements the other.

In this chapter, we will concentrate on the macro—on organizational design. But as we do so we need to be mindful that it is people, not structures, that are ultimately the reason organizations succeed or fail.

ORGANIZATIONAL DESIGN AND STRUCTURE

Organizational *design and structure* may be thought of as analogous to a building's architecture. *Organizational design* may be described as the "blueprint" on which the organization is built—its conceptual framework. Organizational design provides the basis for the development or alteration in *structure*.

Organizational structure refers to the ways in which the organization allocates its resources (human and material) in order to achieve goals that it has set for itself. Organizational structure is the formal arrangement of job responsibilities; it refers to how jobs and tasks are grouped and coordinated (Robbins & Coulter, 1999).

An organization's structure can be viewed at various levels: the overall organization; the departments and units that make up the organization; the individuals who come together in other groups, such as work teams. Each of these levels—small group, department (or division), organization—needs to be considered in the context of the others. For example, as an employee, I may be part of the Accounting Department; but I also work on a team comprised of members of several departments; and I get my overall goals and personnel policies from the organization itself.

Because organizations exist "to get things done," a useful way of looking at them is as a *system* that is comprised of input, process and output functions. This is referred to as the Open Systems Model, or General Systems Model; it is depicted in Figure 1.

Organizations convert resources (inputs) into finished products or services. Inputs can include raw materials such as water or minerals; human resources, both physical and intellectual; or financial resources. The act of converting resources into products or services is the process function, or "organizational technology." Organizational technology can be viewed on a continuum from simple to complex.

Figure 1. General Systems Model

Input ⟶ Process ⟶ Output

The General Systems Model shown in Figure 1 can also be described as an "Open Systems Model." Open systems recognize that organizations do not operate in a vacuum, but rather rely on, interact with, and must respond to, the environments in which they exist.

One benefit of understanding this basic model is that it provides a way of studying how and why an organization is successful. When the value of the output is greater than the cost of the input and process, the company is in a position to make a profit. By contrast, if the cost of materials or labor exceeds the value that can be placed on the sale of outputs produced, the company will be in a deficit position.

American society has shifted from the Agricultural Age, where the emphasis was on the use of natural resources and physical labor; to the Industrial Age, where the emphasis was on the invention and use of machinery; to the Information Age, in which both raw materials and outputs are less tangible. The essential raw materials for this Information Age are not so much resources extracted from the earth, but resources drawn from the mind—from intellectual capital. If the machine was an apt metaphor for the Industrial Age, then a fitting metaphor for the Information Age might be the brain.

From the Agricultural Age. . . . Copyright © Corbis-Bettmann.

. . . To the Industrial Age. . . . Copyright © Corbis-Bettmann.

. . . To the Information Age . . . The Microsoft Campus. Copyright © Microsoft Corporation.

THE RELATIONSHIP BETWEEN ORGANIZATIONAL DESIGN AND STRUCTURE AND MANAGEMENT

Organizing is a management function. Managers are charged with the task of utilizing people and other resources in the interest of achieving collective organizational purposes. Management is itself a process—the process of coordinating and directing the use of resources in an efficient and effective manner so that the organization's goals can be achieved. One might argue that management is the principal activity that makes a difference in how well organizations succeed in achieving the goals that brought them together.

In the definition of organizations it was noted that organizations allow us to do things that as individuals we may not be able to do by ourselves. Organizations take advantage of their numbers by dividing up the tasks ("division of labor") in order to get the work done. Large jobs are divided into smaller, literally more "manageable" tasks. Organizational structure thus refers to the sum of jobs, workflow, reporting relationships, and communication that together link the efforts of the organization's diverse elements.

An organization chart is a visual depiction of the structure. The chart shows who reports to whom, how work is organized, normal channels of communication, and the number of levels in the "chain of command." Figure 2 shows an organization chart.

Figure 2. Organizational Structure

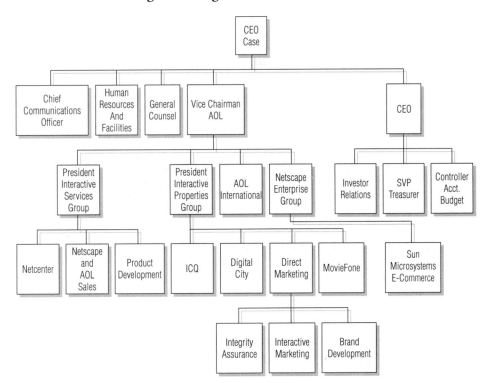

Source: AOL Annual Report (1999), online.

Management is the sum of behaviors and actions undertaken by a manager in order to achieve organizational objectives. As organizations increase in size or complexity, the need for management increases as well. In response, organizations create subdivisions (departments), often along the line of *functions*, such as accounting; or *product* lines; or *geography*. Managers are responsible for seeing that their departments achieve their own goals in a manner that contributes to the organization's goals.

ELEMENTS OF ORGANIZATIONAL STRUCTURE AND DESIGN

Just as the architect uses a recognized vocabulary and symbols in order to depict the building he or she wants to construct, so too organizational structure and design has a vocabulary by which we can describe what makes one organization unique from another. Structural and contextual dimensions comprise just such a vocabulary. They allow us to describe the organization both internally and in the context of the external environment.

Structural Dimensions

The term "structural dimensions" (Daft, 1998) refers to the internal composition of an organization. Structural dimensions include the following:

Formalization refers to written documentation in the form of policy manuals, written procedures, use of written forms, job descriptions and the like. The more elements such as these that are used, the more formalized the organization.

Standardization refers to the degree to which tasks are performed in the same way each time. Standardization became popular with the advent of the assembly line, wherein the same tasks are performed in the same sequence (and often by the same persons) each time. American fast food companies are highly standardized.

Specialization describes the manner in which tasks are subdivided. Specialization is most common in organizations where division of labor is practiced—that is, where tasks are analyzed and broken into simpler activities. The more specialized the organizational processes, the narrower the range of skills required by individual employees.

Hierarchy refers to the organization's chain of command. Who reports to whom? How many "direct reports" does the typical manager have in his or her "span of control?"

Complexity depicts the amount of activities or subsystems in the organization. The more activities, the more subsystems, the more complex is the organization. Complexity can be viewed in three ways:

(1) Vertical complexity (How many levels of hierarchy does the organization have?)

(2) Horizontal complexity (How many departments or job titles are reflected horizontally on the organization chart?)

(3) Spatial complexity (How many geographic locations does the organization have?)

Centralization is used to describe how centrally decisions are made in the organization. In highly centralized organizations, decisions are made only within top management. In decentralized organizations, staff members at varying levels in the organization are given the authority to make and act upon decisions.

Professionalism describes the extent to which employees are formally educated or trained as a condition of employment. A law office, wherein most of the staff has an advanced degree, would be considered highly professional.

Personnel Ratios characterize the assignment of staff members to departments or roles. Ratios compare one category of staff to the overall work force within the organization. For example, if an organization has a total staff of 100, 20 of whom are in clerical positions, we can say that the clerical ratio is 1:5.

Structural dimensions are comparative measures. Organizations that make products in which precision is important (televisions, for example) are likely to be highly standardized and specialized, but low in professionalism. By contrast, organizations in which each product is unique (a group of pottery makers, for example) are likely to be low in standardization and specialization (each potter often makes his or her own product from raw clay to finished, fired product). Consulting firms such as Arthur Anderson or the Boston Consulting Group are often characterized by a high degree of professionalism, with consultants each holding advanced degrees and training.

Contextual Dimensions

Whereas structural dimensions describe certain internal elements within the organization, contextual dimensions describe the overall organization and the "contexts" in which it operates. There are five contextual dimensions: (1) environment, (2) goals and strategies, (3) size, (4) organizational technology, and (5) organizational culture.

Environment

One of the ways in which organizations can be described contextually is to discuss the environment in which the organization must function. As discussed earlier in this chapter, organizations are open systems and must be able to function effectually in the environments in which they find themselves.

One way to consider external factors impacting the organization is through a STEEP analysis:

S	Sociological	Changes in demographics; changes in cultural values.
T	Technological	Trends in technology that may affect how the organization does business.
E	Environmental	"Environment" here refers to the physical environment (and thus to the availability of raw materials); and issues of health (the impact of gene research, for example).
E	Economic	Changes in the stock market; competition.
P	Political	Legislation and regulation; changes in the political makeup of Congress.

Goals and Strategies

A second contextual dimension has to do with the overarching goals that the organization sets for itself and the strategies it undertakes in pursuit of those goals. Goals and strategies include the overall purpose for the organization (its "mission"); organization-wide, longer-range goals; operational goals; and plans of action. Taken together, goals and strategies comprise the organization's range of operations.

Size

As one might expect, organizational size can be measured in terms of employees, total assets, or total sales. Size also can be a comparative measure (e.g., largest bank).

Organizational Technology

Organizational technology is the "combination of knowledge, equipment, and work methods used to transform inputs into organizational outputs" (Schermerhorn, 1999, p. 226). Organizational technology thus refers to any of the processes used by the organization—assembly lines, classrooms, and computers, for example.

Organizational Culture

Organizational culture includes all the values, norms, rituals, rules, and beliefs that characterize the organization. As defined by Edgar Schein (1992), culture is:

> ... *a pattern of shared basic assumptions that the group learned as it solved its problems of external adaptation and internal integration, that has worked well enough to be considered valued and, therefore, to be taught to new members as the correct way to perceive, think, and feel in relation to those problems (p. 12).*

It is important to note that each of the structural dimensions and contextual dimensions noted above is linked—and to some degree dependent—on each of the others. For example, an organization that produces a highly standardized product, such as a television, is also likely to have a high degree of specialization (i.e., division of labor). And because it is often necessary to have written procedures so that each time the product is made, it is made the same way, such an organization is often highly formalized as well. Structural dimensions also can be affected by contextual dimensions. For example, organizational size usually contributes to increased rules and procedures (formalization) as well as to more layers of management (hierarchy of authority) and more use of support staff (personnel ratios). So does the environment affect structural dimensions; for example, an organization that operates in multiple environments may need to have a decentralized decision-making process in order to be responsive to differences in each of the environments.

MECHANISTIC AND ORGANIC STRUCTURES

The environment in which the organization exists also affects the relative uncertainty in which the organization operates. This in turn affects the degree to which tasks can be preplanned and scheduled by management. The more predictable the environment, the more likely it is that the organization can and will structure its activities. The less predictable the environment, the more fluid the organization will need to be (Robey & Sales, 1994).

We refer to organizations that are highly structured as *mechanistic*. In such organizations, decision making tends to be centralized and hierarchical and formalized; jobs are usually narrow in scope, and job descriptions and tasks are well delineated.

By comparison, we refer to organizations that are informally structured as *organic*. Organic organizations typically have a small amount of specialization (division of labor) and standardization. Decisions may be decentralized. Job descriptions are defined more broadly, and if there is an official hierarchy of authority, it is often circumvented in the interest of getting the job done (Robey & Sales, 1994; Nahavandi & Malekzadeh, 1999).

ORGANIZATIONAL DESIGN, STRUCTURE, AND LIFE CYCLES

Organizations go through stages of growth and development in much the same way that people or animals do (although organizations are less constrained by biological factors). Organizations are "born," they grow (and hopefully flourish), they become mature, they grow older, and sometimes they die. The speed with which organizations move through their life cycle is unique to each. Figure 3 presents a life cycle model that relates life cycle stage to issues of structure.

In general, organizations tend to become more formalized and more complex as they mature and grow in size. This is understandable. Formalization and complexity are directly related to the organization's need to divide up the workload as size increases. As work becomes more divided among staff, the need for additional staff grows. As staff size increases, so too does the need for written rules and procedures (Hodge, Anthony & Gales, 1996).

In the *entrepreneurial stage*, the emphasis is on survival, and whatever structure exists tends to be organic. If the organization survives (and most new organizations do not), it may move into the *collectivity stage*, represented by the advent of structure within a climate that is still relatively informal. Top management may begin delegating (decentralizing) the decision-making process as staff members are hired to run major functional areas of the organization.

Figure 3. Organization Characteristics During Four Stages of Life Cycle

Characteristic	1 Entrepreneurial Nonbureaucratic	2 Collectivity Prebureaucratic	3 Formalization Bureaucratic	4 Elaboration Very Bureaucratic
Structure	Informal, one-person show	Mostly informal, some procedures	Formal procedures, division of labor, new specialties added	Teamwork within bureaucracy, small-company thinking
Products or services	Single product or service	Major product or service with variations	Line of products or services	Multiple product or service line
Reward and control systems	Personal paternalistic	Personal, contribution to success	Impersonal, formalized systems	Extensive, tailored to product and department
Innovation	By owner-manager	By employees and managers	By separate innovation group	By institution-alized R & D
Goal	Survival	Growth	Internal stability, market expansion	Reputation, complete organization
Top manage-ment style	Individualistic, entrepreneurial	Charismatic, direction-giving	Delegation with control	Team approach, attack bureaucracy

Source: R. L. Daft, 1998, p. 178

In time, the organization may move into the *formalization stage*. As its name suggests, this stage is characterized by a higher degree of rules and procedures as tasks become more specialized, chains of command (hierarchy) more defined, and the organization generally more complex.

The fourth stage is the *elaboration stage*—so called because the organization often develops elaborate bureaucratic structures (Quinn & Cameron, 1983). If the organization is to be competitive and survive, it may need to undergo major change in its design and structure—downsizing, re-engineering, or streamlining. Senior management may decide the best approach is, in effect, to break up the organization into smaller, more autonomous units, each of which can operate as an organization would in an earlier stage of the life cycle.

ORGANIZATIONAL DESIGN AND STRUCTURE FROM THE PERSPECTIVE OF MANAGEMENT THEORY

In order to understand how concepts of organizational design and structure have evolved, it is important to look at some of the major influences within the history of management thought. This section will briefly describe some of the major schools of management thought, with an emphasis on how management thought emerged in the United States from the work of leaders in industry.

Scientific Management

Management's orientation to design and structure has been strongly influenced by the Industrial Revolution, in which machine resources replaced a portion of the human resources that had driven business and industry up to that point. This change in turn increased the need for managers—to anticipate work flow needs, organize work and develop structures and processes accordingly.

Over 200 years ago, Adam Smith (1937) wrote about the need for division of labor in order to improve efficiency and maximize productivity. His insights spurred the move toward task analysis, which formed the basis of Scientific Management. As described in Chapter I of this text, Scientific Management sought to determine the "one best way" to get the job done. The emphasis of the Scientific Management School, led by Frederick Taylor, was great productivity, and greater productivity could be achieved by applying the principles of scientific method to the workplace. The manager's role was to analyze worker tasks in order to design a streamlined operation.

Classic/Administrative School

As work became more complex and more specialized in the interest of productivity, the need arose for guidelines on how to manage these increasingly complex organizations (Stoner, Freeman & Gilbert, 1995). Led by Henri Fayol, there sprung up what has come to be called the Classic or Administrative School. It looked at the organization from a top-down perspective. Fayol believed there was a "universal process approach" that could be applied to management (Fayol, 1949). It was the job of top management to decide how best the organization should be designed and how work should be allocated.

From the Perspective of American Management History

Many of our organizational models have tended to be based on the study of major organizations. Alfred Chandler looked at some 70 major U.S. companies, including Dupont, General Motors, Standard Oil of New Jersey, and Sears Roebuck (Chandler, 1962). Chandler saw the relationship between *strategy* (what the organization wanted to accomplish and the directions it wanted to take) and *structure* (the means for getting there). Chandler determined that changes in organizational strategy led to changes in organizational structure. Most organizations began with an entrepreneurial structure. This evolved into a vertically integrated structure as the organizations acquired suppliers of materials and distributors. Many organizations then expanded into a multi-divisional structure as they branched out into new product lines.

While he was president of New Jersey Bell Telephone, Chester Barnard had the opportunity to study large organizations, which he came to think of as being comprised of interacting persons. Barnard concluded that it was the manager's role to stimulate those persons to strive for higher achievement (Barnard, 1938).

From the Perspective of How We View One Another

How society views work and the structure of the work environment have been influenced by how we perceive the worker.

Theory X/Theory Y

Theory X and Theory Y (McGregor, 1960) are two, polar views of the worker. Theory X sees the worker as basically lazy and in need of direction. If we favor Theory X, we will be more likely to want an organizational structure that allows for line-of-sight management. Decentralization of authority would be inconsistent with a Theory X mentality. Theory Y, in contrast, assumes that work fulfills a psychological need and that employees will work when given appropriate training and recognition. Thus, the Theory Y manager would be more likely to support the use of cross-departmental teams, telecommuting, and other work conditions that encourage people to reach their potential.

Power

An individual's orientation to work and the workplace is also influenced by his or her perception of power. If power is viewed as finite (as a "fixed pie"), the individual will be inclined to favor a structure that is centralized and probably hierarchical. If he or she views power as expandable, the individual may be more inclined to support decentralized authority and a flatter organizational structure. (Greenberg & Baron, 1997).

Ethics and Social Responsibility

Ethics and social responsibility have come to play an increasing role in recent years in shaping organizational strategy and hence organizational design. Historically, issues such as environmental pollution were considered "externalities," by-products of doing business whose costs were borne by persons not directly involved in the consumption of the product or service (Salvatore, 1993). Although the debate continues over the role of corporations in addressing societal problems, there is fairly widespread acceptance that companies must give due consideration to how their operations affect society at large.

DESIGN AND STRUCTURE IN LIGHT OF KEY MANAGEMENT ISSUES TODAY

There are several issues that require managers to rethink their organization's structure. They are: (1) designing and implementing effective structures for a global organization; (2) chaos and complexity and systems theory; and (3) the learning organization.

Designing and Implementing
Effective Structures for a Global Organization

We have become a global economy. Almost any product can be made in almost any location, and then be shipped and sold in almost any other location. What is driving this change? One factor is the role played by dominant economic forces other than the United States, such as Germany. These powerful economic engines have the wherewithal to expand their sales, acquire necessary resources, and diversify their sales by entering international markets (Daniels & Radebaugh, 1994).

A second factor is growth in newly industrialized countries. Consider, for example, the burgeoning role being played by countries that were once part of the Soviet Union.

Another factor in the rise of the global economy is a resultant shift in market economies and with it a shift in international power. Robert Reich, in *The Work of Nations* (1992) writes:

> We are living through a transformation that will rearrange the politics and economics of the coming century. There will be no national products or technologies, no national corporations, no national industries . . .. All that will remain rooted within national borders are the people who comprise a nation. [A nation's] industries are ceasing to exist in any form that can meaningfully be distinguished from the rest of the global economy. (pp. 3, 77)

Perhaps the most compelling factor in the globalization of the economy is the impact of technology. Futurist Joseph Coates (1999) writes of six "enabling technologies" that will dramatically change the way we live and do business. The six are: (1) information technology, (2) genetics, (3) materials technology, (4) energy technology, (5) brain technology, and (6) environmental impact. According to Coates, changes in these technology areas will lead to:

- A dramatic decrease in the cost of telecommunications, and hence a dramatic increase in its use;
- Opportunities for less-developed nations to acquire the "infrastructure of the advanced nations";
- More decentralization of work;
- Low cost, continual, open-ended access to customer wants and needs;
- An overhaul of the way in which we educate and train employees; and
- Increased life expectancy. (p. 37)

The sum of these changes will have a significant impact on organizational design and structure. The potential will exist for any organization to be a player internationally, meaning organizations will have to rethink how to achieve competitive advantage. Technology will heighten the ability to communicate at all levels, leading to the growth of networks. And as everyone in the organization acquires the ability to access information, organizations will need to rethink how power is shared and where decisions get made. There will truly be no such thing as a "closed system."

It is also becoming more apparent that the economy of one country affects that of all the others. People cannot afford to think of their organization and their country as unique and isolated: A rising tide lifts all boats, and a low tide affects all boats as well.

Structure in a Global Economy

Technology has not only made it possible for companies of almost any size to compete internationally, it has often made it necessary. There is hardly any product or service that cannot be imported or exported.

In *A Manager's Guide to Globalization* (1993), Stephen Rhinesmith speaks of six ways that organizations will have to function differently in order to compete globally. Each of the six has implications for organizational design and structure. Rhinesmith says organizations will need to retool in order to:

(1) *Manage the competitive process.* Organizations will need to be designed as information-gathering and information processing devices, capable of scanning the world for information on trends, best practices and new opportunities.

(2) *Manage complexity.* The traditional definition of an organization suggested that organizations had definable boundaries. It was readily apparent where one organization ended and another began. In today's complex environment, the same organization may be both a competitor and an ally. The definition of organizational structure must change in today's environment, where employees of one company are oftentimes working side-by-side with those of another company.

(3) *Manage organizational adaptability.* In order to be adaptable, the organization needs to rethink which decisions should be decentralized. It also needs to create a global strategy that is at once fixed and flexible.

(4) *Manage multicultural teams.* Very few, if any, managers in the globally competitive company will be able to succeed without cultural sensitivity. Issues of professionalism, horizontal and vertical communication, and formalization of personnel policies, will all be affected by the fact that the organization is comprised of people not of one culture but of many.

(5) *Manage uncertainty.* The ability to adapt, to change structures in order to create opportunities, will be key.

(6) *Manage personal and organizational learning.* In the traditional organization, some staff members are assigned to be "boundary spanners" whose job is to be in touch with the world outside the organization. In this complex era, every person in the organization must be a boundary spanner, and a lifelong learner as well.

What Does It Mean to Go "Global?"

As in architecture, organizational design should heed the maxim, "Form follows function." The type of structure the organization needs depends on the stage of development the organization is in, as indicated in Figure 4.

Figure 4. Stages of Global Evolution

	I. Domestic	II. International	III. Multinational	IV. Global
Strategic Orientation	Domestically oriented	Export-oriented multidomestic	Multinational	Global
State of Development	Initial foreign involvement	Competitive positioning	Explosion	Global
Structure	Domestic structure, plus export department	Domestic structure, plus international division	Worldwide geographic, product	Matrix transnational
Market potential	Moderate mostly domestic	Large multidomestic	Very large multinational	Whole world

Source: Based on R. L. Daft, 1998, p. 259

In the domestic stage, the organization is concentrated on its own country of origin but is beginning to consider becoming involved internationally. In order to do so, the organization may create a separate unit dedicated to exploring the potential for export of products or services. As it moves into the international stage, the organization starts to look at international business more intently. Most of its international activities are country-by-country. What was an exploratory unit dedicated to potential export is now becoming a full-fledged department or division.

If the organization continues to progress in its global commitment, the next stage may be the multinational stage, which is characterized by the organization's having both production and marketing capabilities housed in other countries. This third stage may lead to a fourth, the global stage, in which the organization and its international branches think of themselves in truly global terms—not as an American company operating in Asia, but as an international company operating anywhere and everywhere opportunity presents itself (Holstein, 1990). The design challenge for any organization, as it moves from a domestic to a more global orientation, is to have decisions that reflect a centralized vision but are informed by local factors.

Chaos, Complexity and Systems Thinking

Management theorist Peter Vaill (1993) says that the workplace is in a state of "permanent white water." All timelines are off, all plans are wrong, no objectives are stable, everybody's working too hard, no evaluations are accurate, and Murphy's Law pervades everything.

What Vaill describes as "white water" might also be called "chaos." In recent years, management theory has seen the influence of the science of "chaos theory" and its first cousin, "complexity." Chaos theorists maintain that a close look at the history of organizations reveals unpredictable rises for some companies and unseen failures for others. The true picture, chaos theorists would argue, is that most organizations' histories are replete with false starts and uneven advances, leading to unpredictable outcomes which only occasionally and temporarily settle into a recognizable pattern or order.

Within the chaos, according to some, however, there lies a kind of underpinning of order. While every snowflake is different, there is an order to the making of snowflakes, each of which looks and behaves similarly to the others. Behind this seeming disorderliness is order. However, the complex nature of this order reduces its predictability (Gleick, 1987). The future is not linear, it is multiple.

Not only is there order beneath the disorder; there is also a sense of connectedness—itself a key element of systems thinking. As one writer puts it: "One of the most powerful lessons from the new science called chaos is the concept that everything is totally connected to everything else in unbroken wholeness" (Gelatt, 1995, p. 108).

> *How does all of this relate to the management of organizations? One answer is to think of organizations as "organisms"—as . . . living systems, existing in a wider environment on which they depend for the satisfaction of various needs. . . . Organizations, like organisms, can be conceived of as sets of interacting subsystems. . . . There is no one best way of organizing. The appropriate form depends on the kind of task or environment with which one is dealing. Management must be concerned, above all else, with achieving "good fits." Different approaches to management may be necessary to perform different tasks within the same organization, and quite different types of "species" of organization are needed in different types of environment (Morgan, 1986, pp. 39, 49).*

In sum: No one structure is sufficient. What structure is selected, it must be adaptable.

Systems Thinking

Related to the concept of organizations as organisms is the concept of *systems thinking*. Systems thinking sees the organization as "an entity that maintains its existence and functions as a whole through the interaction of its parts" (O'Connor and McDermott, 1997, p. 2). In order to understand the organization, it must be examined holistically. It must be recognized that for every action, there is a reaction, for every intended consequence, an unintended consequence. When a decision is made about organizational design or structure, the question must be asked: How will this change affect the entire organization?

Management theorist Margaret Wheatley, linking the concepts of chaos and systems thinking, notes: "Organizations are not machines but complex living systems—networks of relationships that thrive on information and are capable of reorganizing themselves in response to dramatic changes in the environment" (Wheatley, 1994, p. 16). What Wheatley and others are implying in linking chaos theory with systems thinking is that organizations are systems much in the same way that bodily organs make up organ systems. These systems are complex, and they are adaptable. Today's managers must focus on that adaptability in order to compete in a complex global environment.

The "Learning Organization"

Organizational adaptability is almost synonymous with organizational learning. In the words of management theorist Peter Senge, an adaptable organization is a learning organization (Senge, 1990). Learning organizations have developed the ability to adapt in response to new information. In the learning organization, almost every employee can and should be a source of information—and hence be a source competitive advantage for the organization. What does this mean in terms of design and structure? It means creating an organization that is as near-ly "boundaryless" as is possible. Physical and structural boundaries that get in the way must be removed, allowing employees to work more collaboratively (Robbins & Coulter, 1999).

IMPLICATIONS FOR FUTURE MANAGEMENT

Issues such as globalization, technology and increasing complexity are driving organizations to rethink how work gets done. The role of the worker—and hence the structure in which the worker functions—are undergoing dramatic change in this Knowledge/Information Age. Theorist Daniel Bell (1976) anticipated this shift over twenty years ago in his book *The Coming of Post-Industrial Society.* He wrote:

> *Every modern society now lives by innovation and the social control of change, and tries to anticipate the future in order to plan ahead. . . . One can say that the methodological promise of the second half of the twentieth century is the management of organized complexity . . . and the development of a new intellectual technology. (Bell, 1976, pp. 20, 28)*

What Bell foresaw was what we now refer to as "intellectual capital," which is the essence of the learning organization. The implications for management and organizational structure are clear: What is needed are organizations that allow individuals to achieve their intellectual potential, that are continually attuned to their environment, that are anticipatory in nature.

Thus, organizational designs and structures must be both adaptive and proactive. Following are some examples.

The Virtual Organization

In the virtual organization (Davidow & Malone, 1992), centralized places of work are giving way to the concept that work is wherever the worker is—in his or her home, in the office of a customer, en route between offices. The virtual organization refers to having a core business function and then *outsourcing* (i.e., subcontracting to other companies) any activities that are not part of the core.

Related to the concept of the virtual organization is the *just-in-time work force*. As just-in-time inventory allows companies to maintain small product reserves by keeping in constant touch with customer needs, so too the just-in-time work force is the result of organizations' anticipating times in which workloads may peak in order to obtain temporary staff members or arrange for additional outsourcing of work.

The notion of the *shamrock organization* (Handy, 1991) is also related. Picture a shamrock—a central stem with petals orbiting off the stem. The central stem relates symbolizes what we might call "core competencies"—those components of the organization that are essential to its mission, the things it does well, the services that are most important to the customer. The petals are those products or services that can be outsourced.

The Protean Organization

Proteus was a god in Greek mythology who was capable of assuming different forms. The protean organization is one that is similarly adaptable and flexible. The concept of the protean organization corresponds with the virtual organization. By keeping the organization lean, focusing on core competencies and Outsourcing the rest, the organization is positioned to reshape itself as opportunities or threats arise (Barner, 1996).

Network Structures

Network structures rely on interorganizational relationships—strategic alliances, joint ventures, coalitions and consortia. The Japanese *kereitsu* (Daft, 1998) is one example. The kereitsu involves a variety of companies, each of which holds shares in the other, but none of which is wholly owned by any other. Companies in the kereitsu come together to work on mutually agreed upon projects. The companies can be said to be neither wholly independent or dependent of one another, but rather interdependent—their individual success is dependent on their mutual success (Ghoshal & Bartlett, 1990).

Organization Ecology Model

The Organization Ecology Model (Baum, 1996)—or "Population Ecology Model"—looks at organizational structure and design in the way that scientists study past cultures. Just as scientists may ask, Why did the Mayan civilization die out?, so are management thinkers asking, Can large, established organizations (e.g., Sears, General Motors) survive in this age of uncertainty and complexity? The model argues that adaptation and the ability to avoid "structural inertia" (Daft, 1998, p. 535) are key.

What kind of structure will best survive? The answer probably is that no one structure, but rather a philosophical frame of reference, will be the determining factor. In the words of Peter Drucker (September–October 1992, p. 97):

Every organization has to build the management of change into its very structure. On the one hand, this means every organization has to prepare for the abandonment of everything it does. Managers have to learn to ask every few years of every process, every product, every procedure, every policy: "If we did not do this already, would we go into it now knowing what we now know?" . . . On the other hand, every organization must devote itself to creating the new. . . . Innovation can now be organized and must be organized—as a systematic process.

No one can say with certainty what the organization of the future will look like. More than likely, it will be not one design or one structure but many. For what we do know is that organizations, like living organisms, need to be able to adapt in order to survive. The successful organizational design will be both dependable and flexible. It may be one location, or many, or none. But whatever its structure, it will provide a facilitating environment in which the potential within human capital can be most realized.

REFERENCES

Barnard, C. I. (1938). *The functions of the executive*. Cambridge, MA: Harvard University Press.

Barner, R. (1996, March–April). The new millennium workplace: Seven changes that will challenge managers—and workers. *The Futurist, 30*, 14–18.

Bell, D. (1976). *The coming of the post-industrial society*. New York: Basic Books.

Chandler, A. (1962). *Strategy and structure*. Cambridge, MA: MIT Press.

Coates, J. F. (1999, Jan/Feb). Opportunities and consequences in science and technology. *Research-Technology Management, 42*(1), 36–42.

Daft, R. L. (1998). *Organization theory and design* (6th ed.). Cincinnati: South-Western College Publishing.

Daniels, J. D. & Radebaugh, L. H. (1994). *International business: Environments and operations* (7th ed.). Reading, MA: Addison-Wesley Publishing Company.

Davidow, W. & Malone, M. (1992). *The virtual corporation: Structuring and revitalizing the corporation for the 21st century*. New York: HarperCollins.

Fayol, H. (1949). *General and industrial management*, trans. C. Storrs. London: Isaac Pitman & Sons.

Gelatt, H. B. (1995). Chaos and compassion. *Counseling and Values, 39*, 108–118.

Ghoshal, S. & Bartlett, C. (1990). The multinational corporation as an interorganizational network. *Academy of Management Review, 15*(3), 603–625.

Greenberg, J. & Baron, R. A. (1997). *Behavior in organizations*, 6th ed. Upper Saddle River, NJ: Prentice Hall.

Hall, R. H. (1999). *Organizations: Structures, processes, and outcomes* (7th ed.). Upper Saddle River, NJ: Prentice Hall.

Handy, C. (1991). *The age of unreason.* Boston: Harvard Business School Press.

Hodge, B. J., Anthony, W. P., & Gales, L. M. (1996). *Organization theory: a strategic approach.* Upper Saddle River, NJ: Prentice Hall.

Holstein, W. J. (1990, May 14). The stateless corporation. *Business Week,* 98–105.

McGregor, D. (1960). *The human side of enterprise.* New York: McGraw Hill.

Morgan, G. (1986). *Images of organization.* Beverly Hills: Sage Publications.

Nahavandi, A & Malekzadeh, A. R. (1999). *Organizational behavior: The person–organization fit.* Upper Saddle River, NJ: Prentice Hall.

O'Connor, J. & McDermott, I. (1997). *The art of systems thinking.* San Francisco: Thorsons HarperCollins Publishers.

Quinn, R. E. & Cameron, K. (1983). Organizational life cycles and shifting criteria of effectiveness: Some preliminary evidence. *Management Science, 29,* 33–51.

Reich, R. (1992). *The work of nations : Preparing ourselves for 21st century capitalism.* New York: Vintage Books.

Rhinesmith, S. H. (1993). *A manager's guide to globalization: Six keys to success in a changing world.* Burr Ridge, IL: Irwin Professional Publishing.

Robey, D. &. Sales, C. A. (1994). *Designing organizations* (4th ed.). Burr Ridge, IL: Richard D. Irwin.

Robbins, S. P. &. Coulter, M. (1999). *Management* (6th ed.). Upper Saddle River, NJ: Prentice Hall.

Salvatore, D. (1993). *Managerial economics in a global economy* (2nd ed.). New York: McGraw-Hill.

Schein, E. H. (1992). *Organizational culture and leadership* (2nd ed.). San Francisco: Jossey-Bass Publishers.

Schermerhorn, J. R., Jr. (1999). *Management* (6th ed.). New York: John Wiley & Sons.

Senge, P. M. (1990). *The fifth discipline: The art and practice of learning organizations.* New York: Doubleday.

Smith, A. (1937). *The wealth of nations.* New York: Modern Library.

Stoner, J., Freeman, R. E., & Gilbert, D. R., Jr. (1995). *Management* (6th ed.). Englewood Cliffs, NJ: Prentice Hall.

Vaill, P. (1993, Nov. 23). Speaking at a Colloquium at the University of Maryland, University College, Graduate School of Management & Technology.

Wheatley, Margaret. (1994, October). Quantum management. *Working Woman, 19(10),* 16–17.

Conclusions

CLARENCE J. MANN

Over the past century and a half, U.S. management theory and practice have developed a distinctive character of their own. Initially, they borrowed heavily from European thinking, for 19th century immigrants were heavily of European origin. But management theory and practice quickly took on American cultural traits of individualism and pragmatism. Further, the rapidly expanding continental market, relatively free of governmental and other environmental constraints, generated professional management styles and organizational designs needed to thrive on a highly diverse and mobile work force. In this sense, the development of U.S. management theory and practice has come to parallel values deeply imbedded in American society and its free enterprise system, for in many respects, the workplace is simply a mirror image of society at large. By the same token, within the scope of these general traits, the diversity and dynamism of American society has yielded a broad range and mix of management practices.

This legacy of management thinking has evolved over time. It has provided individuals and firms with enormous leeway to take risks—for better and for worse—and to exploit their capabilities. In the meantime, the growing complexity and diversity of U.S. industrial—and now post-industrial—society as well as the global marketplace have begun to reshape U.S. management theory and practice. Drawing from the foregoing chapters, these concluding remarks highlight trends that are influencing this change in thought and practice. They also summarize some of the challenges to U.S. managers that these trends suggest.

TRENDS AFFECTING U.S. MANAGEMENT

While by no means intended to be an exhaustive list, the authors have identified in their various chapters five trends as having particular impact on U.S. management theory and practice over the coming decades. These trends represent patterns of events and modes of thinking with a momentum of their own which are forcing or catalyzing changes in the U.S. management environment. For the most part, such trends are well beyond the ability of companies as well as governments to significantly modify over the near term.

- *Convergence of a broad range of technologies.* The post-industrial revolution and knowledge-based economy of the United States is being powered by at least six different, rapidly advancing, converging fields of science and technology: microelectronics, biotechnology, robotics, computers, telecommunications and man-made materials. The breadth, depth and speed of this technological convergence is supported by industry, government and university linkages and by the deliberate, systematic character of private sector and government investment emphasizing everything from medical research to "star wars." As these basic technologies converge, innovative applications create the opportunity for an endless stream of new and often unforeseen products of every kind. The speed of this convergence is also blurring traditional lines separating industries, making it increasingly difficult for firms to gain foresight on future markets and to cost out the risk associated with the investment.

- *Communications/information technology revolution.* This trend is a particular and yet distinct aspect of technology convergence, requiring management to rethink the very nature of business. It is changing the pace of commerce, the rules of engagement for whole industries and the very definition of the organization. The explosion in information technology since the mid-50s has witnessed over a billion-fold improvement in processing and storage capacity—a rate that is expected to continue well into the first part of the next century. Computer-aided design and manufacturing (CAD/CAM) are reinventing the factory, while the Internet has transformed value-chain management and e-commerce is reinventing the retail industry as a whole. IT strategy has become a field of its own. It is particularly critical to success in firms which are globalizing their operations. The result is a rapid pace of change and innovation in almost every part of the value chain, culminating in planned product obsolescence to pave the way for new technology applications. The pace of change and the accelerated pace of work also are bringing increased levels of personal stress at every level of organizations.

- *Globalization of market forces.* The emerging global market was spawned initially by the ever-expanding liberalization of trade, investment and finance that has occurred since the end of World War II. It has been intensified by the establishment of free trade areas in Europe and North America, innovations in transportation (such as containerization and supertankers), and enormous improvements in air travel and telecommunications. With the collapse of Soviet communism, market forces are at work—more or less—throughout the world. The result is, increasingly, a "woven world" (Yergin & Stansilaw, 1998), whose hallmark is a highly mobile and competitive environment. "Capital sweeps across countries at electronic speed; manufacturing and the generation of services move flexibly among countries and are networked across borders; and markets are supplied from a continually shifting set of sources." Between 1989 and 1997, international trade grew at an annual rate of 5.3 percent, nearly four times faster than global output (p. 376). These forces are creating a more transparent yet competitive marketplace, filled with opportunities. Globalization, however, has brought with it a large degree of unpredictability and even volatility, especially for societies without the institutional foundations, regulatory framework and value system necessary for a functioning market economy.

• *Increasing work force diversity.* In the very near future, the percentage of men and women in the U.S. work force will approach parity. By the year 2020, whites will constitute 68 percent (down from 76 percent today), African-Americans will remain constant at 11 percent, and Asians and Hispanics will grow to 6 and 14 percent, respectively. At the same time, the aging of the U.S. population will outweigh these ethnic shifts, for many people will choose to work longer in life. Moreover, the expanding virtual environment of business nationally as well as internationally will increase the diversity of working relationships. These demographic changes are affecting social and business values, product and service markets, and the way people communicate and relate with each other in the workplace.

• *Increasing reliance on systems thinking, open systems analysis, complexity and chaos theory and related concepts* as the basis for effective decision making and organizational change, particularly in high velocity industries. This entails a shift in mindset from mechanistic cause-effect thinking and highly controlled and pyramid-structured organizations that have dominated U.S. management theory and practice since its inception. The relentlessly changing environment requires firms to be innovative and adaptive as well as consistent in executing plans and delivering product quality, neither seduced by the creativity of chaos nor enslaved by a bureaucratic mindset. Systems thinking calls for a holistic understanding of organizations as networks of reciprocal relationships and as complex living and learning organisms capable of self-organization in response to environmental changes. This paradigm shift is a natural companion to the revolution in communications and information technology, making the walls of companies more permeable, markets more transparent and human talent more mobile. Systems thinking is visible in a myriad of practical applications: quality management, crisis planning, stakeholder collaboration, work force development, and the entire range of ecological, environmental and social policy analysis.

CHALLENGES TO U.S. MANAGEMENT

In light of these trends which are shaping the U.S. environment and the analysis in the previous chapters, the following highlights some of the challenges which the authors believe U.S. managers must be prepared to deal with now and in the coming years.

- *Recognize and build on the dynamic value legacies running through the American management character*, such as individualism, pragmatism, the free enterprise system and professional management—all the while enabling the work force at all levels to deal constructively with the accelerating pace of change and the challenges of an emerging transcultural global system. (Overview)

- *Move beyond "quick fixes" and "cook book" reactions toward foresightful management measures* based on sound scholarship rather than reactions to quarterly metrics and anecdotal evidence. Pursue evolutionary rather than traumatic revolutionary organizational changes, i.e., build on strengths and work force talent. (Chapter I)

- *Nurture leadership as well as management capabilities within the organization*, recognizing that these roles encompass a broad range and mix of skills, traits and decision-making styles. These roles and the mix of skills, traits and styles will vary depending on the industry, the life cycle of the firm and the task at hand. Leadership entails followership, managers must be managed—and, at all levels, employees must be encouraged to speak out and be creative as well as productive. In a dynamic industry environment, leadership calls on managers to be facilitators who empower the work force and agents of organizational transformation. (Chapter II)

- *Build trust and balance throughout the organization*, thereby enabling effective working relationships and releasing passion for the task. Trust does not mean individuals necessarily like each other, but rather they share each other's ability and dependability to contribute positively to task accomplishment. Align individual needs and values with those of the organization. Pay attention to the whole worker and his/her mix of intelligences and ways of learning. Encourage employees to achieve balance in terms of both individual and team effort at work and quality of life as among work, family, leisure and personal growth. Given the accelerating pace of change and the uncertainty that this causes among employees, there is greater need than ever for firms to nurture a reliable skilled labor force. (Chapter III)

- *Make diversity an integral part of the workplace and operations management*, not simply a burdensome program to meet minimum legal requirements. It takes coordinated effort on a daily basis to make diversity a business asset. If taken seriously, work force diversity offers firms the opportunity for workplace harmony, increased productivity, product development and market penetration. (Chapter IV)

- *Be sensitive to and take seriously ethical issues at all levels of operations*, rather than viewing them simply as operating and investment constraints. Use audits as a means to monitor social and environmental issues. Be imaginative, where possible, in coupling socially responsible solutions with business opportunity. (Chapter V)

- *Build lean and flexible, rapid-response operating systems, linked closely to suppliers, buyers and the industry environment through IT architecture.* IT strategy should focus on four key challenges: ensure ongoing innovation through knowledge management; improve operations through simulation and computer-aided design and manufacturing and flexible production systems; identify and track evolving needs and customer value; and generate new product and service development. Managers further must develop the ability to tap and glean insight from the extensive information sources already at their disposal. (Chapters VI and VII)

- *Develop the financial system to be the common denominator of the enterprise and all its activities.* Financial managers must become knowledge integrators, providing fiduciary oversight of assets, reporting interface with regulatory bodies, and assembling both financial and non-financial information for planning and performance evaluation. This requires ever more sophisticated financial systems and their management. While the basic data that support financial and accounting analyses will change little, the type of data, the level of details, the sophistication of the analyses, and the methods of retrieval, display and reporting will change dramatically. This in turn will improve management information and decision-making processes. (Chapter VIII)

- *Formulate strategy as a value triad, encompassing buyers, shareholders and stakeholders alike.* This implies a theory of the business built around working assumptions about society and the market, the mission of the firm, and the core competencies where the firm excels. This calls for strategy focused not simply on the firm and its immediate environment, but on the evolution and re-creation of the industry as a whole within the larger ecosystem. Given the complexity and vagaries of a dynamic and globally competitive environment, strategists must continually re-examine a firm's working assumptions, configure its assets across the globe to achieve both efficiencies and market responsiveness, and simultaneously shape and coordinate business processes at the corporate, business unit (or country) and functional levels to achieve maximum effectiveness and learning. (Chapter IX)

- *Think holistically and systematically about organizational structure and design*, considering not simply one design or structure but many. Form should follow function. Build adaptive organizations that balance structure with the need for ongoing innovation. Flatter organizations are needed to ensure responsiveness to customers, to the market, to innovation and among working colleagues. The team-based work force is replacing hierarchy, calling for new styles of leadership. Organizations must be designed around the worker and for teamwork, providing a facilitating environment, in order to realize the full potential of human capital. (Chapter X)

REFERENCE

Yergin, D., & Stanislaw, J. (1998). *The commanding heights: The battle between government and the marketplace that is remaking the modern world.* New York: Simon & Schuster.

About the Authors

John O. Aje is associate professor and Chair of Technology Management Programs at University of Maryland University College Graduate School of Management & Technology. Areas of specialization: project management; R&D management; engineering economic analysis; science, technology, and public policy; productivity and quality management; engineering management. Major professional experience: eight years as laboratory manager, Howard University College of Medicine; two years as research engineer, Monsanto Company. B.S., Clemson University; M.S., North Carolina State University; M.E.A., The George Washington University; D.Sc., The George Washington University.

Glenda J. Barrett is professor and Director of Human Resource Management Programs at University of Maryland University College Graduate School of Management & Technology. Areas of specialization: employee relations, human resource development, contingent work force issues, organizational communication, and change management. Over 20 years of managerial and consulting experience, including Program Manager, Boeing; Customer Relations Director, ACT. B.A., Indiana University; M.A., University of Iowa; M.A. (Education & Human Development), George Washington University; Ph.D., George Washington University.

Kathleen F. Edwards is associate professor and Director of Health Care Administration Programs at University of Maryland University College Graduate School of Management & Technology. Areas of specialization: ethics and social responsibility, conflict management and negotiation, external communication, health care administration, public health administration, health care systems. Over 25 years of management experience in the health care industry, 12 of them in senior management, and consulting in the health care industry. B.S., University of Maryland; M.S., The Catholic University of America; Ph.D., The Catholic University of Maryland.

Michael S. Frank is professor and Chair of General Management Programs at University of Maryland University College Graduate School of Management & Technology. Areas of specialization: leadership, decision making, change management, organization theory, and human resource management. Major professional experience: over 20 years as senior executive and consultant in the public and private sectors, including positions as Human Resource Director and chief labor negotiator for a 4,000-employee organization and Executive Vice President for a major financial institution, guiding strategy, marketing, sales, reorganizations, human resources, and asset management. B.A., M.A. and Ph.D., University of Maryland, College Park.

James P. Gelatt is professor and Program Director of Interdisciplinary Studies in Management at University of Maryland University College Graduate School of Management & Technology. Areas of specialization: organizational theory, leadership, strategic management, decision making, change process and nonprofit management. Major professional experience: chief fund raiser and Director of Planning for Human Resources Center; the Kennedy Institute, Johns Hopkins University; and the American-Speech-Language-Hearing Association. B.A., St. Lawrence University; M.A., Colgate University; Ph.D., University of Southern California.

Clarence J. Mann is professor, Chair of International Management Programs, and Director of the Institute for Global Management at University of Maryland University College Graduate School of Management & Technology. Areas of specialization: strategic planning and negotiation, international business transactions; technology transfer and technology ventures, international law and law of the European Union. Over 20 years of professional experience in corporate and international law practice; General Counsel, Sears Roebuck's International Operations; CEO, A.T. International. B.A., Wabash College; JD, Yale Law School; M.A. (Economics), Yale University; Dr. jur., University of Bonn, Germany.

Salvatore J. Monaco is professor and Executive Director of the Office of Executive Programs at University of Maryland University College Graduate School of Management & Technology. Areas of specialization: systems analysis, innovation and entrepreneurship; information technology, production and operations management. Over 20 years professional experience as Director, New Product Development; Director, Washington Consulting at a division of Standard & Poor's; and research, engineering, and economic analysis, including positions as Chief of the U.S. Air Force's Inertial Guidance Research Division and Chief of the Economic Analysis Division at USAF Headquarters. B.S.E., Manhattan College; M.S.E., University of Michigan; Ph.D., Rensselaer Polytechnic Institute.

Richard D. Neidig is professor and Acting Associate Dean, Academic Affairs at University of Maryland University College Graduate School of Management & Technology. Areas of specialization: human resource management, leadership, organizational communication, conflict management and negotiation, team building, assessment centers and organizational development. Over 15 years professional experience as an entrepreneur and management consultant and seven years as Personnel Research Psychologist at the U.S. Office of Personnel Management. B.A., Pennsylvania State University; M.A., Bucknell University; Ph.D. Industrial Psychology, Pennsylvania State University.

Robert P. Ouellette is associate professor and Director of Technology Management Programs at University of Maryland University College Graduate School of Management & Technology. Areas of specialization: marketing, strategic planning, financial management. Twenty-five years experience in senior managerial positions in marketing, business development, and strategic planning. B.Sc., University of Montreal, Canada; Ph.D., University of Ottawa, Canada; MBA, New York Institute of Technology.

Index

A

Accounting model, 213–214, 229
Activity based costing, 201
Affirmative action, 39, 112, 115, 118–120, 124, 130–132
Amazon.com, 188–190, 198
American management systems, 36, 191
Americans with Disabilities Act, 113, 131
AT&T, 172, 253
Auditing and control, 219

B

Babbage, Charles, 41, 161
Balanced Scorecard, 17, 30, 201
Barnard, Chester, 9, 14, 34, 43, 268
Bennis, Warren, 26, 64
Boeing, 178, 202, 283
Boston Consulting Group's Growth/Share Matrix, 242
Bounded rationality, 24, 44
Budgeting, 65, 217, 219, 227–228, 243

C

CAD / CAM, 167, 174, 184, 251, 278
Canon, 240, 252
Capital asset pricing model (CAPM), 216

Capital structure, 213, 216–217, 219, 221, 229
Champy, James, 55, 170
Chaos theory, 272–273, 279
Civil Rights Act, 114–120, 125, 127
Classical school, 34–35, 41–44
Closed systems, 49
Communication, 3, 11, 22, 24, 26–27, 89–90, 93, 96, 98–99, 109, 134, 136–137, 139–140, 153–154, 178, 190–191, 203–204, 210, 219–220, 238, 249–252, 254, 261, 270, 283–284
Competitive advantage, 37, 53, 57, 61, 86, 185, 188, 191, 193, 198, 232, 237, 239–241, 243–244, 246, 252–253, 256, 269, 273
Complexity, 8, 16, 22, 38, 42, 88–89, 113–114, 152, 218, 235, 251–254, 262, 265, 268, 270–274, 277, 279, 281
Confidentiality, 136, 143
Conflict resolution, 26
Conflicts of interest, 18, 136, 141–143, 155
Contingency theory, 36, 49, 77, 213
Core competencies, 234–235, 242–246, 252–253, 274, 281
Corporate social responsibility, 6, 126, 133, 135, 148–149, 153, 155–156
Covey, Steven, 16, 56, 82

D

Decision making, 8, 15, 28, 35–36, 38, 42, 44, 51, 70, 74–75, 77, 97, 135, 137, 141–142, 147, 154, 183, 187, 209, 213, 217–218, 231, 233, 235, 237, 239, 241, 243, 245, 247, 249, 251, 253–255, 265, 279, 283–284
Dewey, John, 14
de Tocqueville, Alexis, 4
Discrimination, 12–13, 18, 23, 114–118, 120, 124–125, 131, 141, 222
Diversity, 3, 8, 12–13, 16, 18–19, 26–27, 29, 94–95, 111–131, 149, 212, 277, 279–280
Diversity management, 111–112, 114, 120, 123–125, 127, 129–130
Division of labor, 42, 67, 160–161, 261–262, 264–265, 267
Drucker, Peter, 16, 26, 34, 37, 52–53, 188, 252, 274

E

Economic value added, 201
Electronic commerce, 28, 189, 196, 224–227, 229
Empowerment, 11, 49, 54, 76–79, 86, 89–90, 94, 96–97, 108
Encyclopedia Britannica, 58–60, 193
Environmental Protection Agency (EPA), 139
Equal Employment Opportunity Commission, 115, 117, 131
Ethics plans, 146–147
European Union (EU), 210
Expert systems, 175, 223
Expressive individualism, 8–10

F

Fayol, Henri, 43, 267
Federal Express, 188–189
Fiat, 202
Financial accounting, 210, 213

Financial reporting, 212, 218–219, 229
Financial systems, 28, 201, 207–211, 213, 215, 217, 219, 221, 223, 225–227, 229, 281
Flexible manufacturing systems, 167, 174
Follett, Mary Parker, 26, 30, 46, 146, 150, 155
Ford, 43, 53, 161–164, 169, 231
Ford, Henry, 43, 161
Formal organizations, 257
Franklin, Benjamin, 6–7, 14, 220
Free enterprise system, 2, 4, 19, 23, 25–26, 29, 277, 280
Friedman, Milton, 6, 149, 151
Fukuyama, Francis, 6

G

General Electric, 117, 129, 167, 218
General Motors, 14, 24, 43, 53–54, 147, 155, 179, 203, 240, 246, 267, 274
Generation X, 27, 80, 92–94, 104, 109–110
Gilbreth, Frank, 45, 162
Gilbreth, Lillian , 45, 161
Glass ceiling, 125–126, 129
Global marketplace, 3, 135, 172, 177–178, 277
Gulick, Luther, 46

H

Hammer, Michael, 55, 170, 234
Hawthorne Effect, 46
Hewlett-Packard, 244, 249
Human performance technology, 106
Human relations school, 34–35, 45, 47–48

I

IBM, 51–54, 58, 61, 149, 166, 180, 243, 252
Incrementalism, 234, 237–238, 256

Industrial Revolution, 21, 27, 35, 37–38, 40–42, 69, 87, 95, 159–160, 166, 185, 250, 267

Informal organizations, 257

Information Age, 28, 86, 94, 98, 100, 187–189, 191, 193, 195, 197, 199, 201, 203, 205, 259–260, 273

Information Technology (IT), 171, 202, 223

Innovation, 11, 19, 22, 28, 50, 52–53, 58, 60, 94, 104, 186–187, 190, 193, 199–201, 204–205, 223, 229, 234, 247, 250–251, 266, 273, 275, 278, 281, 284

Intel, 21, 249

Intellectual property, 22, 143, 189, 208–209, 226–227, 254

International Accounting Standards Committee, 210

J

Japan, 3, 25, 30, 36–37, 39, 48–49, 51–52, 55, 59, 112, 167, 169–170, 180–181, 185, 251

K

Knowledge management, 28, 190–193, 281

Knowledge-based systems, 223

L

Leadership, 3, 6, 8, 25–27, 37, 46, 49–50, 53, 56–57, 59, 61–84, 107, 124–126, 140, 149, 152, 166, 170, 180, 239–240, 245, 251, 255, 276, 280–281, 283–284

Leadership types, 75

Lean manufacturing, 234, 246

Learning organization, 56, 82, 106, 123, 129, 268, 273

Lincoln, Abraham, 16

Lockheed Martin, 120, 202

M

Management by objectives, 38, 53

Managerial accounting, 208, 213

Market efficiency hypothesis, 213–214

Marketing, 9, 12, 21–22, 53, 121, 135–140, 147, 155–158, 175, 184, 212, 225, 235, 237, 244–247, 253–254, 271, 284

Mass production, 24, 162–163, 165, 167

Mayo, Elton, 45, 165

McCormick, Cyrus, 231

Microsoft, 10, 193, 202, 205, 248–249, 260

Motivation, 18, 26, 39, 44, 46–47, 59–60, 64, 72–73, 80, 84, 87, 94–95, 101, 103, 128, 137, 165, 175, 234

Myers-Briggs Personal Interest Inventory, 8

N

Netscape, 202, 248

North American Free Trade Agreement (NAFTA), 210

O

Open systems, 26, 49, 258–259, 263, 279

Operations management, 27–28, 157–161, 163, 165–169, 171–173, 175–179, 181–186, 280, 284

Operations research, 165

Organizational behavior, 27, 58, 60, 83–84, 87–88, 93, 102, 109, 136, 148, 258, 276

Organizational culture, 66, 84, 89, 96, 103, 107–108, 112, 126–127, 170, 263–264, 276

Organizational design and structure, 28, 257–259, 261, 263, 265, 267, 269–271, 273, 275

Organizational technology, 258, 263–264

Organizational theory, 38, 49, 54, 258, 284

Owen, Robert, 41

P

Peters, Thomas, 34

Pierce, C.S. 14

Population Ecology, 18, 37, 50, 59, 274

Porter, Michael, 34, 53, 56, 193, 233

Portfolio theory, 213, 216

Power, 11, 13, 19, 36, 39, 43, 52, 57, 60, 64, 68–69, 74, 76–77, 81–82, 87–90, 92, 97, 102, 104, 116, 120, 126–127, 130, 145, 160, 162, 189, 212–213, 225, 232, 234, 237–238, 244–245, 252, 268–269

Pragmatism, 2, 4, 14–18, 26, 29–30, 277, 280

Product life cycle, 182

Protean organization, 274

Q

Quality control, 17, 161, 165, 168–169, 234

Quantitative analysis, 16

R

Re-engineering, 170–172, 234, 241, 266

Reisman, David, 8

Risk communication, 136–137, 139–140, 154

Rosenwald, Julius, 231

S

Sampling, 165

Scientific management, 1, 24, 35, 44–45, 62, 161, 212, 267

Sears Roebuck, 231, 253, 267, 284

Sexual harassment, 18, 117, 119–120, 136, 141, 143–144, 154

Singer, 253

Sloan, Alfred, 14, 24, 231

Smith, Adam, 19, 55, 160–161, 211, 214–215, 267

Software agents, 223

Standard Oil of New Jersey, 267

STEEP analysis, 263

Strategic management, 188, 233, 243, 284

Strategic positioning, 241

Strategy, 22, 28–30, 35, 37, 43, 50, 56–57, 61, 88, 97, 103, 114, 127, 141, 171, 182, 192–193, 198, 205, 231–241, 243–245, 247–248, 250–256, 267–268, 270, 275, 278, 281, 284

Supply side economics, 213

Sustainable competitive advantage, 244

Swift, Gustavus, 231

Systems theory, 36, 49, 58, 207, 213, 268

Systems thinking, 26, 56, 271–273, 276, 279

T

Taylor, Frederick, 1, 14, 24, 34–35, 161, 267

Team building, 284

Telecommuting, 86, 98, 102, 122, 268

Texas Instruments, 187

Theory of constraints, 213, 216, 227–229

Theory of the firm, 213–214, 226

Theory Y, 47, 165, 268

Theory Z, 37, 51, 61

3M, 60, 244

Throughput-per-unit accounting, 217

Time to market, 180–182

Total Cost Assessment (TCA), 208

Total Quality Management, 18, 36, 48, 56, 168–169, 219, 241

Toyota, 169, 246

Trait theory, 69

U

U.S. Supreme Court Rulings, 117
Utilitarian individualism, 6, 8, 14

V

Value chain, 22, 28, 190, 198, 233,
    245, 251–252, 254, 278
Value chain analysis, 233
Virtual organization, 94, 273–274
Von Bertalanfly, Ludwig, 49

W

Wal-Mart, 120, 188–189, 241
Walton, Sam, 189
Weber, Max, 39, 41–42, 62
Welch, Jack, 252
Westinghouse, 253
Whitney, Eli, 161
Wood, Robert, 24
World Bank, 191

X

Xerox, 172, 191, 240